EC LAW AND MINORITY LANGUAGE POLICY

EC LAW AND MINORITY LANGUAGE POLICY

CULTURE, CITIZENSHIP AND FUNDAMENTAL RIGHTS

by

Niamh Nic Shuibhne
Lecturer in EC Law,
University of Edinburgh

Kluwer Law International

The Hague / London / New York

A C.I.P. Catalogue record for this book is available from the Library of Congress.

Printed on acid-free paper.

ISBN 90-411-1733-4
© 2002 *Kluwer Law International*
© 2004 *Koninklijke Brill NV, Leiden, The Netherlands*

Brill Academic Publishers incorporates the imprint Martinus Nijhoff Publishers.
http://www.brill.nl

Printed and bound in The Netherlands

Do mo Mháthair

Table of Contents

Table of Cases

1. EUROPEAN COURT OF JUSTICE

A. Alphabetical

B. Chronological

2. EUROPEAN COURT OF FIRST INSTANCE

A. Alphabetical

B. Chronological

3. EUROPEAN COURT AND COMMISSION OF HUMAN RIGHTS

4. PERMANENT COURT OF INTERNATIONAL JUSTICE

5. UNITED NATIONS HUMAN RIGHTS COMMITTEE

6. OTHER JURISDICTIONS

Canada

Germany

Table of Legislation

1. TREATIES AND CONVENTIONS

2. EC DIRECTIVES

3. EC REGULATIONS

4. EC DECISIONS

5. NATIONAL LEGISLATION

List of Abbreviations

CFI	Court of First Instance
CMLR	Common Market Law Reports
EBLUL	European Bureau for Lesser Used Languages
EC	European Community
ECHR	European Convention for the Protection of Human Rights and Fundamental Freedoms
ECJ	European Court of Justice
ECR	European Court Reports
ECSC	European Coal and Steel Community
EEC	European Economic Community
ERDF	European Research and Development Fund
ESF	European Social Fund
EU	European Union
ICCPR	International Covenant on Civil and Political Rights
ICESCR	International Covenant on Economic, Social and Cultural Rights
IGC	Intergovernmental Conference
JO	*Journal Officiel des Communautés Européennes*
MEP	Member of European Parliament
OHIM	Office for Harmonisation in the Internal Market
OJ	Official Journal of the European Communities
OSCE	Organisation for Security and Cooperation in Europe
PCIJ	Permanent Court of International Justice
TEU	Treaty on European Union
ToA	Treaty of Amsterdam
UDHR	Universal Declaration on Human Rights
UN	United Nations

Preface

Language is a concept and function that is largely taken for granted, so that the extent to which its use is regulated is not usually considered. This holds true even for the inherently multilingual European Community. Its fiercely defended—and enduring—language policy means that at least one official language from each Member State is involved in the administration of both the Community institutions and the law which emanates from them. The Treaty of Rome referred to language only in so far as it provided that its four language versions were equally authentic. The principle of the equality of all official Community languages was then derived from this modest declaration; but the position of non-official languages was not addressed. Minority language policy is typically thought of as a matter for domestic regulation. But the way in which the reach of both international law generally and Community law more specifically has evolved in recent decades means that the structures of governance at any level are no longer quite so simple. Throughout the 1980s in particular, the European Parliament called on EC Member States to recognise and provide for the rights of minority language speakers that resided within their territories. The European Court of Justice recognised that national linguistic policy could, in certain circumstances, restrict Community principles on free movement. And the Commission began to finance initiatives geared towards the maintenance of minority languages, especially in the fields of culture and education. The promotion of linguistic diversity was thus emerging as a potentially legitimate constraint on economic and political integration. Minority language groups, in turn, began to channel considerable lobbying energies towards the EC institutions, to seek consolidation and expansion of concessions already tentatively made. But is it actually defensible for the Community to grapple with language planning issues? Answering this question in the particular domain of minority language policy opens a debate on inclusiveness and identity, on competence, on culture and diversity, and on citizenship and fundamental rights; but it is a debate that has thus far tended as much towards establishing the limits of possibility at supranational level as to assessing its potential. The following pages strive, above all, to locate an effective and pragmatic balance between the two. The legal and theoretical background to Community multilingualism is first set out (Chapter 1), questioning why linguistic diversity should be protected by the EC at all and, more specifically, situating minority languages in that context. Early signs that the EC institutions were prepared to recognise minority language claims are then charted (Chapter 2), before the legal bases for Community action, both existing and potential, are assessed in detail (Chapters 3, 4 and 5). Finally, current institutional trends are identified (Chapter 6) and a number of conclusions, on the language policy of the Community and on what that policy says about the EC as a governing entity, are put forward (Chapter 7).

This work originated as a PhD thesis; renewed and genuine thanks for continued help and encouragement are due to all those acknowledged therein, but especially to Anne MacFarlane, Mary-Pat O'Malley, Laura Carthy and Michael O'Neill; to John Usher, then research supervisor; and to the University of Edinburgh and *Comhdháil Náisiúnta na Gaeilge* for financial support. To those who have since come on board—thesis examiners Joe McMahon and Peter Cullen; Robert Lane, for reminding me to learn; Fiona Friel; and in particular, to Christine O'Neill—*mile buíochas.*

The law is stated as at 1 March 2001, on the presumption that the Treaty of Nice will be ratified.

Chapter 1

The European Community and Language Policy: Why do Minority Languages Matter?

1. THE RATIONALE OF LANGUAGE POLICY

The evolution from European Community to European Union reflects an underlying, if not always coherent, commitment to increased economic, social and political integration. Community norms permeate, regulate and often harmonise numerous aspects of domestic law and practice. Yet the diversity displayed by the distinct languages spoken in the Member States stands in marked contrast. To posit the most basic standpoint, there are two prevailing but opposing interpretations of the fact of linguistic diversity: it is either celebrated as a manifestation of humanity and free expression, an invaluable cultural asset; or it is denounced as a divisive obstacle, a hollow —and costly—ideal that thwarts the achievement of true European unity. These arguments can be applied to the internal linguistic politics of most individual states. The ongoing debate is usually poised as a conflict between sentiment and efficiency, yet neither extreme premise is convincing or pragmatic when considered in isolation. While there are relatively few European policies that deal specifically with language, the dynamics of integration and harmonisation more generally have had a discernible impact on language use patterns throughout the Member States. The European Commission has declared that no-one should be penalised, either socially or economically, for using his/her vernacular language, despite the demands of an increasingly multilingual world.[1] But if the effect of European integration on the security of even national languages and cultures can be corrosive, the consequences for speakers of regional, minority and non-official languages are even more acute.

The study of language of language, and of its role in society and government, is undoubtedly an interdisciplinary undertaking, invoking both concepts and terminology often alien to the lawyer. This chapter aims

---

[1]   European Commission, "Language engineering in the European Community", (1992) vol. 16:3 *Language Problems and Language Planning* 249-252.

primarily to introduce some necessary tools, to set a theoretical background against which the language policy of the EC can then be analysed and assessed in a more legal sense. At its most basic level, language is primarily an instrument of communication, fulfilling the need for expression in countless circumstances and contexts. What is usually termed the 'private' use of language covers a virtually infinite sphere of language functions, from personal (and business) interactions to cultural events, including the foundation of educational establishments outwith the domain of public funding. Equally, in any polity or organisation, communication between individuals or groups and the entity that governs them must be made possible, introducing the concept of the public or official use of language. This is a fundamental tenet of language policy and represents its practical application in a variety of public domains, from state-funded schools to courts to local authority offices. But facilitating communication is just one objective within a complex web of cultural, economic, sociological and political concerns. And the boundaries between the private and public use of language are neither clear-cut nor mutually exclusive, especially when public funding for what might be considered 'private' language projects comes into play. In whatever guise, language policy has both practical and symbolic implications. Its formulation introduces the idea of 'planning' for linguistic diversity—the deliberate regulation of languages and of their functions in society. There is a clear distinction between 'corpus planning' (referring to the development of vocabulary, grammar, *etc.*) and 'status planning', which deals with the official recognition of languages and with measures designed intentionally to regulate and influence language use in various domains. Status planning generally merits attention with the occurrence of 'language shift', *i.e.* "...the breakdown of a previously established societal allocation of functions; the alteration of previously recognised role-relationships, situations and domains, so that these no longer imply or call for the language with which they were previously associated."[2] There is a danger that planning deliberately for the survival or revival of a language *per se* can overemphasise language in an abstract sense. This idea is developed in Chapter 5, distinguishing policies based on linguistic survival (language-based) versus those grounded in linguistic security (speaker-oriented). It is important to stress at this stage, however, that language planning cannot, on its own, reverse language shift. Planning can contribute to creating the optimum administrative structures within which language choice can be exercised freely; but it can neither anticipate nor redress fully the myriad of

---

[2]   J.A. Fishman, *Language and Ethnicity in Minority Sociolinguistic Perspective*, (Clevedon: Multilingual Matters Ltd., 1989), p. 212.

human, political and economic factors at play. In other words, language planning is necessary but it is not enough.

If just one language is spoken within a state or other polity, status planning is not relevant, since the same language is used invariably by both the citizens and the governing authorities. The language rights of non-resident groups in this situation (*e.g.* tourists) would be covered generally by international standards, such as those set down in the European Convention on Human Rights, discussed in Chapter 5. But an overwhelming majority of contemporary states have more than one language group resident within their territories and need to devise and implement appropriate language policies as a result. Dealing with more than one language is equally relevant in the context of multi-state organisations, not least from the perspective of internal administration. The European Community is a multilingual, multicultural phenomenon. Accordingly, it has been obliged to develop and put in place an institutional linguistic framework, an 'official languages policy', described in Section 2 below. Opinion on the effectiveness of EC language policy is sharply divided. It reflects the views of those who would reduce the number of languages currently used in the institutions, advocating increased linguistic uniformity, as well as those who argue that the present policy does not go far enough and call for, for example, interventionist protection for minority languages spoken within the Community realm. In forming a compromise, it is sometimes suggested that a non-interventionist or 'survival of the fittest' approach should be encouraged, in the overall spirit of achieving linguistic freedom and in accordance with the free market ethos.[3] This argument introduces two issues or themes that are reflected throughout the book: first, the extent to which the Internal Market can be constrained or delimited on non-economic grounds and second, the dividing line between justifiable intervention and oppressive protectionism. For present purposes, the basic question is whether true linguistic freedom—a balance between the cultural value of languages that are relatively weak and those which are considerably stronger—can be generated in the abstract, independently of deliberate national or supranational government strategies. Just as the provision of state aid is deemed to be objectively justified under certain conditions (notwithstanding the promotion of open competition) in an economic sense, it is difficult to imagine the realisation of linguistic freedom without *some* degree of intervention, given the unequal position of both the 'smaller' official and non-official languages in the first place. Furthermore, given that the EC, just like its Member States, has had consciously to

---

[3] For a discussion on, and argument against, this proposition, see Fishman, *Language and Ethnicity*, pp. 292-3.

determine what its working and official languages would be, there is no such thing in reality as an absolutely neutral or non-interventionist policy. The official languages policy of the EC, the clearest example of language planning within the Community to date, is thus outlined in Section 2; only then can the scope of EC minority language policy more specifically be addressed.

2.   THE (OFFICIAL) LANGUAGE POLICY OF THE EUROPEAN COMMUNITY

A.   Introduction

The first thing that can be noted about EC language policy is that it is not codified as such, its content more derived than regulated systematically. As a starting point, there are eleven official and working languages of the European Community: Danish, Dutch, English, Finnish, French, German, Greek, Italian, Portuguese, Spanish and Swedish.[4] This language grouping includes at least *one* of the official languages of each Member State. It is presumed that these eleven are also the official and working languages of the European Union, since no provision of the Treaty on European Union (TEU) deals specifically with this point.

The linguistic dimension of integration was already apparent at the outset of EEC negotiations, given the complexity associated with preparing Dutch, German and Italian versions from the French language working draft of what became the Treaty of Rome. The requisite co-ordination of terminology was complicated by the very innovativeness of the concepts being codified. In addition, differences between domestic legal systems and traditions had to be overcome. The need to ensure that the Treaty texts were fully harmonised was rooted in one crucial phrase of Article 248 EEC: "[t]his Treaty, drawn up in a single original in the Dutch, French, German and Italian languages, *all four texts being equally authentic*, shall be deposited *etc.*"[5] The equality

---

[4]   Describing these languages as official and working languages of the EC is not strictly accurate; Regulation 1/58, the legislative codification of the EC language regime, refers actually to the 'official and working languages of the *institutions* of the Community' (emphasis added) ([1952-1958] OJ English Special Edition 59); the terms 'official EC language' of 'official languages of the Community' are, however, used widely in both official and academic texts, and are adopted here also.

[5]   Now Article 314 EC (emphasis added). Under international law generally, that different language versions of treaties can be equally authoritative is expressed in Article 33 of the 1969 Vienna Convention on the Law of Treaties. According to the Treaty establishing the

of all of the Community's official languages in a more general sense is inferred from this arguably modest reference; it remains a unique feature of contemporary EC language policy and does not compare with the typical linguistic practice of other international organisations. English and French are the only official languages of the Council of Europe, for example; Arabic, Chinese, English, French, Russian and Spanish are the official and working languages of the United Nations. Apart from the obvious consideration of mutual comprehension, the link between language, sovereignty, and national and political identity explains for the most part why the equality of the official EC languages was and continues to be of fundamental importance; this assertion is explored more fully below. EC and EU enlargement have always resulted in a corresponding increase in the number of official/working languages, in accordance with the doctrine of linguistic equality.[6] When the EEC comprised just six Member States, preoccupied with a vision grounded in a new understanding of international law, language planning was simply not a priority. Furthermore, the predominance of economic integration, in comparison with the present reach of the EC Treaty, did not seem to demand serious contemplation of the consequences in linguistic terms of establishing additional Community competences. But the implications of enlargement, both geographically and otherwise, for already strained translation and interpretation facilities have engendered contemporary concern, discussed further below.

Article 217 EEC (now Article 290 EC) allocated responsibility for determining the linguistic regime of the European Economic Community institutions to the Council, a duty it fulfilled in its very first regulation.[7]

European Coal and Steel Community (ECSC, 1951), only the French version is authentic in a legal or interpretative sense, although there are official translations in the other Treaty languages: see Koen Lenaerts and Piet Van Nuffel, *Constitutional Law of the European Union*, (London: Sweet & Maxwell, 1999), p. 380. Regarding subsequent treaty amendments, Article 34 SEA, Article S (now 53) TEU, Article 15 ToA and Article 13 of the Treaty of Nice all provide expressly that the twelve language versions of these treaties (the eleven official language texts and that in Irish) are equally authentic.

[6] See Acts of Accession 1972/Article 155 (Denmark, Ireland and the United Kingdom), 1979/Article 147 (Greece), 1985/Article 397 (Portugal and Spain) and 1994/Article 170 (Austria, Finland and Sweden). See below, however, on the status of Irish.

[7] Regulation 1/58, [1952-1958] OJ English Special Edition 59. See below, however, on the Rules of Procedure of the Court of Justice. The progress report on IGC 2000, prepared for the Feira European Council (CONFER 4750/00, Brussels, 14 June 2000) did not recommend any substantive amendments to Article 290 EC, beyond changing the reference therein from the Rules of Procedure of the Court of Justice (see below) to the 'Statute' of the Court of Justice (see Annex 5.3, p. 109); this recommendation was enacted via Article 2/45 of the Treaty of Nice. It is worth noting that Article 290 was described in

Article 1 of Regulation 1/58 distinguishes explicitly between the terms 'working' and 'official' language, but neither explains this distinction nor provides for its implementation in practice. The Regulation then proceeds to set out guidelines for communications between Member States and Community institutions (Articles 2 and 3). Member States (and persons subject to their jurisdiction) may write to the institutions in any of the official Community languages and must receive a reply in the language they have chosen (Article 2). These rules effectively confer language choice on the Member States rather than on the institutions.[8] Documents sent by a Community institution to a Member State (or to a person subject to its jurisdiction) must be drafted in the official language of that state (Article 3); if the state in question has more than one official language, selection of the appropriate language is to be governed by the state's internal language rules (Article 8; for example, certain language(s) may be required to be used in sub-national regions). But the ECJ has attached a significant limitation to Article 3: a contested act or measure may not be annulled on grounds of non-compliance with Regulation 1/58 unless the irregularity can be shown to have generated harmful consequences capable of vitiating the administrative procedure. This principle was first established by the ECJ in *ACF Chemie-farma v. Commission*,[9] and has since been followed by the Court of First Instance.[10] Notwithstanding the clear and unambiguous terms of Article 3 itself, the ECJ has never elaborated on the source of the 'harmful consequences' limitation in the context of language specifically. The test almost certainly reflects the Court's application of administrative principles in a more general sense.[11] With respect to breaches of Regulation 1/58, however,

---

the Feira Report as a provision 'which, in view of the *sui generis* character of the European Union may be considered "quasi-constitutional"' (Annex 3.7, p. 90) and as such, was deemed to merit the maintenance of the unanimity requirement provided for already therein.

[8]   See Chapter 5 on the language rights of Member State nationals particularly, which are now bound up with the concept of EU citizenship.

[9]   Case 41/67, [1970] ECR 661 at 686-687, paras. 49-52.

[10] Case T-77/92 *Parker Pen v. Commission* [1994] ECR II-549 at 573-574, paras. 70-74, and more recently in Cases T-25 *etc./95 Cimenteries CBR v. Commission*, judgment of 15 March 2000, not yet reported, paras. 627-646. In both cases, as in *Chemiefarma*, the Court was able to establish that the applicants had not been prejudiced by the Commission's acknowledged breaches of Regulation 1/58. See also Case T-148/89 *Tréfilunion v. Commission* [1995] ECR II-1063, on the classification of documents 'emanating' from the institutions (pp. 1076-1077, paras. 19-21), as applied in *Cimenteries* (paras. 631-640).

[11] On the infringement of essential procedural requirements generally, see Koen Lenaerts and Dirk Arts, *Procedural Law of the European Union*, (London: Sweet & Maxwell, 1999), pp. 189-196. Writing on Community law principles of good administration, Usher

the maintenance of a distinction within two distinct strands of ECJ jurisprudence appears, at least, questionable. The cases relate to the enforcement
of EC competition law (in respect of which Community legislation requires
compliance with detailed procedures prior to the adoption of a decision[12])
and the distinction hinges on what amounts to the infringement of an
essential procedural requirement for the purposes of the annulment of
Community acts under Article 230 (formerly 173) EC. Where a procedural
rule has been breached, the contested act or measure may be annulled, but
this is not an automatic or inevitable outcome; the measure will be annulled
only where it can be shown "...that in the absence of the irregularity in
question the contested measure might have been substantively different, that
the irregularity makes judicial review impossible, or that, on account of the
irregularity which it contains, the act in question breaches a fundamental
institutional rule."[13] In *Commission v. BASF and Others*—which relates in
part to the authentication of different language versions of Commission
documents, a procedure discussed further below—the Court of Justice held
that:

> Far from being...a mere formality for archival purposes, the
> authentication of acts provided for in...Article 12 of the [the
> Commission's] Rules of Procedure is intended to guarantee
> legal certainty by ensuring that the text adopted by the college
> of Commissioners becomes fixed in the languages which are

---

notes that "...a breach even of an express requirement will not lead to the annulment of an
act involving such a breach unless it can be shown that the resultant act would have been
different had the breach not occurred." (John A. Usher, *General Principles of EC Law*,
(London: Longman, 1998), pp. 100-101, citing Case 90/74 *Deboeck v. Commission* [1975]
ECR 1123 at 1133, paras. 11-15); and in the context of the rights of defence (specifically,
the right to be heard), Edward and Lane write that "...an infringement...can result in an
annulment only if it can be established that, but for the irregularity, the outcome of the
proceedings might have been different." (David A.O. Edward and Robert C. Lane,
European Community Law: An Introduction, 2nd ed., (Edinburgh: Butterworths/Law
Society of Scotland, 1995), p. 66, referring to Case 142/87 *Belgium v. Commission* [1990]
ECR I-959 at 1016, para. 48). Moreover, whereas breach of an essential procedural
requirement must be raised by the Community judicature of its own motion, manifest
error of assessment will be examined by the Court only if it is raised by the applicant: see
Case C-265/97P *Coöperatieve Vereniging de Verenigde Bloemenveilingen Aalsmeer v.
Florimex and the Commission*, judgement of 30 March 2000, not yet reported, at paras.
114 *et seq*.

12 Regulation 17/62 [1962] JO 204, Article 19; Regulation 2842/98 [1998] OJ L354/18.

13 Lenaerts and Arts, *Procedural Law*, p. 189, citing relevant case law of the ECJ; see also
pp. 193-196 on the duty to give a statement of reasons for the adoption of a Community
measure, derived from Article 253 (formerly 190) EC.

binding. Thus, in the event of a dispute, it can be verified that the texts notified or published correspond precisely to the text adopted by the college and so with the intention of the author. Authentication of acts...therefore constitutes an essential procedural requirement within the meaning of [Article 230 EC] breach of which gives rise to an action for annulment.[14]

Lenaerts and Arts thus classify the procedural infringement in *BASF* as one in which the irregularity makes judicial review of the contested measure impossible.[15] But the Court went further in its recent decision in *Commission v. ICI*, expanding on the decisive significance of locating the breach in the sphere of legal certainty:

It is the mere failure to authenticate an act which constitutes the infringement of an essential procedural requirement and it is not necessary also to establish that the act is vitiated by some other defect *or that the lack of authentication resulted in harm to the person relying on it*...The Court of Justice [in *BASF*] explained that the authentication of acts was intended to guarantee legal certainty. [This] principle, which is part of the Community legal order, requires that any act of the administration that has legal effects must be definitive, in particular as regards its author and content.[16]

The fact that the existence of harm does not need to be established in these circumstances stands in marked contrast to the line of authority emanating from *Chemiefarma*, where the absence of prejudice or 'harmful consequences' meant that breaches of Regulation 1/58 did not result in the annulment of the contested measures. Can these positions be reconciled? In *BASF*, the infringement of the authentication procedure was not really presented in terms of Regulation 1/58; the procedural breach was linked decisively to the verification of texts for the purposes of judicial review. The fact that the relevant provision of the Commission's Rules of Procedure should be read in conjunction with Regulation 1/58 was simply stated at the outset, in the context of summarising the judgment of the Court of First

---

[14] Case C-137/92P, [1994] ECR I-2555 at 2652-3, paras. 75-76.

[15] Lenaerts and Arts, *Procedural Law*, p. 189 (footnote 84).

[16] Case C-286/95P *Commission v. ICI*, judgment of 6 April 2000, not yet reported, paras. 42-45 (emphasis added); the Court repeated this finding at paras. 52-53; see also the judgment in Cases C-287&288/95P *Commission v. Solvay*, delivered on the same day, at para. 43 *et seq.*

Instance; from that point, the Commission Rules were considered in isolation and any independent implications of non-compliance with Regulation 1/58 were not discussed (although the link to the Regulation, and indeed to Article 314 EC, is clearly implied).[17] From the Court's decision in *Chemiefarma*, it appears that an infringement of Regulation 1/58 *per se* does *not* merit unconditional or automatic annulment; instead, the party affected must show that they have been prejudiced by the procedural breach. Why, though, is an acknowledged breach of Article 3 of Regulation 1/58 not treated as a violation of the principle of legal certainty, as enunciated by the Court in *ICI*? Is it appropriate that a fundamental principle firmly established within the Community legal order can be qualified in this manner? Its violation in *BASF* was deemed sufficient to justify annulment (*inter alia*); establishing the existence of harm was considered superfluous. What distinguishes the line of authority that begins with *Chemiefarma*? In both sets of cases, the eligibility of the contested measures for judicial review was not actually at issue; this process was underway in a substantive sense.[18] Again, the answer seems to lie in general administrative principles and not in a language-specific context. Lenaerts and Arts write that "[i]f a procedural provision is infringed but this does not prevent the aims of the provision from being achieved, no 'substantial procedural defect' will be involved."[19] The cases cited as authority for this proposition relate to breaches of the Staff Regulations; in *Ragusa*, for example, a member of a recruiting committee did not sign the committee's report, an 'irregularity' categorised by the Court as "[r]egrettable [but] it does not, however, constitute, in itself, a substantial procedural defect since it is common ground that that member did in fact take part in the deliberations of the Committee."[20] Both the tenor and phrasing here echo the Court's decision in *Chemiefarma*; but can a breach of the Staff Regulations of this nature be compared realistically to a violation of Regulation 1/58? It hardly seems so, given the tenor of the Court's decision in *ICI*. Moreover, how can this be reconciled with the current position of the Court in *Solvay*, where it was established, once again in the context of authentication, that "…authentication is a formal requirement which must be

---

[17] See *BASF*, p. 2636, para. 11

[18] On the liability of Community acts to judicial review in competition law cases generally, see C.S. Kerse, *EC Antitrust Procedure*, 4th ed. (London: Sweet & Maxwell, 1998), pp. 381-416.

[19] Lenaerts and Arts, *Procedural Law*, pp. 189-190, citing Case 282/81 *Ragusa v. Commission* [1983] ECR 1245 at 1259, para. 22, and Case 207/81 *Ditterich v. Commission* [1983] ECR 1359 at 1373, para. 19.

[20] *Ragusa*, p. 1259, para. 22.

observed *whether or not there is any evidence to cast doubt on the authenticity of the text as notified*."[21] Two lines of reasoning—starting with *BASF* and *Chemiefarma* respectively—have thus developed independently where the value of legal certainty might have been better served had the issues raised in both groups of cases been considered together. In *BASF*, the decision was not framed as an aspect of Regulation 1/58 but, in effect, the supremacy of the Regulation was upheld; in *Chemiefarma*, the facts were considered explicitly in terms of the Regulation, but the efficacy of the institutional obligation laid down therein was limited significantly. Conformity with Regulation 1/58 has not, of itself, been ranked as an essential procedural requirement that demands the annulment of a contested measure on an unconditional basis; thus, adopting the classification set out by Lenaerts and Arts, it could be said that compliance with Regulation 1/58 does not constitute a 'fundamental institutional rule'.[22] Ironically, defective authentication of Community texts—a management practice that was developed precisely because of the EC's official language regime—has been held to render a contested measure void automatically, in order to enable effective judicial review. In *Roquette Frères* and *Maïzena*, the relevant acts were annulled because the Council had failed to consult the Parliament, as it had been required to do under Article 43 EEC (now 37 EC); consultation was classified as a 'fundamental institutional rule' on the grounds that it "...reflects at Community level the *fundamental democratic principle that the peoples should take part in the exercise of power....*"[23] EC official language policy is surely as much a reflection of 'fundamental democratic principles' as it is of legal certainty. Indeed, the maintenance of a multi-lingual administrative structure—the operation of which is undeniably complicated and expensive—is generally accepted as resting on these very principles.

The fragility of the *Chemiefarma* limitation is further exhibited by yet another principle that has stemmed from *BASF*. In *Nakajima v. Council*, the Court had held that "...the purpose of the rules of procedure of a Community institution is to organise the internal functioning of its services in the interests of good administration...It follows that natural or legal persons may not rely on an alleged breach of those rules since they are not intended to

---

[21] *Solvay*, para. 34 (emphasis added), upholding the CFI in *'Solvay I'* (Case T-31/91, [1995] ECR II-1821) and *'Solvay II'*, (Case T-32/91, [1995] ECR II-1825).

[22] See note 13; Lenaerts and Arts cite Case 138/79 *Roquette Frères v. Council* [1980] ECR 3333 at 3360, para. 33, and Case 139/79 *Maïzena v. Council* [1980] ECR 3393 at 3424, para. 34.

[23] *Roquette Frères*, p. 3360, para. 33 (emphasis added).

ensure protection for individuals."[24] The decision in *BASF* places an implicit proviso on that proposition.[25] And ironically, the Court has since strengthened its stance in favour of individuals in this regard: in *Germany v. Council*, it held that the Commission legislative procedures in question were *"...fundamentally different from the acts which are adopted by the Commission and are of direct concern to individuals.* In those circumstances *strict compliance with the formalities prescribed for the adoption of acts of direct concern to individuals* cannot be required for the adoption of such proposals."[26] Again, the approach taken by the Court in *Chemiefarma*— which has had such recent implications in *Cimenteries*—simply does not fit with the more convincing and principled trend emanating from *BASF*. Perhaps the only thing that can be stated with conviction on this question, then, is that confusion reigns. The labyrinthine tangle of cases outlined above certainly produces more questions than answers on the status of Regulation 1/58 in the eyes of the Court. But it is difficult to avoid feeling that a somewhat arbitrary restriction has been placed on Article 3, grounded in isolated and undeveloped reasoning.

Moving to general rules on secondary legislation, regulations and other legislative documents of general application must be drafted in *all* of the official languages (Article 4); in line with the principle of equality, each language version is considered to be equally authoritative in a legal sense. Similarly, Article 5 requires the publication of the *Official Journal of the Communities* in all of the official EC languages. Article 6 stipulates that the Community institutions may determine internal language regulations for specific administrative practices. The Regulation itself does not elaborate on the compatibility of this procedure with the intended equality of the official languages, but it has been provided elsewhere that any internal guidelines

---

[24] Case C-69/89 *Nakajima v. Council* [1991] ECR I-2069 at 2183, paras. 49-50.

[25] The Court of Justice did not deal explicitly with *Nakajima* in *BASF*; a distinction between rules of procedure that have internal application only and those that were intended for the protection of individuals was drawn, however, by both the Court of First Instance (Cases T-79 etc./89 *BASF AG and Others v. Commission* [1992] ECR II-315) and by Advocate General van Gerven (*BASF*, pp. 2259-2628). The Advocate General took a stricter approach than that of the CFI, arguing that situations in which an institution's rules of procedure could be said to have been intended for the protection of individuals were the exception and not the rule (p. 2604, para. 55); his ultimate conclusion that the CFI judgment should be set aside was not, however, followed by the ECJ with regard to the character of the authentication procedure, as seen above.

[26] Case C-280/93 *Germany v. Council* [1994] ECR I-4973 at 5054, para. 36, citing *BASF* (emphasis added).

implemented by the institutions must comply with the linguistic equality formula.[27]

B.   Language in the Community Institutions

Internal arrangements for the everyday use of language in the Community institutions, outlined in the following paragraphs, are one of the primary manifestations of EC language planning in practice. The thematic policies of the institutions on *external* language issues are not detailed at this stage but are assessed in depth in Chapters 2 and 6. Moreover, this section deals only with the use of official Community languages; the status of minority languages is considered separately below. The particular difficulties faced by the EC translation and interpretation services are also considered separately, since they apply in a cross-institutional sense.

(i)   The European Court of Justice[28]

The ECJ is subject to the general guidelines set out in Regulation 1/58 but, according to Article 7, it may develop autonomous rules in respect of language use during proceedings. The relevant rules devised by the Court can be found in Articles 29-31 of its Rules of Procedure.[29] Article 29(1) confirms that the languages that may be used are all of the official EC languages, and Irish. Generally, the language of proceedings is selected by the applicant. But where the defendant is a Member State, or a natural or legal person of Member State nationality, the official language of that State must be used.[30] If a state has more than one official language, the applicant

---

[27]   See Doc. A 3-169/90.

[28]   The language policy of the European Court of Justice applies equally to the Court of First Instance: see Articles 35-36 of the Rules of Procedure of the Court of First Instance (see note 29 *infra*).

[29]   ECJ Rules of Procedure, [1991] OJ L176/9, as corrected ([1992] OJ L383/117) and amended ([1995] OJ L44/61, [1997] OJ L103/1 and Council Decision 97/419, [1997] OJ L103/3). The progress report on IGC 2000, prepared for the Feira European Council in June 2000, did not propose any substantive amendments to the ECJ language rules as codified at present; however, see generally the Protocol Annexed to the Treaty of the European Union, to the Treaty establishing the European Community and to the Treaty establishing the European Atomic Energy Commnity, enacted via the Treaty of Nice (and specifically the Protocol on the Statute of the Court of Justice).

[30]   See also Articles 29(2)(b) and 29(2)(c), which provide that use of another official EC language may be authorised at the joint request of the parties to the proceedings or at the

may choose between them (Article 29(2)(a)). The Rules do not specify expressly that the language selected here must also be an official EC language. On a literal interpretation, this leaves open the possibility that the applicant may select, for example, a minority language that is an official language of the Member State concerned but is not actually recognised by Regulation 1/58; it is more likely, however, that Article 29(1) governs this situation, setting an overriding limitation against the use of non-official (in the EC sense) languages. Article 29(3) stipulates that the language of the case must be used for both oral and written pleadings and for supporting documents; any documents submitted in another language must be accompanied by a translation into the language of the case. Article 29(4) provides that where a witness or expert states that s/he is unable adequately to express him/herself in any of the official EC languages or Irish, the Court may authorise him/her to give evidence in another language. In this situation, the Registrar must arrange for translation of the evidence into the language of the case. For preliminary references sent by national courts to the ECJ in accordance with Article 234 EC, the language used in the ECJ will be 'the language of the national court or tribunal' making the reference.[31] Also, whenever a Member State intervenes in a case before the ECJ, it may use 'its official language' irrespective of the language of the case;[32] responsibility for arranging the translation of these submissions is placed on the Registrar. In respect of both preliminary references and Member State interventions, it would appear from the ambiguous phrasing in the ECJ Rules of Procedure that the language selected in either instance does not have to be one of the official EC languages. Again, it is probable that Article 29(1) establishes a general presumption against languages other than those listed therein (although the literal interpretation to the contrary is arguably more convincing here than when raised in respect of Article 29(2)(a)). Judgments delivered by the Court are of legal effect in the language of the case only, but are subsequently translated into and published in the other official languages (but not Irish).[33] Judgments in staff cases are published only in the

---

request of one of the parties after the opposite party and the Advocate General have been heard.

[31] Formerly Article 177 EC; see Articles 29(2) and 29(3) of the Rules of Procedure of the Court of Justice.

[32] Article 29(3) of the Rules of Procedure of the Court of Justice.

[33] Article 30(2) of the Rules of Procedure of the Court of Justice; but see John A. Usher, "Languages and the European Union", in Malcolm Anderson and Eberhard Bort (eds.), *The Frontiers of Europe*, (London: Pinter, 1998), 222-234 at 225 *et seq*, who notes that some judgments have been published only in the language in which the case was heard. In addition, delays in the translation of judgments have been further exacerbated in recent

language in which the case was heard, with a summary published in the other official languages. The Opinion of the Advocate General is usually delivered in his/her native tongue (bearing in mind, however, that the Opinion must be delivered in an official EC language or in Irish) and is translated subsequently into the language of the case.[34] Illustrating the Court's pragmatic approach to multilingualism, it has *not* applied the maxim that 'ignorance of the law is no defence' where there have been delays in the translation of Community legislation.[35] Similarly, and as discussed above, violation of the language rules does not necessarily invalidate proceedings.[36]

In contrast, the character of judicial deliberations illustrates the divergence between policy and practice in the day-to-day running of the institutions. Since these discussions must be held in closed session, the use of interpreters is necessarily prohibited, requiring judges to communicate in a common working language.[37] The language adopted almost always is French. A judge may request a translation of anything said or written in the course of the proceedings into any of the official EC languages (or Irish), which provides a basic safeguard in case of linguistic confusion.[38] In light of the confidentiality of judicial deliberations, it is difficult to propose any alternative to the internal adoption of a common working language. The adoption of a common language may also contribute to the cohesiveness of an otherwise diversely constituted court. But equally, the practice may operate in a discriminatory manner against judges whose expression in the French language might be somewhat limited, resulting in a possible loss of potency from their arguments. This may become more problematic in the future, given the ever-increasing primacy of English as a second language across Europe. In any event, the *de facto* distinction between official and working languages that is necessarily practised within the Court calls the absolutism of the principle of language equality into question and introduces the case for doctrinal reform.

---

years, given their virtually instant publication on the Court's Internet website (http://curia.eu.int).

[34] Article 29(5) of the Rules of Procedure of the Court of Justice.

[35] Case 160/84 *Oryzomyli Kavallas* [1986] ECR 1633.

[36] Case 1/60 *Acciaieria Ferriera di Roma v. High Authority* [1960] ECR 165 ; Case 41/69 *ACF Chemiefarma. v. Commission* [1970] ECR 661.

[37] Article 27(1) of the Rules of Procedure of the Court of Justice.

[38] Article 30(1) of the Rules of Procedure of the Court of Justice; this facility is also available to the Advocate General and to any party to the proceedings. See also Article 27(4) of the Rules.

(ii)   The Commission and the Council

Both the Commission and the Council are bound generally by the language guidelines established in Regulation 1/58. In reality, both institutions use French and English as working languages for daily communication; German is also used increasingly. The Commission has devised an internal translation and authentication scheme to reflect this pattern of language use, in accordance with Article 6 of the Regulation.[39] This means that deliberations and negotiations are often carried out in a reduced number of languages, with the resulting texts then translated into all of the official EC languages and duly authenticated. The Court of Justice implicitly sanctioned this practice when, in *Commission v. BASF*, it annulled a Commission decision on the grounds that the Commission had not adhered to the authentication procedure in respect of certain texts; but it was this omission, and not the practice of subsequent translation in itself, that was decisive in this case.[40]

The divergence between theoretical language equality and language use in practice was challenged in *Kik v. Council and Commission*, regarding the procedures adopted by the Office for Harmonisation in the Internal Market (trade marks and designs) (OHIM)[41] to deal with applications for Community trade marks.[42] Only English, French, German, Italian and Spanish are recognised as its working languages. An application for a Community trade mark may be filed in any of the official EC languages, but applicants must specify a second language—which must be a working language of OHIM—in which OHIM may send written communications. Furthermore, the applicant is deemed to accept this second language as the language of any subsequent opposition, revocation or invalidity proceedings. If a European trade mark is granted, it is translated into the language of each Member State designated in the application. *Kik* was dismissed on admissibility grounds, because the measure challenged was a general legislative one and was not, therefore, open to challenge by an individual before the Court of Justice.[43]

---

[39]   See Article 16 of the Commission's Rules of Procedure (the present Rules were adopted on 17 February 1993, [1993] OJ L230/16).

[40]   Case C-137/92P *Commission v. BASF and Others* [1994] ECR I-2555.

[41]   In 1994, the Translation Centre for Bodies in the European Union was set up in Luxembourg; it provides translation services for most EU agencies and other bodies, including OHIM.

[42]   Case T-107/94, [1995] ECR II-1717; upheld by the ECJ on appeal, Case C-270/95, [1996] ECR I-1987; see also Article 115 of Regulation 40/94, [1994] OJ L11/1.

[43]   See generally, on the principles of direct and individual concern, Case 25/62 *Plaumann v. Commission* [1963] ECR 95 and Case C-309/89 *Codorniu v. Council* [1994] ECR I-1853.

But, as with the character of judicial deliberations, this case highlights yet another instance within the administrative structure of the Community where an adjustment to the absolute equality of languages has been employed, ostensibly on grounds of pragmatism. The situation in *Kik* is not as straightforward as that in *Commission v. BASF*; in the latter case, the employment of a reduced number of languages had been chosen by the Commission itself for its own internal administration, but in *Kik*, the relevant procedural framework has been imposed by a Community body on those who communicate with it. This has serious implications for applicants who do not have competence in the languages of the Office, heightened by the fact that the 'second' language is to be employed for any subsequent opposition, revocation or invalidity proceedings. The two cases highlight the difference between the internal and external effects of language policy, considered in more detail below, and suggest that the paper equality of the official EC languages has not secured their equality in practice. And more especially, the facts of *Kik* reveal that differing linguistic standards apply for the Community institutions on the one hand, and for other Community agencies or bodies on the other. Regulation 1/58 binds only the 'institutions of the Community', and so there is no legal barrier to the OHIM linguistic framework. But is this acceptable within an ethos of linguistic 'equality'? It is at least arguable that the doctrine of the linguistic equality in a generic sense is contravened by the Community language rules. If this cannot be said to have legal force, it will at least pose a thorny political obstacle for the Court. There lies also to be considered more openly the relationship between language rules and the fundamental principle of legal certainty. Moreover, the selectivity involved in the OHIM language regime raises the possibility of discrimination on grounds of nationality. And while a Community body is not in a strict or technical sense classified as an 'institution', it may still be treated as being in a position analogous to that of an EC institution.[44] The Court may yet have to face the substantive issues raised here; in May 1999, the applicant in *Kik*—having since had her application for a Community trade mark turned down on the grounds that the second language specified therein (Dutch) was not one of OHIM's five working languages—applied for a review by the Court of First Instance of the decision of the OHIM Board of Appeal, arguing,

---

[44]   See John A. Usher, *EC Institutions and Legislation*, (London: Longman, 1998), pp. 12-14, citing Case 110/75 *Mills v. European Investment Bank* [1976] ECR 955 and Case C-370/89 *SGEEM v. European Investment Bank* [1993] ECR I-2583.

once again, that the relevant language procedures violate Article 12 EC (non-discrimination on grounds of nationality) and Regulation 1/58.[45]

(iii)   The Parliament

There is arguably a special significance attached to the observation of multi-lingualism in the European Parliament. First, since proceedings of the Parliament are held in public, it provides a unique forum for open discussion on proposals for Community legislation. Second, the Parliament is a directly-elected body whose members are entitled, on democratic principles, to understand proceedings within the institution. It is thus imperative that the debates be mutually comprehensible. Whether the attachment to the office of MEP of language competence requirements could actually be justified (or successful) is not something that has yet received serious attention. It may become more of a live issue, however, as a consequence of EU enlargement. At present, the European Parliament Rules of Procedure allow each MEP to use his/her official language for both written and oral communications.[46] Additionally, Parliament sometimes authorises, in special circumstances, the use and interpretation of languages other than the official Community languages. Advance notice of an intention to use other languages, which may include minority languages where appropriate, must be given, to enable the appointment of interpretation staff competent in the selected language(s). To date, then, where language reform (and essentially, streamlining) has arisen for discussion, Parliament has been considered in a somewhat different light to the other institutions whose representatives are not directly elected by Union citizens; in particular, the function of the Parliament as a deliberative, public assembly has been taken into account. But whether this 'exemption' will continue to hold sway under the strain of enlargement remains to be seen.

---

[45]   Case T-120/99 *Kik v. Office for Harmonisation in the Internal Market (OHIM)*, lodged on 19 May 1999; see [1999] OJ C246/35.

[46]   See rule 117 of the European Parliament Rules of Procedure (amended version, [1999] OJ C175/95; renumbered version, [1999] OJ L202/1); see also Resolution of the European Parliament on multilingualism in the European Community, 14 October 1982, [1982] OJ C292/96 and Resolution of the European Parliament on the right to use one's own language, 6 May 1994, [1994] OJ C205/528.

C.   Implications for Translation and Interpretation

The functioning of EC administration is wholly dependent on the lifeline services of translation and interpretation. The Community, as a multinational organisation, had to make arrangements from the outset for both the translation of texts and documents and the interpretation of oral speech. The execution in practice of its official language (equality) policy was not always the immense technical feat it has now become; but over the past decades, with more than double the original number of Member States now accommodated—and almost three times the original number of languages—the demands placed on these services have been greatly intensified; inevitable and increasing delays have for some time been considered to have reached crisis point, not least from the angle of effective administration. As the EU prepares for further enlargement, the need to rethink already problematic arrangements becomes all the more urgent.

(i)   *Practical Impact on Translation and Interpretation Services*

As noted in the context of the Treaty of Rome, the co-ordination of several language versions of legal texts is a tremendously difficult process, producing a considerable quantity of printed documents. Translation and interpretation staff are required to be competent in at least two Community languages; other qualification requirements may differ having regard, for example, to the institution for which the services will be provided. The Commuity translation service has established its own Terminology Office, to harmonise legal and other subject-specific vocabulary. It has also created a multilingual terminology data-bank.[47] Community research programmes on the potential of electronic translation are ongoing but not yet operative, mainly because the practical difficulties associated typically with automated comprehension and word recognition have not yet been overcome satisfactorily. Interpretation services currently operate on a relay system, which necessitates groups or teams of interpreters working together and, in turn, requires high staff numbers. And difficulties can sometimes arise when the subject matter at issue involves a highly specialised vocabulary.

Perhaps the most controversial aspect of translation and interpretation requirements is the corresponding drain on Community finances. It is regularly pointed out that these services consume more than forty per cent of the EC administrative budget, an unacceptable figure that renders an

---

[47]   *i.e. EURODICAUTOM.*

admittedly well-intentioned idea no longer practicable; and it is arguably ironic that an organisation in which economy and efficiency are the primary objectives pays such a high price for linguistic politics.[48] But few who argue in this vein acknowledge that the administrative budget of the EC amounts to a far smaller proportion of *total* Community expenditure. It is a plain fact that several languages are spoken throughout the Member States and it is simply to be expected that facilitating mutual comprehension must be a basic EC concern. Moreover, even though EC policies are developed by centralised institutions, they still have to be implemented in linguistically diverse Member States. The debate on costs raises the question of just what kind of polity the EC should be; does the pursuit of economic objectives represent an impermeable ambition, so that all other competing values are ultimately irrelevant? As discussed in subsequent chapters, the Member States have railed against this interpretation; furthermore, decisions of the Court of Justice show that the EC itself has never required it. What must be faced up to, however, is that current EC language policy, framed in terms of 'equality', does not reflect the linguistic reality. Reform of the official languages policy may therefore be necessary, but the case for it should not be made on economic grounds alone. Each and every Community document does not end up in eleven language versions; not all gatherings are served by interpretation services (predominantly in the interests of confidentiality, but also efficiency). Pragmatism demands that arrangements of this kind are necessary; but honesty demands that they be acknowledged more openly and that the doctrine of linguistic 'equality' is reassessed accordingly.

(ii)   Interpretation of Multilingual Texts

Interpreting several different, but equally authoritative, versions of a legislative act has serious implications for the uniform application of Community law.[49] Textual discrepancies have to be considered carefully, since opting for one interpretation over another can affect the outcome of the proceedings at hand. The EC database of specialised legal and other terminology has

---

[48]   See for example, Florian Coulmas, "European integration and the idea of the national language", in Florian Coulmas (ed.), *A Language Policy for the European Community*, (Berlin: Mouton de Gruyter, 1991), 1-44; Robert Huntington, "European unity and the Tower of Babel", (1991) 9 *Boston University International Law Journal* 321-346.

[49]   That all language versions of EC legislation are equally authentic stems from the obligation in Article 5 of Regulation 1/58 to publish the *Official Journal* in all of the official EC languages; see also Case 283/81 *CILFIT v. Ministero della Sanità* [1982] ECR 3415 at 3430, para 18.

certainly facilitated the successful harmonisation of official texts. But the Court of Justice has sometimes been faced with the interpretation of two or more equally authentic yet inconsistent provisions. It has adopted a purposive, teleological approach to avoid the stalemate likely to result from strictly literal interpretation.[50] This means that the Court attempts to discern the purpose or intention behind the legislation in question, so that the most likely interpretation of the disputed term or phrase becomes evident. Though pragmatic in inspiration, some are sceptical of this practice, arguing that the Court may thus determine that words, in certain instances, should not be accorded their usual meaning. But the multilingual drafting and inter-pretation process also has certain advantages.[51] Both drafting and subsequent translation can require more careful contemplation of the terminology used, arguably resulting in a more considered text than might otherwise have been possible. Moreover, a provision that seems difficult or unclear can be clarified by comparison to another language version; and the actual composi-tion of the ECJ means that there may be a representative of each official language on hand to facilitate this process. Significantly, notwithstanding the volume and often specialised nature of official EC texts, the number of instances where linguistic anomalies have had discernible legal con-sequences is relatively low; this statistic reinforces rather than defeats the value of multilingual drafting in the first place.

(iii)   Conclusion

It is obvious that the EC's translation and interpretation services have an enormous workload and are often strained. Indeed, most calls for reform come from those directly involved in their provision. But that argument should not hinge primarily on costs. Reducing the number of official languages would certainly reduce costs but would necessarily transfer responsibility for the translation of legislation and other publications to the individual Member States. This procedure would have considerable implica-tions for the uniform application of Community law, given that even centralised translation is itself susceptible to harmonisation difficulties. In

---

[50]   The Court itself has confirmed the application of this approach: see Case 61/72 *Mij. PPW International v. Hoofdproduktschap voor Akkerbouwprodukten* [1973] ECR 301; see also, Geert Van Calster, "The EU's Tower of Babel: The interpretation by the European Court of Justice of equally authentic texts drafted in more than one official language", (1997) 17 *Yearbook of European Law* 363-393.

[51]   On this point, see Mala Tabory, *Multilingualism in International Law and Institutions*, (Alphen aan den Rijn; Rockville MA: Sijthoff and Noordhoff, 1980), pp. 227-230.

addition, the self-executing character of directly applicable Community law, examined further below, strengthens the case in favour of maintaining centralised translation. The EC Member States are diverse. This is an enduring truth that the abolition of tariffs and customs duties does not and should not overcome. But it is also essential that language policy should be guided by pragmatism. In the context of the EC, this would not require a very radical reform of existing practices and, in reality, would largely reflect the way in which internal day-to-day administration is already carried out. In other words, the practice would not be new but its formalisation would be. The political implications of this are discussed further below, especially against the backdrop of EU enlargement. Above all, however, reformation of the language regime should continue to be guided by the principle that arbitrary restrictions on free choice of language must be avoided, particularly where an individual's linguistic expression would be compromised as a result.

D.   The Language Dimension of Fundamental Community Freedoms

The use of language in the institutions was described above as the primary manifestation of EC language policy. But there is a linguistic dimension to virtually *any* policy initiated at Community level, in that the rippling effect of EC law has innumerable consequences for languages and for their speakers. The converse of this argument is that far more spheres of life are affected by considerations of language than is usually realised or acknowledged. This idea is reflected throughout this chapter, especially in terms of whether resulting linguistic imbalances can or should be redressed. Arguments of this kind also relate more generally to the wider debate on the nature and theories of European integration, introduced separately below. Finally, the legal competence of the Community to take more direct action on language issues is assessed in subsequent chapters. But, in the first instance, the following paragraphs sketch briefly some of the implications for language use patterns that are generated by the implementation of fundamental Community freedoms, while striving to identify any common trends that could, in effect, add up to an 'indirect' EC language policy.

(i)   Free Movement of Persons

The EC Treaty guarantees the right of EU citizens to move freely among, to reside and to work in all of the Member States.[52] It is probable that a person who moves from his/her native country to another Member State will also cross language frontiers. The Community has addressed the linguistic aspect of free movement from two perspectives: first, by supporting preparatory language education and second, by anticipating and dealing with difficulties that may arise after resettlement in the new country. A number of language education programmes have been established to promote the learning of the official Community languages, *LINGUA* being the most comprehensive.[53] Recognising that the decision to move to another Member State can occur at any stage in life, language education is not confined to school and university curricula; it is also promoted in the context of continuing adult education. Community policy on the education of children of migrant workers has evolved gradually from one favouring passive assimilation into the host state, towards the view that mother-tongue education should also be provided on cultural and identity grounds, as well as to prepare children for eventual reintegration into their countries of origin where relevant.[54] Significantly, a shift in emphasis now seems to reflect a concern for fundamental rights and citizenship not readily apparent in earlier, more assimilative measures. The philosophy behind general EC involvement in language education can be interpreted in two ways. First, by ensuring that all official EC languages are included in the various programmes, the Community is confirming its commitment to linguistic diversity and to the doctrine of the equality of the relevant languages. Alternatively, the promotion of language

---

[52]   See Articles 18 and 39-42 EC; the extent to which the right to freedom of movement and of residence extends beyond the sphere of economic activity is arguably in a state of ongoing flux but see generally Directives 90/364, 90/365 and 93/96 ([1990] OJ L180/26 and L180/28, and [1993] OJ L317/59 respectively), and the decisions of the Court of Justice in Case C-85/96 *Martínez Sala v. Freistaat Bayern* [1998] ECR I-2691, Case C-274/96 *Criminal Proceedings against Bickel and Franz* [1998] ECR I-7637 and Case C-378/97 *Criminal Proceedings against Wijsenbeek*, judgment of 21 September 1999, not yet reported.

[53]   Established by Decision 89/489, [1989] OJ L239/24; for information on *LINGUA* and other language education programmes, see Joseph A. McMahon, *Education and Culture in European Community Law*, (London: The Athlone Press, 1995), Chapter 2; see also, the website of the Education and Culture Directorate General for details of updated programmes, at http://europa.eu.int/comm/education/newprogr/index.html.

[54]   See Holly Cullen, "From migrants to citizens? European Community policy on intercultural education", (1996) 45 *International and Comparative Law Quarterly* 109-129.

education can be attributed solely to the functional requirement that the free movement of workers should be facilitated by comprehensive linguistic training. In truth, it is likely that both ideologies have influenced EC action in this field. The promotion of bilingualism and multilingualism through language education receives strong support in general. But whether time and public money should be allocated to the promotion of smaller national and non-official/minority languages, as well as to the languages of wider communication, or in what proportion this allocation should occur, remains a contentious issue; EC funding in the minority language context is discussed particularly in Chapters 2, 3 and 6.

It has been accepted by the Court of Justice that a foreign national may be susceptible to the language policy requirements of the host state, so long as the basic principles of free movement—proportionality and non-discrimination—have not been breached.[55] By recognising that a Member State may legitimately pursue language planning at national level, within the limits of these established standards of fairness, the ECJ attached considerable significance to the inherent value of linguistic diversity. Moreover, it adopted this position *before* the Community was required to respect either the national identities of its Member States (Article 6(3) (formerly F) TEU) or their cultural diversity (see Article 151 (formerly 128) EC, introduced by the TEU, analysed in Chapter 3). In *Ministère Public v. Mutsch*, the Court held that language rights granted by a Member State to its nationals must be extended to *all* Community workers resident in that State.[56] The implications of *Mutsch* for Community language policy are discussed in Chapter 2, but it should be emphasised that this case does not require Member States to introduce a language rights regime *per se*: rather, it demands non-discriminatory implementation where such rights have already been provided for. In certain limited circumstances, however, the principle of free movement may result in the granting of language rights to non-nationals over and above those enjoyed by nationals of a Member State.[57]

---

[55] Case 379/87 *Anita Groener v. Minister for Education and the Dublin Vocational Education Committee* [1989] ECR 3967; this case, which centred on linguistic competence as a precondition of employment, is analysed in detail in Chapter 2.

[56] Case 137/84, [1985] ECR 2681.

[57] See Case C-274/96 *Criminal Proceedings against Bickel and Franz* [1998] ECR I-7637, discussed in Chapter 6.

24   *Chapter 1*

(ii)   *Right of Establishment and Freedom to Provide Services*[58]

As with free movement of persons, EC law on both the right of establishment and the freedom to provide services prohibits direct and indirect discrimination against non-nationals. Essentially, Member States may still impose linguistic competence conditions on the exercise of trades and professions, but these requirements must apply equally to both nationals and non-nationals. They must also comply with the principle of proportionality, in that the measures adopted must be proportionate to the objectives of the language policy pursued. Language rules and the freedom to provide services were considered in *Bickel and Franz*, discussed in detail in Chapter 6.[59] The Court of Justice has recently, in *Haim*, addressed language requirements in the context of freedom of establishment.[60] Article 18(3) of Directive 78/686 (on the mutual recognition of dentistry qualifications) provides that "Member states shall see to it that, where appropriate, the persons concerned acquire, in their interest and in that of their patients, the linguistic knowledge necessary for the exercise of their profession in the host Member State."[61] One of the questions referred to the ECJ related to whether Member State authorities could make the appointment as a social security scheme dental practitioner of a national of another Member State (who is established in the first Member State and is authorised to practise there but does not have the qualifications mentioned in Article 3 of the Directive) subject to a linguistic competence requirement.[62] The Court answered the question in the affirmative, justifying the attachment of a linguistic competence requirement in these circumstances as an 'overriding reason of general interest' in respect of the reliability of communication with patients, and with the relevant administrative authorities and professional bodies.[63] It did, however, issue a reminder that any such requirement was subject to proportionality.[64] In this context, the Court made the fairly open-ended statement that it was "...in the interest

---

[58]   Articles 43-48 (Establishment) and 49-55 (Services) EC.

[59]   See Case C-274/96 *Criminal Proceedings against Bickel and Franz*, [1998] ECR I-7637.

[60]   Case C-424/97 *Haim v. Kassenzahnärztliche Vereinigung Nordrhein*, judgment of 4 July 2000, not yet reported.

[61]   Directive 78/686, [1978] OJ L233/1.

[62]   *Haim*, para. 50.

[63]   *Haim*, para. 59, referring to paras. 105-113 of the Opinion of Advocate General Mischo (which had been delivered on 19 May 1999). The interpretative approach adopted here by the Court is discussed further in Chapter 2, in respect of derogations from the free movement principles.

[64]   *Haim*, para. 60.

of patients whose mother tongue is not the national language that there exist a certain number of dental practitioners who are also capable of communicating with such persons in their own language."[65] This statement could be said to lean subtly towards the identification of a positive duty on Member State authorities to take into account, given the dominant ethos of movement that pervades EC law, the linguistic needs of those who do not speak the national language of the state in which they find themselves. That the Court made this remark in the first place is surprising, especially given that the language in question (Turkish) is neither an official nor indigenous minority EC language; that it did not elaborate further is perhaps disappointing but, politically, wise.

(iii)   Free Movement of Goods[66]

In the context of the free movement of goods, attention has been focused primarily on the competing value of consumer protection, especially regarding the language(s) used on product labels *etc.*[67] If every Member State had its own language requirements for all products available within its territory, thus requiring different product labels for each market, suppliers of imported goods would face additional costs; this becomes still more onerous where a Member State recognises sub-national language regions (*e.g.* the Basque country, Catalonia and Galicia in Spain). Setting specific language requirements could, therefore, be interpreted as an indirect obstacle to the free movement of goods.[68] But this must be balanced with one of the fundamental principles of consumer protection, and in particular the right of the consumer to information on the functions and properties of products available on the market. The Court of Justice has addressed this conundrum on a number of occasions and its case law was recently consolidated in *Colim and Bigg's*.[69] Belgian consumer law requires that "[t]he particulars to appear on the labelling...are to be given at least in the language or languages

---

[65] *ibid.*

[66] Articles 23-31 EC.

[67] A range of EC Directives are relevant here; see principally, Directive 79/112, [1979] OJ L33/1, as amended by Directive 97/4, [1997] OJ L43/21; Directive 83/189, [1983] OJ L109/8, as amended by Directive 88/182, [1988] OJ L81/75; see also Directives 92/159, [1992] OJ L228/24, 94/10, [1994] OJ L100/30 and 1999/44 [1999] OJ L171/12.

[68] See generally Case 120/78 *Rewe-Zentrale AG v. Bundesmonopolverwaltung für Branntwein (Cassis de Dijon)* [1979] ECR 649.

[69] Case C-33/97, 3 June 1999, not yet reported.

of the area in which the products are placed on the market."[70] Two
department stores in the province of Limburg were found to have numerous
products for sale that had no information in Dutch—the language of the
area—on either the packaging or labelling. The primary issue to be decided
in this case was whether the national legislation should have been notified to
the Commission under Directive 83/189, as a draft technical regulation.[71] But
two key questions on the free movement of goods were also referred to the
ECJ:

> Where specific Community rules exist concerning the particu-
> lars which must appear on specific products, may a Member
> State require imported products to carry other information in the
> language of the area in which the products are sold or in a
> language readily understood by the consumer?

> In respect of products for which there are no specific Commun-
> ity rules, may a Member State require all or certain (and if so
> which) information on the imported products to be given in the
> language of the area in which the products are sold or in a
> language readily understood by the consumer?[72]

The distinct situations envisaged by these questions reflect the different
standards that apply within the exercise of shared Community/Member State
competence. The Court summarised the implications of this division of
powers as follows:

> [F]or certain categories of product, Community directives
> require the national language or languages to be used in order to
> enhance consumer or public health protection. When those
> directives fully harmonise the language requirements applicable
> for a given product, the Member States cannot impose addi-
> tional language requirements. By contrast, where there is only
> partial Community harmonisation or none at all, the Member
> States in principle retain the power to impose additional
> language requirements.[73]

---

[70] Article 13 of the Law of 14 July 1991 on Trade Practices and Consumer Information and
Protection.

[71] Directive 83/189, [1983] OJ L109/8, on the provision of information on technical standards and regulations.

[72] *Colim and Bigg's*, questions 2 (a) and (c), para. 18.

[73] *ibid.*, paras. 33-35.

But, as noted above, the competence of a Member State to impose additional language requirements is limited by the fact that conditions of this nature can constitute a barrier to intra-Community trade "...in so far as products coming from other Member States have to be given different labelling involving additional packaging costs."[74] Such restrictions are directly at odds with the principle of the free movement of goods and are prohibited by Article 28 EC. But the Court pointed out that rules of this kind can be saved where their application can be justified by a public interest objective taking precedence over the free movement of goods.[75] Additionally, they must apply without distinction to all national and imported products, and must be proportionate to the objective pursued. The public interest objective typically identified in this context is that of consumer protection, based on the premise that product information is of no practical value unless it is given in a language that the consumer understands. The concept of a 'language easily understood' has been applied consistently by the Court.[76] But this too has provoked the criticism that since consumers are not necessarily entitled to information in the nationally designated official language(s) of the state or area in question, the EC is prepared, in effect, to subordinate national language requirements in the interests of trade. It is equally arguable, however, that in treating the matter as one of consumer protection, emphasis has properly been placed on the fundamental requirement that consumers should be able to understand *whatever* language is used on product labels. This stance focuses on the rights of individuals, over and above the more abstract or aesthetic properties of language. Viewed in this light, the approach adopted does not seem quite so dismissive.[77] But one crucial question remains under either interpretation: can the pursuit of language policies at

---

[74] *ibid.*, para. 36, referring to Case C-51/93 *Meyhui v. Schott Zwiesel Glaswerke* [1994] ECR I-3879. In Case C-385/96 *Goerres* [1998] ECR I-4431, the Court held that Article 14 of Directive 79/112 ([1979] OJ L33/1) does not preclude national legislation that prescribes the use of a specific language for the labelling of foodstuffs so long as that legislation also permits the use of another language, as an alternative, that is easily understood by consumers.

[75] *Colim and Biggs*, para. 38, referring to *Meyhui* (p. 3898, para. 10). See also, Case C-315/92 *Verband Sozialer Wettbewerb v. Clinique Laboratories and Estée Lauder* [1994] ECR I-317 at 335, para. 13.

[76] See Case C-85/94 *Piageme II* [1995] ECR I-2955, especially at 2976, para. 15.

[77] Although criticism has also been levelled equally at the Court's faith in labelling as a mechanism for fulfilling the interests of consumer protection; see for example, J.H.H. Weiler, "Prologue: Amsterdam and the quest for constitutional democracy", in David O'Keeffe and Patrick Twomey (eds.), *Legal Issues of the Amsterdam Treaty*, (Oxford: Hart Publishing, 1999), 1-19 at 16.

national level *per se* amount to a public interest objective taking precedence over the free movement of goods? In other words, can non-economic values that are grounded in maintaining diversity sometimes override the goal of economic harmonisation? This question cuts to the heart of the evolving functions and priorities of the EC. It has not been addressed directly within the case law on free movement of goods although it would appear implicitly that the interest of consumer protection trumps where the two have come into conflict. But it has arisen in other strands of jurisprudence, considered further in Chapters 2 and 6, where derogation from the Treaty has been sought expressly on the basis of preserving linguistic and/or cultural diversity.

E.   Conclusion: Should EC Language Policy be Reformed?

At present, EC language policy is confined largely to managing the use of the official languages in the institutions; the language dimension of other Community policies is certainly relevant but, to date, has been dealt with in an incidental or secondary manner. The apparent theme of EC language policy is a commitment to linguistic equality. But the rigidity of this doctrine is often circumvented in administrative practice. Clearly, the eleven official languages are not always used 'equally'. It must be asked, then, whether retaining an absolutist approach benefits either the Community or the languages themselves. The principle of linguistic equality has always had, and retains, intense political symbolism, fuelling a broader sense of equality and participation among the Member States; this is explored further in the next section. But it is not practical to use all the official languages for all purposes; and reform will become even more necessary if EU enlargement proceeds as anticipated. The administration of the EC using just one or two languages to the exclusion of all others, often proposed on grounds of—usually economic—efficiency, is not feasible either in an inherently multi-cultural, multilingual entity; a droll answer often rendered in response to suggestions of this kind is that no-one, then, should be allowed to use his/her own native language, to allow for an even distribution of the inevitable linguistic handicap. But a more appropriate alternative may lie between the extremes of both existing arrangements and draconian alternatives. An obvious starting point is the division between official and working languages, which emphasises also the distinct internal and external implications of language policy. Regulation 1/58 makes an explicit reference to both 'official' and 'working' languages but this distinction has not been exploited fully. In reality, just one or two of the official EC languages are used regularly as *de facto* working languages within the institutions. The continued employment of pragmatism, in this *internal* context, alleviates pressure on translation and interpretation services without trespassing needlessly on political sensitivities. The Working with just one or two languages is managed already by the Commission, and by the Council (or more accurately, by its administrative staff) where appropriate. This practice should be acknowledged more openly and extended where possible, accompanied by the proviso that any individual who is unable to express him/herself in, or understand, the selected language(s) could avail of translation and interpretation services where required. The distinct features and functions of the European Parliament should arguably continue to demand more comprehensive language arrangements if necessary, in the interests of accessibility and participatory democracy.

The external impact of language policy is, however, quite different. In terms of contact with the institutions, Regulation 1/58 (as noted above and considered further in Chapter 5) demands that Member States and their nationals should be able to use the official EC language of their choice, reflecting once again the distinction between internal administration and external communication. It also brings to mind the different issues at play in *BASF* and *Kik*, discussed above. But the scope of language policy in an external sense extends further still. Should the EC continue, for example, with its present regime of translating official documents into all eleven EC languages? Given that Community law is implemented by fifteen Member States and, in consequence, by numerous national, and sub-national or regional, authorities, the centralised translation of EC legislation and other official documents is innately justifiable. Community law is unique—even in terms of its volume—by international standards; in particular, regulations are directly applicable in each Member State without the need for separate domestic implementation, irrespective of Member State approaches to the incorporation of international law in a more general sense.[78] As already noted, delegating the translation of Community law to each Member State individually creates a real risk of non-uniform application, since the potential for textual and interpretative divergence would be greatly increased. Indeed, the need for both accountability and precision arguably justifies the centralised translation of *all* legislation, judgments and other official documents, and not just regulations. The rights resulting from citizenship generally and European Union citizenship more specifically, as well as persisting political tensions, are also relevant. In other international organisations, obligations are imposed initially on contracting state parties only.

---

[78] Case 34/73 *Variola v. Amministrazione delle Finanze* [1973] ECR 981.

The consequences for individual citizens, and for legal persons, are thus wholly different. How a state chooses to give effect to its international obligations more generally is a matter that it may decide for itself, in contrast to the long-established principle of the supremacy of EC law.[79] The more limited language policies of other international organisations cannot really be compared, then, with that of the Community. It is noteworthy that originally, the UN had two working and five official languages; this number was gradually expanded to the current total of six working and official languages. The increase was not supported unanimously. Several delegates despaired the introduction of additional languages into what had been intended as a forum for greater understanding and it was perceived more as a political than functional necessity. But whatever the impetus or ensuing reaction, the fact remains that a minimalist language policy did not suffice to meet either the linguistic or political needs of the UN Member States. The Council of Europe uses just two working and official languages but it has, and indeed always had, far more Member States (currently, forty one) than the EU. Moreover, the differences between the nature of the obligations arising from membership, the extent to which national sovereignty has been ceded and the differing breadth of subject matter covered by both organisations must be borne in mind. The distinct nature of EC law is, therefore, one of the most compelling justifications for maintaining its admittedly complex translation system. There are alternatives, including a deferred translation filing system (similar to the authentication procedure followed internally by the Commission), translation on demand only or the translation of abstracts only.[80] But these are compromises and not necessarily effective ones, having limited legal value from the perspective of national courts; they also diminish the protection presently afforded to individuals and legal persons from the perspective of legal certainty. The imminent enlargement of the EU will undoubtedly call into question the translation at central level of each and every official document. Due consideration should, however, be given to the role played by language in building and maintaining the unique legal structure of the Community. Could EC law have permeated domestic jurisprudence to the extent now evident without, for example, the availability of legislative texts and case law in languages readily comprehensible from the perspective of lawyers and the judiciary throughout the Member States?

---

[79] See in particular Case 26/62 *Van Gend en Loos v. Nederlandse Administratie der Belastingen* [1963] ECR 1 and Case 6/64 *Costa v. ENEL* [1964] ECR 585.

[80] For consideration of these alternatives, see Chartered Institute of Patent Agents, "Translations: Costs and compromise", (1996) vol. 25:3 *Chartered Institute of Patent Agents Journal* 177-190.

Can it hope to do so within new member states, if a similar starting point is not made available to them? The Commission indicated in 1992 that for 'reasons of principle' legal acts and other 'important documents' would continue to be translated into all official EC languages even after enlargement; its primary source of concern at that time was to find ways for more effective and pragmatic communication in an internal, institutional sense.[81] In the interim, the mandate of IGC 2000 was established to deal specifically with the likely institutional implications of enlargement. Realistic language arrangements are essential to the efficient working of an enlarged Union but, on the whole, there is an almost ghostly absence of serious debate on reform of the official language policy. The assumption is that the doctrine of linguistic equality will persist, on paper at least, even with more than double the present number of languages involved. Apart from limited procedural references to Article 290 EC and to the Rules of Procedure of the ECJ and CFI mentioned earlier, the 'half-way mark' progress report on IGC 2000 did not discuss language at all, a vacuum thus carried through to the eventual Treaty of Nice.[82] The practice of clinging to linguistic equality in principle while striving to circumvent its implications in practice on grounds of efficiency seems to have been the preferred way for the IGC itself to function.[83] And this is discernible also from other official publications. For example, the language question is raised perhaps more comprehensively than elsewhere to date in a working party report on the *Operation of the Council with an Enlarged Union in Prospect*.[84] The discussion on what are termed 'logistic and linguistic functions' is, in effect, a manifesto for an official/working language distinction, in spirit if not in law. The report notes that "[a] European Union of twenty five to thirty members would involve such an increase in requirements as to make the Council infrastructure possibly unmanageable unless appropriate adjustment measures were promptly taken."[85] But rather than engaging in a detailed and serious discussion of language policy reform, the succeeding recommendations urge the exploration of

---

[81]   European Commission, *Europe and the Challenge of Enlargement*, EC Bull. Supp. 3/92, p. 16.

[82]   See the progress report on IGC 2000 at Annex 3.7, p. 90 and Annex 5.3, p. 109.

[83]   See paragraph 51 of the Helsinki European Council Presidency Conclusions, 10 and 11 December 1999, Annex III ("An Effective Council for an Enlarged Union: Guidelines for Reform and Operational Recommendations"), at http://europa.eu.int/council/off/conclu/dec99/dec99_en.htm.

[84]   Council of the European Union, SN 2139/99, Brussels, 10 March 1999; see especially, Chapter 12 on the General Secretariat and Chapter 13 on 'The Practical Framework'.

[85]   *ibid.*, p. 95.

ways in which what is, in effect, an official/working language distinction might be practised (almost subversively) where possible.[86] It is not that the recommendations themselves are problematic; the need to research technological innovations in translation and interpretation, the possibility of using external translation services for less sensitive material and a sliding-scale classification for documents regarding translation priority are just some of the clearly sound ideas mooted.[87] But by trying to evade an honest debate and dealing more openly with what is actually going on regarding language use in the EC/EU institutions, the already mendacious doctrine of linguistic equality is just becoming further entrenched as an untouchable ideology. Its absence from the Nice agenda is a critically missed opportunity. Language was never going to be "the" issue for consideration at IGC 2000, but its artificially low priority rating may well be forced to be altered in time.

It is clear that reform of EC language policy is necessary; but possible alternatives, as well as the motivations behind them, must be evaluated carefully. While framing language policy in linguistic 'equality' in a superficial sense has been criticised above, building on linguistic diversity as a basic premise remains a legitimate ambition. To ensure an efficiently operational Union, a careful balance between efficiency and diversity will need to be struck. We are already at a stage in European integration where long-established language arrangements have become problematic; left unchecked, they will become critically so. And thus goes the case for reform, attempting to achieve linguistic efficiency but not at all costs (recalling the different impact of language policy internally and externally). But if reform is to be undertaken sincerely, then attention must also be focused on languages *not* currently recognised at all. Diversity is, after all, an inherently inclusive concept. A selective language policy can work, but only where speakers of the languages *not* then selected for specific purposes can be shown to be no worse off in linguistic terms than they would otherwise have been. Crucially, thinking on language use should not be confined to the abstract, irrespective of broader societal concerns and in isolation from the needs of speakers. How the EC accommodates non-economic objectives in a general sense is relevant here; in the particular context of language, economic variables must somehow compete alongside claims based on culture, democracy, citizenship and fundamental rights. The primary purpose of this study is to trace the legal bases for minority language policy from which the Community has drawn in the past, and to consider those upon which it could

---

[86]   *ibid.* See for example, pp. 98, 101 (para. 137(c)), 102 (para. 139).

[87]   *ibid.*, especially at 101.

rely in the future. But the value and significance of linguistic diversity must be established more clearly in the first instance. In other words, before we can ask *how* minority languages might feature in EC policy, we must first consider why linguistic diversity should be defended at all.

3.   SUSTAINING LINGUISTIC DIVERSITY: THE ROLE OF THE EC

A.   Introduction

The emergence of the discipline of sociolinguistics has encouraged widespread, interdisciplinary study of the role of language in society. This fits neatly with more general thinking in social and legal theory which questions the relationship between law and social change. To deal with the reality of global mobility and with competing versions of nationalism and attachment, concepts like diversity, identity, pluralism and inclusion have become contemporary catch-phrases. But a backlash against this school of thought materialised almost simultaneously, with the criticism that those who sought to promote the ideal of diversity were deluded sentimentalists rather than rational, objective realists. It is undeniably difficult to delve into the lexicon of diversity without descending into clichéd jargon. But, whether we like it or not, it is equally plain that issues of identity have coloured how we think and act at many levels, including the collective and political. The nation-state was rarely, if ever, the logical entity it was once supposed to be and many now struggle with an inherent 'national identity' ambiguity. 'Nation-states' increasingly face an intensifying drive towards devolved or regional government, which in turn both competes with and complements the evolution of supranational polities. Managing these rival claims to or levels of identity and attachment has become one of the primary tasks of contemporary political strategy and it is here that battles between diversity and assimilation, as well as majorities and minorities, surface almost involuntarily. But however jaded the associated terminology might have become, it is not possible simply to dismiss the concepts themselves as unimportant, to pretend that identity doesn't really matter.

Language can be classified as an indicator or subset of identity in a broad sense, or as an independent constituent of 'linguistic identity' in itself. The assumption that an international political entity would need to have a comprehensive language policy is far from realised in the EC context. As noted above, despite the formal equality of the official languages, just one or two function as day-to-day vernaculars within the Community institutions.

This trend has inevitable repercussions for the languages *not* generally used. It is unlikely that individual Member State policies can grapple sufficiently with the disruption to language use patterns that is linked to the structure of the EC itself and to the very process of European integration; but to what extent is the Community under a duty to redress negative consequences of its own integration? The charge that language issues are inherently related to the fairly ambiguous and even potentially troublesome notion of identity is not enough to discount the fact that the value of linguistic diversity may be worthy of protection at EC level; neither, on the other hand, does it rule out the need for an objective assessment of that worth. So just what exactly can the EC be expected to accomplish in this field? Arguments that the Community had no competence to develop a language policy above and beyond providing for its own internal administration were seemingly dispelled by the introduction of Article 151 EC, which provides that "[t]he Community shall contribute to the flowering of cultures of Member States while respecting their national and regional diversity and, at the same time, bringing the common cultural heritage to the fore." Does this provision establish an effective legal foundation for Community involvement in language planning, at least at the level of shared competence? Can the EC legitimately supplement national initiatives, in accordance with the principle of subsidiarity? These questions demand a thorough assessment of available legal bases, which are detailed in Chapters 3, 4 and 5, as well as setting out the range of potential EC involvement in the first place; but first, the responsibility of the Community to contribute to linguistic diversity is analysed from (mainly) political and economic perspectives.

B.   Is Linguistic Uniformity Necessary for 'True' European Unity?

This question is often cited as a stumbling block to the promotion of diversity. The European Union is anchored in economic, political and social integration, eroding many distinctions between inherently diverse Member States. If diversity is interpreted as the antithesis of unity, it is arguable—to take the most extreme hypothesis first—that a truly united Europe would speak one language. At its most literal, the effects of adopting a one-language policy of this kind would be dramatic, to say the very least; they would not be confined to the Community institutions, but would affect the everyday lives of everyone resident in the EU, beginning with mass education programmes promoting the selected language. It is doubtful that many other languages could withstand the pressure of 'the' European language, which would inevitably become associated with economic, political and social advancement. Supporters of a 'one language Europe' usually advocate that English should be the language of European communication, given its existing position as the second language of most bilingual and multilingual Europeans, its growing role in the Community institutions and its ever-increasing employment as a language of wider communication on a world-wide scale. But is monolingual Europe necessarily the key to united Europe? Or is the connection between uniformity and solidarity being overstated? The adverse consequences of a monolingual Europe far outweigh its dubious potential as a vehicle for greater unity. Language and diversity are contentious issues at the best of times. Forced or involuntary linguistic assimilation would inevitably threaten rather than fortify European unity. And its deliberate realisation would amount in reality to cultural genocide. Instead of simplifying mutual comprehension, monolingual planning would restrict free expression for, at the very least, an entire generation. Even leaving these considerations aside, history has shown time and time again that ideologies which are imposed rarely flourish in any event, and instead breed bitter opposition. Those who participate directly in the running of the EC institutions are usually bilingual or multilingual, constituting an elite group by any standards. While this may be a way of life for a growing number of Europeans, it is not the typical one. Moreover, these administrators have *chosen* their occupations in full awareness of the corresponding linguistic conditions. Drastic reform of EC language policy may be justifiable, in economic and pragmatic terms, for the bilingual Community policy maker, but the situation appears quite differently outside that specific circle. Moreover, this course of action would hardly alleviate the acknowledged Community concern that the EC can seem too remote from its citizens, discussed further in Chapter 5.

In contrast to absolute monolingualism, the concept of selective multilingualism or 'diglossia' provides a less extreme alternative.[88] Diglossia is an established sociolinguistic concept that refers to a systematic distribution or hierarchy of languages. Essentially, vernacular languages are retained for traditional 'home and hearth' functions *i.e.* for personal interactions and for limited local functions. The so-called languages of wider communication are then designated for specifically defined 'outside' functions, mainly in political and economic domains. More specifically in the present context, the selected language(s) of wider communication would be assigned to domains of language use related to the EC. In other words, this would mean applying

---

[88] See Fishman, *Language and Ethnicity*, pp. 177 *et seq.* on the properties of diglossia from a sociolinguistic perspective.

internal Community language arrangements for external purposes also. From a sociolinguistic perspective, diglossia can be a completely stable condition; the example usually cited is the successful control of Dutch/English functions in the Netherlands.[89] But several of the arguments endorsing diglossia do not hold up when applied to multilingual Europe. First, it is generally argued that selective multilingualism works best where the allocation of functions is specific and is, in particular, cushioned by the protection of national boundaries. If the explicit regulation (or even covert promotion) of diglossia is exercised at supranational level, the allocation of language functions is obviously beyond the control of the language groups affected. Furthermore, the very character of the Community seeks to diminish the validity of national boundaries in the first place. Second, it is naive to assume that the dynamics of language can be neatly allocated and controlled; given that EC law is implemented primarily by a variety of national authorities, it is virtually impossible to contain or even define exactly the actual range of language functions involved. Finally, control of popular culture is considered essential to the stability of diglossia, which presents an inherent flaw in terms of its application to multicultural Europe. While Article 151 EC does refer to a 'common cultural heritage', preservation of cultural *diversity* sits alongside this objective and, as supported by an amendment introduced via the Amsterdam Treaty, probably represents the dominant objective.[90] It is acknowledged within sociolinguistics that diglossia *can* go wrong, where it then marks the first stage of language shift. In these circumstances, the increased status and utility of the language(s) of wider communication first compete with but subsequently erode the functions allocated originally to the vernacular language. And as noted above, in the EC context, language functions cannot even be allocated systematically in the first place. The acute concern felt by speakers of smaller national languages, although within the language 'equality' framework, and of minority languages throughout the Member States dispels the notion that the citizens of Europe are prepared simply to give up their languages. European unity has a far better chance of being realised if this fact is accepted and taken as a starting-point rather than challenged. Stable diglossic bilingualism must be desired, not imposed or perceived as a burden. Another consideration relates to the utility of languages in terms of vocabulary. It is argued that certain, less evolved languages simply cannot, for example, deal with technological innovations. But the origin of this

---

[89]   *ibid.*, pp. 225 *et seq.*

[90]   This question is considered in detail in Chapter 3.

reasoning is rooted firmly in historical attitudes and not in linguistic fact. Languages that were selected as state or official languages acquired enhanced status; they became associated with prestigious language domains such as public administration and education and, in turn, commerce, science and technology. The evolution of their vocabularies thus reflected their increased relative utility. In this historical context lie the roots of diglossia. But if sociolinguistics as a discipline has taught us anything, it has been to demonstrate empirically that no language or dialect is inherently 'better' than any other. Accordingly, there is no linguistic reason why corpus planning cannot cope with the evolution of any language.

The supposed link between uniformity and effective integration is connected also to discussions on ethnicity and the influence of nationalism. Does nationalism affect the capacity of the EC Member States to integrate successfully? Here, once again, there is a sharp divergence of views between the 'realists' and the 'sentimentalists'. There is an undeniable logic to be drawn from reasoning which suggests an irreconcilable conflict between nationalism, particularly the potent variant of linguistic nationalism, and economic and political integration. The enduring sense of national loyalty exhibited by most 'Europeans' arguably inhibits the path to unity, and only when this outdated ideological burden is shrugged off can a genuine European identity be forged. The expression of nationalist identity has caused the geo-political map of Europe to be redrawn more than any other impetus in recent history. Like language attachments, nationalist feelings cannot be explained rationally. Both the impact and mythology of nationalism are usually brought to attention through fundamentalist channels, meaning that the concept is typically characterised by the worst atrocities committed in its name. But nationalism has a far more pervasive and subtle impact on all political structures. The notion that the Member States might one day be consumed by European integration has not been realised; in truth, integration has proceeded because of rather than without their support. Thus, for whatever reasons, 'national' identity continues to carry weight, even where this is arguably an artificial construct in itself; if this can be accommodated instead of repressed, the impression that something valued has had to be sacrificed is rendered false, lessening the need for resorting to a misapplied nationalist philosophy at all. Conversely, the push towards 'nation-ism' must also wrestle with demands for regional recognition and minority justice. As sources of attachment, national and regional identities are more often than not in competition with one another. This is further complicated at supranational level, in that different Member States have different 'attachment' configurations; some have devolved regional structures, others follow a staunchly centralised, unitary philosophy. The momentum of supranational integration heightens issues of self-awareness at all of these levels. Accession to the EU by states in central and eastern Europe, where nationalism has had more recent consequences, will introduce another dimension to this equation, and will perhaps force an even more acute awareness of nationalism at EU level than has been the case to date. Identity-based attachments affect human experience in a profound way which, in turn, affects the organisation of civil society at all levels. It is tempting to dismiss the whole debate as a fashionable collective identity crisis, but the past century alone provides more evidence to refute that attitude than we should need. Language is critically relevant to this analysis. Southall documented this truth in 1893, but his observations remain cannily accurate today:

> Modern life is supposed to tend to break down all the barriers of nationality, of race and even of language, and to weld the nations of the earth into one mighty mass. That something like this may not be witnessed in a future stage of the world's history I am not prepared to deny.... However...side by side with the levelling tendency which annihilates distinctions and which would have one law, one language, one cosmopolitan character throughout...there is a counter tendency of a natural and involuntary character constantly emphasising distinctions and building up local differences, tending to make languages.[91]

Arguments advanced against the promotion of monolingualism, the questionable stability of selective multilingualism (diglossia) and the automatic disregard of 'sentimental' attachments have another common basis *i.e.* that language choices should never be imposed from the top down. Rather, a governing polity, at whatever level, must strive to accommodate, within reason, the language choices of its constituents. There must also be a reassessment of the presumed link between nationalist sentiment and territorial ambition. Linguistic nationalism is often an ideological defence in the campaign for more effective language rights within an existing polity and has nothing whatsoever to do with the establishment of a separate state. On the whole, this position veers away from the more traditional focus on the status of languages *per se*, attention being directed instead towards the needs and rights of speakers. While language policy must always be injected with a healthy dose of pragmatism, this should not be accomplished at the expense

---

[91]   J.E. Southall, *Wales and her Language*, (1893), reproduced in Fishman, *Language and Ethnicity*, pp. 314-315.

of effectiveness. The practical expression of this argument was set out above, where reform of EC language policy was proposed. Because supra-national government has as much a role to play in the organisation of language structures as national and sub-national administrations. This argument was accepted by the Commission in the *Euromosaic Report*, which states unequivocally that "[t]he future...must involve a reorientation of integration within the context of diversity and that the emergence of the supra-state affords an important opportunity to realise this goal."[92] The EC has a distinct role to play in sustaining linguistic diversity, a value that does not need to be abandoned to secure European unity more generally. What that role actually demands of the Community is something that has never really been explored in a substantive sense. In reality, however, attempts to generate loyalty to supranational government are far more likely to be successful at this civic or administrative level than attempts to manipulate some sort of shared European 'ethnicity'; this idea is developed further below, in the context of sovereignty and integration.

C.   The Sovereignty Dimension

Closely linked to nationalism, though almost from the inverse perspective, is the question of state sovereignty. International law has eroded the boundaries of sovereignty to a remarkable extent. Most states have gradually become more tolerant of the external role played by international organisations in certain aspects of what were seen traditionally as domestic matters. But alongside this reassessment of sovereignty, a countertendency to preserve distinct characteristics is also much in evidence. The degree of sensitivity surrounding EC language policy is illustrative of this friction. Debate on pragmatic, even minor, amendments to the principle of linguistic equality is usually hindered by sovereignty-related linguistic nostalgia. It is often justifiable that respect for diversity should transcend the requirements of economic efficiency. But where promotion of national difference mas-querades as chauvinism, the exploitation of Community language policy cannot be excused. It is arguable that political sanctification of the present arrangements is in fact counterproductive and that resisting change for purely political reasons might even perpetuate linguistic inequality. In reality, some official languages *are* more equal than others, since just one or two usually fulfil internal communicative requirements in the Community

---

[92] European Commission, *Euromosaic: The Production and Reproduction of Minority Language Groups in the European Union*, (Luxembourg: Office for Official Publications of the European Communities, 1996), p. 13.

institutions. An effective EC language policy should be based to a certain extent on accommodating the different functions of different languages; but, in contrast to diglossia, this doesn't just require a basic division of functions between available languages; rather, providing for different language functions both internally *and* externally should be the primary guiding factor, as outlined above; this in turn should involve a more considered contemplation of languages *not* typically used for more (linguistically) prestigious language functions. It was noted that reforming the internal institutional language arrangements along more pragmatic lines would not demand substantive deviations from current practice; the main change would be that a system already operating would be formalised. The degree of resistance to any such move is, in political terms, overwhelming, which begs the question: to what extent is such opposition fuelled by recurring ideologies over and above genuine linguistic interest? Even Member State representatives in the Council, perhaps one the most ephemeral group involved in the EC law-making process, must surely negotiate and take decisions in a reduced number of languages on a frequent basis; this renders objections to formalised reform more philosophical than practical. That is not in itself an objectionable stance, except that dogged maintenance of current language arrangements arguably does more harm than good. Once again, however, a comprehensively reformed regime should also take into account the position of non-official languages, which should not be consigned to the realm of *laissez faire*. Ironically, strict deference to national sovereignty can sometimes operate to exclude from the principle of multilingualism languages *not* presently recognised by the EC. The attachment of Member States to their national languages propagates, on the one hand, the Community's own commitment to multilingualism; yet it is often the fervour with which the national or official language of a country is promoted that precludes domestic recognition of any other languages. Under this construction, it is arguable that the EC doctrine of linguistic 'equality' has actually been conceived from the suppression of minority languages.[93] As detailed in Chapters 2 and 6, Community strategy on minority language issues has taken on something of a direction of its own, clearly distinguishable from national biases. It is not wholly accurate, then, to project the motivations of the Member States onto the emerging EC ethos. Furthermore, while state sovereignty may have been more problematic in the absence of express Community competence, Article 151 EC, as well as other legal bases

---

[93]   On this point, see Harald Haarmann, "Language politics and the new European identity", in Coulmas (ed.), 103-120 at 103.

examined at a later stage, may yet transcend these concerns to a certain extent.

The course of European integration more generally is inextricably bound up with the cession and retraction of sovereignty and various theories have been developed in explanation.[94] It is a path marked by a number of legal milestones, most notably the Single European Act, Treaty on European Union and the substantive amendments achieved at Amsterdam and Nice, all undeniably fleshed out by landmark decisions of the Court of Justice. But, notwithstanding the express commitment to pursuing an 'ever closer union' in the Preamble to the Treaty of Rome, the forces of integration have at times seemed to act somewhat independently of legitimising structural measures. The trend towards supranational government was initially explained on the premise of functionalism, a theory grounded in needs that transcend national boundaries and could, therefore, be better provided for by establishing some form of joint government. The resulting entity would be task-specific in the initial stages, although its structure would be flexible both in terms of membership and assigned subject matter. But this flexibility, inherent in functionalist theory, did not really correspond with how European integration was proceeding in actuality; in particular, a loosely-based opt-out system could not have supported the movement from economic to political alliance. In hindsight, the main contribution of functionalism was probably its promotion of the *possibility* of positive interdependency between sovereign states, based on an appreciation of the advantages of cooperation. Critics of the theory were quick to point out that cooperation did not necessarily alleviate the strain of inter-state contact: while the issues had changed, from territorial disputes to trade, the underlying political tensions remained. Yet despite the shortcomings of functionalism as an explanatory framework, the reality of intensified integration had nonetheless become apparent. To redress the theoretical deficit, the theory of neo-functionalism was developed. More normative in character than its predecessor, neofunctionalism presupposes a fixed supranational authority with appropriately centralised institutions. As has occurred actually with the EC, integration would begin in the economic sector, leading to the growth of solidarity among the Member States. It was argued that this, in turn, would automatically lead to further integration. Initially, the process would occur without mass support—again emphasising the automatic or inevitable character of integration—but, eventually, popular support would ensue. The

---

[94] On the history and theories of European integration generally, see Martin Holland, *The Community Experience*, (London: Pinter, 1993); William Wallace (ed.), *The Dynamics of European Integration*, (London: Pinter, 1990).

central premise of neofunctionalism is the idea of 'spillover'. This means that integration in one sector, such as trade in goods, inevitably produces advantages and disadvantages in other sectors. Centralised competence to introduce corrective measures where appropriate would then inevitably 'spill over' into other policy spheres. Under this interpretation, the TEU, when introducing a number of 'new' competences, merely formalised the preceding occurrence of spillover, as the Community had already taken some action in most of the policy areas then codified. Once again, however, there was a problematic gap between theory and the direction integration had actually taken. Essentially, neofunctionalism assumed that spillover was inevitable, but this did not allow for political dynamics within the Member States. This critique is expressed primarily via neo-realism; the unfulfilled potential of the originally pro-integration climate in the 1960s, which virtually ran aground under the constrictive Luxembourg Accords voting arrangement in the Council, illustrates this flaw.[95] The European Parliament's 1984 Draft Treaty on European Union is also significant. It was quite a radical document, challenging the existing EEC structures in a fundamental way. At that time, Member States were neither prepared nor willing to contemplate such a drastic acceleration in the process of integration; the political and public backlash against the Maastricht Treaty provides a more recent example. So while the interrelated effects on secondary policy areas (*i.e.* functional spillover) may themselves be an automatic consequence of organised collective action, the acquisition of centralised competence to deal with these effects (*i.e.* political spillover) is not. Rather, EC competence to act is dependent on the formulation of an explicit legal basis via political negotiation. Thus, spillover is an external catalyst in the initiation of negotiations, but it is not the expression of a firm political will in itself. Allowing for this political dimension also provides a framework for considering how supranationalism and intergovernmentalism have vied for prevalence over the years in the EU context.

Discussion on European integration has forced the contemplation of two key issues: first, how and why does European integration actually work and, second, how can growing concerns about centralisation, increasingly prevalent among some Member States, be accommodated without thwarting the process of integration itself? In the fertile domain of legal theory, this debate is in progress; a wealth of commentary, continuing to assess both the process of integration and the character of the resulting structures, has introduced

---

[95]   See EEC Bulletin, 1966, No. 3, p. 9.

concepts like neo-federalism, institutionalism and consociationalism.[96] Theorists question also the extent to which the EU is a typical governing entity and whether it is one based principles of democracy and constitutionalism. In constitutional terms, the introduction and application of subsidiarity is highly significant, and is discussed in Chapter 4. The legitimisation of flexibility and closer cooperation marks yet another stage in the attempt to match legal structures with the momentum of integration.[97]

From the perspective of identity, the issues raised by state sovereignty effectively mirror the conclusions drawn above on nationalism. Given the current socio-political climate, European unity is far more likely to be achieved by recognition and not subordination of national differences. It has been suggested that when national groups develop a sense of security within the larger EU polity, this could in itself bring about an acquiescence towards the loss of national identities, leading to enhanced integration and, eventually, fostering of and attachment to a European identity.[98] But it should not be presumed that there is an *inherent* link between further integration, to whatever extent, and the surrender of national identities. This assumption did not hold true for neofunctionalism and spillover; it is also of limited application in the more specific province of identity. The predicted acquiescence towards further integration would probably *not* occur where any perceived threat to identity became apparent, since it is far from certain that national groups would be prepared to let go of the very guarantees that encouraged their sense of security in the first place. The reality is that shared sub-national, national and supranational loyalties is a more credible expectation than an outright European solidarity which leaves no room for any other group or characteristic-based (*e.g.* language) sense of identity. In short, the notions of 'us' and 'it' will probably persist, but that in itself is not fatal to developing a more workable construct of integration; it may, in fact, prove to be its central premise.

---

[96] See in particular Neil Walker, "European constitutionalism and European integration", (1996) *Public Law* 266-290 and Damian Chalmers, "Judicial preferences and the Community legal order", (1997) vol. 60:2 *Modern Law Review* 164-199, both of which outline the evolving debate and associated concepts. See most recently, the essays collected in Zenon Bankowski and Andrew Scott (eds.), *The European Union and its Order: The Legal Theory of European Integration*, (Oxford: Blackwell Publishers, 2000).

[97] Title VII (Articles 43-45) TEU and Article 11 EC on the mechanics of closer cooperation were introduced via the Treaty of Amsterdam; all stand to be amended by the Treaty of Nice (see Article 1/10-14 and Article 2/1 of the Treaty of Nice).

[98] See Paul Howe, "A community of Europeans: The requisite underpinnings", (1995) vol. 33:1 *Journal of Common Market Studies*, 27-46 at 37 *et seq.*

D.   Issues of Democracy and Citizenship

The extent to which the law can be ascertained is a key attribute of democratic government, taking in principles of openness, transparency and sound administration, in the interests of legal certainty and the rule of law. As noted at various points above, one of the most compelling arguments for translating EC legislation into all of the official EC languages is derived from this line of reasoning, in the sense that people should be able to understand the laws by which they are affected. This extends also to judges and legislators, who must be able to grasp the laws that they are called upon to apply or implement. 'Understanding' the law, for present purposes, denotes comprehension in a basic linguistic sense, as distinct from understanding the law in substance, which is a more ambiguous idea. It has already been noted that the maxim commonly applied in the latter case—*i.e.* ignorance of the law is no defence—was not adopted by the Court of Justice in cases relating to linguistic understanding, to reflect and enable pragmatic interpretation of multilingual legislation; against this background, the rights of citizens to understand the law in a literal or linguistic sense would seem assured.[99] The attempts made earlier to locate coherence in the *Chemiefarma* and *BASF* jurisprudence does not, however, encourage a similar degree of confidence. The Court of Justice has addressed the value of legal certainty in the express context of language and the individual; in *Farrauto*, it held that:

> [a] special problem concerning legal certainty may arise if the decision is notified to the person concerned in a language which he does not understand. Certain provisions of Community rules on social security for workers take account of the difficulties of a linguistic nature by providing either that the institutions and the authorities of a Member State may not reject claims or other documents submitted to them on the grounds that they are written in an official language of another Member State...or that certain decisions shall be notified to the claimant in his own language...but these provisions do not apply in the present case. *The national courts of the Member States must nevertheless take care that legal certainty is not prejudiced by a failure*

---

[99]   On legal certainty and substantive clarity more generally, see Lenaerts and Nuffel, *Constitutional Law*, p. 536 *et seq.*

arising from the inability of the worker to understand the language in which a decision is notified to him.[100]

What is especially striking about this extract is the extent to which the Court has implied a general consideration of legal certainty in respect of language not only in the context of EC measures, but also regarding national procedures in the sphere of EC law implementation. Community responsibility in this field was arguably strengthened by the introduction of EU citizenship via the Maastricht Treaty (Articles 17-22 EC). To fulfil the idea of citizenship in real terms, the expansion of associated rights must reflect the integrity of various identity-forming characteristics. Language is typically presented as an obvious constituent of identity. The implications of EU citizenship for language policy are, therefore, considerable and are discussed in Chapter 5. In particular, the recognition of language rights as fundamental rights, bearing in mind the Community's intensifying involvement in fundamental rights issues more generally, reinforces the argument that EC language policy should be influenced by and directed towards the needs of its citizens. To the extent that language policy is primarily a domestic or Member State concern, the role of the Community is essentially, of course, a secondary one, in line with the basic rationale of international intervention more generally. This conforms also with the restricted powers of the EC in cultural affairs and with the principle of subsidiarity, detailed in Chapters 3 and 4 respectively. From the perspectives of constitutionalism and government, however, the Community must also assess how it, as a governing authority, communicates and interacts with its citizens, introduced above as the external aspect of language policy and discussed again in Chapter 5. The strong expression of legal certainty in *Farrauto* contrasts sharply with the inconsistencies evident in competition law jurisprudence, outlined earlier, which projects once again the incoherence of EC language policy; this debate is returned to in Chapter 5. The more specific construction of cultural democracy is examined below, in connection with the accommodation of minority rights into majoritarian structures.

E.   Economic Considerations

Language choice can be portrayed within a metaphorical marketplace, where different languages compete with each other in terms of usage, and where

---

[100] Case 66/74 *Farrauto v. Bau-Berufsgenossenschaft* [1975] ECR 157 at 162, para. 6 (emphasis added), referring to Article 45 of Regulation No. 3 and Article 84(4) of Regulation No. 1408/71 (as amended, now re-issued as an annex to Regulation 118/97, [1997] OJ L28/1), and Article 48(1) of Regulation No. 574/72 ([1972] OJ L74/1) respectively.

consumption of non-official and minority languages is more costly than that of languages of wider communication. But, even aside from the direct costs of multilingualism, choice of language can also affect and be affected by actual economic variables. There is particular concern, for example, that increased intra-EC trade, fuelled by monetary union, will accentuate the need for and status of the *de facto* Community working languages, reducing the viability of maintaining other national and non-official languages. This process is more likely to accelerate than decline and is one of the most obvious examples of how the EC has the potential to impact on language use patterns in the Member States. Community rules on trade and competition are also relevant. Given the diminished competitiveness of the more peripheral languages on the cultural market, should the Community rectify resulting imbalances in the form of subsidies? In other words, should it intervene in an economic sense to compensate for linguistic damage caused by the dynamics of European integration? That integration can have negative as well as positive consequences is not at issue; but what must be asked is whether negative side-effects demand a retreat from the integrative momentum, as some Member States would favour and as has arguably been legitimised by Title VII TEU on closer cooperation, or whether, on the other hand, it is better to proceed but to acknowledge and actually deal with detrimental corollaries. From yet another perspective, the considerable economic advantages enjoyed when Member States promote instruction in their languages are not often taken into account; the United Kingdom in particular has gained substantial economic benefits from 'English as a Foreign Language' (EFL) programmes. This contrasts sharply with the negligible economic value of the smaller national languages, bringing to mind once again the idea of compensatory or re-distributive policies. The feasibility of granting centralised Community linguistic subsidies is questionable on the grounds that there is no appropriate legal basis in the EC Treaty; furthermore, such protectionist measures might contradict EC competition law. But these arguments are more likely stretching the application of competition rules far beyond their intended or even logical remit. The EC already co-ordinates and finances various language education programmes: does this constitute an unacceptable linguistic subsidy? Domestic support given to languages would also be potentially invalid under a literal interpretation of the competition rules. On this issue, however, the Treaty does provide guidelines. Given the wording of Article 87 EC, which provides that impermissible state aid is that which affects *trade* between Member States, it is unlikely that language support is inherently suspect. In particular, Article 87(3)(d) EC, introduced by the TEU, provides that "...aid to promote culture and heritage conservation where such aid does not affect trading conditions and competition in the Community to an extent that is contrary to the common interest..." is compatible with the common market.[101] The related issue of extending regional policy to cover minority language issues is discussed separately below. Corrective intervention is regularly dismissed as being overly protectionist, although this is not a concern voiced only with respect to linguistic policy. It is important here, once again, to avoid terminology fatigue. Some values are simply worth protecting, whether it is popular to say so or not, and related intervention is often justifiable.[102] There is, of course, an optimum balance between 'survival of the fittest' and protectionist ideologies that should be sought out. On the whole, the contribution that multilingualism can potentially make to the prosperity of the EC in economic terms is regularly overlooked, if not dismissed. It is almost as if the policy boundaries have been drawn too rigidly, in an exercise of needless overcompensation—that the symbolic sanctity of language should not be polluted by considerations of pounds and pence on the one hand, against the entrenched view that anything intrinsically 'human' has no place in an economic polity on the other. Viewing language within a strictly economic framework is arguably more in keeping with the original objectives of the EEC but does not then reflect the continually evolving nature of those objectives. Equally, as discussed already in terms of policy reform, while language does have an economic dimension, language planning should not hinge on financial considerations alone. The EC founding fathers curtailed their integrative ambitions to concentrate on economic goals, but it is widely accepted that this was due to political necessity and not absence of vision; thus, excessive reliance on economic values to the exclusion of any others is both artificial and prohibitive in the broader framework of Community evolution. Significantly, the traditional assumption that monolingualism is preferable for the encouragement of economic growth and that multilingualism is linked causally to debility does not hold up under empirical scrutiny. In particular, the *Euromosaic* Report, initiated by the European Commission, is the first study to investigate the economic dimension of languages that do not come

---

[101] Article 87 EC is addressed again in Chapter 3, which deals with the scope of EC cultural policy.

[102] In the language context, see the *Euromosaic* Report, discussed again in Chapter 6. On parallel arguments to justify a Community responsibility regarding race discrimination exacerbated by EC integration, see Tamara K. Hervey, "Putting Europe's house in order: Racism, race discrimination and xenophobia after the Treaty of Amsterdam", in O'Keeffe and Twomey (eds.), *Legal Issues of the Amsterdam Treaty*, 329-349 at 331 *et seq.*

within the EC official language policy; the findings published therein link diversity clearly to economic *development* and not disadvantage.[103]

F.   Conclusion

Language issues are not typically identified as a significant aspect of the debate on EC competence and are rarely deemed a priority. Yet the acrimonious nature of recorded opinion, the real fears of many language groups, the diversity of the concerns raised and the degree of political sensitivity pertaining to both national and linguistic sovereignty defy this omission. The EC is not merely a union of policy makers, it is a union of millions of diverse, individual people. Language choice affects everyone. It is not surprising that linguistic concerns *should* feature on the Community agenda; rather, it is incredulous that they do not figure to the extent that has become critically necessary. Imminent EU enlargement underscores this obligation. In a climate leaning towards enhanced globalisation in economic (and other) spheres, the additive learning of languages of wider communication is not just advisable, it is absolutely necessary and ignoring this fact carries serious consequences. But the price often paid by other languages should not be taken for granted as an inevitable, even if regrettable, side-effect. Subtractive language learning, which replaces knowledge of all other languages, is not an inevitability. The EC has a clear role to play in securing linguistic diversity, since language problems are not contained within national boundaries. Serious consideration will have to be given to the questions outlined in the preceding paragraphs, in light of the particular influence of European integration on all European languages, both official and non-official, and on their continuing utility. Nothing less can be expected if the evolving European society is truly a civil one.

4.   MINORITY LANGUAGES: A PARTICULAR CONCERN?

A.   Definitions and Terminology: What is a Minority Language?

The principles of diversity, language shift and language planning have already been introduced. The following sections set out the heightened relevance of these ideas when the languages in question are minority languages.

---

[103] European Commission, *Euromosaic*, especially Section V.

There is no universally recognised definition of a minority language, a concept that is related inherently to the existence of a minority language group. This has not actually precluded the recognition of minority languages and their speakers in various international instruments. For example, Article 27 of the United Nations International Covenant on Civil and Political Rights (ICCPR) provides *inter alia* that "[i]n those states in which ...linguistic minorities exist, persons belonging to such minorities shall not be denied the right, in community with the other members of their group...to use their own language"; but there are no guidelines in the provision, or elsewhere in the Covenant, as to what constitutes a linguistic minority in the first place. The European Bureau for Lesser Used Languages (EBLUL) have defined a minority language as:

> ...a language which, as a result of its structures, its sounds, its words, its characters and its history, differs and is distinguished from the dominant language of a State and is spoken and/or written within a certain territory, by a smaller number of persons.[104]

The phrase 'lesser used language' was itself coined in an attempt to avoid the negative connotations of 'minority' terminology, an exercise of questionable value when the underlying perceptions that generate these attitudes still influence society as a whole.[105] The Council of Europe's European Charter for Regional or Minority Languages (1992) contains one of the few codified definitions, in Article 1:

> For the purposes of this Charter:
>
> a. 'regional or minority languages' means languages that are:
>
> i. traditionally used within a given territory of a State by nationals of that State who form a group numerically smaller than the rest of the State's population; and
>
> ii. different from the official language(s) of that State;

---

[104] EBLUL, *Key Words: A Step into the World of Lesser Used Languages* (Dublin: EBLUL, 1995), p. 37. The foundation and work of EBLUL is set out in Chapters 2 and 3.

[105] For example: "I use my language just as much as any speaker of a majority language [so] the problem of comparison is still there: lesser used than what?... I think that we must accept the term 'minority language' in spite of its connotations, the way forward is to give it higher status and better connotations." (Michael Reuter, "Summing up", in Gearóid Mac Eoin, Anders Ahlqvist and Donncha Ó hAodha (eds.) *Third International Conference on Minority Languages: General Papers*, (Clevedon: Multilingual Matters, 1987), 213-218 at 216.

it does not include either dialects of the official language(s) of the State or the languages of migrants.

These definitions embody the criteria of assessment, both objective and subjective, that are normally applied in an attempt to define any minority group. Objective criteria include the existence of a distinct group, its relative numerical constitution and the incidence of a non-dominant position (usually be reference to the political context). On the latter point, the *Euromosaic* study offers a more complex, sociological interpretation:

> The concept of minority by reference to language groups does not refer to empirical measures, but rather to issues of power. That is, they are language groups, conceived of as social groups, marked by a specific language and culture, that exist within wider societies and states but which lack the political, institutional and ideological structures which can guarantee the relevance of those languages for everyday life of members of such groups.[106]

This construct indicates how minority languages are affected directly by the Community's administrative and legislative choices, and also indirectly, given the impact of the EC on the character of its Member States. Minority language groups typically do not have their own political or institutional structures; their claims and ideologies must thus be somehow incorporated into those of the polities by which they are governed, which takes in regional authorities (where relevant), Member States and the EC.

The EBLUL and Charter definitions specify additional objective criteria also, including a territorial restriction and, in the Charter, the requirement that minority language speakers should be nationals of the state in question. The former condition relates to the possible derivation of minority language rights from either territorial or personality principles, which is discussed further in Chapter 5. The nationality requirement introduces a distinction between indigenous or autochthonous languages and the languages spoken by migrant groups. In the EC context, both the accommodation of migrant languages and the specific needs of their speakers relate directly to the free movement of persons; in a sense, then, the involvement of the Community in this aspect of language policy is not such a contentious issue *per se*, although the policy direction taken may itself be. At present, EC policy seems to be grounded in reconciling the integration of migrant workers into the host state while respecting and maintaining the cultural identity associated with the

---

[106] European Commission, *Euromosaic*, p. 1.

state of origin; this philosophy was outlined above in the context of education. But the accommodation of indigenous minority language groups is more usually perceived as an internal or domestic policy issue and it is here in particular that the role of the EC, especially in terms of an effective legal basis, is yet to be confirmed. For this reason, while affirming strongly the particular responsibilities associated with migrant languages and the validity of the claims of their speakers, this study focuses on Community involvement with indigenous minority languages. Finally, the exclusion of official languages in Article 1 of the Charter is effectively countered by Article 3(1), which allows that "[an] official language which is less widely used on the whole or part of [a State's] territory" can also come within the scope of the Charter. The separation of official and non-official minority languages in this way reflects a compromise that was secured for political reasons, allowing states to ratify the Charter without ceding the constitutional or legislative integrity of officially-recognised minority languages; but in terms of the Charter's implementation and effect, there is no difference between minority languages that are officially recognised in domestic law and those that are not.

Subjective criteria, on the other hand, refer to a group's self-perception as a minority, based on notions such as a shared sense of community and a desire, whether explicit or implicit, to preserve or maintain the distinguishing characteristics of the group, which can include a language. These factors are often considered essential to the definition of minority groups but are not taken into account in the Charter, confirming the assertion that the process of defining a minority language is far from settled. Both objective and subjective criteria do provide welcome guidelines but they are not subject to uniform application. This will become clearer when other international instruments are considered in Chapter 5. The definition outlined in Article 1 of the Charter is, in any event, relevant to the application of the Charter itself only. In broader terms, there is more a general understanding than strict definition of what constitutes a minority language. A flexible approach to definition can be advantageous, in that very different linguistic situations can be recognised and provided for accordingly; but the danger that definitions can be manipulated to exclude legitimate minority language situations must also be borne in mind.

B.   The Status of Minority Languages in the EC

EBLUL has classified the minority languages spoken within the EC as follows:

1. the national languages of two Member States which are not official languages of the EU (*i.e.* Irish and Letzeburgesch);
2. languages of communities residing in a single Member State (*e.g.* Breton in France; Welsh in the United Kingdom);
3. languages of communities residing in two or more Member States (*e.g.* Basque in France/Spain; Occitan in France/Italy/Spain);
4. languages of communities which are minorities in the state in which they live but are the majority languages of other Member States (*e.g.* German in Belgium; Swedish in Finland);
5. non-territorial languages (*e.g.* Roma, Yiddish).[107]

Although estimates do vary, it is probable that over fifty million EU citizens, from an approximate total of 365 million, speak a minority language. At present, however, these languages are not recognised in EC language policy to any effective extent. The status of two of them, Irish and Letzeburgesch, is somewhat different and, accordingly, is considered separately.

(i)   Irish and Letzeburgesch

Irish and Letzeburgesch are both national languages in their respective Member States but neither has been accorded full status as an official Community language. The Irish language, a minority language in real terms, is constitutionally designated as the national and first official language of Ireland, but it is not an official EC language.[108] It does have a quasi-official function, however, in that the texts of the treaties are required to be made available in Irish and are thus equally authentic as regards versions in the official EC languages (see Article 314 EC). And significantly, the inclusion of Irish in Article 314 has had indirect consequences for its status and utility in respect of other aspects of EC language policy which are grounded in that provision, explored further in Chapter 5. Irish is also a working language of the European Court of Justice and the Court of First Instance, although it has not been used in any proceedings to date. And, as already noted, there is no obligation on either Court to publish their judgments in Irish. The *Official Journal* has, on occasion, been published in Irish, where texts have been of

---

[107]   EBLUL, *Unity in Diversity*, 2nd ed., (Dublin: EBLUL, 1996).

[108]   See Article 8 of the Irish Constitution (1937). After a limited but controversial debate, the Irish government itself decided not to seek official status for Irish on accession to the Community in 1972. The position of Irish as a constitutional/minority language arose in Case 379/87 *Anita Groener v. Minister for Education and the Dublin Vocational Education Committee* [1989] ECR 3967, examined in Chapter 2.

particular importance generally or of special relevance to Irish interests. Irish has also been included in Community language-education programmes, such as *LINGUA* and *SOCRATES*. In addition, official documentation issued in Irish, *e.g.* passports and driving licences, is accepted as valid within the Community. Letzeburgesch is the national language, but not an official language, of Luxembourg. It has not been endorsed as a 'treaty language' to a similar extent. It has, however, been included in Community language-education programmes and is mentioned in a number of Community documents as the national language of Luxembourg. Significantly, the Court of Justice has recognised the value of Letzeburgesch as a constituent of national identity and has confirmed the legitimacy of related state policy.[109]

(ii)   The Position of Minority Languages Generally

As noted, over fifty million EU citizens are thought to speak a language other than the primary vernacular of the state in which they live. Minority languages enjoy varying degrees of legal support domestically, from full official recognition with practical implementation, to hostility and denial; this holds true also for the EC Member States.[110] Minority languages do not have either working or official status in the European Community. In an incidental sense, special provision may be made in ECJ and CFI proceedings for those who feel unable to express themselves adequately in any of the official EC languages. It was also suggested above that some anomalies in the ECJ Rules of Procedure might allow for the use of minority languages by the back door in certain limited instances (although this is unlikely to pan out in reality). It is arguable that the Community's virtual dismissal of minority languages contradicts its proclaimed commitment to multilingualism and to the equality of languages. It would not, of course, be practical to include *all* European languages in the linguistic equality policy as it is designed presently. But a reformed EC language policy should take the special position of minority languages and their speakers into account where this can be shown to be appropriate. This argument is developed in the following paragraphs and is tested against the competence of the EC in cultural matters, and in fundamental rights and citizenship, in subsequent chapters. It can be noted at this stage, however, that the scope of the European Year of Languages (2001), organised jointly by the Council of Europe and the

---

[109] Case C-473/93 *Commission v. Luxembourg* [1995] ECR I-3207; this case is analysed in Chapter 6.

[110] See Appendix I, which sets out the constitutional provisions of Member States relating to minority language recognition.

European Union and discussed further in Chapter 3, does bring minority languages within the scope of its anticipated programmes and projects.

C.   Determining Cultural Democracy

Any espousal of the value of linguistic diversity must include an appreciation of minority languages, in the overall interest of cultural democracy. These languages have often persisted in the face of overwhelming assimilative trends. But minority languages, or more specifically their speakers, have also paid a heavy price to regimes of intolerance and injustice, both deliberate and covert. The suppression of minorities, including linguistic minorities, can produce grave political consequences, a fact that has been somewhat forced onto the agendas of international organisations in recent years. The traditional response to minority claims has been the blanket guarantee of non-discrimination. In linguistic terms, this means that a speaker of a minority or non-official language should not be discriminated against because of the language s/he speaks. The principle of non-discrimination on linguistic grounds is an element of the all-inclusive non-discrimination clauses of most international human rights instruments.[111] The extent to which this approach can bring about the implementation of genuine cultural democracy is considered in Chapter 5.

Siting minority rights within liberal democratic political theory raises a particular and inherent irony, in that it is more often than not the majoritarian aspect of democratic rule that causes marginalisation of minority groups in the first instance. A clear example of this has been documented in the USA, where referenda initiated to introduce 'English-only' laws in certain states have succeeded on the 'majority rules' tenet.[112] The accommodation of justice for minorities into liberal democracy is an ongoing controversy in contemporary jurisprudence, giving rise to the construction of various theoretical models for liberal multiculturalism.[113] It is essential that traditional assumptions relating to power are challenged in this context. Minorities cannot be considered to exist merely on the sufferance of the

---

[111] *e.g.* Article 14—European Convention on Human Rights (1953); Article 2.1—International Covenant on Civil and Political Rights (1976); Article 2.2—International Covenant on Economic and Social Rights (1976); Article 2.1—United Nations Convention on the Rights of the Child (1989).

[112] See Michele Arington, "English-only laws and direct legislation: The battle in the States over language minority rights", (1991) 7 *Journal of Law and Politics* 325-352.

[113] See particularly, Will Kymlicka, *Multicultural Citizenship: A Liberal Theory of Minority Rights*, (Oxford: Clarendon Press, 1995).

majority; the ethos of multiculturalism is that of unbiased coexistence. By addressing the situation of minorities as a concern of its own governance, the EC would be participating in one of the key jurisprudential challenges of present times, a theoretical dilemma with immense practical implications, whether strived towards from the perspective of utopian idealism, the prevention of outright conflict, or any point in between these extremities. What exactly the EC can do is, of course, limited by the scope of its competence.

The contention that cultural democracy can only ever be an academic ideal is also open to challenge. It is arguable that the principle of harmonious coexistence may be all very well in theory but is virtually impossible to attain in practice; providing for cultural democracy in the abstract is far removed from the reality of the (often historically entrenched) attitudes involved in any given situation, where tensions can range from mild disquiet to sheer hatred. Perceived differences, from religion to ethnic origin, can and do divide, and are exacerbated when the setting is also a majority/minority one. Language is more usually thought of as a constituent of broader ethnic identity and is often manipulated as a potent symbolic weapon in such cases; it can also be an independent source of group tension in itself. Inter-group conflict is a reality; but the misconception that there is a *causal* link between groups and disharmony is not sufficiently confronted in contemporary political debate. The withholding of minority rights, including minority language rights, has been justified on the grounds that encouraging manifestations of difference disturbs national unity and results in bitter conflict. It is also generally assumed that minority-based conflict will lead to claims for independence and secession. But majoritarian insecurity is what often lies at the heart of the conflict thesis. With specific reference to minority language situations, the roots of conflict are traced by Nelde as follows:

> [A] dominant language group...controls power in the areas of administration, politics and economy, and gives employment preference to those applicants who have command of the dominant language. The disadvantaged language group is then left with the choice of renouncing social ambition, assimilating or resisting. While numerically weak or psychologically weakened language groups tend towards assimilation, in modern societies numerically stronger, more homogenous language groups having traditional values, such as their own

> history and culture, prefer political resistance, the usual form of
> organised language conflict this century.[114]

Within this paragraph lie the reasons why conflict can occur in the first place. The dominant language group in this scenario has absolute control over prestigious domains for language use; other language groups are forced into an involuntary alternative of assimilation, which compromises their basic, legitimate rights. Alternatively, they might choose resistance. But confining analysis to these options projects an incomplete impression of the behaviour of minority groups. Because then, the assimilative, monolingual climate is presented as a given; its legitimacy is not questioned. Focusing on choices at the extremities of any spectrum and presenting them as the norm is a misleading exercise, as concluded also on the question of nationalism and identity more generally. It has been shown empirically, for both historical and contemporary minority situations, that while a diversity-conflict link can certainly develop, it is by no means a *causal* phenomenon.[115] The realisation of a fully-fledged multicultural democracy is without doubt an aspiration, even an incurably idealistic one; but that in itself is not reason enough to warrant its dismissal as a legitimate policy objective. The alternative of redrawing maps and boundaries witnessed throughout the twentieth century, slicing territories into supposedly feasible units, has not worked. Moreover, the underlying philosophy of absolute separatism no longer fits with the evident contemporary trend towards international and supranational cooperation. The fact that the realisation of harmonious, inclusive coexistence remains, at best, elusive is not enough to defeat its validity as an ambition that can inform policy direction. If the EC really is committed to the values of democracy, diversity and fundamental rights, it too has to take responsibility for the achievement of cultural democracy.

D.   The EC and Minority Languages: Framing Responsibility

Analysis of EC involvement in minority language issues can be approached from two perspectives. First, notwithstanding the cultural significance of linguistic diversity *per se* and the distinct contribution of minority languages in particular, why should minority concerns feature specifically in *Community*

---

[114] Peter Hans Nelde, "Language conflicts in multilingual Europe", in Coulmas (ed.), *A Language Policy for the European Community*, 59-74 at 60-61.

[115] See Robert Phillipson and Tove Skutnabb-Kangas, "Linguistic rights and wrongs", (1995) *Applied Linguistics* 483-504; T.R. Gurr, *Minorities at risk: A Global View of Ethnopolitical Conflicts*, (Washington DC: United States Institute of Peace Press, 1993).

language policy? Second, given that, to date, EC intervention in this field has been largely peripheral and not usually legally binding, why do minority language groups continue to attach significance to the potential benefits of Community action? For example, in spite of the recent deadlock on related EC funding, speakers of minority languages tend to place considerable faith in the effectiveness of a Community policy over and above progress achieved under the auspices of the Council of Europe.[116] The present official languages structure has not stabilised the position of even official EC languages against the increasing strength of French and English, even though all eleven languages are, in theory at least, full and equal participants in that regime. Non-official languages are thus relatively in an even more precarious position. Minority languages are equal contributors to the cultural diversity of the Member States and, as such, ought to come within the ambit of EC interest as much as their official counterparts. The idea that 'languages will take care of themselves' has already been discounted in the Community context, where open market forces, in a literal as well as linguistic sense, threaten cultural diversity to a discernible extent. This is heightened for minority languages; they are subject to varying degrees of recognition, or indeed rejection, at Member State level and have not yet been placed within an alternative EC framework.[117] A state or other governing entity endorses a particular language or languages in countless ways, from its administrative system to its road signs, so the idea that the language market is a free one is ultimately fictitious. Even in purely economic terms, the vast divergence between official and minority languages merits more than an *ad hoc* outlook. The allocation of resources as 'compensation', was introduced above and in the case of minority languages, its practice is already more widespread than in respect of languages generally. The allocation of funds to minority language publishing, for example, is extremely unlikely to affect the balance of trade between Member States, since it is essentially a domestic market. The compensation thesis takes on yet another dimension in light of EC regional policy, opening up an additional possibility for Member States when relying on Article 87(3). Linguistic diversity is an obvious and fundamental element of regional difference and this should be reflected in related EC policy. The Committee of the Regions has an important role to play

---

[116] The precarious situation regarding EC funding for minority language projects, linked to concerns over its legal basis, is discussed in Chapters 3 and 6. The European Charter for Regional or Minority Languages places emphasis on state duty in respect of minority languages rather than on the rights of the speakers themselves. Commentators are divided on its potential effectiveness for this reason; the Charter is discussed in Chapter 5.

[117] Although, see Chapters 3 and 6 for potential plans in this regard.

here.[118] But there are certain difficulties with a minority languages framework grounded *entirely* in the regional mindset. In a report commissioned by the EC Commission, the *Istituto della Enciclopedia Italiana* warned against treating regional-oriented policies as mere concessionary measures without appreciating their independent justification.[119] Policies that cannot source an autonomous legal basis are necessarily dependent on political benevolence for their existence and thus also for their continuance; by extension, assigning minority language policy to the EC regional framework exclusively leaves it open to amendment and even annulment against the priorities of a much broader programme. In any case, not all minority language groups are concentrated entirely in closed geographical regions; strict application of regional criteria might thus exclude otherwise legitimate minority language groups. There is also the overriding criticism that extending the application of regional policy falls well short of developing a comprehensive, standalone perspective on minority language issues. But what remains essential is that it must be within rather than outside the EC structure that solutions to the 'problem of peripheralism' are sought: as declared in *Euromosaic*, "[t]he Single Market exists and it is within that context that the solution must be found."[120]

Concern over the legal competence of the EC in language issues is arguably relieved to some extent by the introduction of Article 151 EC, evaluated in Chapters 3 and 4. Difficulties that ensue from the ambiguous wording of the provision should, however, be raised briefly at this stage. It is arguable, for example, that since the EC is compelled to respect the national and regional diversity of the Member States (Article 151(1); Article 151(4)) —a commitment made more explicit since the Amsterdam Treaty—cultural protection is a matter that remains within exclusive Member State competence. But this construction is somewhat contrived. A provision that requires the EC to bring the 'cultural heritage of Europe to the fore' must surely necessitate respect for diversity in *that* actual context: diversity is as much, if not more, an element of European cultural heritage as it is of domestic cultural heritage. The application of the principle of subsidiarity, set out in detail in Chapter 4, is also relevant. Interpreting subsidiarity as a virtually arbitrary devolution of power to the Member States could inhibit the

---

[118] The role ascribed to the Committee of the Regions under Article 151 EC is discussed in Chapter 5.

[119] Istituto della Enciclopedia Italiana, *Linguistic Minorities in Countries belonging to the EC*, (Luxembourg: Office for Official Publications of the European Communities, 1986), p. 234.

[120] European Commission, *Euromosaic*, p. 49.

feasibility of minority claims where a national government is not sympathetic to the language group(s) in question. Domestic policy on minority languages varies considerably throughout the Member States and often, speakers are denied basic language rights because of the absence of effective domestic recognition. Against this background, it is arguable that Community action is justifiable *because* of, rather than despite, the application of subsidiarity. Moreover, rectifying the linguistic inequality that results from the momentum of supranational integration necessarily demands corrective action at that level. Practical steps that the Community could take in the domain of minority languages have already been put forward by the EC institutions, especially the European Parliament; its recommendations are outlined and assessed against the legal powers of the Community in Chapters 2 and 6.

From the perspective of minority groups themselves, the ambiguous nature of EC language policy to date does not seem to have displaced the optimism with which the promise of Community intervention is usually viewed. This can be explained by the interaction of several distinct factors. There are certain practical advantages pertaining to minority language protection at EC level in conjunction with domestic measures that cannot be attributed to a national regime on its own. Standards of protection proposed by the Community are going to be international, based on cooperation and collaboration, and the persuasive moral effect of international standards on human rights issues more generally provides a favourable precedent in this regard. Attention could be focused on areas where national policy has been ineffective or even completely absent. An EC mechanism might even provide another forum for adjudication in disputes between speakers and national authorities. Language groups have also been encouraged by past receptiveness to their claims within the institutions (discussed in Chapters 2 and 6). It is rarely proposed that the EC should usurp the role of the Member States here; but the involvement of the Community where justified and appropriate is perceived to have a far better chance of encouraging effective change than relying on national initiatives alone. In particular, the collective, combined strength of minority language groups as a trans-European lobbying force can be far more influential than piecemeal, individual campaigns. In contemporary European society, language issues relate just as much to access to economic and social advancement as to grammar and syntax. Speakers of minority languages are perhaps more aware of this fact than most others; and they have asked that European society should re-structure its access systems to encompass equal opportunity in the linguistic as well as any other sense. Formal equality of languages has not achieved this; but neither will the continued exclusion of the fifty million EU citizens who choose to speak a minority language.

5.   CONCLUSION

The issues highlighted in this Chapter reflect a divisiveness of opinion on the optimum future development of EC language policy. But one truth is unanimously clear: the present arrangements cannot be maintained without comprehensive revision. Striving for the equality of eleven languages in a plainly unequal array of circumstances simply doesn't make sense. Equally, dismissing decades of a fundamental linguistic doctrine without giving serious consideration to the shape of proposed alternatives would be un-acceptable. The different internal and external implications of EC language policy provide a logical starting point for the necessary administrative review, which should be guided by considerations of pragmatism, fairness and effectiveness. The reality of EU enlargement will not excuse the ongoing failure to grapple with this aspect of institutional reform. Considerations of finance and efficiency are obviously relevant but cannot be allowed to consume the less quantifiable value of linguistic diversity, primarily in the interests of language speakers but also for language evolution and, not least, for the Community itself in terms of successful integration, political expediency and economic development. The EC must undertake an objective review of its present language practices; but expanding this remit, as well as tackling the obvious need for administrative reform, it must also face up to its responsibilities in the fields of cultural diversity, fundamental rights and citizenship. The position of non-official languages rests on an extremely fragile premise, which urgently needs to be assessed and strengthened. Even if the current language regime persists indefinitely, the Community must acknowledge its shortcomings in respect of languages left outside that structure, and begin to resolve the resulting deficits. In Chapter 2, the growing awareness within Community institutions that minority languages do matter, even prior to the changes in EC competence brought about by the TEU, is charted, showing that the foundations supporting reform of the present language regime are, in fact, already long established.

Early Days:
The Origins of EC Minority Language Policy

1. INTRODUCTION

The expansion by Treaty amendment of the legal bases for Community action has, at times, legitimised a pre-existing pattern of legislative, judicial and political endeavour. This idea was introduced in Chapter 1 as the concept of 'spillover'. While its merits as an explanatory theory for political integration are debatable, the occurrence of spillover in a functional sense retains descriptive legitimacy at least. Early EC involvement in minority language issues, which can be traced back to more than a decade before the ratification of the TEU, provides a clear example of how the unpredictable reach of EC law caused the remit of the institutions to be blurred at the boundaries of competence. This Chapter outlines developments in the European Parliament and Court of Justice that, taken together, reveal the piecemeal but creative evolution of a Community perspective on minority languages.[1] Emphasis is placed on first, emerging trends in institutional reaction to minority language claims and, second, sources of legal competence derived by the institutions, in light of the absence at that time of directly relevant Treaty provisions.

2. INITIATIVES IN THE EUROPEAN PARLIAMENT

The European Parliament is often perceived as the champion of minority language rights within the EC. This reflects its function as a directly elected, representative body, in that it brings the concerns of its electorate to the fore more visibly than any of the other institutions. The following paragraphs outline initiatives introduced by the Parliament throughout the 1980s,

---

[1] Cultural policy measures that relate to minority languages, often in an incidental or secondary manner, are outlined separately in Chapter 3; the role of the Commission, in particular, is considered in that context.

analysed particularly from the perspectives of motivation and legal basis. The texts of the Resolutions discussed below are reproduced in Appendix II.

A.   Arfé Resolution (1981)

Resolution on a Community Charter of Regional Languages and Cultures and on a Charter of Rights of Ethnic Minorities.[2]

(i)   Background

In the late 1970s, there was growing support within the European Parliament for developing a Community charter on the protection of minority cultures; a number of motions were tabled in favour of producing a report on the feasibility of such a course of action.[3] This awareness of minority concerns—cultural, linguistic, economic and political, among others— corresponded with the drive towards closer European union that permeated the institutions more generally, which had culminated in the preparation of the Tindemans Report.[4] These apparently conflicting trends are in fact manifestly compatible, as exemplified by one basic question: where would minority cultures fit in a more determinedly united Europe? Thus, even in a predominantly pro-integration political climate, reconciliation of unity and diversity was becoming a corollary, albeit lesser, item on the Community agenda. In December 1979, the Parliamentary Committee on Youth, Education, Information and Sport appointed M. Arfé as *rapporteur*, instructing him, in February of the following year, to draw up a report on the viability of a Community charter on regional languages and cultures, and the rights of ethnic minorities. The resulting Resolution was adopted on 16 March 1981. Its preamble provides further insight into the motivations behind its endorsement. The Parliament was clearly aware that minority rights had become a matter of increasing importance, as well as controversy. The reference to 'the most recent political, legal and anthropological theories' could include the growing corpus of writings on minority justice and sociolinguistics, as well as the preparatory report drawn up by M. Arfé. Crucially, the Preamble frames the Resolution's basic premise, that the diversity of cultural identities throughout the Member States is an essential

---

[2] European Parliament, 16 October 1981, [1984] OJ C287/106.

[3] See, for example, the motion tabled by John Hume MEP on 26 October 1979, Doc. 1-436/79.

[4] Tindemans Report on European Union, [1976] EC Bull. Supp. 1.

element of the cultural heritage of Europe. The Parliament thus spurned the notion of enforced linguistic and/or cultural conformity which, as noted in Chapter 1, is sometimes deemed a linchpin of 'true' political unity. The Preamble also recognises the fundamental rights dimension of language choice, referring to 'declarations of principle' on this subject already made by the United Nations and Council of Europe.[5] More specifically, it was acknowledged that all Member State governments had recognised the right of ethnic and linguistic minorities to freedom of expression 'in principle', and that 'most' had initiated legislative programmes to ensure the realisation of that objective. The pragmatic link between the preservation of linguistic diversity and prevailing economic conditions, particularly in the case of regional languages, was stated expressly. What is most notable by its absence, however, is any attempt to derive a Treaty-based competence for Community action, notwithstanding the fact that the Resolution was actually conceived as a feasibility report. Language rights were positioned in a vague context of culture and heritage, and characterised as an inherently 'human' issue; this latter view is demonstrated by the reference to cultural identity as one of the most important contemporary 'non-material, psychological needs'.

(ii)   Content and Commentary

The Parliament sought primarily to encourage national, regional and local authorities to promote the use of minority languages in the fields of education, the media/communications and public life. The Commission was called upon to provide funding for appropriate projects, to collect information on the minority languages of Europe and 'to review all Community legislation or practices which discriminate against minority languages' (Article 6). The latter clause is particularly noteworthy. It demonstrates that language use is affected by a broad spectrum of policy initiatives and, more particularly, that Community law affects a number of random and purportedly peripheral subject fields; it also foreshadows similar provisions that were later included in the EC Treaty for various 'new' competences, including culture.[6] The Parliament acknowledged the 'wide differences' in the situations of minority language groups across the Community, but called for the implementation nonetheless of some common objectives in the traditional language planning domains listed above. Given that the

---

[5]   Details on the language-related provisions of international instruments can be found in Chapter 5.

[6]   Article 151(4) EC; see Chapter 3.

Resolution was the first significant institutional proclamation on minority languages, its provisions are understandably cautious, but they do contain some progressive innovations. The role of regional and local as well as national and international government was stressed, for example, highlighting the potential for co-operation between these various levels of authority. This approach signifies an early flavour of subsidiarity in Community policy-making; the idea that the EEC Regional Fund should contribute to 'the financing of regional economic projects'—in the interests of preserving regional population bases and, in turn, regional cultures—draws this philosophy to a practical conclusion. Another innovation is that the Resolution looks at the provision of minority language education not only in the primary school sector, but right up to (and including) university level. Also in the domain of education, the Parliament called for the incorporation of minority languages into the existing Community language education programmes. The Parliament envisaged a coordinating role for the Commission, based primarily on the collection of data and the funding of research and pilot studies. By encouraging communication between linguistic groups and the EC institutions, the transnational and/or cross-border dimension of language issues was emphasised, thus implicitly substantiating the need for Community intervention in this field and, again, presaging the conditions later adopted for the mechanics of subsidiarity.

The phraseology employed suggests a more proactive role for the Member States, however, asking that they 'provide for', 'promote' and 'take steps to ensure'—in addition to 'allowing'—the execution of the initiatives proposed. This illustrates a recognition by the Parliament that conscious government action is necessary for the effective implementation of language choice; the degree to which this contributes to the ultimate success of language planning in a purely linguistic sense is quite another matter, addressed in Chapter 5. But what is clear is that, from the outset, different roles were envisaged for the Community and the Member States. The primary responsibility for policy realisation was placed squarely on the Member States themselves, with the Community acting more as coordinator. The Resolution—which is not, of course, legally binding in any event—can thus be interpreted as a declaratory instrument. This interpretation does not render the absence of reasoning on competence or legal basis quite as damning as might otherwise be expected. A basic standard for language rights, measures below which were not acceptable, was defined and a number of language-use domains requiring attention at both national and supranational levels were identified. The Arfé Resolution cannot be interpreted as an attempt to contrive legally binding duties for either the EC institutions or the Member States. But a distinct policy stance was articulated, confirming, at least, the desirability of further action; and it is also obvious that the Parliament envisaged a definite role for the Community in this context, out of very little indeed.

(iii)   Impact of the Resolution

In October 1981, approximately six months after the Resolution was adopted, the European Bureau for Lesser Used Languages (EBLUL) was founded to conserve and promote autochthonous minority and regional languages in the EC Member States. It is funded by subventions from the Community and from the governments of certain Member States.[7] Examples of its wide-ranging activities include publication of the *Contact Bulletin*, the coordination of research projects and the collection of relevant data. It is, in effect, an executive personification of the numerous minority language communities scattered throughout the Community, establishing a vital political link with the EC institutions (and with other international organisations) on their behalf. Its continued existence has, however, been threatened in recent years, in that the legal basis for minority language funding more generally has been called into question, as detailed in Chapter 6. In 1986, the *Istituto della Enciclopedia Italiana* produced a report on linguistic minorities in the EC, at the request of the Commission (Committee on Youth, Culture, Education, Information and Sport) and based on questionnaires that had been dispatched to the Member States.[8] On its analysis of the responses received, the Commission recommended *inter alia* the recognition of minority languages in the constitutions of the Member States, implementation of that status in a real sense, the formation of a Minorities Commission at EC level and the provision of appropriate economic aid for research and study programmes. The Report considered that "...the treatment of linguistic minorities is by its very nature a political problem, and secondarily a problem of language policy."[9] Several of the recommendations made, such as the constitutional recognition of linguistic minorities, were quite far-reaching from the perspective of their potential impact on national

---

[7]   Currently Ireland, Luxembourg, the Provincial Government of Friesland and the Germanophone community in Belgium; in addition, rent-free accommodation for the EBLUL Brussels office is provided by the French-speaking community in Belgium (EBLUL has a second office in Dublin).

[8]   *Istituto della Enciclopedia Italiana*/European Commission, *Linguistic Minorities in Countries belonging to the EC*, (Luxembourg: Office for Official Publications of the European Communities, 1986).

[9]   *ibid.*, p. 232.

governance. Concrete action towards the achievement of these objectives was not, however, undertaken. Overall, given that the Arfé Resolution marked the very early stages of the Community's foray into minority language protection, its impact on the EC institutions is at once both superficial and extensive: superficial as regards the measures and projects actually undertaken, which stopped short of investigating legal competence and were framed in a suggestive rather than imperative format; but extensive in that neither the Commission nor the Parliament hesitated when reminding Member State governments of their responsibilities towards minority language groups, notwithstanding the absence of a substantive Treaty provision upon which this 'interference' into domestic political practice could be grounded. It is more difficult to assess the impact of the Resolution from the perspective of the minority language speakers themselves. It is true that it is widely referred to in contemporary language rights campaigns, but promotion of the European Parliament measures has been relatively recent and can be traced particularly to the growth and influence of EBLUL; moreover, *Arfé* is usually alluded to in a collective sense, as one element within a series of measures, rather than for its distinct significance. That public awareness has developed over time rather than at the outset is substantiated by a survey conducted among Breton speakers which posed questions on the impact of *Arfé* specifically: it was found that most respondents had not even known that the Resolution existed.[10]

B.   Arfé Resolution (2) (1983)

Resolution in favour of Minority Languages and Cultures[11]

The second Arfé Resolution, adopted on 11 February 1983, is primarily a reminder—or arguably a reproof—that Parliament's proposals had not really been taken up by the other Community institutions. Reference is also made in the Preamble to the 'resurgence of special movements by ethnic and linguistic minorities'. The original recommendations were summarised and restated, but more intensely in some instances. For example, the proposed review of Community legislation, called for in Article 6 of *Arfé* (1), was replaced by the statement that 'all Community *and national* legislation *and practices*' that discriminate against minority languages should be reviewed

---

[10]   Rosalind M. Temple, "Great expectations? Hopes and fears about the implications of political developments in Western Europe for the future of France's regional languages" in M.M. Parry, W.V. Davies and R.A.M. Temple, *The Changing Voice of Europe*, (Cardiff: University of Wales Press, 1994), 191-211 at 202-4.

[11]   11 February 1983, [1983] OJ C68/103; see Appendix II for text.

by the Commission (emphasis added). Moreover, the Resolution called upon the Commission to 'prepare appropriate Community instruments for ending such discrimination'. This is a particularly striking provision, since it implies that the Commission should tackle not only discriminatory EEC measures, but also those enacted by the Member States (although, most probably to be read with the implied limitation that this would cover national laws and practices only in so far as they were connected to the implementation of Community law). This signifies a certain impatience within the Parliament. But once again, it did not establish or even consider whether the Community had the competence to introduce such measures in the first place. The Commission was required to report to the Parliament by the end of 1983, on the outcome of any action taken, but this did not materialise in practice.

C.   Kuijpers Resolution (1987)

Resolution on the Languages and Cultures of Regional and Ethnic Minorities in the European Community.[12]

(i)   Introduction

The Kuijpers Resolution was adopted on 30 October 1987, more than four years after the adoption of *Arfé* (2). The lengthy preamble suggests that Community interest in minority language issues had intensified rather than waned in the interim period. But still, no Treaty provision was identified as a legal basis for *any* of the measures proposed, although the extensive list of national and international instruments cited is possibly an alternative attempt to buttress the legitimacy of Community action in the field. The Resolution reiterates and elaborates on the principles outlined in both of its predecessors. Language rights are placed firmly within the ambit of international human rights, with stronger references to the work of both the United Nations and the Council of Europe. Relevant international instruments had been referred to as 'declarations of principle' in the earlier Resolutions, but are cited in *Kuijpers* as 'basic principles regarding the rights of minorities formulated and approved'. In particular, the Council of Europe's Charter on Regional and Minority languages, in preparation at that time, was supported expressly. It was also acknowledged that the implementation of minority language rights contributes to the prevention of discrimination. The Parliament alluded to strengthening the autonomy of the regions, and yet creating a 'more politically unified European Community'. It advocated especially

---

[12]   30 October 1987, Doc. A 2-150/87; see Appendix II for text.

the need to improve economic conditions at regional level, as a corollary of the maintenance and development of localised cultures and languages. The Resolution expressed 'regret' that the Commission had failed to 'deal comprehensively' with the rights of minorities since the adoption of *Arfé* (1). But this admonition belies Parliament's own failure to flag any Treaty provisions upon which comprehensive action could actually be based. Notwithstanding this oversight, the Resolution calls expressly for the full implementation of both Arfé Resolutions, and proceeds to restate and expand the principles endorsed originally therein.

(ii)   Content and Commentary

At the outset, the Parliament described legal recognition at Member State level as 'the basic condition for the preservation of regional and minority cultures and languages' (Article 2). The phraseology used here is cautious to begin with. The Parliament 'points out' the need for constitutional recognition but does not demand or require it. In Article 3, however, it 'calls on the Member States whose Constitutions already contain general principles on the rights of minorities to make timely provision on the basis of organic laws, for the implementation of those principles'. It is arguable that this ostensibly strong demand is weakened by the fact that it was directed only at the Member States that have *already* made some provision for the protection of linguistic minorities and have, therefore, displayed a sympathetic predisposition to minority concerns. But it must be remembered that the Parliament called upon Member States to act on *national*, constitutional provisions: this casts the Resolution in a more radical light, skirting the principle of non-interference in domestic affairs: although it was suggested above that an implied proviso could be read into *Arfé* (2), the laws of the Member States that deal with minority languages are specified expressly here, and it is difficult to link such provisions with the implementation of Community law to any meaningful extent. Though more or less confined to the traditional domains of language use—education, law and administration, the media, cultural events, and social and economic measures—the Kuijpers Resolution went further in a substantive sense than either of its precursors. It contains both general, sweeping principles and more specific calls for action. For example, the use of minority languages for administrative and legal purposes (Article 6) was associated with local authorities 'in the first instance'. This does not preclude the adoption of measures by *national* authorities, where speakers of a minority language are not contained geographically in a specific region or where local authorities do not have the requisite legislative autonomy to manage linguistic policy in the first place. The Resolution advocated that the language(s) through which decentralised government services are provided should be determined by the linguistic structure of the geographical area served. But it is arguable that minority languages should also be incorporated into the services provided by centralised state authorities, so that a basic level of service, at least, can be provided where requested.[13] This principle can also be adapted to supranational authorities, given the internal *and* external implications of language policy, introduced in Chapter 1 and discussed further in Chapter 5. Article 7 of the Resolution deals with the media. It contains general principles on access to broadcasting for minority language groups. More specific opportunities for direct action were also outlined, such as supporting the training of journalists and technical staff who work through the medium of a minority language, as well as ensuring that the latest broadcasting technology is available to them. Cultural infrastructure is addressed in Article 8. The Parliament recommended the foundation of cultural institutes to undertake studies, to co-ordinate and gather information, and to provide and supervise education through the medium of minority languages. The reference to the banking and consumer sectors in Article 9 is especially striking in that it relates to domains largely *outside* the ambit of government services. This is significant given the trend towards the privatisation of utilities formerly controlled by states (*e.g.* telecommunications, power supply), which has removed more and more services from the protective realm of the 'official' use of language. The remaining provisions deal largely with the role of the Community institutions. The long-expressed ideal that the Commission should treat minority languages in a broader context, considering the impact of *all* legislative initiatives on culture and language patterns, was reaffirmed. The Resolution recommended strongly that the institutions and the Member States support the work of EBLUL, particularly in terms of financial assistance. In Article 12, Parliament called on the Commission to take every action to implement the Resolution 'within its terms of reference', yet it did not attempt to identify what those constraints might actually be. Interestingly, minority languages were located within the ambit of 'cultural and educational policy' but it is debatable whether even this Community competence existed at the time. Article 128 (now 151) EC on cultural policy only came into being after the ratification of the TEU; the original Article

---

[13] In Ireland, for example, in preparation for the drafting of imminent language legislation, all central and local government departments were required to draw up a customised language plan, based on the demand for services through Irish experienced by each individual department: see Niamh Nic Shuibhne, "Rethinking Language Policy: A Legal Perspective", (2000) 3 *Contemporary Issues in Irish Law and Politics* 36-53.

128 EEC (now 149 EC), which dealt with vocational training, had been extended by the ECJ to apply to education in a wider sense, but this development was still fairly controversial in 1987.[14] In Article 15, Parliament stressed '...categorically that the recommendations contained in this Resolution are not to be interpreted or implemented in such a way as to jeopardise the territorial integrity or public order of the Member States'. Finally, it was recognised that migrant workers and overseas minorities have specific but different needs as minority groups that should be addressed separately.

D.   Conclusion

The series of resolutions outlined above chronicles the early stages of the European Parliament's work on minority languages. But it could not draw upon any substantive Treaty provisions to bolster its calls for action. The breadth of issues covered, particularly in the Kuijpers Resolution, demonstrates an appreciation of the main difficulties faced by minority language speakers, as well as a commendable comprehension of both the potential and limits of language planning. It is clear from the tone of the later texts that Parliament had not been able to influence the other EC institutions as much as it had intended. A number of reasons traditionally associated with resistance to the granting of minority rights might be relevant here. Minority 'problems' are, in any context, among the most contentious aspects of the contemporary fundamental rights debate. The Commission may have evaded adopting a definite policy stance to avoid trespassing on the undoubtedly diverse political circumstances within the Member States. The fact that the Parliament was not acting on the basis of any discernible Community competence provides a more fundamental explanation as to why its initiatives were not, and indeed could not be, translated into concrete programmes of action, above and beyond the coordination of funding and data collection that did result. Given the unease expressed over the ECJ's generous interpretation of Article 128 EEC (vocational training) around the same time, the Commission was unlikely to land itself knowingly in the midst of yet another 'Community versus Member State' competence contest. It must be remembered that throughout the 1980s, the European political climate was characterised by strong movements both in favour of *and* against intensified European unity. The ratification of the Single European Act was not achieved without resistance, and the build-up to the Maastricht negotiations

---

[14]   The position was later clarified in Case 24/86 *Blaizot v. University of Liège* [1988] ECR 355; see now, Articles 149-150 EC on 'Education, Vocational Training and Youth'.

in particular revealed even further the deep-rooted objections in a growing number of Member States to the escalation of supranational integration. In this light, it is surprising that the three Resolutions did not actually generate much controversy within the Parliament itself, on arguments of national sovereignty for example. But resolutions do not have legal effect. This reflects the cynical truth that policy makers are far more willing to declare principles than policy actors are to implement them in turn. Supporting a relatively innocuous resolution would not cause too many political ripples—and might gain favourable publicity and, in turn, sympathy from those affected—yet would not require much substantive action to be undertaken. This analysis does not detract from the ambitions of the Parliament; rather, it sheds light on why the recommendations it made were not subsequently acted upon. In short, it would not have been possible to adopt legally binding texts on the protection of minorities, linguistic or otherwise, at Community level. This is reflected even more acutely by considering the pre-Maastricht jurisprudence of the Court of Justice.

3. JURISPRUDENCE OF THE EUROPEAN COURT OF JUSTICE

In Chapter 1, it was observed that language use is affected by a multitude of direct and indirect factors which, on the surface, seem otherwise unrelated. It was also noted that, at least in the Pre-Maastricht era, the EEC Treaty did not authorise the Community to determine language policy beyond structuring its own official languages regime. As seen above, this limitation did not hinder the work of the Parliament. But the European Court of Justice, as the author of legally binding decisions, is bound by the parameters of the Treaties in quite a different way—or is it? The interpretative developments in respect of vocational training referred to above illustrate that the ECJ is not immune to the employment of judicial activism, a charge that has been levelled against it on a fairly consistent, and infamous, basis.[15] Against this background, the first cases in which the Court was obliged to consider the interaction of EC law with minority language issues are analysed below.

---

[15] See in particular, Hjalte Rasmussen, *On Law and Policy-Making in the European Court of Justice*, (Dordrecht: Nijhoff, 1986) and the abundance of derivative commentary, *e.g.* Takis Tridimas, "The Court of Justice and judicial activism", (1996) vol. 21(3) *European Law Review* 199-210.

A.   *Ministère Public* v. *Robert Heinrich Maria Mutsch*[16]

(i)   Facts

The applicant, a Luxembourg national, resided in a German-speaking municipality in Belgium. In 1981, he was charged with a criminal offence, related to a late-night dispute with members of the Belgian police force. He was questioned by the police through the medium of German; all forms and records relating to the charge were also completed in German. The trial summons was issued in French, but it was accompanied by a German translation. Initially, the applicant was convicted and fined *in abstentia*, but he applied to have that judgment set aside. He also requested that the appeal proceedings take place in German. Both requests were granted by the Belgian criminal court. The Public Prosecutor's office appealed against the latter part of the decision, however, maintaining that since the accused was a Luxembourg national, he did not have the right to be tried through German. Article 17(3) of the relevant Belgian statute[17] provides that an accused person of Belgian nationality residing in a German-speaking municipality is entitled to request that court proceedings be conducted through German. Although the accused in this case asserted that he spoke only German, or at least expressed himself more easily in that language, the Prosecutor argued that only Belgian nationals could avail of the rights granted by Article 17(3). The Belgian Court of Appeal was unsure whether this restriction was compatible with EEC law and referred the following question for a preliminary ruling under Article 177 EEC (now 234 EC):

> Does the third paragraph of Article 17...on the use of language in the courts...comply with the principles referred to in Article 220 of the Treaty, which is intended to secure the protection of persons and the enjoyment and protection of rights under the same conditions as those accorded by each Member State to its own nationals, that is to say, in the case in point, is it or is it not necessary, in a criminal case, to grant a German-speaking EEC national, and in particular a Luxembourg national residing in...a German-speaking municipality, the right to require that the proceedings take place in German?[18]

---

[16]   Case 137/84, [1985] ECR 2681.
[17]   Law of the 15 June 1985, on the use of languages in the courts.
[18]   *Mutsch*, p. 2693, para. 5.

Article 220 EEC (now 293 EC) set out that "[M]ember states shall, so far as is necessary, enter into negotiations with each other with a view to securing for the benefit of their nationals the protection of persons and the enjoyment and protection of rights under the same conditions as those accorded by each State to own nationals...." In this context, the Commission observed that "...a Member State is not obliged to grant the nationals of other Member States the rights referred to in Article 220 so long as the Member States have not entered into an agreement as referred to in that article."[19] The Commission did suggest, however, that other provisions of the EEC Treaty, on the free movement of workers and the right of establishment, might be relevant. In particular, it concluded that the legal status of the applicant as a migrant worker from another Member State ensured his right to be tried in German, in accordance with the rights granted to Belgian nationals in similar circumstances. Significantly, the tone of the submission made by the Italian Government placed the case in the context of minority language rights, but argued for a restrictive interpretation thereof:

> [N]ational legislation for the benefit of language minorities applies only to members of the minority in question and to the area where the language is spoken. A member of a recognised language minority can not therefore require the use of his language in legal proceedings outside the area where his language is spoken. Nor can a national of another Member State require that the minority language be used on the grounds that he speaks the minority language (which is not the national language of the State in which he lives) and lives in the area where the minority language is spoken. In such proceedings, interpreters must be used.[20]

It was noted that the employment of interpreters in the circumstances of this case would fulfil the requirements for criminal proceedings set down in the European Convention on Human Rights.[21]

---

[19]   *ibid.*, p. 2684 (Opinion of Advocate General Lenz).

[20]   *ibid.* The Italian Government argued on the basis of the territorial principle of language rights, explained in Chapter 5; see also Case C-274/96 *Criminal Proceedings against Bickel and Franz* [1998] ECR I-7637, discussed in Chapter 6.

[21]   The relevant provisions of the ECHR are outlined in Chapter 5.

(ii)   Judgment of the Court

The Court of Justice adopted the approach put forward by the Commission in respect of Article 220 EEC *i.e.* given that an agreement on the mutual recognition of language rights did not exist between Belgium and Luxembourg, it was not possible for the applicant to employ that provision in the present case. However, the Court also applied the broader reasoning suggested by the Commission, based on the rights of migrant workers. It classified the right to use a particular language in the courts of another Member State under the same conditions as nationals of that State as a 'social advantage', within the meaning of Article 7(2) of Regulation 1612/68.[22] Specifically, the Court referred to its earlier decision in *Ministère Public v. Even*, where it defined 'social advantages' as "...all advantages 'which, whether or not linked to a contract of employment, are generally granted to national workers primarily because of their objective status or by virtue of the mere fact of their residence on the national territory'."[23] Applying this interpretation to the present case, the Court stated that "[t]he right to use his own language in proceedings before the courts of the Member State in which he resides, under the same conditions as national workers, plays an important role in the integration of a migrant worker and his family into the host country, and thus in achieving the objective of free movement of workers."[24] Furthermore, the Court cited Article 7 EEC (now 12 EC), which prohibited discrimination on grounds of nationality. In a terse but significant statement, the Court declared that "[i]n the context of a Community based on the principles of free movement of persons and freedom of establishment the protection of the linguistic rights and privileges of individuals is of particular importance."[25]

(iii)   Commentary

To what extent was the decision in *Mutsch* coloured by minority language rights? The Court did not address this question directly, but there is some evidence in the judgment of an implicitly supportive stance. As just noted, for example, the Court regarded the protection of linguistic rights in the Community as being 'of particular importance'. It is significant also that the

---

22   [1968] OJ Special English Edition, L257/2, p. 475.

23   *Mutsch*, p. 2696, para. 17, referring to Case 207/78, [1979] ECR 2019.

24   *ibid.*, p. 2696, para. 16.

25   *ibid.*, p. 2695, para. 11.

only barrier to the application of Article 220 EEC ('enjoyment and protection of rights') was the absence of a relevant inter-state agreement, implying that the Court viewed the use of a particular language in criminal proceedings as a *right* and not just a privilege. Advocate General Lenz tackled the language rights dimension more overtly. He concentrated on the nature of 'social advantages' under Regulation 1612/68, to which Community workers are entitled without discrimination. He argued that there are two specific categories of rights and duties: first, those involving a 'special relationship of allegiance' to the state in question and, second, social rights that must be guaranteed to all workers without discrimination. In the context of the present case, he stated that "[c]riminal proceedings certainly do not involve a 'special relationship of allegiance', so safeguarding the rights of the defence, which includes choice of language of the proceedings, cannot be made dependent on nationality."[26] He did not elaborate further on the nature of a 'special relationship of allegiance', however, so it is not certain that *all* language issues are exempt from this criterion. One language more than any other is often intrinsically connected with a particular state or regional identity; taken to extremes, a state could conceivably argue that because of this close association or 'special allegiance', there cannot be an official role for any other language(s), in the interests of unity and solidarity, for example. Traces of this philosophy can be identified in Article 2 of the French Constitution when read in conjunction with related legislation (outlined in Appendix I), which has had a detrimental effect on the recognition of language rights for those who speak a language other than French (the national language), such as Breton.[27] The ECJ has never been called upon to consider this hypothetical argument but it would certainly amount to a tough political decision, bringing national sovereignty and the multicultural ethos of the Community into direct conflict.

The Advocate General referred interchangeably to language/minority rights. In a statement that reflects the position of the European Parliament at the time, he stressed that linguistic discrimination based on nationality "...is certainly not in keeping with the establishment of a 'Citizen's Europe'. Nor does it contribute to the integration of the worker in the host country, in

---

[26] *ibid.*, Opinion of Advocate General Lenz, pp. 2685-6.

[27] The force of constitutional resistance to the promotion of any language other than French has been felt most recently as a result of the decision of the Constitutional Council that effectively prevents France from ratifying the European Charter for Regional or Minority Languages: see Chapter 5; see also (2000) vol. 16:3 *Contact Bulletin* 1.

particular in the linguistic region in which he lives."[28] Referring to established case law, the Advocate General pointed out that the Court has always interpreted the principle of non-discrimination broadly, and noted that while equal treatment is based on an individual's status as a Community worker, the principle can also be applied to situations *outside* the employment relationship.[29] Applying this precedent to the present case, he concluded that:

> ...it cannot be assumed that [social] advantages...are inapplicable merely because they are granted in order to protect minority rights...The requirement of equal treatment...applies in areas which are not primarily governed by Community law but on which Community law may have indirect effects...[The possible application of Article 7(2)] cannot be dismissed with the simple statement that matters concerning the organisation of the courts or the use of languages in criminal proceedings are not governed by Community law.[30]

The last sentence in this passage reflects the idea of the 'spillover' of Community competence. The Advocate General recognised that because the effects of EC law cannot be contained precisely, its impact is often wider than the achievement of the specific goals or objectives outlined in the Treaties or in secondary legislation—in fact, a Community *responsibility* to deal with these 'side-effects' can be derived from the above extract. He thus laid the jurisdictional foundations for the Court to examine national language policy in respect of its compliance with Community law, followed through in *Groener*, discussed below.

It may be recalled that the Italian Government had submitted a number of arguments based on minority rights criteria, but these arguments were not addressed by the Court. Somewhat paradoxically, however, Advocate General Lenz asserted that minority rights criteria could not apply in *Mutsch*, since the languages referred to in the Belgian legislation—Dutch, French and German—were not classified as minority languages therein: "[e]xpressions

---

[28] *ibid.*, p. 2689; it was noted in Chapter 1 that motivation for Community protection of the language rights of migrant workers could be attributed to a desire to ensure the successful integration of workers and their families into the host state, as well as to the value of linguistic and cultural diversity *per se.*

[29] *ibid.*, pp. 2688-9; see Case 15/69 *Südmilch v. Ugliola* [1969] ECR 363, Case 9/74 *Casagrande v. Landeshaupstadt München* [1974] ECR 773, Case 32/75 *Cristini v. SNCF* [1975] ECR 1085 and Case 65/81 *Reina v. Landeskreditbank Baden-Württemberg* [1982] ECR 33.

[30] *ibid.*, p. 2689.

such as national language, native language, linguistic minority and so on are not to be found in [the statute]. I therefore do not consider it correct...to rely on general principles of law regarding the protection of linguistic minorities, as was done by [the Italian Government]."[31] This is an extremely narrow interpretation, relying on the domestic classification of languages as a precondition to the application of international standards. This literal approach has, in fact, been rejected by even the more conservative minority rights theorists.[32] On the Advocate General's reasoning, the protection of language rights by an international entity is wholly dependent on the categorisation of languages applied internally by a state, which defeats the very purpose of international intervention in the first place. This automatic and disappointing deference to the Member States casts an unwelcome shadow on attempts to unearth a coherent Community policy on minority languages. Moreover, the rest of the Advocate General's comments on language rights simply do not fit with this aspect of his analysis. For example, although within the framework of national rules on the use of languages, the Advocate General recognised the principle of language choice, stating that "[i]t would be inconsistent and incompatible with the principle that workers from other Member States must be treated in the same manner as national workers if [the applicant] were suddenly to find that in criminal proceedings he could no longer use the language *which he can use in everyday life* and in which workers who are Belgian nationals may, *if they wish*, be tried."[33] This comment presupposes the existence of a domestic language choice regime, but it nonetheless determines that language rights come into play well before the criteria outlined in the European Convention on Human Rights; these benchmarks are discussed in detail in Chapter 5, but it may be noted at this stage that an accused must be unable to *understand* the language of court proceedings before interpreters will be appointed. This is a much weaker standard, from the perspective of language rights, than that of *choosing* a language 'used in everyday life'. The Advocate General expressly rejected the argument put forward by the Italian Government that the use of interpreters would suffice in the present case. In a remarkable passage, he

---

[31]   *ibid.*, p. 2690.

[32]   See Chapter 5 on international fundamental rights standards; the United Nations Report on Ethnic, Religious and Linguistic Minorities, for example, [Francesco Capotorti, *Study on the Rights of Persons belonging to Ethnic, Religious and Linguistic Minorities*, (New York: United Nations, 1979), p. 121, para. 61] concludes the exact opposite to Advocate General Lenz, stressing that the absence of domestic recognition of minority languages does *not* prevent the application of international protection mechanisms.

[33]   *Mutsch*, p. 2689 (emphasis added).

clarified the relationship between the Community and the Council of Europe as follows:

> In the area of fundamental rights, the Court has certainly drawn from the Convention, in the sense that it has treated the Convention as supplying common minimum standards. It is not contrary to the European Convention on Human Rights for Community law to grant more extensive protection to individual rights. Indeed, the Court has held that Community law takes precedence over other agreements concluded within the Framework of the Council of Europe in so far as it is more favourable for individuals.[34]

This interpretation has immense implications for EC fundamental rights policy generally and for language rights in particular, as the Council of Europe has not yet established a legally enforceable framework for the rights of minority language speakers.[35] But the Advocate General's remarks must be appraised in terms of potential rather than effect since, as he was careful to point out in the closing paragraphs of his Opinion, "…there is no question of requiring the Member State to permit the use of other languages in addition to those already available [under its language policy regime]. In this case the question is whether a worker from another Member State can rely on a legal provision regarding language use which exists in the Member State concerned and is available to its own nationals."[36]

It is clear that both the Advocate General and the Court were decidedly more reluctant to issue pronouncements on minority language rights than the European Parliament was at that time. This demonstrates a fundamental difference between the two institutions, in terms of both function and impact. Decisions of the ECJ contrast sharply with non-binding European Parliament

---

[34]   *ibid.*, p. 2690; see Case 187/73 *Callemeyn v. Belgium* [1974] ECR 553 and the Opinion of Advocate General Lenz in Case 157/84 *Frascogna v. Caisse des Depôts et Consignations* [1985] ECR 1740.

    In the present case, Advocate General Lenz pointed out that, prior to the intervention by the Public Prosecutor, the Belgian Court had been quite happy to proceed with the case through German and that the introduction of an interpreter would have added needless cost and inconvenience.

[35]   The most recent expression of the principle outlined by Advocate General Lenz is contained in Article 52 of the Charter of Fundamental Rights of the European Union (Charte 4487/00, Brussels, 28 September 2000): see Chapter 5.

[36]   *Mutsch*, p. 2690; see also Article 51(2) of the Charter of Fundamental Rights, which confirms, in a similar vein, that the Charter "…does not establish any new power or task for the Community or the Union, or modify powers and tasks defined by the Treaties".

resolutions. The determination of legal basis is, therefore, far more problematic for the Court. In *Mutsch*, it avoided the minority language issue altogether—which it could easily do, given the scope of the question referred by the domestic court and the fact that Belgium already had an official languages regime in place. All that the Court needed to decide was whether non-Belgian nationals could benefit from that pre-existing regime; it did not have to examine the substance of the Belgian policies. Advocate General Lenz, on the other hand, was willing to use minority rights terminology, but his far-reaching statements on the limitations of the ECHR do not match his conclusive reliance on the domestic classification of languages, which has been virtually disregarded in international law more generally. Curiously, there are no references in the Opinion to the work of the Parliament, which had already adopted both Arfé Resolutions by that time. The Advocate General was prepared to frame the case in a language rights context but was obviously constrained by the ambit of the EEC Treaty. He may also have been conscious of offending Member State sensibilities, seeking to avoid an interference into what are typically regarded as 'internal' matters. So while his conclusions on this point are not especially satisfactory, his compliance with the internal classification of language may at least be considered politically expedient; in Chapter 1, it was seen that the European Charter for Regional or Minority languages includes, in effect, two definitions of a minority language, so that languages recognised officially at domestic level can remain separate to some extent from those that are not—notwithstanding that this differential is relevant for definition purposes only and not for the substantive breadth and implementation of the Charter. The overall impression in *Mutsch*, then, is one of a vague sympathy within the Court that was not (capable of being) translated into justiciable effect. At any rate, the Court was able to reach the conclusion that vindicated the language rights of the applicant without having to explore language rights *per se*. And despite the anomaly referred to above, the Advocate General's reasoning can be noted for its broad interpretation of language rights—not based on linguistic competence, but on choice—and for his significant comments on the authority of the ECJ to grant more extensive fundamental rights protection than that provided by the ECHR, on the basis that an individual should benefit from the most extensive safeguards available. These ideas laid the seeds for the bolder interpretative approach apparent in more recent ECJ judgments that deal directly with minority language issues as raised, considered in Chapter 6.

B.   *Anita Groener v. Minister for Education and the City of Dublin Vocational Education Committee*[37]

McMahon observes that the decision in *Groener* reflects the tension between a number of competing interests—cultural and economic, national and supranational, individual and Community.[38] The Court of Justice had to negotiate a thorny political predicament: how would it balance the market-based free movement of Community workers with a Member State's constitutional language policy? It may be commonly thought of as a 'constitutional court',[39] but the ECJ does not actually function as the judicial apex in an overtly federal arrangement. In truth, it has clashed openly with national constitutional courts on occasion and its authority may even be said to rest, ultimately, on their forbearance.[40] The following paragraphs outline how the ECJ balanced established Community principles on free movement with national constitutional law in the specific—and contentious—province of state language policy. But the decision in *Groener* throws light on questions of much broader application also, from the shifting priorities of the EEC to the evolution of the Court's interpretative principles.

(i)   Facts

The applicant was a Dutch national who had resided in Ireland since 1982. She worked as a part-time art teacher at the Dublin College of Marketing and Design, which was under the authority of the second respondents. In 1984, she applied—successfully—for a permanent full-time lecturing post at the

---

[37]   Case C-379/87, [1989] ECR 3967.

[38]   Bryan McMahon, case comment, (1990) vol. 27:1 *Common Market Law Review*, 129-139 at 130.

[39]   The ECJ itself has tacitly set out its constitutional role: in Case 294/83 *Parti Ecologiste 'Les Verts' v. European Parliament* [1986] ECR 1339 (at 1365, para. 23), the Court stated that "...the EEC is a Community based on the rule of law, inasmuch as neither its Member States nor its institutions can avoid a review of the question whether the measures adopted by them are in conformity with the basic constitutional charter, the Treaty." See also *Opinion 1/91* [1991] ECR 6079 at 6102, para. 21.

[40]   See Chapter 5, for example, on the background to the ECJ's acceptance of fundamental rights protection as an element of Community law; see also the decision of the German Federal Constitutional Court in *Brunner v. The European Union Treaty* [1994] 1 CMLR 57. In Case C-159/90 *S.P.U.C. v. Grogan* [1991] ECR I-4685, the ECJ had to consider whether abortion, which was considered unlawful under Article 40.3.3° of the Irish Constitution, could be classified as a service in terms of the application of EC law (discussed further in Chapter 5).

College but, in accordance with procedures established by the Minister for Justice,[41] the appointment was conditional on her passing an oral Irish language examination. According to Article 8 of the Irish Constitution, Irish is the national and first official language of the State (English is recognised as a second official language); in reality, however, Irish is a *de facto* minority language.[42] The applicant first requested that the examination requirement be waived in her case, on the grounds that she would not actually be obliged to teach any courses through the medium of Irish, but this petition was refused. She then followed a four-week beginners' Irish course, proceeding to take, but fail, the oral examination. At this point, she wrote directly to the first respondent, asking once again that the language requirement be waived. The Minister replied that this was not possible in her case as other fully qualified candidates had applied for the position. The applicant initiated proceedings in the Irish High Court for a judicial review of the Minister's decision. She asserted that the relevant administrative procedures were contrary to the free movement of workers as protected by Community law (Article 48 EEC, now Article 39 EC) and, in particular, by Regulation 1612/68, Article 3(1) of which provides:

> Under this Regulation, provisions laid down by law, regulation or administrative action or administrative practices of a Member State shall not apply:
>
> (i) where they limit application for and offers of employment, or the right of foreign nationals to take up and pursue employ-

---

[41] Two national administrative measures had been adopted in accordance with the powers granted to the Minister by the Vocational Education Act, 1930: (1) Memorandum V7 (1 September 1974) established that a person could not be appointed to a permanent, full-time post in certain areas of teaching, including art, unless that person held a *Ceard Teastas Gaeilge* (a certificate of competence in the Irish language) or had an equivalent qualification recognised by the Minister. Candidates from outside Ireland could be exempted from the Irish language requirement provided that there were no other fully qualified candidates for the post. (2) On 26 June 1979, the Minister issued Circular Letter No. 28/79, which provided that appointees for permanent, full-time posts could be required to undergo a special oral Irish examination. The appointment could not be made unless the selected candidate passed this examination but, once again, the Minister reserved the right to exempt candidates from this requirement where there were no other fully qualified candidates for the position.

[42] Official census statistics (1996) estimate that approximately one-third of the population has some competence in the Irish language; figures on the use of Irish as a first or vernacular language are more difficult to gauge, however, and estimates can range from 2-10% of the total population of the State.

ment or subject these to conditions not applicable to their own nationals; or

(ii) where, though applicable irrespective of nationality, their exclusive or principal aim or effect is to keep nationals of other Member States away from the employment offered.

This provision shall not apply to conditions relating to linguistic knowledge required by reason of the nature of the post to be filled.

The High Court, in turn, referred the following questions to the ECJ, for a preliminary ruling under Article 177 EEC (now Article 234 EC):

1. Where provisions laid down by law, regulation or administrative action make employment in a particular post in a Member State conditional upon the applicant having a competent knowledge of one of the two official languages of that Member State, being a language which nationals of other Member States would not normally know but would have to learn for the sole purpose of complying with the condition, should Article 3 of Regulation (EEC) No. 1612/68 of the Council be construed as applying to such provisions on the ground that their exclusive or principal effect is to keep nationals of other Member States away from the employment offered?

2. In considering the meaning of the phrase "the nature of the post to be filled" in Article 3 of [the Regulation], is regard to be had to a policy of the Irish State that persons holding the post should have a competent knowledge of the Irish language where such knowledge is not required to discharge the duties attached to the post?

3. (1) Is the term "public policy" in Article 48(3) of the EEC Treaty to be construed as applying to the policy of the Irish State to support and foster the position of the Irish language as the first official language?

(2) If it is, is the requirement that persons seeking appointment to posts as lecturer in vocational educational institutions in Ireland, who do not possess "An Ceard Teastas Gaeilge", shall undergo a special examination in Irish with the view to

satisfying the Department of Education of their competency in
Irish, a limitation justified on the grounds of such policy?[43]

The applicant argued that while the exclusion of non-nationals from
lecturing posts was not the exclusive or principal aim of the administrative
measures, it was, in reality, their principal effect. It was contended that the
phrase 'nature of the post to be filled' amounted to a derogation from Article
48 EEC; as such, it should be interpreted narrowly to apply only in cases
where the linguistic competence required could be related directly to the
performance of duties after appointment. In other words, while not opposed
to the cultural and linguistic policies of the Irish State *per se*, the applicant
argued that they could not be used to justify the negation of Article 48 EEC
and Regulation 1612/68 in the circumstances of her case.

The Irish Government sought, on the other hand, to establish that the
language requirement *could* be justified 'by reason of the nature of the post
to be filled'. No attempt was made to exhibit an illusory status for the Irish
language: it was acknowledged openly that Irish was not spoken universally
throughout the State. The submissions focused principally on the more
abstract properties of language; it was argued in particular that Irish is
central to the identity of the Irish State. The policies of successive governments to preserve and promote the language were presented as a corollary of
its constitutional status; the education system was, and remained, the domain
chiefly targeted and, in consequence, competence in Irish was considered
central to the regulation of teaching appointments. This argument was
developed, somewhat creatively, to embrace a situation such as that faced by
the applicant, where instruction was not actually required to be provided
through the medium of Irish. The Government submitted that "...Irish will
never become a living language if it is treated simply as a school subject. It
would be an abandonment of its policy if the State did not attempt to create a
supportive environment for the use of Irish outside formal classes. In [this
respect] the requirement that all teachers have a knowledge of Irish is fair
and reasonable."[44] It was stressed that both the direct and indirect influence
of teachers on their students cannot be distinguished in this context. As
regards the applicant's assertion of indirect discrimination, the Government
countered that competence in Irish was required for both nationals and non-
nationals alike. Interestingly, it did not claim that Community law simply did
not apply to its domestic language policy. This is somewhat unusual, as it is
generally observed that "[w]herever it is alleged that a measure taken by a

---

[43] *Groener*, pp. 3990-1, para. 10.
[44] *Groener*, Report for the Hearing, p. 3972.

Member State is contrary to one of the basic prohibitions of the Treaty...
[the] first line of defence should be to assert that the measure under attack
does not fall within the scope of the Treaty."[45] In this case, the Government
accepted that the applicant's rights under Article 48 EEC and Regulation
1612/68 were relevant, but claimed that her rights had not been infringed. It
was stressed that "...the exclusive or principal effect of the circular letter is
not to exclude non-Irish nationals from full-time posts but rather to ensure
that the persons engaged are suited for those posts."[46] Moreover, competence, not fluency, was the required standard, and other non-Irish nationals
had already passed the oral examination.[47] As an alternative argument, it was
submitted that even if the Court did find discriminatory treatment, the
administrative measures fell within the public policy exception in Article
48(3) EEC. In its final statement, the Government reasoned as follows:

> [A] condition requiring knowledge of the national language of
> the host country, applied in a manner proportionate to the
> intended objective and without discrimination as regards nation-
> ality, is in the public interest since it is pursuing an objective
> (the maintenance of cultural diversity in the Community and
> respect for linguistic pluralism) which is worthy of being
> recognised and furthered by the Community authorities...The
> Community institutions must respect a Member State's choice
> of its national language or languages and the measures suited to
> giving effect to that choice.[48]

In one respect, it is surprising that this argument was tacked on as an
addendum, since it encapsulates the pivotal—and novel—question to be
decided in this case. But the Irish government could not have predicted
whether the ECJ would be receptive to such arguments and probably sought
to avoid forcing an unfavourable determination. The strongly-worded

---

[45] AnneMarie Loman, Kamiel Mortelmans, Harry Post and Stewart Watson, *Culture and
Community Law: Before and After Maastricht*, (Boston: Kluwer Law and Taxation
Publishers, 1992), p. 23.

[46] *Groener*, Report for the Hearing, p. 3973.

[47] It was noted that from a total of six non-Irish nationals (including the applicant) who had
taken the examination, four had passed at the first attempt and another on the second
attempt; the applicant was, at that time, the only non-national who had failed the
examination.

It was also noted that there were 1723 Irish nationals teaching in vocational education
establishments, compared with 189 nationals from other Member States.

[48] *Groener*, Report for the Hearing, p. 3974.

submission of the French Government on the same issue stands in clear contrast:

> [A] condition requiring a knowledge of the national language of the host country is legitimate. Ireland is entitled to adopt measures to ensure that Irish is respected and used in conformity with its constitution...*No provision of Community law can preclude those rights*...The desire to achieve plurilingual communities is an imperative reason which must justify a language requirement of the kind at issue. The maintenance of cultural diversity in the Community and respect for linguistic pluralism enrich both the Community and the Member States. Those fundamental principles have been clearly affirmed by the Community, both in the Parliament and in the Council.[49]

(ii)   Judgment of the Court

In line with the approach taken by the Irish Government, the Court looked initially at the second question referred *i.e.* whether the 'nature of the post' justified the imposition of an Irish language competence requirement. The Court reasoned that if this question was answered in the affirmative, the outstanding issues of discrimination (question one) and public policy (question three) would not be relevant. It confirmed that while the applicant's teaching position did not require her to provide instruction through Irish, "...that finding is not in itself sufficient to enable the national court to decide whether the linguistic requirement in question is justified 'by reason of the nature of the post to be filled'....."[50] The Court placed strong emphasis on the constitutional status of Irish, and on the continuing policies of consecutive governments to maintain and promote the language. In a key statement, the Court declared that "[t]he EEC Treaty does not prohibit the adoption of a policy for the protection and promotion of a language of a Member State which is both the national language and first official language. However, the implementation of such a policy must not encroach upon a fundamental freedom such as that of the free movement of workers."[51] Several aspects of the decision hinge on this brief paragraph. First, the Court confirmed that language policy is primarily a matter of Member State competence. Second, emphasis was placed expressly on the legal status of Irish as a national and

---

[49]   Observations of the French Government, *ibid.* p. 3973 (emphasis added).

[50]   Judgment of the Court, p. 3992, para. 16.

[51]   *ibid.* p. 3993, para. 19.

official state language. But most remarkably, and in contrast to the non-interventionist arguments put forward by the French Government, the ECJ clearly envisaged a Community jurisdiction and responsibility in this field—to ensure that domestic language policy does not wipe out free movement rights gained under Community law. To this end, the Court applied its customary guiding principles; it confirmed that requirements imposed by national measures "...must not in any circumstances be disproportionate in relation to the aim pursued and the manner in which they are applied must not bring about discrimination against nationals of other Member States."[52] It did not apply these tests to the facts of the present case in any great detail, but was satisfied that the language requirement contested was legitimate. The Court's reasoning was based on an understanding that teachers fulfil both direct and indirect teaching functions. It was stressed also that the level of knowledge required was proportionate to the language restoration objective pursued by the Irish Government.[53] The second question was, therefore, answered in the affirmative—*i.e.* the linguistic requirement *was* justified by reason of the nature of the post to be filled—meaning that the Court did not have to consider the merits of the other questions referred. It did provide examples of situations that would amount to discriminatory treatment, however, such as the Government's insisting that the linguistic knowledge be acquired in Ireland only or preventing non-nationals from re-taking the examination.[54]

(iii)   Commentary

The decision of the ECJ in *Groener* had one irrefutable result: ultimately, the applicant was prevented from taking up a teaching job because of a language competence requirement, even though she would not have been required to use that language in the performance of her teaching duties. The Court focused on the 'nature' of the teaching appointment, in accordance with Regulation 1612/68, rather than on the specific tasks associated with it. But does this outcome really fit with the ECJ's renowned stance on free movement and integration, and on non-discrimination more generally? In effect, the Community principle of the free movement of workers was subordinated

---

[52]   *ibid.*

[53]   The Court did not, however, discuss explicitly the competence/fluency distinction: this argument is examined below in the context of the Advocate General's Opinion.

[54]   This aspect of the decision in *Groener* has been confirmed recently in Case C-281/98 *Angonese v. Cassa di Risparmio*, judgment of 6 June 2000, not yet reported; see Chapter 6.

to a Member State's official language policy, but the judgment raises more questions than it answers. Can the Court's reasoning be justified objectively? Does it set a precedent of wider application or should *Groener* be read strictly within its factual parameters? Is the scope of the decision confined to national and/or official languages, or was the status of Irish as a *de facto* minority language significant? These issues will now be considered.

(a)   The 'nature of the post to be filled'

The decision of the ECJ in *Groener* pivots entirely on a certain construction of teaching functions, yet the conclusion reached on this point is one of the most questionable aspects of the judgment. The applicant had argued that if she was appointed on a permanent, full-time basis, her duties would not differ substantively from those she was already carrying out as a part-time teacher. In particular, she stressed that she would not be required actually to use Irish in the new post. Thus, her appointment had been made conditional on knowledge of a language that was not required for the fulfilment of her responsibilities. The resulting paradox was addressed directly by Advocate General Darmon:

> [I]t does not seem to me necessary to embark upon a complex analysis to ascertain whether lack of knowledge of the Irish language may in fact create difficulties in the efficient teaching of the subject concerned for—and we are now at the heart of the matter—*it is a question of drawing a line between the powers of the Community and those of the Member States and of considering whether or not a policy of preserving and fostering a language may be pursued, having regard to the requirements of Community law.* [Regulation 1612/68] attempted to reconcile those apparently conflicting requirements by excluding conditions relating to linguistic knowledge from the scope of the principle of non-discrimination when the nature of the post to be filled requires such knowledge.[55]

This interpretation relates the particular facts of *Groener* to its broader conceptual context and is returned to in the next section. But it is clear that, in any event, the wording of the Regulation ('the *nature* of the post to be filled') was open to the liberal construction put forward by the Irish Government and accepted ultimately by the Court. A stricter provision could have specified that the language(s) must be *used* during the course of the

---

[55]   *Groener*, Opinion of Advocate General Darmon, p. 3980, para. 11 (emphasis added).

employment, but this cannot be assumed from the phraseology actually adopted. As the Court reasoned, determining that a language is not required for the performance of the duties of a post is *not* the same as determining that knowledge of a language cannot be justified by the *nature* of the post.[56] Advocate General Darmon considered that two conditions must be satisfied before the 'nature of a post' exception can apply: "[f]irst, the language requirement must meet an aim and, secondly, it must be strictly necessary in order to achieve that aim."[57] Ireland's language policy was adjudged to fulfil both criteria. The second condition is an expression of proportionality.[58] The use of alternative procedures was considered for the purpose of meeting this 'strictly necessary' test—*e.g.* acquisition of the language *after* appointment —but the Advocate General was not convinced that this option would be effective: "[f]irst, the learning of the language would not be immediate and secondly, the teachers involved would undoubtedly be less conscious of the necessity of having a knowledge of the Irish language."[59] But this reasoning is not persuasive. Even where a non-national studies a language prior to his/her appointment, language acquisition is an ongoing process and could hardly be seen as 'immediate'. Second, the Advocate General did not address the possibility of retaining the examination structure, but allowing the examination to be taken *after* employment had commenced. If an appointment remains ultimately contingent on proof of language compet-ence, then it hardly matters whether the examination is taken before or during employment, especially in cases such as *Groener* where the appointee will not, in all likelihood, have to teach through the relevant language in any case. This latter fact should have been recognised as a key aspect of the proportionality question; but this would, in a political sense, have been disastrous and so emphasis was placed instead on the abstract properties of culture and the indirect influence of teachers on their students—tenuous arguments at best. An employee in the interim or provisional situation described above is not going to be any 'less conscious' of the necessity of learning the language(s) concerned. While this alternative structure inevitably raises employment law issues, it is not a novel idea: many 'permanent' jobs are at first probationary, contingent on reviews of various kinds. This option could, at the very least, have been considered. From this perspective, it is difficult to maintain the argument that a pre-employment

---

[56]   Judgment of the Court, p. 3992, paras. 15-16.

[57]   Opinion of Advocate General Darmon, p. 3983, para. 26.

[58]   The first condition—the 'aim' of language policy—is discussed in section (b).

[59]   As note 57.

examination was 'strictly necessary' in the given circumstances. The key to the 'nature of the post' reasoning is not, therefore, proportionality;[60] rather, it requires the contemplation of education in a much broader sense, as outlined by Advocate General Darmon in the following extract. Significantly, he introduces the terminology of language rights and puts forward a more concrete case as to why the performance of duties through Irish was not the deciding factor:

> Once a constitution...recognises the existence of two official languages without limiting their use to specific parts of the national territory or to certain matters, each citizen has the right to be taught in those two languages. *The fact that only 33.6% of Irish citizens use the Irish language is no justification for sweeping away that right altogether, for its importance is measured not only by its use but also by the possibility of preserving its use in the future...To limit the requirement of a knowledge of Irish to posts involving the actual teaching of Irish would be to treat it as a dead language* like ancient Greek or Latin and as a language incapable of further development... Every Irishman has the right—enshrined as we have seen in the Irish State's most fundamental legal instrument—to be taught any subject at all, including painting, in Irish if he so desires. Whatever the official language used in educational institutions, a State is entitled to ensure that any citizen can express himself and be understood in another language, which is also an official language and which is also a repository of and a means of transmitting a common cultural heritage.[61]

This is a remarkable passage. The Advocate General identified the right of Irish citizens to be educated through a minority language, basing his reasoning on the fact that the language was recognised constitutionally and was a medium of cultural transmission. He then derived a correlative state duty to provide education through Irish where sought—something which has never actually been declared expressly by the Irish courts. But once it is

---

[60] In contrast to *Groener*, see the later decision in Cases C-259/91, 331-332/91 *Allué and Coonan* [1993] ECR I-4309, in which the measures contested—relating to the restricted duration and structure of teaching contracts at Italian universities for foreign language teaching assistants (who were primarily non-Italian nationals)—were held to infringe the principle of proportionality.

[61] *Groener*, Opinion of Advocate General Darmon, pp. 3982-3, paras. 21-24 (emphasis added).

accepted that a citizen has the right to be taught any subject through Irish, the State can reasonably require *all* teachers to demonstrate Irish language competence; in other words, the mere potentiality of the citizen's right being taken up was deemed sufficient to justify the blanket policy measures. The ECJ did not follow this line of analysis and did not, therefore, have to address the issue from the perspective of citizens' rights; it focused more on state powers than on state duties. McMahon remarks that to have done otherwise "...might have opened up too many possibilities and created too great a loophole for self-regulation by national governments."[62] A citizenship-based analysis might arguably have had the opposite effect, however, had the Court applied international rather than national standards; but the framework of EU citizenship had not yet been incorporated into the (then) EEC Treaty and the protection of fundamental rights within the ambit of Community law more generally, discussed in Chapter 5, had not yet evolved fully. Against this political background, an ECJ discussion on state duty and citizens' rights would have been unthinkable, despite the *dicta* in *Mutsch* on the furtherance of individual protection. McMahon notes yet another implication of the Court's concentration on teaching functions, that "[i]t is by no means certain whether a similar requirement would be justified in the case of nurses, doctors, postmen, lawyers, or others."[63] The 'nature of the post' criterion was relied upon to construe an eclectic interpretation of teaching functions only. As seen, this was tied to a philosophy of language education rights by the Advocate General but not by the Court itself. The Court must have been influenced by this logic, however, in its discussion on direct and indirect teaching duties. It referred tersely to 'the participation [of teachers] in the daily life of the school and the privileged relationship they have with their pupils.'[64] Here, the Court's reasoning seems lacking; yet on this weak and abstract basis, it condoned an indiscriminate policy measure that was arguably disproportionate in terms of the aim to be achieved. Advocate General Darmon provided a more coherent model for justifying the measures at issue. But the Court would have entered murky political waters had it openly applied his reasoning, given that the delineation of state duty on language matters is a contentious issue even internally.[65] So even if it is

---

[62] McMahon, case comment, p. 137.

[63] *ibid.*, p. 136.

[64] *Groener*, p. 3993, para. 20.

[65] On the situation in Ireland, for example, see Niamh Nic Shuibhne, "State duty and the Irish language", (1997) 19 *Dublin University Law Journal* 33-49, and "The Constitution, the courts and the Irish language", in Tim Murphy and Patrick Twomey (eds.), *Ireland's*

accepted that Ireland's official language policy can be used to augment the 'nature' of the teaching function, there are serious residual doubts from the perspectives of proportionality and non-discrimination on grounds of nationality. These issues are examined further below, after a consideration of the other element of Advocate General Darmon's test *i.e.* the aim of the language requirement.

(b)   The legal status of the language

> [This] case relates to one of the most sensitive aspects of cultural identity. The importance of the Court's reply and its consequences for the Member States and for the diversity of the Community as a whole are so evident that I need not dwell upon them, for at issue here is the power of a State to protect and foster the use of a national language.[66]

The ECJ relied heavily on the constitutional status of Irish as the national and first official language of the State.[67] Aside from an acknowledgment that Irish was not spoken by the whole population, the Court took its official status at face value. By classifying Irish as a constitutionally protected national language, the ECJ was spared from having to articulate a Community viewpoint on regional and minority languages. In this sense, it is misleading to regard *Groener* as a landmark decision on EC minority language protection.[68] But while the Court did not refer expressly to minority rights principles, the gist of its decision, as argued above, reflects the implicit influence of that ideology. Can these two strands of reasoning be reconciled? The Court acknowledged the validity of language planning as a government objective, a legitimate 'aim' in itself, but does this apply only when coupled with a particular constitutional status? This is the crux of the decision. The Court did not establish an absolute link between cultural diversity and national autonomy; as pointed out, it did not consider itself

---

Evolving Constitution 1937-1997: Collected Essays, (Oxford: Hart Publishing, 1998), 253-263.

[66]   *Groener*, Opinion of Advocate General Darmon, p. 3979, para. 1.

[67]   Interestingly, neither the Court nor the Advocate General commented on the status of Irish within the Community's language regime: Irish is a 'Treaty language', but not an official EC language (see Chapter 1).

[68]   McMahon has written that while "[t]hose who favour cultural diversity and national autonomy in these matters were undoubtedly pleased with the [judgment]...[t]heir initial euphoria...might be modified when they note the limits of the Court's decision." (McMahon, case comment, p. 135).

precluded from testing a Member State's language policy against the Community principles of proportionality and non-discrimination. Express reference to minority ideology is more visible in both the submission of the Commission and the opinion of the Advocate General. The Commission regarded the language requirement as discriminatory, discussed below, but accepted that its imposition could be justified by the 'nature of the post' clause. In a variation of the two-pronged test set out by the Advocate General, the Commission considered that language examinations as a pre-condition to employment were *prima facie* defensible in three situations: first, where knowledge of the language was required as a practical necessity, irrespective of the language's legal status; second, where the language is generally spoken in the work environment, even though not necessarily for carrying out the job itself; third, on the basis of the language policy of the relevant national authority.[69] The applicant had established that neither the first nor second condition applied in her case so the Commission focused on official language policy, stating that "[a] dynamic policy of fostering and protecting a *minority* language might justify the obligation in question, even if knowledge of that language is not widespread in the relevant Member State."[70] Thus, the Commission took on board the actual—and not just legal—status of Irish. It consolidated this approach, referring to:

> ...the importance of Irish as the historical language of the Irish people and the constant policy pursued by the Irish State to re-establish it as a generally spoken language in the face of real threats to its survival. The education system occupies a central role in this policy. Even if the level of knowledge required and the ubiquity of the English language make it unlikely that Irish students can be instructed entirely in Irish, it remains worth-while to ensure that communication can take place, at least on a one-to-one basis, in the native tongue of the minority language student. *The Community has a general interest in protecting minority languages....*[71]

This paragraph is firmly rooted in the philosophy of minority rights. The Commission condoned state intervention where a language not spoken by the majority of the population faces 'real threats to its survival'. Moreover, it not only approved of language planning at national level, but declared a

---

[69] *Groener*, Report for the Hearing, p. 3975.

[70] *ibid.*, (emphasis added).

[71] *ibid.*, p. 3976 (emphasis added).

general Community interest. It is surprising, then, that when forwarding its recommendations, the Commission referred only to 'the policy of a Member State to promote an official language'; it did not cite the minority-based arguments from which it had actually derived its conclusions. This omission reinforces the argument that the Court itself must have been influenced by the status of Irish as a *de facto* minority language, notwithstanding the absence of any direct references to this in its judgment. The antithesis of this position is, of course, that the Court would not have issued a decision in favour of the national measures *but for* the constitutional position of Irish as national and first official language, and that its *de facto* status was wholly irrelevant. On this basis, it is arguable that the Court would have reached a similar decision in respect of any national language, such as French in France or English in the United Kingdom. The Advocate General, in contrast, referred to the Arfé and Kuijpers Resolutions to illustrate institutional awareness of *minority* language issues. He sought to rationalise the status of Irish as a national, but minority, language:

> Certainly, Irish cannot be described as a regional language. Indeed, the Irish Constitution gives it the status of a national language. However, *since it is a minority language*, such a language cannot be preserved without the adoption of voluntary and obligatory measures. *Any minority phenomenon, in whatever field, cannot usually survive if appropriate measures are not taken.*[72]

The Advocate General thus looked beyond official status, acknowledging that it does not necessarily reflect the linguistic reality. His reasoning is a clear indication that the legitimacy of language policy is *not* contingent on the legal status of language(s) at domestic level; this explains why the measures adopted by the Irish Government were evaluated against the principle of language *preservation*, in addition to proportionality and non-discrimination. It is also consistent with his remarks on language policy as an ingredient of cultural heritage. Finally, it marks a welcome advance from the contrasting view taken by Advocate General Lenz in *Mutsch*, criticised above. The Court's acceptance of the 'paper' status of Irish was, in comparison, misplaced. The constant regurgitation of state policies has not bridged the gap between the constitutional prominence of Irish and its actual minority standing, so that citizens who wish to transact legal and official business through Irish, for example, often do so under considerable

---

[72] Opinion of Advocate General Darmon, p. 3982, para. 18 (emphasis added).

disadvantage.[73] In any event, whether feasible or not, constitutional recognition may well have saved the language measures challenged, so a plausible consequence of the Court's approach is that non-official languages are excluded from the ambit of its decision. The fact that Irish is a minority language could be seen as purely coincidental. This does not correspond, however, with the logic applied by either the Commission or the Advocate General; moreover, given doubts expressed above with regard to proportionality, it is hard to justify the result in *Groener* without relating it to some broader ideological context. And although the Court clearly based its decision on the constitutional status of Irish, it did not declare that such recognition would *always* be necessary before Member State language policy could be justified. Even if it is claimed that this is implied, is the particular classification of *national* language the imperative standard? Or would an express constitutional reference to minority languages suffice? Thus, the extent to which the ECJ set a fixed limit to be applied in subsequent cases is far from settled. What the judgment ostensibly reflects is the concern evident in the Advocate General's Opinion, quoted above *i.e.* that 'at issue here is the power of a State to protect and foster the use of a national language'. In truth, the minority language dimension means that there was a lot more 'at issue'. *Groener* was not just about a state fostering its national language; it related to the preservation of a very particular type of language. If the judgment is seen to apply only to languages having constitutional status, then non-official languages, arguably the most in need of recognition, are effectively excluded; in this sense, the decision in *Groener* would go against its own underlying spirit. But the need to reassure Member States of their competence in language issues more generally took precedence, and resulted in an unfortunate dearth of reasoning on the fundamental questions raised here. In this sense, the legitimacy of the language requirement was arguably distorted, because the aim of the judgment itself was far more about 'protecting' national languages from the Community momentum than preserving a language, of whatever status, domestically.

---

[73] See Nic Shuibhne, "State duty"; in 1998, the Irish Government finally indicated a commitment to the introduction of language legislation to implement Article 8 of the Constitution—more that sixty years after its enactment; progress on its preparation to date has, however, been disappointing.

(c)   Competence versus fluency

The respondents in *Groener* argued that the language examination was designed to determine a candidate's competence in Irish; demonstrating fluency was not necessary. It was submitted, in turn, that other non-nationals had successfully attained this level of 'competence'. Criticism has been levelled at this aspect of the decision, however:

> According to the Court, for the national measure…to be compatible with [Community law], the *level* of knowledge required for this purpose must not be disproportionate to [the language policy] objective. It is submitted that, given the fact that knowledge of…Irish in this case bore no functional relationship to the post concerned, the Court should have applied the proportionality test, not to the level of knowledge required but to the fact that this knowledge was set as an entry requirement as such…After all, it is not unreasonable to require Irish nationals to learn their language in order to preserve their national cultural heritage, to require Community workers with a completely different cultural heritage to do the same or otherwise refuse them employment is a wholly different matter.[74]

Legitimate concerns can be identified in this extract, but feed more appropriately into the discussion above on the 'nature of the post' exception, and the existence of discrimination, discussed below. The Court did not actually refer expressly to the competence/fluency distinction, and did not exploit either standard to illustrate what it considered to be a proportionate language requirement.[75] In other words, it did not deal with the issues raised here in the context of the *level* of knowledge required, since it had already interpreted teaching functions broadly to satisfy 'the nature of the post' criterion. The respondents' argument was picked up more directly by the Advocate General; he agreed that "…the level of knowledge required is not so high as to make it impossible for a foreigner to pass the examination."[76] Overall, however, the competence/fluency distinction is more properly dealt with as an aspect of a broader question: did the language requirement infringe the principle of non-discrimination on grounds of nationality?

---

[74]   Loman *et al*, *Culture and Community Law*, pp. 57-8.

[75]   The Court referred only to 'a certain knowledge of the Irish language' (*Groener*, p. 3993, para. 18) and 'an adequate knowledge [of Irish]' (p. 3393, para. 20), without any discussion on what that level of knowledge might be, or how it might be attained or assessed.

[76]   Opinion of Advocate General Darmon, p. 3983, para. 25.

(d)   The free movement of workers and the question of discrimination

The decision in *Groener* makes it clear that Member State language policies are not entirely autonomous, but are subject to review by the ECJ in respect of their compatibility with Community law. As stated at the outset, the judgment effectively endorsed the exclusion of a non-Irish national from a permanent teaching post because she did not have competence in the Irish language. This must be squared with the fact that she would not have been required actually to use that language in the performance of her duties. The Court defended this anomaly using the 'nature of the post' proviso in Regulation 1612/68. But the legitimacy of this reasoning was called into question above, mainly on the grounds of proportionality. Because it decided that the language requirement could be justified in this way, the Court did not have to examine the question of discrimination in any depth. The background to the case shows, however, that discrimination was central to the applicant's claim. The Commission, prior to the initiation of the domestic judicial review proceedings and acting under Article 169 EEC,[77] had written to the Irish authorities for information and observations on the applicant's particular situation. The Commission concluded at that time that the language requirement *was* contrary to certain provisions of the EEC Treaty on grounds of discrimination. The measures challenged applied to both nationals and non-nationals; this means that if discrimination is relevant, it comes within the ambit of indirect or covert discrimination—*i.e.* while the measures did not discriminate in law, they had the potential to discriminate in effect. This echoes the Court's decision in *Seco and Desquenne Giral* v. *Etablissement d'assurance contre la viellesse et l'invalidité*, in which it confirmed that Community law "...prohibit[s] not only overt discrimination based on the nationality of the person...but also all forms of covert discrimination which, although based on criteria which appeared to be neutral, in practice lead to the same result."[78] The Irish Government argued that the language test presented difficulties for Irish nationals as well as for non-nationals, since the majority of the population does not actually speak Irish fluently. But the Commission countered that most Irish people have studied the language at school for several years and, while they may not have attained fluency, this placed them at a clear advantage over non-nationals. Though accepting that Irish could be studied in a number of locations

---

[77]   Now Article 226 EC.

[78]   Cases 62 and 63/81, [1982] ECR 223 at 235, para. 8.

outside Ireland,[79] the Commission concluded that while the aim of the measures was "...to ensure a certain level of competence in the national language, the principal effect is to create a greater obstacle for non-Irish nationals, likely to keep them away from the employment in question."[80] It has been argued that since the national rules challenged in *Groener* were implemented *before* Ireland's accession to the EEC, they were not actually geared towards keeping other Community nationals away from teaching posts.[81] This fact was emphasised by the Advocate General, although it has been pointed out that the absence of an intention to discriminate is not conclusive in instances of indirect discrimination.[82] Statistics submitted by the Irish Government at the request of the ECJ show that, from a total of 189 nationals of Member States other than Ireland teaching in the vocational education sector, 183 had been exempted from the language requirement. These figures, more than anything else, cast doubt on the supposition that the language requirement had a dissuasive effect on the employment of non-nationals.[83] Both the Advocate General and the Court pointed out that the discrimination threshold would be crossed where, for example, the Irish government refused to recognise competence in or knowledge of the Irish language gained in another Member State.[84] The ECJ had already determined in *Robert Fearon & Co.* v. *Irish Land Commission* that it is not sufficient, in order to establish that a particular measure is discriminatory, to show that it has had a greater impact on non-nationals than on nationals if the measure in question is intended to achieve certain important policy objectives.[85] Ironically, the Commission relied on this decision in its eventual submission

---

[79] Aberystwyth, Bonn, Brest, Paris and Rennes were mentioned specifically.

[80] *Groener*, Report for the Hearing, p. 3975. On more 'direct' nationality restrictions, see Case C-473/93 *Commission v. Luxembourg* [1995] ECR I-3207 (see Chapter 6); see also Case C-123/94 *Commission v. Greece* [1995] ECR I-1457.

[81] McMahon, case comment, pp. 137-8.

[82] *Groener*, Opinion of Advocate General Darmon, p. 3981, para. 15; see Josephine Shaw, "Equality of treatment for teachers under European Community law", (1991) vol. 3:1 *Education and the Law*, 35-38 at 36.

[83] Shaw points out also that "...measures had been put in place by the Irish Government to facilitate non-nationals surmounting the barrier posed by the Irish proficiency condition [making] it difficult to argue that the principal aim of the provision was truly protectionist...." (*ibid.*)

[84] As noted, this aspect of the decision in *Groener* has since come to pass (Case C-281/98 *Angonese v. Cassa di Risparmio*, judgment of 6 June 2000, not yet reported; see Chapter 6).

[85] Case 182/83, [1984] ECR 3677.

in *Groener*, notwithstanding its earlier inclination towards a finding of *prima facie* discrimination at the pre-litigation stage.

The key to negating the charge of discrimination, then, is to establish that the national measures were introduced 'to achieve certain important policy objectives'. Leaving aside, once again, the minority dimension, the Court stated concisely that a Member State may 'adopt a policy for the protection and promotion of a national and first official language'.[86] Although its analysis was restricted to Article 3(1) of Regulation 1612/68 (and the 'nature of the post' criterion), Shaw considers that the Court identified an implied limitation to the free movement of workers—namely policies promoting cultural diversity and national identity—in addition to the express derogations on grounds of public policy, security and health set out in the Treaty itself.[87] She cautions against a broad interpretation of this implied derogation, in keeping with the narrow construction usually applied to the express derogations listed in Article 39 EC, and thus regards the result in *Groener* as "...a most unusual position for the Court to take."[88] Certainly, the Court's approach contrasts sharply with its earlier stance in *Leclerc* v. *Au Blé Vert*, for example, where it confirmed that derogations from fundamental Treaty rules "...must be interpreted strictly and cannot be extended to cover objectives not expressly enumerated therein."[89] In that case, relating to the free movement of goods, the ECJ stated expressly that 'the protection of creativity and cultural diversity' was not mentioned in Article 36 EEC (now 30 EC) and could not therefore be construed as an additional derogation from Community law. It is important at this point, however, to separate two issues that have become mistakenly enmeshed *i.e.* the difference between direct and indirect discrimination and, more specifically, the different consequences that ensue in respect of their attempted justification. To take direct discrimination first, it is generally the case that, as exemplified by *Leclerc*, any arguments put forward in justification must be drawn directly—and only—from the express derogations provided for by the Treaty. But for indistinctly applicable measures—or more precisely, where indirect rather than overt discrimination is at issue—the possibility for justification does go beyond express Treaty derogations.[90] Taking the free movement of goods

---

[86] *Groener*, p. 3393, para. 19

[87] Shaw, "Equality of Treatment", p. 37; see also Article 39(3) EC (then Article 48(3) EEC).

[88] *ibid.*

[89] Case 229/83, [1985] ECR 1 at 35, para. 30.

[90] On the free movement of goods, see Case 120/78 *Rewe-Zentrale* v. *Bundesmonopol-verwaltung für Branntwein (Cassis de Dijon)* [1979] ECR 649 and subsequent case-law on 'mandatory requirements' that have been held to justify indirectly discriminatory

first, the establishment of the protection of cultural heritage as a 'mandatory requirement' (that could justify an indirectly discriminatory breach of Article 28 EC) can be traced through ECJ case law. In *Cinéthèque*, the Court upheld—on grounds of the promotion of the cinematographic industry—an indistinctly applicable French law that ostensibly contravened Article 30 EEC (now 28 EC).[91] In *Stoke-on-Trent and Norwich City Councils v. B&Q*— one of the 'Sunday trading' cases—Advocate General van Gerven contemplated the existence of a "...general, less specific category of grounds of justification—that is to say...those which reflect certain political and economic choices...[in accordance] with national or regional socio-cultural characteristics...."[92] In respect of what is now Article 28 EC, he argued that "...certain further special mandatory requirements may be added to the list of mandatory requirements inherent in Article 30 of the EEC Treaty (which may be relied upon solely in order to justify non-discriminatory national provisions)... *i.e.* requirements which are consistent with specific objectives or interests of the Community Treaties."[93] The continuing development of an implied 'cultural heritage' derogation, its extension beyond the free movement of goods—and perhaps even beyond indirect discrimination—can be

---

breaches of Article 28 EC (see, as examples, Case 302/86 *Commission v. Denmark* [1988] ECR 4607 (environmental protection) and Case C-368/95 *Vereinigte Familia Press v. Heinrich Bauer Verlag* [1997] ECR I-3689 (press diversity)). On the free movement of workers, see for example Case C-237/94 *O'Flynn v. Adjudication Officer* [1996] ECR I-2617, especially at pp. 2637-8: in paras. 17-18, the Court sets out the instances in which conditions imposed by national law will be regarded as indirectly discriminatory; and in paras. 19-20, it is stated that '[i]t is otherwise only if those provisions are justified by objective considerations independent of the nationality of the workers concerned, and if they are proportionate to the legitimate aim pursued by the national law.' (para. 20, citing relevant case law). In the context of the justification of direct discrimination, however, there are some anomalies in the case law, where even direct discrimination seems to be weighed against objective criteria above and beyond those provided for expressly in the Treaty: see for example, Case C-415/93 *Union Royale Belge des Sociétés de Football Association ASBL v. Jean-Marc Bosman* [1995] ECR I-4921. See also the discussion below on Case C-17/92 *Federacion de Distribuidores Cinematográficos (Fedicine) v. Spanish State* [1993] ECR I-2239, in the context of services. On discrimination in Community law generally, see Nicolas Bernard, "Discrimination and free movement in EC law", (1996) 45 *International and Comparative Law Quarterly* 82-108 and Chris Hilson, "Discrimination in Community free movement law", (1999) vol. 24:5 *European Law Review* 445-462.

[91]   Cases 60-61/84 *Cinéthèque v. Fédération Nationale des Cinémas Français* [1985] ECR 2605.

[92]   Cases C-306/88, 304/90 and 169/91 *Stoke-on-Trent and Norwich City Councils v. B&Q plc* [1992] ECR I-6457 at 6577, para. 23.

[93]   *ibid.*; see also Robert Lane, "New Community competences under the Maastricht Treaty", (1993) 30 *Common Market Law Review*, 939-979 at 955-7.

traced through a more recent opinion of the same Advocate General, in
Fedicine v. *Spanish State*.[94] This case involved a dispute over the circulation
of films in Spain; legislation imposed certain conditions on film distributors
in respect of dubbing licences, which meant effectively that films in the
official languages of Spain, as opposed to those of other countries, were
required to be favoured. The applicants claimed that this infringed their freedom to provide services under Community law. When considering whether
the Spanish legislation constituted a legitimate derogation from Community
law, Advocate General van Gerven confirmed initially that "[t]he Court has
consistently held that national rules involving discriminatory treatment as
regards provision of services from another Member State can be compatible
with Community law only if they can be brought within the scope of an
express derogation of the Treaty."[95] He then considered whether Spain could
avail of the public policy derogation in Article 66 EEC (now 55 EC). Having
concluded that this provision did *not* vindicate the Spanish legislation, the
Advocate General went on to deliberate "...whether...it is not possible to
find in Community law some other ground of justification than public
policy, in particular reference to an overriding reason of general importance
connected with the protection of the cultural heritage."[96] At first glance, this
approach contrasts directly with the general rule that only express, Treaty-
based derogations should be considered; once again, however, the discrimination complained of in the present case was of an indirect and not overt
nature.[97] The Advocate General was clearly influenced by the increasing
importance attached to cultural heritage in the TEU, by then adopted but not
yet in force. He quoted from Article 128 (now 151) EC, in respect of the
Community's expected contribution to the 'flowering of the cultures of the
Member States', and referred to the new Article 92(3)d (now 87(3)d) EC on
state aid in the cultural domain. He observed that, even before the TEU was
ratified, "[m]any judgments show that the Court too is not insensitive to
[cultural] diversity and the specific requirements of policy which the effort
to preserve cultural individuality involves."[98] In support of this claim, he

---

[94] Case C-17/92 *Federacion de Distribuidores Cinematográficos (Fedicine)* v. *Spanish State*
[1993] ECR I-2239.

[95] *ibid.*, pp. 2257-8, para. 15.

[96] *ibid.*, p. 2259, para. 22.

[97] *ibid.*, p. 2257, para. 13.

[98] *ibid.*, p. 2260, para. 23. Note, however, that in Case C-415/93 *Union Royale Belge des
Sociétés de Football Association ASBL* v. *Jean-Marc Bosman* [1995] ECR I-4921, the ECJ
held that Article 151 EC cannot itself—in a substantive sense—be used to limit the scope
of a fundamental Community freedom such as freedom of movement for workers: see

listed a number of cases, including *Groener*, where national cultural policy was deemed to constitute an overriding requirement of general interest that justified the restriction of Community freedoms once the general tests of proportionality and non-discrimination were satisfied.[99] It is not altogether clear from the Opinion if the Advocate General intended that the implied 'cultural heritage' derogation should be restricted to indirect discrimination only, however, or whether it might apply also even to directly discriminatory measures[100]—a controversial proposition although one which seems to be gaining some (implied) credence in recent case law.[101] But, in any event, when slotting *Groener* into this discussion, it is essential to bear in mind that if any discriminatory restriction on the free movement of workers is being considered, then it falls within the ambit of indirect discrimination—*i.e.* where the national measures in question apply to both nationals and non-nationals, but may be discriminatory in effect if not in law. And for indirect discrimination, the criteria for justification go beyond express Treaty derogations. The pivotal decision in *Bosman* extends the potential for justification still further in terms of 'non-discrimination'; here, the Court held that obstacles to the free movement of workers which were neither directly nor indirectly discriminatory were still prohibited by Article 48 (now 39) EC, but could be saved where they "...pursued a legitimate aim compatible with the Treaty and were justified by pressing reasons of public interest."[102] In *Groener*, whether from the perspective of promoting a national language (the tender dealt with explicitly) or the preservation of a minority language (presented here as a more subtle influence on the Court), the EEC Treaty

---

p. 5064-5, para. 78. This is *not* the same thing as arguments grounded in cultural concerns constituting independently a dergogation from Community freedoms, which is what is being discussed here.

[99] Advocate General van Gerven did not, however, agree that this overriding requirement applied in the present case, "...since it has not been shown that the contested [legislation] seeks in the first place to preserve and promote Spain's own culture." (*ibid.*, p. 2264, para. 28).

[100] See in particular, p. 2264, para. 27.

[101] Again, see Case C-415/93 *Union Royale Belge des Sociétés de Football Association ASBL v. Jean-Marc Bosman* [1995] ECR I-4921, pp. 5073-8, paras. 115-137, dealing with nationality clauses in respect of foreign players; the anomaly is even more striking in the Opinion of Advocate General Lenz, who had remarked that "[n]o deep cognition is required to reach the conclusion that the rules on foreign players are of a discriminatory nature. They represent an absolutely classic case of discrimination on grounds of nationality." (p. 4976, point 135).

[102] Case C-415/93 *Union Royale Belge des Sociétés de Football Association ASBL v. Jean-Marc Bosman* [1995] ECR I-4921 at 5070, para. 104; the Court stressed also that the principle of proportionality would apply here.

could not at that time provide the Court with an appropriate legal basis for a more thorough and comprehensive analysis. Consequently, it inevitably appears as though the applicant's rights were subordinated to some bigger policy picture—or indeed political agenda—but an unacceptably vague one, and that the existence of discrimination was not dispelled effectively. But in light of interpretative trends since consolidated—that cut across the principles of free movement in a collective sense—it is equally arguable that the decision in *Groener* was not so much arbitrary as early.

(e)   The public service exception

Article 48(4) EEC (now 39(4) EC) stipulates that "[t]he provisions of [Article 48] shall not apply to employment in the public service." The Court has long held, however, that this proviso relates only to:

> ...a series of posts which involve direct or indirect participation in the exercise of powers conferred by public law and duties designed to safeguard the general interests of the state or of other public authorities. Such posts in fact presume on the part of those occupying them the existence of a special relationship of allegiance to the state and reciprocity of rights and duties which form the foundation of the bond of nationality.[103]

Applying this test, it is doubtful that the public service exception can apply to teaching posts.[104] But, as the Commission pointed out, the Court was never likely to accept the argument in any event, since it would only be relevant where discrimination was shown to exist and where the measures could not be justified by the 'nature of the post' clause. Moreover, the public service exception "...[presupposes] 'the existence...of a genuine and sufficiently serious threat to the requirements of public policy affecting one of the fundamental interests of society'."[105] The Commission went on to argue that a Member State policy designed to promote an official language was unlikely to fulfil the criterion of a 'fundamental interest of society' in the Community law sense. But this aspect of its submission, although not central to the decision ultimately handed down in *Groener*, is questionable, given that the

---

[103]   Case 149/79 *Commission v. Belgium*, No. 1, [1980] ECR 3881 at 3900, para. 10.

[104]   On this point, see Case 66/85 *Lawrie-Blum v. Land Baden- Württemberg* [1986] ECR 2121.

[105]   *Groener*, Report for the Hearing, p. 3976 (submission of the Commission), referring to Case 30/77 *R. v. Boucherau* [1977] ECR 1999.

Court relied heavily on the existence and importance of such a policy to justify the language requirement under the 'nature of the post' exception.

(iv)   Conclusion

> The *Groener* decision is to be welcomed as recognising the desirability of having a multilingual society in Europe and in allowing Member States a reasonable measure of autonomy in these matters. Cynics might say that the Court recognised the political necessity for such a decision and realised the cultural backlash which would have been inevitable if it had refused to recognise the legality of the Irish measures.[S]uch critics might point to the narrow approach of the Court...as an indication of [its] reluctance. A more gracious and generous view, however, might be that we are here witnessing a real recognition of the legitimacy of national concerns in relation to national cultural heritage and a tentative move by the Court towards Community elaborated demarcation guidelines. The bureaucrats and the economists will have to recognise that cultural diversity cannot be indiscriminately swamped in the name of economic unity.[106]

This paragraph has been extracted from McMahon's concluding remarks on *Groener*. The first perspective, dubbed the cynical view, implies that any positive implications derived from the decision resulted more by accident than by design. The latter approach suggests quite the opposite. In truth, both views are probably legitimate. The Court was adjudicating on a policy area that it had not previously dealt with directly and was undoubtedly aware of the political consequences of its decision. But it did not succumb to the view that language policy remained *entirely* within the realm of exclusive domestic competence, as had been advocated by the French Government. Boch has reasserted this argument, stating that *Groener* "...establish[ed] that the Community 'hands off' policy is over."[107] It is far from clear, however, that a 'hands off' policy could really have been implied in any case, since *Groener* marked the first direct conflict between national language laws and fundamental Community law principles of this kind that reached the ECJ; it may be recalled that the earlier decision in *Mutsch* did not merit a substantive assessment of Belgium's language legislation. Moreover, the

---

[106] McMahon, case comment, p. 139.

[107] Christine Boch, "Language protection and free trade: The triumph of the *Homo MacDonaldus?*", (1998) vol. 4:3 *European Public Law*, 379-402 at 391.

linguistic knowledge 'exception' provided for in Regulation 1612/68 was always required to be justified 'be reason of the nature of the post to be filled'; so why the ECJ's taking on that very task in *Groener* should be seen as inappropriately invasive is difficult to support. But while it is clear that Member State language polices must be checked against Community law, it is the idea of relative national autonomy that prevails in *Groener*. And, in any event, the principles of non-discrimination and proportionality are extensively applied as benchmark standards in both national and international law generally, on the premise of the protection of fundamental rights. The 'narrow' approach adopted by the Court can be justified to a certain extent by the limitations of the Article 177 EEC (now 234 EC) procedure itself. More than this, however, the Court's reticence to delve any further into the content of Member State language policies is essentially a political choice. Boch summarises the various strands of the decision, writing that:

> In its eagerness to promote linguistic diversity as a valued cultural asset, as opposed to an obstacle to mobility, the Court was willing to forego fundamental principle of interpretation. In view of the symbolic importance of its judgment for the promotion of linguistic diversity, the Court is also prepared to endorse the arbitrary character of the national linguistic policy. Ms Groener can be refused a job, because she does not speak a language, which she does not need to speak to do the job. Neither Ms Groener's individual rights nor the needs of market integration require abandoning national linguistic policies. The judgment is all the more remarkable as no reference to national identity or cultural diversity was then included in the Treaty.[108]

This paragraph highlights the many contradictions evident in *Groener*. By focusing exclusively on the second question referred to it, the Court was able to sidestep the more fundamental and contentious aspects of proportionality and non-discrimination. But it is misleading to assume that, in doing do, the Court renounced a 'fundamental principle of interpretation'. Identifying and upholding non-economic policy limitations to the market integration principles of free movement has evolved as a more pervasive and legitimate interpretative principle in itself; and the indistinctly applicable character of the national measures under scrutiny allowed for consideration of such 'objective' justificatory criteria. Bearing in mind the ideological maelstrom

---

[108] *ibid.*, p. 392.

skirting the decision, if the reasoning in *Groener* can really be said to fall down on any point, then it is on the application of proportionality. The language requirement at issue may still have been saved within a more substantiated discussion on the principle; what is most regrettable is that this discussion was never going to happen.

C. Conclusion

The decisions in *Mutsch* and *Groener* have established that Member States are relatively free to determine their own language policies, but that these polices are subject to review by the ECJ in terms of their compatibility with Community law where relevant. The Court ensured the exercise of an individual's language rights in *Mutsch* and condoned Member State measures in favour of a *de facto* minority language in *Groener*. Neither decision could be said to reveal a *coherent* EC minority language policy. The Belgian legislative arrangements did not actually have to be appraised in *Mutsch*; and in *Groener*, the minority language at issue was probably shielded by its arguably unrepresentative, but legally valid, constitutional status. In both decisions, the Advocates General deliberated more openly on the role of the Community in both the cultural and fundamental rights aspects of (minority) language issues. This reflects an awareness within the EC institutions of the minority dimension to linguistic pluralism; but it also highlights the absence at that time of any justiciable legal basis that could have secured the translation of well-disposed leanings into law.

4. CONCLUSION

In general terms, EC Competence has evolved significantly since the judgments discussed in this Chapter were delivered and the European Parliament drafted its first minority language resolutions. The analysis undertaken here has uncovered themes, conflicts and struggles with which neither institution was equipped to deal at the time. An underlying question, introduced in Chapter 1, is also clearly evident: just what is the EC both expected and empowered to achieve on behalf of minority languages and their speakers? The answer is undeniably complex, and is necessarily tempered by both economic and political factors. But what is already clear is that whether and how the EC evaluates what its Member States have implemented in the context of internal language policy is to some extent a key aspect of its *own* language policy; this applies equally, and perhaps especially, in the domain of minority languages. The next section of the book delves into the substance of minority language policy from an EC perspective and looks at three critical aspects in particular—cultural policy, the boundaries of Member State/Community competence in this regard, and the impact of fundamental rights and citizenship—in light especially of subsequent Treaty amendments. The most recent jurisprudence of the Court of Justice and the continuing work of other EC institutions will then be assessed, to see whether the initial Community pointers in favour of minority language claims identified here have been articulated and applied more directly in light of enhanced EC competence.

Chapter 3

Language and EC Cultural Policy

1. INTRODUCTION: DEFINING CULTURE IN A COMMUNITY CONTEXT

The relationship between the European Community and the languages that it currently recognises, as well as those it does not, is outlined in Chapter 1. Issues associated more specifically with minority languages were identified as challenges that the Community needs to confront, but what it should—or even can—do in this context remains largely to be determined. As seen in Chapter 2, the absence of an appropriate legal basis proved problematic for both the European Parliament and the Court of Justice throughout the 1980s. Minority languages were not dealt with in any provision of the EEC Treaty; subsequent Treaty amendments have not changed this fact. To pursue any kind of minority language 'policy', the EC institutions must necessarily draw from other competence domains. And changes introduced over the past decade do help here, the key provisions being those that deal with culture, fundamental rights and citizenship. Of these, perhaps the most obvious starting point is culture, a concept not easily divorced from that of language. But do language matters fall within the remit of culture in its Community incarnation? And even if they do, what can actually be achieved within the parameters of EC cultural competence? These questions will have to be answered by the Commission before long, as it prepares its first multiannual programme on minority language funding, discussed below and in Chapter 6; can a legislative measure of this kind be grounded successfully in Article 151?

The fourth recital of the Preamble to the TEU outlines the desire of the Member States to "...deepen the solidarity between their peoples while respecting their history, their culture and their traditions." Article 3 EC lists activities for the Community, including, at paragraph (q), "...a contribution to education and training of quality and to the flowering of cultures of the Member States." In accordance with this general principle, Title XII or Article 151 EC (introduced by the TEU) sets out the role of the EC in cultural matters:

1. The Community shall contribute to the flowering of the cultures of the Member States, while respecting their national and regional diversity and at the same time bringing the common cultural heritage to the fore.

2. Action by the Community shall be aimed at encouraging cooperation between Member States and, if necessary, supporting and supplementing their action in the following areas:
- improvement of the knowledge and dissemination of the culture and history of the European peoples;
- conservation and safeguarding of cultural heritage of European significance;
- non-commercial cultural exchanges;
- artistic and literary creation, including in the audio-visual sector.

3. The Community and the Member States shall foster cooperation with third countries and the competent international organisations in the sphere of culture, in particular the Council of Europe.

4. The Community shall take cultural aspects into account in its action under other provisions of this Treaty, *in particular in order to respect and to promote the diversity of its cultures.*[1]

5. In order to contribute to the achievement of the objectives referred to in this article, the Council:
- acting in accordance with the procedure referred to in Article 251 and after consulting the Committee of the Regions, shall adopt incentive measures, excluding any harmonisation of the laws and regulations of the Member States. The Council shall act unanimously throughout the procedures referred to in Article 251;
- acting unanimously on a proposal from the Commission, shall adopt recommendations.

As noted above, there was no equivalent provision in the EEC Treaty but the adoption of Article 151 did not activate an entirely new range of Community activity; rather, as will be seen below, it codified an existing, albeit ambiguous, policy direction. The way in which the provision has been drafted reflects an attempt by the Community to balance its involvement in cultural

---

[1]   The phrase in italics was added to Article 151 EC by the Amsterdam Treaty.

affairs with the maintenance of an appropriate level of autonomy for the Member States. Significantly, culture is not actually defined.[2] This could be interpreted as a way of ensuring open-ended scope in the application of Article 151. It is equally arguable, however, that the provision, when read as a whole, is more concerned with setting down boundaries, with establishing what the Community *cannot* do in this domain. Article 151(2) in particular seems to fix some prohibitive definitional limits. In this sense, the often unfettered optimism displayed by proponents of an EC minority language policy, regarding the potential of Article 151 to bolster and legitimate their claims, seems misplaced. Another inherent tension is reflected by the idea that while the Community is charged with fostering a common European consciousness, to emphasise synthesis and unity, the drafters have been equally careful to affirm an appreciation of and respect for diversity. The latter point is now assured expressly, via an Amsterdam Treaty amendment to Article 151(4) that has both cultural and political import. From one perspective, the diversity of Europe's heritage and traditions is a vital component of its driving cultural energy; ensuring that cultural diversity can thrive in the throes of economic and political centralisation is thus a fundamental concern for the Community, its Member States and its citizens. In the political sense, guarantees of respect for diversity have astute symbolic significance, as an additional reassurance that state sovereignty is not being consumed by the European ideal. This argument is enhanced when Article 151 EC is read in conjunction with Article 6(3) (formerly Article F) TEU, which commits the Union to respecting the national identities of its Member States. Both seemingly polar outlooks can, in any event, be reconciled: there is nothing in either Article 151 EC or Article 6(3) TEU to prevent the encouragement of a common consciousness based on respect for diversity, on a common appreciation of difference. In other words, 'common' does not coincide intrinsically with 'same'. The challenge now faced by the Community is the implementation of the objectives of Article 151 EC in a way that respects the sovereignty and identities of the Member States, yet compromises neither economic and political ambition, nor the delineation of a competence in cultural matters in the first place, to a degree of ineffectiveness. Article 151 clearly has its limitations, but it also has potential; both

---

[2] This omission and the drafting style of Article 151 more generally have generated mixed reaction from commentators; for example, Lane observes that "...its 'flowering [is] more botanical than justiciable..." (Robert Lane, "New Community competences under the Maastricht Treaty", (1993) 30 *Common Market Law Review*, 939-979 at 953), while Dashwood lauds the 'new' provisions, including Article 151, as welcome examples of 'tight drafting' (Alan Dashwood, "The limits of European Community powers", (1996) 21 *European Law Review*, 113-128 at 122).

angles tend to compete for prevalence, however, as is evident throughout this Chapter.

Community cultural policy, both before and after Maastricht, has been concentrated largely on what might be termed the 'tangible' aspects of culture *i.e.* cultural property (such as art treasures), archaeological heritage, literature and, more recently, the broadcast media, particularly film and television. From an initial reading of Article 151 EC, it would appear that this theme was effectively codified in 1992. How relevant, then, is the provision to language? Before analysing the scope of Article 151 specifically, it is worth considering how culture is usually defined in a more general sense. It is arguably, of course, an entirely subjective concept, capable of meaning many things to different people and in different contexts. But a survey of the literature in which culture is defined in a general Community context—as distinct, for the moment, from definitions discernible within Article 151 EC—reveals that where its scope is characterised more objectively, definitions fall mainly within two strands. In setting the margins for their study on EC cultural policy, Loman, Mortelmans, Post and Watson consider that 'culture' includes:

> ...all activities which in the Member States are commonly considered as being a legitimate object of their cultural policies, such as the promotion of the contemporary arts (including film and audio-visual products, literature, dance and ballet, music, architecture and drama), the preservation of the national cultural heritage and *the promotion of the national language and cultural identity*.[3]

In arriving at this construction, they distinguish between traditional and anthropological approaches. Prott is referred to as epitomising the traditional position; he defines culture as "...the highest intellectual achievements of human beings: the musical, philosophical, literary, artistic and architectural works, techniques and rituals which have most inspired humanity and are seen by communities as their best achievements."[4] In contrast, the society-based, anthropological definition is typified by Guillaumin, who defines culture as:

---

[3]   AnneMarie Loman, Kamiel Mortelmans, Harry Post and Stewart Watson, *Culture and Community Law: Before and After Maastricht*, (Deventer: Kluwer Law and Taxation Publishers, 1992), p. *x* of the Preface (emphasis added).

[4]   Loman *et al*, *Culture and Community Law*, p. 1, referring to Lyndel V. Prott, "Cultural rights as peoples' rights in international law", in James Crawford (ed.), *The Rights of Peoples*, (Oxford: Clarendon Press, 1992), 93-106 at 94.

...the totality of the knowledge and practices, both intellectual and material, of each of the particular groups of a society, and—at a certain level—of a society itself as a whole. From food to dress, from household techniques to industrial techniques, from forms of politeness to mass media, from work rhythm to the learning of family rules, all human practices, all invented and manufactured materials are concerned with and constitute, in their relationships and totality, 'culture'.[5]

The conservation and promotion of minority languages clearly fits with this second approach. Loman *et al*, though their definition conforms more with the traditional position, adapted that outlook to include an express reference to language concerns; thus, a pragmatic definition of culture does not have to be tied exclusively to either the traditional or anthropological school of cultural philosophy. But language was included only in terms of promoting 'the national' language and cultural identity, which most likely excludes minority languages, at least if read literally. Church and Phinnemore developed a similar, multifaceted definition of culture, which can "...mean either the fine arts and literature or, *as in the Community context*, those wider practices and patterns which help to define national identity."[6] This definition does not suggest one homogeneous 'national' identity. And even under the more limited approach, it is arguable that the promotion of linguistic diversity can itself constitute a central feature or characteristic of a state's 'national' identity, as evidenced by the relevant constitutional provisions of many EC Member States (listed in Appendix I). The rationale here can be extended, to argue that regional languages exemplify regional cultures; this was recognised by the Commission in the context of mother tongue education for the children of migrant workers, when it confirmed that "[t]he Commission justifies the teaching of mother tongues to migrants as part of the TEU's guarantees of protection of national identities, by extending the

---

[5]   Loman *et al*, *Culture and Community Law*, p. 1, referring to C. Guillaumin, "Women and cultural values: Classes according to sex and their relationship to culture in industrial society", (1979) *Cultures* 41.

[6]   Clive H. Church and David Phinnemore, *European Union and European Community: A Handbook and Commentary on the Post-Maastricht Treaties*, (Hemel Hempstead: Harvester Wheatsheaf, 1994), p. 507 (emphasis added); see also A. Forrest, "La dimension culturelle de la communauté européene: Les ministres de la culture explorent le terrain", (1987) 307 *Revue du Marché Commun*, 320-332 at 327. Joseph H. Kaiser has argued that since "...Europe is rich and pluralistic in its culture, the culture of the European policy should be pluralistic too, and the dimensions should be many." (from "Final conclusions" in Jürgen Schwarze and Henry G. Schermers (eds.), *Structure and Dimensions of European Community Policy*, (Baden-Baden: Nomos, 1988), 237-8 at 238.)

concept of national identity to include the cultural identities of *all* citizens of a Member State."[7] This express emphasis on pluralism in the cultural context is arguably another positive indicator of concern at Community level for minority as well as national languages. More particularly, it displaces the notion that 'national'—in connection with culture, identity and language— must only be read literally. The resulting, more inclusive understanding of culture has been expressed cogently by O'Toole:

> Culture is not merely about works of art, and it follows that the cultural dimension of the European Community is about much more than aesthetics. Culture is the ground on which people are empowered to participate in their society. Culture is both the social contribution to the formation of the individual person, and the collective tools—values, language, means of commun- ication, ideas of excellence, the imaginative sympathy by which one individual can make sense of the experience of another individual—by which an individual can contribute to society. The question of culture and the European Community is there- fore intimately bound up with the question of democracy and the European Community.[8]

This overview projects at least one common factor: language can come within the remit of cultural policy, in a general EC context at least. What must be considered now is whether Article 151 allows for the application of a similarly broad understanding in respect of Community competence in this field or whether, on the contrary, that possibility was closed off by the enshrining instead of a more specific and limited interpretation. Ultimately, the matter will probably fall to be decided by the Court of Justice. It has already had to deal with this question indirectly, in *Parliament v. Council.*[9] The European Parliament, acting under Article 230(3) (formerly 173) EC, sought the annulment of Council Decision 96/664 on the adoption of a multi- annual programme to promote the linguistic diversity of the Community in the information society.[10] The measure had been adopted on the basis of Article 130 (now 157) EC, with which the Parliament did not have difficulty

---

[7]   Commission of the European Community, *Report on the Education of Migrants' Children in the European Union*, COM (94) 80 Final (Brussels, 25 March 1994), p. 6 (emphasis added).

[8]   Fintan O'Toole, "Culture and media policy", in Patrick Keatinge (ed.), *Ireland and EC Membership Evaluated*, (London: Pinter, 1991), 270-276 at 270-1.

[9]   Case C-42/97 *European Parliament v. Council of the European Union* [1999] ECR I-869.

[10] [1996] OJ L306/40.

as such, but it claimed that Article 151 should have been specified also. In rejecting the application, for reasons discussed more fully in Section 3 below, the Court did not have to pronounce directly on the scope of culture under Article 151. But certain paragraphs of the decision provide some implicit guidance as to how it might yet answer that question. First, to determine the correct legal basis, the Court focused on establishing whether the essential component of the contested measure was industrial or cultural; thus, it did not rule out the application of Article 151 to language matters *per se*. It is worth noting that the argument on Article 151(2) put forward by the Council, discussed below, had reflected the more restrictive view. Second, the Court concluded that language did not constitute an element of cultural heritage in the context of the measure adopted; this is not the same as saying that language can *never* constitute an element of cultural heritage within the meaning of Article 151.[11] Finally, the Court confirmed that while Article 151 was not the correct legal basis for the decision under scrutiny, the Council was right to take the cultural aspects of the proposed programme into account, in accordance with Article 151(4).[12] The Court's decision hinged on a construction of the 'essential' and 'incidental' components of the contested measure, but also on a clear assumption that language was relevant to Article 151. While its reasoning on the key essential/incidental issue is itself questionable (examined below regarding Articles 151(2) and 151(4)) the Court did not, at least, actually rule out the application of Article 151 to language matters. The Opinion of Advocate General La Pergola is less coherent, however, as exemplified by the following paragraph:

> I do not consider that in this case 'linguistic diversity' displays the cultural importance attached to it by the applicant institution. The promotion and safeguarding of such linguistic diversity is intrinsically neutral; it only involves ensuring that the groups of people concerned have an opportunity to express themselves in their own language. It remains to be seen whether the provisions of the decision were inspired by cultural aims, in the sense that linguistic plurality was seen as an element 'of cultural heritage of such significance' under…Article [151](2); or whether such linguistic diversity was taken into account as regards its commercial applications: it represents a cost for undertakings and sometimes an obstacle to the penetration of

---

[11] *Parliament v. Council*, p. 900, para. 53; see also, p. 900, para. 56.

[12] *ibid.*, p. 602, para. 62.

foreign markets, particularly for small and medium-sized economic operators.[13]

The Advocate General opted for the latter interpretation, using the essential/
incidental test later employed by the Court. But there are anomalies in this
extract. It is not at all clear why 'ensuring that the groups of people
concerned have an opportunity to express themselves in their own language'
is not a matter of 'cultural importance' or indeed, why it is described as
'intrinsically neutral'. When *would* the promotion of linguistic plurality
come within 'cultural heritage of such significance'? This is discussed
further below, in the context of Article 151(2), but it can be noted at this
stage that the Advocate General's logic is far from apparent. Certainly, it
contradicts O'Toole's line of argument that 'culture is the ground on which
people are empowered to participate in their society', set out above. The
explanation seems to lie in the statement that language does not come within
Article 151(2) because "...[it] is not treated by the [Council] decision as part
of the 'cultural heritage' but as a means by which undertakings conduct
business."[14] This suggests a disappointingly literal interpretation of the
contested measure and of language functions, insofar as it distinguishes
between language as an expression of culture and language as an independent constituent of culture in itself. But the Court did not take up this
particular line of reasoning. Nonetheless, even though its borders remain
uncertain, Article 151(2) may now control the definition of culture for the
purposes of ascertaining Community competence. The following paragraphs
summarise, first, how EC cultural policy was developed prior to the adoption
of the Maastricht Treaty; this will help to establish what was presumably
intended to come within the Community conception of 'culture'. Then,
Article 151 will be evaluated, to assess whether what had been accomplished
coincides with what was eventually ratified. In this way, the limits of the
provision—both real and purported—can, at least, be estimated.

2. DESTINATION MAASTRICHT: TRACING COMMUNITY ACTION IN THE FIELD OF CULTURE

It is not really surprising that construction of the Community's cultural
policy has been relatively disjointed. There was no appropriate legal basis in

---

[13] *ibid.*, Opinion of Advocate General La Pergola, p. 877, para. 6.
[14] *ibid.*, pp. 879-80, para. 7.

the Treaty of Rome; consequently, the institutions were acting initially at the peripheries of EEC/Member State competence. The concept of functional spillover comes closest to describing both why and how the Community involved itself in the various cultural projects outlined below. But while spillover might have been a legitimate phenomenon in integration theory, its validity is more complex in reality. Even a perceived attempt to corrode or usurp the autonomy of the Member States in a domain so closely linked to national sovereignty would have been ill-starred politically. This is the background against which the development of Community cultural policy must be considered.

A.   'Essential and Incidental': Where Culture meets Trade

Why does the EC need an autonomous cultural policy? The most obvious answer is that if the Community is going to take direct action in the cultural domain, there must be a correct legal basis in which the implementing measures can be anchored. But apart from direct action, it is inevitable that the cultural sector—which includes, for example, trade in cultural goods, and the free movement of cultural workers and service providers—is going to be affected by the implementation of the EC Treaty economic freedoms.[15] What must be established, then, is whether the general rules and principles that govern these freedoms cater effectively for the specific character of cultural transactions. It was noted that in Chapter 1 that the impact of EC law on the cultural sector is a good example of functional spillover. Since the theoretical corollary of political spillover has been rejected as a legitimate means of attributing powers to the Community, a Treaty-based cultural policy must be the feasible alternative. Otherwise—apart from the limited recognition of cultural diversity in Article 30 EC, outlined below—there cannot be an effective or coherent response to the distinct needs of the cultural sector, especially in light of its inherent link with the national and regional identities of the Member States. Not unlike the direct/indirect action rationale, the distinction between 'essential' and 'incidental' cultural content was employed to decisive effect by the ECJ in *Parliament v. Council*, introduced

---

[15]   For more specific examples of the intersection between Community freedoms and the cultural sector, see Loman *et al*, *Culture and Community Law*, as follows: free movement of goods, pp. 24-50; free movement of workers, pp. 50-66; freedom of establishment, pp. 67-75; freedom to provide services, pp. 75-90; and free movement of capital, pp. 90-93. Culture and competition law—*e.g.* restrictive agreements and practices, dominant positions, merger control, *etc.*—is dealt with at 95-121 (but see below regarding Article 87(3)(d) EC, which sets out the special position on state aid in the cultural context; see also, Chapter 1).

above and discussed further in Section 3. For present purposes, a brief overview of institutional response to an 'incidental' cultural issue prior to the adoption of Article 151 EC exhibits the alternative to coherence. The provision of state aid is especially significant for the cultural sector. While subsidies in this domain may now be legitimate via Article 87(3)(d) EC, both individual governments and the EC itself have long granted financial aid to cultural undertakings, although, as argued in Chapter 1, this is unlikely to infringe the requisite criterion of affecting trade between Member States in any event. State aid for the film and television industries is a particularly sensitive political issue. Its provision is usually decreed necessary for the maintenance of both quality programming and cultural diversity, even though it generates ample potential for the contravention of Community freedoms. The Commission has been open to Member State arguments based on the promotion of cultural diversity in this context. For example, it has authorised aid granted for programming initiatives involving minority languages.[16] And in the context of the 1989 'Television without Frontiers' Directive on the transmission of 'European works', it reached a bilateral agreement with the French Government on a domestic quota for the broadcasting of French works.[17] The Commission emphasised, however, that while the Community acknowledges the role of television in the development of national language policies, such policies must remain within the limits of Community law and, in particular, must be in proportion to the linguistic objective to be achieved. This echoes the Court of Justice's decision in *Groener*, discussed in Chapter 2, which is a clear example of how national measures pursuing cultural objectives will be assessed for their compatibility with fundamental Community freedoms.[18] In *Groener*, however, the ECJ did not apply a typically strict interpretation to its analysis of cultural objectives as a derogation from the free movement of workers; it was also asserted that a more general cultural policy 'exception' can be traced through case law on the free movement of goods and the free provision of services. Lane argued in 1993 that the justification of national measures on cultural policy grounds was *not* generally accepted by the ECJ, referring to cases on product labelling rules and the audio-visual sector in particular, where national

---

[16] See, for example, the Commission's authorisation of aid granted by the British Government for the production of programmes in the Welsh and Gaelic languages, 30 January 1992, [1992] OJ C23/3; see also (1991) *Europe* No. 5530, 8/9 July, p. 13.

[17] Directive 89/552, [1989] OJ L298/23; see (1991) *Europe* No. 5555, 29 August, p. 7; see also, Loman *et al*, *Culture and Community Law*, pp. 155-158.

[18] Case 379/87 *Groener v. Minister for Education and the City of Dublin Vocational Education Committee* [1989] 2 ECR 3967; see Chapter 2.

limitations on Community freedoms could not be justified on the grounds of the protection of cultural pluralism.[19] But in respect of the audio-visual sector, the Court's decision in *Veronica* stands in contrast.[20] In the same vein as the earlier Dutch *Mediawet* cases,[21] the facts in *Veronica* exemplify the conflict between the cultural aspect of television broadcasting (which comes within national interests) and the cross-border provision of services, falling under Community competence. It is difficult to discern the ultimate basis for the decision. Essentially, the Court had to decide on the compatibility with EC law of Dutch legislation that precluded *inter alia* a broadcasting organisation established in the Netherlands from investing in a broadcasting company established in another Member State. The ECJ reiterated principles it had developed in the earlier *Mediawet* cases, affirming that the Dutch legislation was "...designed to establish a pluralistic and non-commercial broadcasting system and thus forms part of a cultural policy intended to safeguard, in the audio-visual sector, the freedom of expression of the various (in particular social, cultural, religious and philosophical) components existing in the Netherlands."[22] Moreover, it classified such objectives as "...relating to the public interest which a Member State may legitimately pursue by formulating the statutes of its own broadcasting organisations in an appropriate manner."[23] But the Court did not explain *why* cultural policy objectives were accepted here as justifying—in contrast to the earlier *Mediawet* decisions—the contested provisions of the Dutch legislation. In *Veronica*, the Court drew also from the principle that "...a Member State cannot be denied the right to take measures to prevent the exercise by a person whose activity is entirely or principally directed towards its territory of the freedoms guaranteed by the Treaty for the purpose of avoiding the professional rules of conduct which would be applicable to him if he were

---

[19] Lane, "New Community competences", p. 954, referring to Case 27/80 *Fietje* [1980] ECR 3839 and Case C-369/89 *Plageme v. BUBA Peeters* [1991] ECR I-2971, and p. 955, citing Case C-288/89 *Stichting Collectieve Antennevoorziening Gouda v. Commissariaat voor de Media* [1991] ECR I-4007 and Case C-353/89 *Commission v. Netherlands* [1991] ECR I-4069 (the *Mediawet* cases, relating to the implementation of Dutch broadcasting legislation); he does concede, however, that the Court did make 'sympathetic noises' in these decisions (p. 955). See Chapter 1 on the stance adopted by the ECJ regarding language and national labelling rules.

[20] Case 148/91 *Vereniging Veronica Omroep Organistatie v. Commissariaat voor de Media* [1993] ECR 487.

[21] See note 19.

[22] *Veronica*, p. 518, para. 9.

[23] *ibid.*, p. 518, para. 10.

established within that State...", established in *Van Binsbergen*.[24] It then combined both streams of argument, effectively adding a condition or proviso to the *Van Binsbergen* test, *i.e.* the legislative prohibitions must also be "...necessary in order to ensure the pluralistic and non-commercial character of the audio-visual system introduced by [the] legislation."[25] This is unsatisfactory in the sense that the scope of *Van Binsbergen* was limited somewhat arbitrarily; but more particularly, the 'cultural policy objectives' aspect of the Court's decision is completely undeveloped, which detracts considerably from its efficacy as a useful precedent given the conflicting stance taken in the *Mediawet* decisions. It is arguable that lack of competence rather than vision had precluded a result more favourable to cultural concerns, as argued in more detail in Chapter 2 with regard to *Groener*. Significantly, the TEU would have been ratified, though not yet in force, when the decision in *Veronica* was handed down and, in a sense, the decision pre-empts the influence of Article 151 EC. In any event, it is clear that this 'incidental' aspect of state aid had been dealt with on an *ad hoc* and improvised basis to the detriment of consistency. The following paragraphs concentrate more on the evolution of direct action in cultural affairs, but the involuntary impact of Community law on the cultural sector introduced here must likewise be acknowledged as a catalyst in the demand for a more coherent EC cultural policy.

B.   The Evolution of EC Cultural Policy[26]

Political integration is usually described as an implicit, though delayed, facet of European integration more generally; while the realisation of political ambition was initially subjugated to the achievement of economic goals, this is typically attributed to reasons of pragmatism rather than priority. The origins of Community cultural policy can be traced using similar reasoning, in the sense that a tendency, at least, towards cooperation in this domain can be discerned even at the inception of the EEC project. The 1948 General

---

[24] *ibid.*, p. 519, para. 12; Case 33/74 *Van Binsbergen v. Bestuur van de Bedrijfsvereniging voor de Metaalnijverheid* [1974] ECR 1299.

[25] *Veronica*, p. 520, para. 14.

[26] As will become apparent, the Community did not usually deal with language issues in its cultural policy initiatives. The following paragraphs outline the principal stages of EC cultural policy development, highlighting relevance to language where possible; on cultural policy more generally, see Loman *et al*, *Culture and Community Law*; Joseph A. McMahon, *Education and Culture in European Community Law*, (London: Athlone Press, 1995).

Report of the Hague Congress, for example, established that any model for European union should respect ideological pluralism, cultural diversity, and the liberty and rights of all human beings.[27] This philosophy (which continues to fuel the ideology of European unity) reflected the paramount concerns of post-War Europe, but its realisation was not the immediate focus of the primarily economic Treaty of Rome. A cursory allusion to culture can be derived from Article 36 EEC, which permitted restrictions to the free movement of goods that were legitimately grounded in (*inter alia*) 'the protection of national treasures possessing artistic, historic or archaeological value'.[28] This early concession to cultural pluralism is confined to the protection of cultural property. But both the European Parliament and European Council envisaged a more extensive role for the Community in cultural affairs.[29] Throughout the 1960s and 1970s, cultural co-operation was regarded as an aspect of political unity more generally, though economic and other political concerns dominated, if not monopolised, the Community agenda. Eventually, the Commission codified the nascent intentions of the EEC institutions, issuing a series of official communications and declarations. The first of these, *Community Action in the Cultural Sector*, was published in 1977.[30] In line with the 'incidental' approach described above, the Commission identified elements of cultural policy that were interlaced with more general Community competences, including free trade in cultural goods, prevention of the theft of cultural goods, the preservation of archaeological heritage, free movement and establishment for cultural workers, taxation in the cultural sector and the harmonisation of copyright laws. The legitimacy of more culturally focused intervention was derived from the creation of "...a more propitious economic and social environment."[31] Furthermore, the scope of the 'cultural sector' was expressly limited to persons and undertakings involved in the production and distribution of

---

[27] See Françoise Massart-Piérard, "Limites et enjeux d'une politique culturelle pour la communauté européene", (1986) 293 *Revue du Marché Commun*, 34-40 at 34.

[28] Now Article 30 EC; see McMahon, *Education and Culture*, p. 12. In another context, Article 131 EEC (now Article 182 EC) refers to 'cultural development' in respect of associations with overseas countries and territories that have special relations with certain Member States.

[29] See for example, Resolution of the European Parliament calling for a Community policy on culture ([1974] OJ C62/5); statement issued by the Summit of Heads of State and Government at The Hague in 1969, recognising the need to preserve Europe as 'an exceptional seat of development, culture and progress' (EC Bulletin I-1970, Part One, Ch. 1).

[30] EC Bulletin Supp. 6/77.

[31] *ibid.*, p. 5.

cultural goods and services, thereby already coming within general economic policy to a large extent. In other words, the Commission did not try to design an autonomous cultural policy; its vision at that time was a sector-specific application of the general rules and principles *already* set out in the Treaty of Rome. It could not have been otherwise, since a legal basis for 'independent' cultural action did not exist. Significantly, it was established that the most appropriate role for the Community was encouraging transnational co-operation between the Member States and between the cultural authorities therein; the potential for co-operation with the Council of Europe was also highlighted. A draft Council Resolution, based on the Commission's proposals, was drawn up but never adopted, notwithstanding support from both the European Parliament and the Economic and Social Committee. Despite this setback, the Commission went on to publish *Stronger Community Action in the Cultural Sector*, in 1982.[32] It focused once again on trade in cultural goods, free movement and establishment for cultural workers, enlarging the cultural audience and the conservation of archaeological heritage. Notwithstanding the title of the communication, the Commission was careful to point out that the role of the Community in cultural issues was necessarily a limited one:

> There is no pretension to exert a direct influence on culture itself or to launch a European cultural policy; what stronger Community action in the cultural sector means in effect is linking its four constituents...more closely to the economic and social roles which the Treaty assigns to the Community, to the resources—mainly legislative—that it provides, and to various Community policies.[33]

But the 1982 initiative, despite this guarded philosophy, did have important practical consequences. A series of informal meetings between the Member State representatives with responsibility for culture got underway that same year, followed, in 1984, by the first formal Council meeting of this kind. Crucially, discussions began to evolve from the original view that cultural policy was just a peripheral dimension of economic policy. In 1983, the European Council issued a *Solemn Declaration on European Identity*, identifying the need to promote widespread awareness of the 'common European cultural heritage' in order to boost public support for European unity.[34] This

---

[32]   EC Bulletin Supp. 6/82.

[33]   *ibid.*, p. 32.

[34]   EC Bulletin 1983/6.

text introduced a new impetus for the pursuit of cultural co-operation, relating it to the broader, indeed ongoing, attempt to legitimise further economic and political integration; the 1984 Council meeting was seen as a crucial step in its implementation. Language issues did merit some consideration at Council meetings, usually in the context of promoting language education and developing translation facilities. This conservative theme can be contrasted with the minority language initiatives presented by the European Parliament at the same time, detailed in Chapter 2. But consideration by the Council of any aspect of cultural policy was predictably cautious. Legal competence and financial costs were obvious restrictions, along with the suspicions of Member States that feared the seemingly relentless ascendancy of a standardised, assimilative 'Euroculture'. In this sense, the origins of cultural policy epitomise the innate discord between supranational ambition and intergovernmental restraint that frequently besets, and even disables, the work of the Council. The decision of the ECJ in *Groener* was something of a mixed blessing in this context: the Court acknowledged the authority of the Member States to determine domestic language policy, yet affirmed its own jurisdiction to assess the resulting measures for conformity with Community law.

A gradual acceptance that cultural policy was likely to be codified, to some extent at least, was reflected by the inclusion of the following provision in the 1984 Draft Treaty on European Union:

> 1) The Union may take measures to:
> - promote cultural and linguistic understanding between citizens of the Union;
> - publicise the cultural life of the Union both at home and abroad;
> - establish youth exchange programmes.
>
> 2) The European University Institute and the European Foundation shall become establishments of the Union.
>
> 3) Laws shall lay down rules governing approximation of the laws of copyright and the free movement of cultural goods.[35]

In terms of scope, this provision was drafted along much the same lines as the Commission documents published to that date, except that culture and language were expressly adjoined. The emphasis on 'mutual understanding' is firmly rooted in the European Council's 'common cultural heritage' ideology that would, it was assumed, renew the dynamism of integration.

---

[35]   [1984] OJ C77/33.

This conviction was substantiated in the 1985 Adonnino Report on a 'People's Europe'; it was reasoned, for example, that it is "…through action in the areas of culture and communication, which are essential to European identity and the Community's image in the minds of its people, that support for the advancement of Europe can and must be sought."[36] Grounded in similar terminology, and with the added incentive of completing the internal market by 1992, *A Fresh Boost for Culture in the European Community* was published by the Commission in 1987.[37] As well as reiterating objectives already stated, this communication significantly strengthened the role of the Community in the audio-visual and technological sectors. Efforts on behalf of the book trade were also intensified, with specific reference to minority languages regarding the translation of important literary works.[38] Once again, the Community styled itself as the co-ordinator of national and regional cultural authorities. It seemed, then, that the Commission had succeeded in assembling an effective framework for Community cultural policy, endorsed and expanded by the Member States acting through the Council. But it is arguable that the absence of a provision dealing with culture in the Single European Act illustrates the ultimate sterility of the Commission's efforts, articulated in a more general sense by de Witte:

> [G]overnments like to adopt grandiose declarations on the imperative need of promoting European identity. They also manage to agree on those implementing measures that are at the same time highly symbolic and highly innocuous. But when they are presented with more ambitious, and arguably more effective, proposals which it is perfectly within their powers to adopt, they decline to do so. The impression therefore prevails that the policy of promoting European identity is no more than an effort to spread a favourable image of Europe, without any substance backing it. Such a pretence is of dubious value, and might even be counter-productive.[39]

It should be borne in mind that charges of insularity have been levelled continually at the SEA in any case; the defence usually furnished is that it

---

[36]   EC Bulletin Supp. 7/85, p. 21.

[37]   EC Bulletin Supp. 4/87.

[38]   This objective was supplemented by a separate Council Resolution—[1987] OJ C309/3— and deals with the translation of works both into and from minority languages.

[39]   Bruno de Witte, "Building Europe's image and identity", in A. Rijksbaron, W.H. Roobol and M. Weisglas (eds.), *Europe from a Cultural Perspective*, (The Hague: Nijgh en Van Ditmar Universitair, 1987), 132-139 at 137.

was introduced to arrange for and invigorate the very specific task of completing the internal market, that negotiating another treaty—what became the TEU—was foreseen as the proper means of extending the Community's competences in a more comprehensive, and political, direction. But even taking this into account, it is difficult not to subscribe to the views elicited by de Witte, which portray some disenchantment with the EC political process. The resulting sense of frustration must be tempered, however, by the complex political resonance of the policy domain at issue. The cautious demarcation of cultural priorities by the Community institutions reflects, as noted, an inherent friction between the forces of unity and diversity. The significance attached to a common European cultural heritage by the Commission and European Council, for example, would have done little to alleviate the misgivings of some Member States, who feared the promotion of uniformity in the absence of a co-ordinated institutional response to the contrary. The scant, albeit increasing, references to respect for cultural diversity did not clarify its relationship to the more established ambition of European integration, which was taken—rightly or wrongly—as a synonym for homogeny. The separateness of the European Parliament's campaign for minority language recognition illustrates a lingering lack of cohesion that perpetuated recourse to a restrictive interpretation of culture. Nevertheless, there were some noteworthy manifestations of the Commission's work. The ongoing success of various programmes designed to coordinate cross-border language and education exchanges is perhaps one of the most enduring inheritances of pre-TEU cultural policy.[40] The EC institutions have all participated, at one level or another, in supporting cultural projects of this kind, in accordance with the official communications outlined above. In 1988, the Commission established the Committee on Cultural Affairs, to monitor the implementation of any actions to be decided upon by the Council. The Commission appointed a Commissioner for Cultural Affairs and set up the Department of Cultural Affairs within DGXXII, which covered the audio-visual sector, information, communication and culture.[41] The Parliament established a Committee on Youth, Culture, Education, the Media and Sport, as well as an Intergroup on Minority

---

[40] See McMahon, *Education and Culture*, pp. 21-49, detailing a number of specific Community programmes, particularly *Erasmus*, *Lingua*, *Comett* and *Tempus*; see also Chapter 1.

[41] Following the reorganisation of the Directorates-General in 1999, cultural policy is now dealt with by the Education and Culture Directorate General, discussed further in Section 3.

Languages. It adopted numerous resolutions on cultural questions, not least those detailing its views on minority languages outlined in Chapter 2.

It is arguable that the Council consistently avoided making a genuine or substantive commitment to the development of cultural policy, despite its perfunctory support for the work of the Commission. Again, this is hardly surprising given doubts over legal competence, along with the defensive attitude of most Member States towards their sovereignty in the cultural domain. In what is commonly regarded as a seriously under-funded sector at all levels—local, regional, national and international—financial assistance approved by the Council, over and above more abstract commitments to developing a cultural policy, was particularly welcomed. A number of projects and initiatives received support from the European Social Fund (ESF), the European Research and Development Fund (ERDF), and the European Investment Bank. Community institutions have also granted specific subsidies for cultural activities, including aid allocated to the following projects that promoted minority languages and cultures:

- funding for the European Bureau for Lesser Used Languages (EBLUL), (including the maintenance of the *Mercator* language information network);

- pilot experiments in the field of education (*e.g.* teaching methods);

- projects aimed at promoting the use of minority languages in information technology and the mass media;

- translation of contemporary literary works both into and from minority languages;

- support for language information centres throughout the Community.[42]

The provision of financial assistance is crucially important although it does not, on its own, constitute a complete cultural strategy. But what is markedly significant about Community expenditure on cultural projects is that, prior to the enactment of the TEU, it was effectively devoid of legal basis. Indeed, funding for EBLUL still rests on a precarious premise, having regard to the principle that every significant Community expenditure must be grounded in the prior adoption of a legislative act.[43] The role of the Court of Justice in the development of EC cultural policy is somewhat more unsettled, evidenced

---

[42] See Loman *et al*, *Culture and Community Law*, pp. 164-167.

[43] Case C-106/96 *United Kingdom and others v. Commission* [1998] ECR I-2729; see Chapter 6.

by the existence of decisions that both facilitate and restrict the promotion of cultural diversity. The absence of an express legal basis is, again, an obvious consideration here, but the Court's contemporaneous stance on other so-called peripheral policies—especially, its initiatives in the related field of education—refutes the absolutism of that argument.[44] The Court repeatedly avoided pronouncing on the Community's cultural agenda, opting instead to deal with the principle or freedom raised in each case in that specific context only. The resulting web of cases has seemed curiously erratic at times, as consideration of the decisions in *Mediawet* and *Veronica* has revealed; whether Article 151 EC has had a converging effect on the ECJ's more recent jurisprudence is examined in Chapter 6.

In its final communication before the ratification of the TEU—*New Prospects for Community Cultural Action*, in 1992—the Commission urged that renewed consideration should be given to the role of the Community in cultural affairs, given the 'unprecedented opportunity for cultural co-operation and support' that was deemed to exist at that time.[45] Reflecting the eventual wording and content of Article 151 EC, the Commission directed its attention to three areas: a 'Community contribution to the flowering of culture in the frontier-free area', promotion of the common cultural heritage, and co-operation with third countries and international organisations. The Commission advocated the retention of a restrictive conception of culture on

---

[44] Education policy under Article 149 EC is not discussed in detail here, although its evolution as a Community competence is similar to the development of cultural policy in many ways. The Commission dealt originally with culture and education within two distinct Directorates-General, under the authority of two separate Commissioners (Directorates-General X and XXII respectively; now education and culture are joined under the ambit of the Education and Culture Directorate-General); meetings of the Council that deal with education and culture are also entirely discrete, notwithstanding the fact that the Member State representatives often share both portfolios at domestic level and, as a result, attend both Council meetings. In practice, it is often difficult to separate the two areas, as with, for example, the Community programmes on language education (*e.g. LINGUA*). Although activity in the education sphere preceded that in the cultural arena by almost a decade, both policies developed along a functional basis. Both were originally thought to be outside the ambit of Community law. And both areas fundamentally reflect the identities of the Member States, which has led to the curbing of Community ambition by the now relevant provisions of the EC Treaty. The implementation of Article 149 is, however, governed by less draconian procedures than those contained in Article 151(5), the latter of which requires unanimous rather than qualified majority voting. Another difference between the two provisions is that Article 149 does not contain a policy integration clause (Article 151(4), see below); thus, the Community is not obliged to take educational interests into consideration when legislating in other policy areas.

[45] COM(92) [1992].

the basis of past Community action; it could not yet predict whether Article 151 would warrant expansion in this regard. But at a formal Council meeting that same year, the Member State representatives went further, stating expressly that the cultural agenda of the Community was not categorically fixed.[46] It was noted explicitly that future Community programmes might include "...increasing awareness of different cultures *and safeguarding the Community's linguistic diversity*, as well as promoting respect for shared values."[47] In objective terms, the 'Community's linguistic diversity' must surely include its minority languages. It is fair to say that, on the whole, the EC institutions have all contributed in some measure to the animation of the Commission's cultural policy framework, perhaps even generating a mutual persuasion to act. But this fragmentary construction—infused with problems of legal basis and political complexity—has not really shed definitive light on its probable reach. In truth, each of the institutions seems to have a different understanding of where the boundaries of competence lie, and that too appears to change over time. Article 151 EC is the answer that has been codified. Ironically, the argument that the provision is itself an uncertain reference point has been strengthened by reviewing the path to its inception. On the other hand, a more positive interpretation of this hypothesis is that the scope of Article 151 may be more inclusive—and thus functional—than is usually assumed.

3.   ARTICLE 151 EC: AN APPRAISAL

A.   Introduction

Lane remarks that the TEU "...not only broadens quantitatively and qualitatively the pantheon of Community competences; it also confers upon them legitimacy, flesh, coherence, new direction—and not a little confusion."[48] Article 151 EC fits neatly into this description. Its objectives reveal a mass of multiple interests, from the preservation of relative Member State autonomy, to the challenges posed by the completion of the single market and the likelihood of EU enlargement. The notion of the Community as a coordinator had to be reflected, as did the desirability of and potential for cooperation with other international organisations. Perhaps most crucially, a balance between the ideologies of cultural pluralism and common cultural

---

[46]   [1992] OJ C366/1.

[47]   *ibid.*, para. 4 (emphasis added).

[48]   Lane, "New Community competences", p. 944.

heritage needed to be struck, a potentially Byzantine equation that the idiom of non-differentiation which nourishes EC policy more generally was not going to resolve. The text as drafted is habitually slated: the provision is either too narrow or too broad; it goes too far, it doesn't go far enough. And certainly, there are difficulties. But by focusing on these shortcomings alone, it is too easy to lose sight of the undeniable significance of Article 151 in the first place; its incorporation into the EC Treaty was achieved despite fundamentally diverging views on critical precepts, including the scope of culture itself, the differing extent and priorities of cultural policy throughout the Member States, even the titles and portfolios of the government representatives under whose administration cultural policy falls. The following paragraphs attempt to dissect and evaluate the textual layers of Article 151 EC, to ascertain its effectiveness as the legal basis for EC cultural policy generally but, more particularly, to gauge whether or not it can authorise more deliberate and coherent Community action in favour of minority languages, bearing in mind that at the time of writing, the Commission is likely to employ the provision as the legal basis for its proposed minority language funding programme.

B.   Article 151(1)

The Community shall contribute...
The idea of the Community 'contributing' to cultural policy is not a new one given the analogous function of 'coordination' already endorsed by the Commission, as outlined above. That the role of the Community is described as a contribution rather than a delineation is wholly appropriate; as discussed in Chapter 1, the Member States do and should retain primary responsibility in this domain. But does the word 'contribute' mean that the institutions can act only where the relevant aspect of cultural policy is already enunciated, or to be enunciated, by the Member States? A literal reading along these lines would effectively preclude any initiation of policy at EC level, rendering the *raison d'être* of Article 151 entirely meaningless. For that reason alone, it is clear that the institutions are *prima facie* empowered to formulate cultural policy measures of their own volition; in other words, the concepts of contribution and instigation are not necessarily mutually exclusive.

...to the flowering of the cultures of the Member States...
Despite predictable—and arguably understandable—criticism levelled at this choice of words,[49] the expression has generated a remarkable degree of

---

[49]   See note 2.

confidence among proponents of cultural and linguistic diversity.[50] The word 'flowering', though it seems unusual and even eccentric, can be traced to discussions long preceding the adoption of the TEU; its etymology derives from the French term *épanouir*, which does mean 'to flower or blossom', but can also be read as 'to open up or open out'. It is particularly significant that culture is written in its plural form, surely quelling some apprehension of a harmonising cultural absolutism within the EC. A key, if ostensibly superfluous, question is whether the term 'cultures' includes 'languages' in the first place. Various schools of thought on the definition of culture were outlined in Section 1; it was argued that language is an intrinsic component of practically all variations on the concept. Language is an essential medium for the transmission of culture generally, but it is also an independent and fundamental constituent of culture in itself. Documented institutional involvement in language (including minority language) issues consolidates their claim for inclusion in the Community concept of culture. It is true that language did not figure initially in the Commission's framework documents, but this is as much a reflection of the situation regarding legal competence and political strategy as of the status or qualities of language *per se*. Moreover, this deficit was seen to be redressed somewhat as Community cultural policy evolved. The European Parliament invariably classes language as an aspect of culture, not least in its post-TEU work on minority languages (examined in Chapter 6), and Article 151 has been central to cases before the ECJ that relate to language, exemplified by *Parliament v. Council*. It is important to realise, however, that while cultural policy does encompass language, it is not a panacea; language issues are broader than can be dealt with by any cultural policy, and not just the EC variation.

...while respecting their national and regional diversity...
This phrasing differs from the requirement in Article 149(1) EC that the Community must respect the 'cultural and linguistic diversity' of the Member States in its contribution 'to the development of quality education'. Again, on a literal interpretation, it is arguable that 'cultural and linguistic diversity' may not then be covered by Article 151.[51] This fear is unfounded. Article 151 deals *specifically* with culture; respect for national and regional diversity must necessarily relate back to the theme of the provision. Any other construction would be erroneous. And it has been argued repeatedly that 'culture' includes 'language' in the majority of contexts. Moreover, as

---

[50] See, for example, the Preamble to the 1994 Killillea Report ([1994] OJ C061/110; see Appendix II), discussed in Chapter 6.

[51] See Lane, "New Community competences", p. 953.

noted, the employment of the term 'cultures' reinforces the implication of pluralism and diversity. The express reference to regional as well as national diversity provides an additional safeguard for minority cultures. This has been ignored by those who regard Article 151 as a vehicle for respecting *national* cultures and identities only; in a sense, Article 151 EC goes further than Article 6(3) TEU, which refers only to 'national identities' (although, as argued in Section 1, that phrase is itself open to generous construction). Article 151(1) might have been more complete if the words 'cultural and linguistic' had been included explicitly, but there is no reason to doubt their implication.

...and at the same time bringing the common cultural heritage to the fore.
Respect for diversity is not the only condition set down in Article 151; it rests alongside a concurrent endorsement of collective cultural identity. The most obvious question to ask is whether a 'common cultural heritage' exists at all in the EC context. And if it does, how can its promotion be reconciled with the apparently competing value of cultural diversity? The 'official' or institutional view is typified by the following paragraph, taken from a speech delivered by Commission president Romano Prodi to the European Parliament:

> We have created a customs union and a single market based on the free movement of goods, services, capital and people. We have built an economic and monetary union with a single currency. We have laid the foundations of a political union with shared institutions and a directly-elected European Parliament. What we now need to build is a union of hearts and minds, underpinned by a strong shared sentiment of a common destiny —a sense of common European citizenship. We come from different countries. We speak different languages. We have different historical and cultural traditions. And we must preserve them. But we are seeking a shared identity—a new European soul.[52]

The idea of a common cultural heritage is exploited widely to confer legitimacy on political entities, or indeed, to incite the formation of new ones; it is based on an often tenuous notion of shared history and traditions, including a

---

[52] Romano Prodi, President of the Commission, addressing the European Parliament on 14 September 1999; see http://europa.eu.int/comm/commissioners/prodi/speeches/designate/140999_en.htm.

mutual conception of culture. As outlined in Section 2, this logic was adapted by the (then) EEC in an attempt to validate the momentum of supranational integration.[53] The language used for this purpose is often chosen to conjure up the mystic character of identity, akin to the 'common destiny' and 'European soul' imagery depicted above. The underlying circular reasoning is that while identification with a 'European' conscious-ness can be said to derive from some sort of shared loyalty, this affinity is equally necessary for its continued fabrication. This is unquestionably ironic given that such symbolism is more usually associated with nationalist argument, a philosophy displaced in the furtherance of a common European heritage. The ideologies associated traditionally with national political structures have thus been modified to reflect collective identity, an approach that, paradoxically, reinforces rather than dispels the potency of nationalist fable in the first place. But do the peoples of the EC Member States really share a 'common cultural heritage'? Does the existence of a relatively universal appreciation of culture suffice here? If so, how is a 'European' appreciation of culture to be differentiated from that of any other human grouping? Or, even if something uniquely European can be said to exist, will the imminent enlargement of the EU cause that assumption to be re-considered? Howe argues bluntly that "[i]n matters of ethnicity, culture and history, there is little, if anything, uniquely European, and certainly nothing as compelling as that which sustains existing national sentiment."[54] He suggests that even the policy-makers that advance this illusion are aware of its ultimate futility. As a philosophical compromise, he discusses the likeli-hood that a 'future-oriented' European identity will be created, spawned by the development of a widespread sense of security within the EC, discussed in Chapter 1 and somewhat similar to the idea that a shared heritage must yet be constructed—which fits with the gist of Romano Prodi's aspirations, outlined above. Certainly, future-oriented identity could transcend both ethnic and historical differences, and might forge a more tenable foundation than the fiction of shared, past-rooted heritage. Does this approach offer a

---

[53] The European Foundation, for example, was set up for the precise purpose of "...fostering a common European identity which in turn would reinforce the political solidarity among the Member States." (Bruno De Witte, "The scope of Community powers in education and culture in the light of subsequent practice", in Roland Bieber and Georg Ress (eds.), *The Dynamics of European Law*, (Baden-Baden: Nomos, 1987), 261-278 at 277). Similarly, Lane considers that the 1989 'Television without Frontiers' Directive, based on the promotion of 'European works', is grounded in the same philosophy (Lane, "New Community competences", p. 955; Directive 89/552, [1989] OJ L298/23).

[54] Paul Howe, "A community of Europeans: The requisite underpinnings", (1995) vol. 33:1 *Journal of Common Market Studies*, 27-46 at 31.

reasonable alternative to more implausible, usually past-rooted, hypotheses?[55] The main difficulty, as asserted in Chapter 1, is the implicit criterion of inevitability, given that it has been consistently hopeless to prejudge the course of integration in any event, or the reactions of those who consider that their cultural identity is somehow at risk. If the gestation of common European consciousness is to become a reality, it would better be based on a collective respect for diversity; political situations throughout the world demonstrate repeatedly that forced assimilation and the annihilation of pluralism have grave consequences. A shared will to accommodate diversity can itself be constitute a common objective or characteristic. This applies equally in the linguistic domain.[56] A rich variety of cultures—including languages—is what is certainly 'common' to the heritage of Europe. What exactly the institutions intended to 'bring to the fore' through Article 151(1) is not at all clear, though this impetus is both long-established and still employed; what can, however, be stated is that cultural uniformity is neither demanded nor inferred.

C.   Article 151(2)

Action by the Community...
The word 'action' confirms a functional role for the EC in cultural policy, perhaps even more than the reference to 'contribute' in Article 151(1). But Article 151(2) goes on to delineate specific areas in which the Community may actually act; it is arguable that these areas are more limited than the general objectives introduced in Article 151(1), a claim examined in detail below.

...shall be aimed at encouraging co-operation between Member States...
As seen in Section 2, the Commission has always been careful to frame the role of the EC as that of coordinator—gently nudging the Member States to partake in the Community conception of culture, but staying in the wings.

---

[55]   As an example of alternative justifications, Howe refers to the tenuous idea put forward by Anthony Smith that a 'common cultural heritage' could be built on the fact that most languages spoken in the Member States belong to the Indo-European language family: *ibid.*, p. 31.

[56]   Linguistic stability within the Swiss Confederation is usually cited as an illustration in this context. From the perspective of minority languages, the Romantsch language was recognised constitutionally, in 1996, as an official language for communications between the Confederation and Romantsch citizens; it had previously been recognised as a national, but not official, language of the Confederation. Furthermore, the constitutional amendment included express support for measures taken by the Cantons to safeguard and promote the Romantsch and Italian languages.

Culture is usually still classified as a 'new' Community competence; but it has now been codified in the Treaty for almost a decade. However unwelcome Community 'interference' may once have seemed, the encouragement of cultural co-operation between Member States is a legitimate Treaty objective, which can no longer be queried on grounds of legal basis.[57] Nevertheless, not least because of the way in which the role of the EC was carved out, the ongoing involvement of the Member States is critical. It has been suggested that Member States are more amenable to Community intervention in some aspects of cultural policy, particularly the audio-visual sector, than in others, such as the book trade.[58] If this claim is defensible, the priorities implied arguably reflect the primacy of economic concerns, given that audio-visual products contribute far more to the economy than books. The role of the Community would be especially meaningful if it succeeded in steering Member State attention towards less commercial cultural projects, thus providing an external balance against more habitually dominant interests. But where is the dividing line between encouragement and coercion, or, the more likely dispute in the EC context, between encouragement and submission? In other words, it is vital to establish just how proactive the Community can be; otherwise, the already—justifiably— vast powers of Member States in the determination of cultural policy will nullify the advancement secured (some would say concessions made) at Maastricht. As is the case for any international intervention, the guiding principle must be that the EC should take action where national or more local initiatives are somehow lacking, to the extent that the achievement of objectively justifiable cultural aims or principles is being impeded; more specifically, EC action must be measured against both the limitations set down expressly in Article 151, discussed below, and, ultimately, the principle of subsidiarity.

...and, if necessary...
This phrase evokes the application of subsidiarity, in accordance with the second paragraph of Article 5 EC, which provides as follows:

> In areas which do not fall within its exclusive competence, the Community shall take action, in accordance with the principle of subsidiarity, only if and insofar as the objectives of the proposed action cannot be sufficiently achieved by the Member

---

[57] The possibility that Member States may even be required to cooperate, in full contemplation of the principle of subsidiarity, is explored in Chapter 4.

[58] See McMahon, *Education and Culture*, p. 164.

States and can therefore, by reason of the scale or effects of the proposed action, be better achieved by the Community.

Article 5 does not create competence; it regulates the *exercise* of competence regarding objectives contained in other provisions of the EC Treaty. The substantive issues raised by subsidiarity—which have a fundamental impact on the effectiveness of Article 151—are discussed in Chapter 4, but some preliminary points should be made here. Effectively, what is at issue is the determination of the appropriate actor for any given aspect of cultural policy. As highlighted in Chapter 1, the effects of Community law cannot be boxed neatly into discrete categories; measures taken in one policy area impact on a range of others. In addition, Article 151(4) provides expressly that the Community is required to take cultural aspects into account in its action under other Treaty provisions; thus, cultural policy is broader than Article 151 and the application of subsidiarity is more complicated as a result. But again, it has to be stressed that despite the reservations of certain Member States, primarily related to sovereignty, and notwithstanding legitimate concerns over how the Community will handle what are seen as inherently localised matters, an EC contribution to cultural policy is a Treaty-based objective. Subsidiarity cannot reverse this. Language may be a politically sensitive issue, but it is also a cultural, sociological and economic one. EC policies affect all of these domains and, consequently, they affect language. Individual state policies are not sufficient to check the linguistic fallout stemming from transnational integration; Member States insisting on the rectitude of national measures as a means of redress claim that to permit otherwise presents a threat to national identity. But two basic facts are being ignored here. First, national identity may be subject to a far greater threat by *not* enacting EC measures to deal with the European dimension of language displacement. Second, focusing on *national* identity exclusively can operate to the detriment of minority cultures, and this includes speakers of minority languages. A feature of the EC competences introduced at Maastricht is that the conditions under which the Community may act are set out in exceptionally considered detail. For example, harmonisation of the laws and regulations of Member States is explicitly prohibited; the Community should instead encourage co-operation between Member States, possibly adopting incentive measures and recommendations, and setting minimum standards, but only 'if necessary'. The role of the Community is visualised as supplementary, creating a significant bias in favour of national action. It is even arguable that the constraints placed on Community initiative within Article 151, read in conjunction with Article 5, render the provision virtually benign and entirely dependent on the goodwill of national representatives via the

Council. The value of the minimum standards approach is often overlooked, however; this may have been the only way to have various policy issues recognised by the Treaty at all. The (fairly routine) inclusion of a non-preemption clause in directives allows Member States to adopt stricter rules than the minimum standards set at EC level in any case. Moreover, the European Council has encouraged the philosophy of minimum standards across the spectrum of Community activity, in accordance with the principle of proportionality.[59] These ideas are fleshed out below when looking at Article 151(5), but it would be erroneous to assume that the Maastricht competences were deliberately afflicted with an impossible impediment to their realisation, at odds with EC legislative trends more generally. Viewed from this perspective, Toth's reservations seem misdirected where he questioned whether the 'new' competences had been worth the 'price' paid, *i.e.* the codification of subsidiarity.[60] His remarks in a subsequent publication pin down the real danger in this context *i.e.* constraining the potential of the EC by the misappropriation of Article 5: "[r]elegating matters to Member State action where Community action is required has serious constitutional implications for the division of the exercise of competences and is just as contrary to the principle of subsidiarity as taking Community action where the Member States should act."[61] It has already been argued, in the context Article 151(1), that the role of the Community as co-ordinator is the right one, but this classification does not imply that it must relinquish all powers of initiative; similarly, then, the restraints put in place by Articles 151(2) and 5 EC should not be presumed to rule out Community enterprise automatically or in all circumstances.

...supporting and supplementing their action...
The remarks made above in respect of encouraging co-operation between Member States apply equally to this subsection. But the word 'supplementing' invokes more expressly the proactive role envisaged for the Community in the cultural domain, potentially going beyond what has been achieved by the Member States acting autonomously. This is arguably dependent on the existence of a Member State initiative in the first place ('supplementing *their*

---

[59]   European Council, *Conclusions of the Presidency*, (Edinburgh Summit, December 1992), Annex 1, Part A, EC Bulletin 12-1992, pp. 8-9; the ethos of these conclusions is now contained in the Protocol on the Application of the Principles of Subsidiarity and Proportionality, attached by the Amsterdam Treaty and considered in Chapter 4.

[60]   A.G. Toth, "The principle of subsidiarity in the Maastricht Treaty", (1992) vol. 29:6 *Common Market Law Review*, 1079-1105 at 1094.

[61]   A.G. Toth, "Is subsidiarity justiciable?", (1994) 19 *European Law Review*, 268-285 at 275; this theme is explored in depth in Chapter 4.

action'). But once again, such a literal reading of Article 151 would render the provision effectively useless, removing the need for any Community input in the first place, and is therefore refuted; at any rate, even on a literal interpretation, the Member States have all taken *some* action in the cultural domain.

...in the following areas...

- **improvement of the knowledge and dissemination of the culture and history of the European peoples;**

- **conservation and safeguarding of cultural heritage of European significance;**

- **non-commercial cultural exchanges;**

- **artistic and literary creation, including the audio-visual sector.**

This subsection forms, at first glance, the nucleus of EC competence in the cultural sphere. Although Community 'encouragement' of Member State co-operation does not seem to be limited to particular areas, those in respect of which the Community may take action are set down explicitly; yet this has the potential to stunt the development of cultural policy. It was certainly necessary to establish the boundaries of competence; but does this express stipulation of areas for EC action prevent the Community from acting on any other aspects of culture? This is why reliance on Article 151(1) without any reference to Article 151(2) (as practised by many supporters of minority languages, including the European Parliament) may be an overly confident aspiration.[62] It is especially remarkable that in Article 151(2), 'culture' is denoted in its singular form, with the ideological balance thus tipped in favour of promoting shared heritage and identity. The topics listed are extraordinarily narrow in focus. They concentrate on the artistic dimension of culture—which is, of course, worth protecting and promoting—in isolation from aspects of culture in its broader sense, such as language. Even if language is an element of cultural heritage, for the purposes of 'conservation and safeguarding', the proviso that this heritage must be of 'European significance' is open to differing interpretations. On a narrow construction, something might only be of 'European significance' based on sheer size or pervasiveness throughout the Community. Alternatively, on a broader view, diversity of languages could itself come within the concept of 'European significance'. But would this imaginative interpretation find

---

[62]   The post-TEU European Parliament stance on minority languages is examined in Chapter 6.

favour within the narrow remit on cultural matters likely to be preferred by the Member States? In *Parliament v. Council*, the applicant institution argued that "...the Community's linguistic wealth forms part of the cultural heritage which the Community is responsible for conserving and safe-guarding...in accordance with Article [151](2)."[63] The Council disagreed with this interpretation on the grounds that "[t]he persons directly benefiting from the programme are not cultural figures such as...novelists, playwrights and literary translators...."[64] As already noted, the Court dealt with these claims on the essential/incidental distinction, and so held that the content of the contested decision did not come within the scope of 'safeguarding cultural heritage'; that is not to say, however, that language issues could *never* satisfy this criterion. The potential application of Article 151(1) was neither raised nor considered.

Loman *et al* do not, however, hinge the entirety of Article 151 on its second subsection.[65] First, and perhaps most importantly, they cite Article 151(5), discussed below, which refers to implementation 'the objectives referred to in this Article'; and Article 151(1), not subsection (2), is considered to stipulate these general objectives. Or, it could be argued that *both* subsections contain distinct sets of Community objectives. Second, they note the importance of 'mixed' cultural activities, provided for under Article 151(4) and explained below. Finally, they argue that, in any event, Community action in the cultural sphere is *not* restricted to that which may be taken under Article 151: "...Article 3[q] EC in a general way states that one of the activities of the Community will be to contribute to the flowering of cultures of the Member States. There is no reason to hold that these activities are only restricted to those made possible under Article 151 EC."[66] Moreover, they argue that the exclusion of the majority of aspects relating to culture from Article 151(2), such as the media, may ensure more comprehensive action outwith the restrictive methods of implementation outlined in Article 151(5). In respect of the media, the audio-visual sector is mentioned explicitly in Article 151(2), in terms of 'artistic and literary creation'; whether that term can encompass general media policy is open to interpretation initially by the Member States, but ultimately by the Court of Justice. Despite arguments in favour of liberal interpretation, however, Loman *et al* conclude that

---

[63]   Case C-42/97 *European Parliament v. Council of the European Union* [1999] ECR I-869, at p. 893, para. 26

[64]   *ibid.*, p. 895, para. 33.

[65]   See Loman *et al, Culture and Community Law*, p. 194 *et seq.*

[66]   *ibid.* (formerly Article 3(p) EC).

notwithstanding the creation of Community competence in cultural matters, Article 151 has enabled the Member States "...to draw the line there, in that it can be seen as an attempt to block the more or less spontaneous further expansion of Community law in this area...."[67]

The notion of developing cultural policy independently of Article 151 merits discussion on whether or not the Community has powers in the cultural sphere under Article 308 (formerly 235) EC.[68] It is arguable that culture falls outside the scope of Article 308, which is concerned with measures deemed 'necessary in the course of the operation of the common market'. But this qualification has not always been adhered to in a strictly literal sense.[69] Moreover, it must be remembered that culture and economics cannot easily be neatly dissociated. The real stumbling block here is that successful employment of Article 308 is effectively dependent on the attainment of consensus among the institutions and the Member States, which is often elusive on questions of culture. It is also arguable that even if the application of Article 308 was once viable, this potential has been nullified by the codification of an express competence in Article 151 itself.[70] But this cannot be taken for granted. Drawing again from ideas raised above, the inclusion of culture as a *general* Community objective (in Article 3(q) EC) is what makes recourse to Article 308 possible at all.[71] And if Article 151 is interpreted narrowly, it is arguable that 'specific powers' have *not* been provided in respect of a number of facets of cultural policy.[72] The legislative options available under the residual powers provision is another key issue. Article 308 can only come into play where there is an economic dimension to cultural policy but in such instances, its use could conceivably lead to the

---

[67]   *ibid.*, p. 195.

[68]   Article 308 EC provides: "[i]f action by the Community should prove necessary to attain, in the course of the operation of the common market, one of the objectives of the Community and this Treaty has not provided the necessary powers, the Council shall, acting unanimously on a proposal from the Commission and after consulting the European Parliament, take the appropriate measures."

[69]   See, for example, De Witte, "The scope of Community powers", pp. 270-1, referring to Directive 79/409 ([1979] OJ L103/1), on the protection of wild birds and endangered species.

[70]   See Renaud Dehousse, "Community competences: Are there limits to growth?" in Renaud Dehousse (ed.), *Europe After Maastricht: An Ever Closer Union?* (München: Law Books in Europe, 1994), 103-125 at 106.

[71]   See Loman *et al, Culture and Community Law*, p. 191 *et seq.*

[72]   Although Loman *et al* contend that the use of Article 308 is not precluded by the existence of more specific objectives in Article 151 at any rate: see *Culture and Community Law*, p. 191 (footnote 32).

evasion of the non-harmonisation condition in Article 151(5) for mixed cultural/economic activities. This would depend on the Community's interpretation of mixed undertakings. It is submitted, however, that, in reality, the Article 308 question is a moot point. It is unlikely that the Commission will resort to the provision to circumvent the intransigence of the Member States, or indeed, of Article 151(5) itself. Any actions taken under Article 308 still require a unanimous Council decision. Furthermore, the Community did take action on mixed cultural/economic issues prior to the adoption of the TEU, but without relying on Article 308 EC. The general provisions of Community law were simply applied to the cultural sector and this practice is likely to continue, particularly in light of the policy integration clause in Article 151(4). And the continued implementation of pre-Maastricht initiatives remains a valid objective, in accordance with Article 47 (formerly M) TEU.

If Article 151(2) has fixed the Community's cultural agenda, it is remarkably disappointing, yet this has attracted scant attention from those who laud Article 151(1) in isolation; furthermore, the Commission proposals enacted *since* the enactment of Article 151 do not suggest that the provision has had a substantive impact on the content of EC cultural policy at all, one way or the other.[73] Using Article 151 as the legal basis for a multiannual programme on minority languages is generating controversy at present, discussed below and in Chapter 6. In light of the functional origins of EC competence in cultural matters, Article 151(2) is a firm slap on the wrists for the institutions. The Community is restricted to encouraging Member State co-operation by the first phrase of Article 151(2); and it may only go further than this—'supplementing' Member State action—in the areas listed expressly, which themselves represent a mere slice of cultural scope. The ultimate fate of Community initiatives is dependent on the disposition of the

---

[73] See for example, the *Kaleidoscope* (Decision No. 719/96/EC of the European Parliament and Council, 29 March 1996, [1996] OJ L99/20), *Ariane* (Decision No. 2085/97/EC of the European Parliament and Council, 6 October 1997, [1997] OJ L291/26) and *Raphael* (Decision No. 2228/97/EC of the European Parliament and Council, 13 October 1997, [1997] OJ L305/31) programmes, on cultural cooperation in the arts, literature and cultural heritage fields respectively, the predecessors to the *Culture 2000* programme, discussed below. Perhaps the most noteworthy advance in Community cultural policy relates to the prospect of EU enlargement: the preamble to the *Culture 2000* decision, for example, refers to the conclusions of the 1993 European Council at Copenhagen, which called for the opening of EC cultural programmes to the countries of Central and Eastern Europe that have signed association agreements with the Union (see recital 14 of the preamble to Decision No. 508/2000/EC of the European Parliament and Council, 14 February 2000, establishing the *Culture 2000* programme, [2000] OJ L63/1; see in particular Article 7 of the Decision).

Member States acting through the Council. Given the independent commitment to subsidiarity in Article 5, which secures their position in any event, the prohibitive tenor of Article 151(2) confirms both insecurity and scepticism on the part of the Member States. Neither Articles 151(1) EC nor 6(3) TEU were seen as sufficient guarantees against the expected encroachment of 'Euroculture'. No provision could account comprehensively for the infinite span of cultural meaning. And it must be reiterated that the areas of cultural policy identified in Article 151(2) are deserving of both recognition and protection. Moreover, the value of having even a limited EC cultural competence enshrined in the Treaty has been reinforced in light of the ECJ decision in *United Kingdom v. Commission*, which established that every 'significant Community expenditure' must be grounded in a legal act; the functionalist, pre-TEU development of EC cultural policy might not have outlived this decree.[74] But if EC cultural competence must stop there, it is simply inadequate. Locating in Article 151(1) more general cultural objectives to which the Community can 'contribute' is an infinitely preferable outlook. In *Parliament v. Council*, the content of the decision at issue fell to be discussed under Article 151(2) only, so we are none the wiser as to whether the Court of Justice will accept a broad or narrow construction of Article 151(1). Either way, the impact in practice of the policy integration clause in Article 151(4) takes on particular significance.

D.   Article 151(3)

The Community and the Member States shall foster co-operation with third countries and the competent international organisations in the sphere of culture, in particular the Council of Europe.
This subsection reflects, once again, the trend of evolved practice, especially in relation to the jurisdiction of the Council of Europe. The succession of Commission publications dealing with culture all accorded precedence to the Council of Europe in the cultural domain. Article 151(3), when read with Article 151(5), does not confer a general power on the EC to enter into treaties with third countries or international organisations, given the limited range of legal instruments available to the Community for the implementation of cultural policy, although it is arguable that the EC in cooperation with the Member States could conclude treaties relating to the limited objectives contained in Article 151(2).[75] A potentially negative result of Article 151(3),

---

[74]   Case C-106/96 *United Kingdom and others v. Commission* [1998] ECR I-2729 at 2755, para. 26 (see Chapter 6).

[75]   See Loman *et al, Culture and Community Law*, p. 199

if the phrasing is considered to represent the Community's yielding to other international actors, is that it would restrain Community participation to more symbolic, prestige-gaining cultural projects than to programmes of substance.[76] In this way, Community action would be peripheral not only to that taken by the Member States but also to the accomplishments of other international organisations and, particularly, of the Council of Europe. Does the Council of Europe actually have superior capacity to develop cultural policy? In the domain of minority language rights, this question is considered in more depth in Chapter 5. In a more general sense, cultural policy is included explicitly in the Council's range of activities.[77] It is sometimes contended that the Council of Europe is a preferable forum for matters of cultural policy with an international aspect.[78] It would be a mistake, however, to become complacent about true potential in this arena. De Witte writes as follows about the Council's attempts in the related province of education:

> The Council's role in education has already been marginalised. The results achieved in a few years within the European Community, on matters like the recognition of diplomas, the equal treatment of foreign nationals, the mobility of students and teachers, and international exchange programmes, are more impressive than anything that has happened in thirty years of the Council of Europe.[79]

These observations do not inspire complete confidence in the Council's capacity to tackle individually the challenges posed by the complexities of cultural regulation, a viewpoint reinforced by its approach to minority language rights (outlined in Chapter 5). In particular, the Council's European Charter for Regional or Minority Languages has granted an extensive degree of discretion to the state signatories regarding options for implementation;

---

[76] See McMahon, *Education and Culture*, p. 174.

[77] See Article 1(b) of its Statute. The Council of Europe's European Cultural Convention (ETS No. 18) was opened for signature in Paris on 19 December 1954 and entered into force on 5 May 1955. The Preamble to the Convention reflects a balance between "...the study of the languages, history and civilisation of the [Member States] and of the civilisation which is common to them all...." All of the Council of Europe Member States have signed and ratified the Convention; further information is posted on the Council's website, at http://www.coe.fr/eng/legaltxt/18e.htm.

[78] See, for example, Ferdinando Albanese, "Ethnic and linguistic minorities in Europe", (1991) 11 *Yearbook of European Law*, 313-338 at 331 *et seq.*

[79] De Witte, "Cultural linkages" in William Wallace (ed.), *The Dynamics of European Integration*, (London; New York: Pinter, 1990), 192-210 at 203.

yet notwithstanding the potentially insubstantial obligations imposed thereby, few EC Member States have proceeded actually to ratify the Charter. The respective contribution made by both the Council and the EC to the realisation of language rights is determined in Chapter 5, as is the relationship between the two organisations in the domain of fundamental rights protection more generally. It is far from self-evident that the EC should defer to the Council of Europe in all matters cultural. Cooperation rather than submission is the better platform from which to develop relations in this sphere, as recognised explicitly in Article 151(3) EC. That 2001 has been designated European Year of Languages in a joint project undertaken by the European Union and Council of Europe exemplifies the spirit—and potential—of this provision.[80]

E.   Article 151(4)

The Community and the Member States shall take cultural aspects into account in its action under other provisions of this Treaty, *in particular in order to respect and to promote the diversity of its cultures.*[81]
It is precisely because policies can rarely be completely divorced from one another that the EC absorbed to a certain extent an initial competence in culture; to have provided formally for this demonstrates the prevalence of pragmatism on the part of the Community institutions, but more especially among the Member States. Article 151(4) confirms that cultural policy goes beyond Article 151, representing a means by which sensitivity to the ancillary effects of Community law can be encouraged. The Member States —who are expressly and equally obliged to take cultural aspects into account when Community law is at issue—have, however, ensured dual safeguards for the protection of their interests: first, the very fact that the EC institutions must take cultural aspects into account so pervasively at all and, second, the insertion of an express assurance of cultural pluralism via the Amsterdam Treaty. Here once again, 'culture' is written in its plural form and must, objectively, include minority cultures; in this regard, the Article 151(4) EC

---

[80]   The European Year of Languages, preparations for which are ongoing at the time of writing, has been pitched as a celebration of diversity and multiculturalism, focusing on the need to make individuals across Europe 'more aware of the linguistic and cultural advantages of learning other languages': see (2000) vol. 16:3 *Contact Bulletin* 6; for details on the range of programmes and activities involved, see http://culture.coe.fr/AEL2001EYL/; see also the website of the European Commission at http://europa.eu.int/comm/education/languages/actions/year2001.html. Significantly, regional and minority languages have been included within the scope of the project to a certain extent.

[81]   The phrase in italics was added to Article 151(4) via the Amsterdam Treaty.

proviso is wider than Article 6(3) TEU, its counterpart on 'national' identities. Ultimately, the Court of Justice will decide the extent to which the general requirements of Community law can be limited by the application of Article 151(4).[82] How potent is a policy integration provision likely to be in reality? The first clause of this type was included in what was Article 130r EEC, the environmental protection provision introduced by the SEA. The environment integration clause was strengthened by the TEU and, significantly, integration clauses—phrased in similar but not identical terms—were introduced for five of the 'new' policy areas: culture,[83] public health,[84] industry,[85] economic and social cohesion,[86] and development cooperation[87].[88] The Amsterdam Treaty has effected further changes in this context: the integration of environmental protection requirements was moved from Article 130r (now 172) EC and restated as Article 6 EC in Part One of the Treaty ('Principles'); and Article 3(2) EC establishes, for the first time, the requirement of policy integration in respect of the elimination of inequalities (and promotion of equality) between men and women. Although thought initially to be relatively benign, there is some evidence that policy integration in the environmental domain does have an appreciable impact in reality.[89] A 1997 Council Resolution on the integration of cultural aspects into Community measures provides some insight into the application of what was then Article 128(4) EC, but more precisely, reiterates reasons *why* cultural aspects should

---

[82]   Lane, "New Community competences", p. 956, has urged caution in this context, stressing the relative inexperience of both the Court and the political institutions in dealing with this complex, predominantly national, policy area, and highlighting the dangers of succumbing to ideological rather than economic analysis. These arguments are similar to those challenged in Chapter 4, addressing the Court's (in)ability to interpret and apply the principle of subsidiarity.

[83]   Article 151(4) (formerly 128(4)) EC.

[84]   Article 152(1) (formerly 129(1)) EC.

[85]   Article 157(3) (formerly 130(3)) EC.

[86]   Article 159 (formerly 130b) EC.

[87]   Article 178 (formerly 130v) EC.

[88]   Integration clauses were *not*, however, included in the other 'new' competence provisions *i.e.* education (Articles 149-150 (formerly 126-127) EC and consumer protection (Article 153 (formerly 129a) EC.

[89]   Recent examples include the Communication from the Commission to the Council and the Parliament, *Indicators for the Integration of Environmental Concerns into the Common Agricultural Policy*, COM(2000) 20 Final (26 January 2000), and the Commission's Proposal for a European Parliament and Council Regulation on Measures to Promote the Full Integration of the Environmental Dimension in the Development Process of Developing Countries, COM(2000) 55 Final (2 February 2000).

be taken into account in more general policy-making in the first place.[90] The Resolution notes that, in 1992, the Council (and the Member State representatives with responsibility for culture meeting in the Council) concluded that "...it should become standard practice on a case by case basis to take account of cultural aspects under [other] provisions of the Treaty...at the earliest possible stage of preparation of any new action or policy...."[91] A number of principles that seek to justify this dictum, thus indirectly affirming the need for Article 151(4) in the first place, are then listed; the link between cultural participation and effective citizenship is a discernible theme throughout. The Resolution refers also to the first Commission Report on the consideration of cultural aspects in EC action, which identified policy areas that were most likely to have a cultural dimension; these included free movement issues, audiovisual and telecommunications policies, external relations, and economic and social cohesion (with special emphasis on structural funds).[92]

The Court of Justice was called upon to consider the implications of Article 151(4) in *Parliament v. Council*.[93] As noted, Parliament was seeking to have a Council decision on annulled on the grounds that Article 151 should have been (co)specified as its legal basis; the decision provided for a multiannual programme to promote the linguistic diversity of the Community in the information society (referred to in the judgment as the 'MLIS' programme), aimed particularly at the needs of small and medium-sized enterprises facing different language markets within the EC.[94] The Commission had identified Article 157(3) (formerly 130(3)) EC as the legal basis for the measure. When Parliament was consulted by the Council, as required by Article 157(3), it proposed a number of amendments that enhanced the cultural and linguistic aspects of the programme, including that of dual legal basis. The Council did not, as seen, amend the measure prior to its adoption, leading to Parliament's action for annulment under Article 230 EC. Essentially, the question to be decided was whether the main aim of the programme was the promotion of cultural and linguistic diversity—thereby going beyond cultural 'aspects' per Article 151(4), and triggering the

---

[90] Council Resolution of 20 January 1997 on the integration of cultural aspects into Community actions, [1997] OJ C36/04.

[91] *ibid.*, (referring to the Council meeting of 12 November 1992).

[92] Commission of the European Communities, *First Report on the Consideration of Cultural Aspects in European Community Action*, (1996) COM(96) 160 Final.

[93] Case C-42/97 *European Parliament v. Council of the European Union* [1999] ECR I-869

[94] See [1996] OJ L306/40; for details of the action proposed, see especially Articles 1(1) and 2(1), and Annex I.

application of Article 151(2) as an additional legal basis—or whether the programme was founded on primarily economic and industrial objectives; in this latter case, as argued by the Commission, there would be cultural and linguistic 'spin-offs' but this would not require Article 151 to be employed. The Court first stated that the objectives of the measure could not be determined solely by reference to the wording of its title; rather, the Court would consider "...whether, according to its aim and content, as they appear from its actual wording, the contested decision is concerned, *indissociably*, both with industry and culture."[95] The Court went on to distinguish between the 'essential' and 'incidental' components of a measure as follows:

> [I]t is not sufficient for the contested decision to pursue a two-fold purpose or for an analysis of its content to disclose the existence of a twofold component. If it were apparent from an examination of the decision that its 'industrial' component is identifiable as the main or predominant component, whereas the 'cultural' component is incidental, it would follow that the only appropriate legal basis for it was Article [157] of the Treaty. *This interpretation conforms with the actual text of Article [151](4) of the Treaty....* It is clear from that provision that not every description of the cultural aspects of Community action necessarily implies that recourse must be had to Article [151] as the legal basis, where culture does not constitute an essential and indissociable component of the other component on which the action in question is based but is merely incidental or secondary to it.[96]

This is a completely sensible construction; an alternative interpretation would, in effect, render Article 151(4) entirely impotent. But in going on to find that the cultural aspects of the contested measure *were* incidental, and thus affirming that the Council was right to have taken the cultural dimension into account under Article 151(4) only, the Court wavered between pragmatism and a potentially restrictive understanding of culture. In particular, the Court considered that the 'marginalisation of languages that remain excluded from the information society' was not a 'risk of a specifically cultural nature'; the Court clarified this logic, stating that "...the aim 'to contribute to the promotion of linguistic diversity of the Community' mentioned in [Article 1(1) of the decision]...does not express a cultural aim

---

[95]   *Parliament v. Council*, p. 896, paras. 37-38 (emphasis added), referring to Case C-300/89 *Commission v. Council* [1991] ECR I-2867.

[96]   *ibid.*, pp. 896-7, paras. 39-42 (emphasis added).

pursued as such.... Language in that context is seen not as an element of cultural heritage but rather as an object or instrument of economic activity."[97] "The phrase at issue here is contained in the twelfth recital of the preamble to the Council Decision, *i.e.* 'languages that remain excluded from the information society would run the risk of a more or less rapid marginalisation'. The Advocate General was blunt on this point: "[t]hat phrase is referred to by the Parliament, which considers that the protection of less-widely spoken languages has a clearly cultural dimension. It is wrong to do so, however: the danger which the legislature sought to ward off is that of marginalisation in the commercial sphere, not the cultural sphere."[98] But it is difficult to be sure of the precise meaning intended here. On the one hand, the clear wording of the preamble does not rule out an interpretation that 'marginalisation' refers to a commercial or economic context. But it is also arguable that the Court's reasoning in this direction reflects that eschewed by Advocate General Darmon in *Groener*, where he cautioned against treating languages as 'dead' instruments 'incapable of further development'.[99] Not all language issues relate primarily to cultural heritage. And it is disappointing that the Court did not comment on the risks to linguistic diversity caused by the momentum of the information society, a real and pertinent concern in itself. Furthermore, by concentrating on the Article 151(2) 'cultural heritage' premise, the Court did not explore the more general objective set out in Article 151(1). It cast the main aim of the MLIS programme as one of ensuring "...that undertakings do not disappear from the market or have their competitiveness undermined by communications costs caused by linguistic diversity."[100] Again, the Court did not comment on the implications for language of creating a competitive market in the first place. Instead, the phrasing used portrays the fact of linguistic diversity in a negative light, as a troublesome economic burden, which stands at odds with more typical Community rhetoric—and indeed, ECJ jurisprudence—on this point. There may not have been cultural questions at stake here if culture is defined narrowly; but there were certainly linguistic questions, and these were treated as neither autonomously significant nor constitutive of culture in a less rigid sense. Actually providing for these concerns was, of course, a matter for the details of the contested decision, but it is regrettable that the Court did not take the opportunity even to affirm their legitimacy. The judgment boiled

---

[97] *ibid.*, p. 900, paras. 52-53.

[98] *ibid.*, Opinion of Advocate General La Pergola, p. 877, para. 6.

[99] See *Groener*, pp. 3982-3, paras. 21-24.

[100] *Parliament v. Council*, p. 901, para. 57.

down to an assessment of intention and emphasis, an inevitably subjective exercise: Parliament argued that the contested decision was intended to safeguard linguistic diversity, the Council and Commission disagreed; the wording of the measure itself was not conclusive one way or the other. The Court made some useful statements on the purpose of Article 151(4), but it is regrettable that its analysis was clouded by some curiously deficient reasoning on culture and linguistic diversity in the process. Both the Court and Advocate General were careful to point to the value of the Article 151(4) mechanism; Advocate General La Pergola considered that "[it] shows that culture is regarded, in the Treaty, as a...'transversal' value, which potentially touches upon every sector of activity in the Community."[101] And the Commission's Report on the integration of cultural aspects into Community actions, cited above, suggests that Article 151(4) has been taken on board to some extent. Yet the danger that the institutions could side-step a policy integration clause remains a very real one. How can the cultural aspects of each and every proposed Community measure be assessed in reality? And, without actions such as that initiated in *Parliament v. Council*, how can the potentially countless evaluations of both the Commission and Council in this respect be appraised? The input of both the Committee of the Regions and European Parliament, as conceived in Article 151(5), could be valuable here. It might also be viable to establish a body of some sort— involving either the Committee or Parliament, or both—to examine all proposed legislation from the cultural perspective specifically. Such a body would be more attuned to the cultural dimension of any given measure and might thus identify potential concerns more readily, securing an operative rather than token execution of the provision. The assignment of a policy integration clause to Article 151 is certainly to be welcomed; it does, as Advocate General La Pergola pointed out, recognise that cultural aspects 'potentially touch upon every sector of activity in the Community'. As with any such clause, however, its true value comes to be realised more through implementation than ratification.

F.   Article 151(5)

In order to contribute to the achievement of the objectives referred to in this Article...
To reflect the distinction put forward earlier, it is submitted that this phrase can refer to the general objective of 'contributing to the flowering' of the

---

[101]   *ibid*, Opinion of Advocate General La Pergola, pp. 879-880, para. 7.

cultures of the Member States, set out in Article 151(1), as well as to the specific objectives listed in Article 151(2).

...the Council—acting in accordance with the procedure referred to in Article 251 and after consulting with the Committee of the Regions... (The Council shall act unanimously throughout the procedure referred to in Article 251)...
Article 251 EC outlines the co-decision legislative procedure, whereby the European Parliament must approve the Council's common position before a proposed measure may be adopted. In light of its documented commitment to the promotion of minority languages, the involvement of Parliament is especially significant here. Article 151(5) goes on to require, however, that the Council must act unanimously throughout; Curtin regards this as a 'highly anomalous' exception to the co-decision procedure, given the narrow legislative scope of Article 151 in the first place.[102] The requirement of unanimity in the Council has the potential to negate the likely ambitions of Parliament, but the involvement of the Committee of the Regions—which could effect representation of various regional and minority interests— confirms support for regional as well as national diversity. As suggested above, an additional way for the Committee to fulfil its role here would be for it to participate in the implementation of Article 151(4) if possible. The progress report on IGC 2000 had recommended that Article 151(5) should be considered (as just one of a list of other Treaty provisions) for a switch to qualified majority voting, without the need for substantive revision of the remainder of the provision; the implications of this are considered below although it should be pointed out that the proposal did *not* come to fruition at the Nice Summit and so the provision remains unchanged for the foreseeable future.[103]

...shall adopt incentive measures...
The character of incentive measures, a phrase first introduced to the EC Treaty by the TEU, is not actually defined therein. The Commission has also used the phrase 'encouragement actions', which suggests a predominantly soft law approach.[104] It is more or less agreed, however, that this legislative option best reflects the Community's role as contributor to cultural policy (Article 151(1)) and co-ordinator of Member State cooperation (Article

---

[102] Deirdre Curtin, "The constitutional structure of the Union: A Europe of bits and pieces", (1993) vol. 30:1 *Common Market Law Review*, 17-69 at 37 (footnote 84).

[103] Progress report on IGC 2000, prepared for the Feira European Council (CONFER 4750/00, Brussels, 14 June 2000), see Annex 3.1, p. 74.

[104] European Commission, *First Report on the Consideration of Cultural Aspects*, p. 1.

151(2)) in any event, covering, for example, the provision of financial assistance and the organisation of cultural events. Dashwood refers to the *Erasmus* education exchange programme as an example of an incentive measure.[105] But he suggests that "...it is now clear, as it was not before, that Member States are *under no obligation* to adapt their systems, so as to allow individuals and educational establishments to enjoy the full advantage of Community programmes."[106] This position is difficult to reconcile, however, with the general obligation on Member States to implement Community objectives, grounded in Article 10 EC and discussed further in Chapter 4.[107] Although Article 151 leaves relative power largely in the hands of the Member States and does not elaborate on any sort of implementation time-frame, it unequivocally denotes cultural policy as a Community objective. Thus, even at the level of incentive measures, the duties and obligations of the Member States that stem from Article 10 EC cannot be so readily dismissed.

...excluding any harmonisation of the laws and regulations of the Member States...

This subsection could curb the trend of past Community practice to some extent, in that a number of harmonising directives enacted in other policy areas have had implications for the cultural sector (*e.g.* directives on VAT); and the Community has also enacted harmonising directives based *primarily* on cultural matters (*e.g.* film, architecture and broadcasting).[108] Even before Article 151 was enacted, these directives contained express references to the interests of the Member States in respect of preserving cultural diversity.[109] It is arguable that the exclusion of the media (generally speaking) from the objectives listed in Article 151(2) allows the Community to continue with

---

[105] Dashwood, "The limits of Community powers", p. 122.

[106] *ibid.*

[107] Article 10 EC provides that "Member States shall take all appropriate measures, whether general or particular, to ensure fulfilment of the obligations arising out of this Treaty or resulting from action taken by the institutions of the Community. They shall facilitate the achievement of the Community's tasks. They shall abstain from any measure which could jeopardise the attainment of the objectives of this Treaty."

[108] See Loman *et al*, *Culture and Community Law*, pp. 145-158.

[109] See for example, Directive 89/552, on the facilitation of cross-boundary broadcasting, [1989] OJ L298/23 (the 'Television without Frontiers' Directive), which dealt with the transmission of 'European works' yet allowed the Member States, for purposes of language policy, to impose stricter rules on broadcasters within their jurisdictions, where the Member States themselves deemed this to be necessary (Article 8). The decision on how far the Member States could go in this regard would, however, rest ultimately with the Court of Justice.

some aspects of its harmonisation programme; but there are also compelling arguments against this interpretation since Article 151(2) makes express reference to 'the audio-visual sector' as a medium for 'artistic and literary creation'. Moreover, the general objective of 'contribution to cultures' in Article 151(1) would include the media, meaning that the more generous interpretation of Article 151(1) that has been advocated does have the consequence of subjecting *all* cultural policy measures to the constraints of Article 151(5), apart from mixed activities linked clearly and primarily to economic concerns of the type at issue in *Parliament v. Council*.[110] Thus, while Community directives implemented before the ratification of the Maastricht Treaty are unaffected, it is not likely that similar harmonisation programmes could now be enacted. The decisive factor here, applying the reasoning of the Court of Justice, is the determination of a measure's 'essential' and 'incidental' effects on the aspect of cultural policy at issue in any given case. For this reason, the provision of financial assistance for cultural activities remains the most significant way in which the Community can fulfil directly (or 'essentially') the realisation of its cultural competence; indeed, the Commission's *Culture 2000* programme—operative from 1 January 2000 to 31 December 2004, and billed as a 'single financing and programming framework for cultural cooperation'—was devised primarily to channel the provision of finance for cultural purposes.[111] It is largely a continuation of the Commission's established blueprint on coordination and financing for cultural projects and initiatives. Its scope is considerably broad, making it difficult to predict how successful and effective it will be in practice. The objectives stated in its preamble imply, on the one hand, that its ambit is quite open-ended, but this means equally that its reach could be curtailed arbitrarily. Minority language questions do feature to some extent; for example, the sixth recital of the preamble provides that 'special attention should be devoted to safeguarding the position of Europe's small cultures and less widely-spoken languages'. Annex 1 ('Activities and Implementing Measures') attempts to set out the types of projects that can be supported under *Culture 2000*; section 1.2 lists subject areas that can form the basis of 'cooperation agreements, including 'projects aimed at the highlighting of

---

[110] In its *First Report on the Consideration of Cultural Aspects*, the Commission confirmed that Article 151 EC "...in no way affects the underlying basis of a number of legislative harmonisation documents relating to other objectives but which include a cultural dimension or have an impact in the cultural field." (p. 2)

[111] See Decision No 508/2000/EC of the European Parliament and Council, establishing the Culture 2000 programme, [2000] OJ L063/1. *Culture 2000* replaces the cultural programmes cited in note 73 above, following on from the Council's calling on the Commission to devise a single cultural framework (see [1997] OJ C305/1).

cultural diversity *and of multilingualism*, promoting awareness of the history, roots, common cultural values of the European peoples and their common cultural heritage' (emphasis added). This incredibly nebulous (and arguably contradictory) phrase is, in effect, a summary of the objectives of Article 151 EC, although with an added reference to multilingualism. The only more specific guidelines on how multilingualism should feature in Community cultural policy can be found with respect to the book sector,[112] intimating that *Culture 2000* is an exercise in more of the same and not one that will push back the boundaries of EC cultural competence to any great extent; on the other hand, its loosely defined objectives lean noticeably towards the more general ambitions of Article 151(1), so the possibility that the scope of cultural competence may yet shift as a result of *Culture 2000* cannot be ruled out. More specifically, Article 151 EC is currently being considered as a legal basis for a multiannual programme (known at this stage as *Arcipelago-Archipel*) to secure and coordinate funding for minority language projects.[113] It is not expected that formal legislative proposals will be introduced by the Commission before Autumn 2001, at the very earliest. Delays that have already stalled the introduction of the programme have been pinned primarily on the unanimity requirement in Article 151(5), discussed above and in Chapter 6. The outcome of IGC 2000 has obvious repercussions here, given that the unanimity requirement stays with us. But the fact that Article 151 has otherwise been deemed (even assumed to be) an appropriate legal basis for the programme bodes well as an indication of ascribing a broad interpretation to the provision. And ironically, while the exclusion of harmonisation codified expressly in Article 151(5) may have been intended as a concession to Member State disquietude, it is probably the most appropriate setting in which to develop a truly pluralist cultural policy. Harmonisation of legislation eliminates national measures in conflict with EC law and supplants a uniform Community regime. Given that cultural, linguistic and administrative policies differ vastly throughout the Member States, the conception and establishment of homogenous cultural standards would be inherently misconstrued and certainly counterproductive. The philosophy of 'Europeanisation' is simply out of place in the cultural context, and the exclusion of harmonisation via Article 151(5) can be read as a means through which a different approach can be maintained.[114]

---

[112] See, for example, section 1(b) of Annex 2 ('Vertical and Horizontal Approaches').

[113] See (2000) vol. 16:2 *Contact Bulletin* 1; 4-5.

[114] Lane has argued that 'Europeanisation' and homogenisation are "...necessary products of the Treaty and the internal market..." ("New Community competences", pp. 953-4), but

Furthermore, 'Europeanisation' is not necessarily a product of the Treaty; it arises more where the reality of accentuated cross-cultural interaction is left unchecked. As argued in Chapter 1, it cannot be taken for granted that national and sub-national authorities can manage this phenomenon without some level of supranational intervention; thus, the Community has both a pragmatic and particular role to play here as coordinator of Member State policy. But it is equally essential that the legislative limits of Article 151 are not misappropriated to the extent of rendering the provision completely ineffective, a consideration reflected throughout this chapter and returned to below.

... - acting unanimously on a proposal from the Commission, shall adopt recommendations.
This phrase exemplifies the dual character of Article 151. It ensures that the Community has a second legislative mechanism at its disposal for the development of cultural policy but, at the same time, it secures Member State supremacy in two ways: first, recommendations are the weakest form of Community legislation and are not legally binding and, second, unanimity is again required in the Council. The latter condition in particular intimates the intensity of Member State insecurity, given the legal weakness of recommendations in the first place. As noted above, however, the Article 151 unanimity requirement was up for debate at IGC 2000. Certainly, qualified majority voting might cut through political impasses, leading to more effective use of the provision. But, as with the exclusion of harmonisation, the unanimity requirement can be viewed in a more positive light, despite its apparent ideological and political background; it could in particular constitute a protection mechanism for (typically smaller) Member States having special needs in the cultural and linguistic sectors that might not otherwise be defensible. Thus, unanimity generates both advantages and disadvantages in the implementation of cultural policy, as would a switch to qualified majority voting; what remains essential is that neither method falls foul of political gamesmanship. The 'moral' force of recommendations should not be discounted, especially once they have been published in the wider public domain. But while the veto embedded in Article 151(5) may prove beneficial to the preservation of cultural diversity, it could also direct the Council to a complete stalemate. De Witte has argued that "...one should...not attempt to merely *prevent* the Community from entering the [cultural] field, but also to *steer* its policy in the appropriate direction [since]

---

the wording of Article 151 EC, and the trend towards minimum harmonisation in EC policy more generally, refute this contention.

both national and regional identities may sometimes better be protected by closer formal interaction at the European level than by the separate policies of each Member State"[115] From this perspective, cooperative participation is crucial, provided that the Member States do not use the power of veto as an instinctive defence mechanism against objectively positive change.[116] Given that some Member States deny the recognition of, or subsequent support for, linguistic minorities resident within their own territories, it may take some time before any substantive progress is made in this sphere. But Article 151 provides, at least, for the first time a basis from which the EC can begin to grapple more openly with these issues.

4.   CONCLUSION

Article 151 EC reflects the ideological cross-roads reached at the Maastricht negotiations; it attempts to strike a balance between the cession of Member State sovereignty and the maintenance of Member State control. To what extent can the provision be used as a legal basis for the development of (minority) language policy? Article 151(2) is the more limited paragraph, in that it sets out express areas for EC action and it remains uncertain as to whether that provision can encompass the development of an autonomous language policy. Article 151(1) contains an arguably independent objective, committing the Community to contribute to cultural diversity in more general terms. The concurrent obligation to promote common European heritage can be placed in a broader context and does not have to conflict with the ambition of safeguarding cultural pluralism. Language policy, including minority language concerns, could therefore fall within the ambit of Article 151(1), but only if an inclusive definition of cultural diversity is applied. Institutional consideration of Article 151 as a legal basis for the *Arcipelago-Archipel* minority languages funding programme supports this view. Even then, there are limitations. The Community may 'contribute' to

---

[115] De Witte, "Cultural linkages", p. 205.

[116] It is arguable that the EC Treaty mechanism for closer cooperation introduced by the Amsterdam Treaty *i.e.* Article 11 EC, which sets out a procedure to be followed where a majority of Member States 'intend to establish closer cooperation between themselves' (subject to Articles 43 and 44 TEU), might provide a way forward in case of institutional deadlock in the cultural context. The prohibitive provisos built into Article 43 TEU (as amended by the Treaty of Nice)—including that closer cooperation 'respects the *acquis communautaire* and the measures adopted under the other provisions of the…Treaties' (Article 43(c) TEU) must, however, be borne in mind; furthermore, Article 43(d) requires that closer cooperation must remain 'within the limits of the powers of the Union or of the Community'.

the 'flowering of cultures' but only by enacting incentive measures and recommendations, requiring a unanimous Council decision. But the employment of this legislative machinery can also be interpreted as fortuitous, in that it yields procedures for the maintenance of pluralism; in light of the diversity of cultures and languages throughout the Community and the multifarious needs deriving therefrom, harmonisation would be unworkable in any event. The policy integration clause in Article 151(4) could result in more culturally sensitive Community law as a rule, but only if draft legislative measures are examined consistently and deliberately for that purpose. It was also noted that while cultural policy is not confined to Article 151 where a measure has significantly 'mixed' elements, it is unlikely that Article 308 EC will be employed habitually in this context; the Community has traditionally dealt with mixed activities by deploying the relevant sectoral provisions of the Treaty, as exemplified in *Parliament v. Council*. The discretion accorded to the Member States via Article 151 is considerable and its exercise will determine how the provision evolves. The Community's current cultural framework—*Culture 2000*—does not mark a substantial advance from the pre-Maastricht programmes; but within its vague formulations, as within those of Article 151 itself, lie the possibilities for strengthening the arguably standalone objectives on cultural diversity found within Article 151(1). The approach of the Court of Justice in *Parliament v. Council* makes clear that neither the Community nor its Member States are yet ready to explore that potential. But that decision also reflects a pragmatic distinction that should be restated here. Article 151 EC has to date been drawn from where culture is presented as a predominantly aesthetic concept; language and multilingualism have been included here, especially for initiatives involving the book sector. This is what the Court of Justice characterised as policy having an 'essential' cultural content. Measures having 'incidental' cultural impact were held to be more properly based on the relevant substantive Treaty provision(s), with the application of Article 151(4) intending that due account would be taken of what might be called secondary cultural aspects. This is a useful distinction, in that it implies correctly that not all language questions are rooted necessarily in the domain of 'cultural heritage'. But what is unfortunate is that the Court of Justice failed to grasp that language issues falling outwith this characterisation are not inherently 'incidental' either; so where can legal basis be sought in such instances? Building more ambitious cultural and linguistic programmes on the uncertain foundations of Article 151(1) is possible but, in truth, would require a fundamental shift in Member State attitudes. That this might still occur cannot be ruled out although debate on the *Arcipelago-Archipel* programme is likely to be intense once the Commission introduces its substantive proposals. Finally, the limitations contained in Article 151(5), bolstered by Article 6(3) TEU, provide considerable safeguards against genuinely intrusive Community action. But it is most likely that, ultimately, the principle of subsidiarity will prove decisive here. For this reason, Chapter 4 now examines how the application of Article 5 EC might actually pan out in reality, since any conclusions drawn in respect of Article 151 are necessarily tied up with how this 'shared' competence might actually be assigned.

Chapter 4

Cultural Policy and the Principle of Subsidiarity

1. INTRODUCTION

In any organisation based on a system of shared powers, one of the fundamental questions to be determined is the allocation of competence. As well
as the obvious need to decide on which level of authority does what, the
division of functions presents an opportunity to set limits, both actual and
potential, to the exercise of relative power. This concept must be formalised
to some extent to avoid excessive disagreement over purportedly *ultra vires*
actions. In federal unions, for example, competence is usually delimited
explicitly in a written constitution. But the distribution of competence within
the EC is not quite so clear-cut. The activities of the Community are set out
in the EC Treaty, but respective EC/Member State obligations are not listed
expressly.[1] For example, so-called Community objectives are not pursued by
the Community alone; Member States must sometimes take action—
although more usually, refrain from taking unilateral action—on the basis of
shared competence. This fairly fluid division of powers has become
increasingly complicated as the impact of EC law reaches consistently
beyond the predominantly economic goals set down in the original Treaty of
Rome. It is arguable that it was never intended to confine the scope of the
Community to economic issues in any case; but it must be conceded that the
express assignment of additional EC powers sparked contentious opposition
which almost thwarted the ratification of the TEU. The trend towards
intensified supranationalism evident at that time contrasted directly with a
renewed determination to protect and promote the national identities of the

---

[1] The distinction between the competences of the Community and the Union must always
be borne in mind: essentially, the former are subject to the rules and principles of
Community law and to the jurisdiction of the Court of Justice, while the latter are
exercised within an intergovernmental framework; see generally Deirdre Curtin, "The
constitutional structure of the Union: A Europe of bits and pieces", (1993) vol. 30:1
Common Market Law Review 17-69, and Ulrich Everling, "Reflections on the structure of
the European Union", (1992) vol. 29:6 *Common Market Law Review* 1053-1077. A 'more
precise' delimitation of Community/Member State competences has, however, been
flagged as an item for the agenda of the next IGC, to be held in 2004.

Member States, and one of the most perplexing challenges still facing the Union is the accommodation of national and regional diversity in the context of common goals and a shared institutional framework. Article 6(3) TEU, which provides that the Union is obliged to respect the national identities of its Member States, is an example of how this concern was reflected in the Maastricht Treaty. An additional response to tensions associated with the division of powers was the codification of subsidiarity as a principle of Community law. But while this might have been intended to simplify the allocation of competence, two preliminary observations can be made. First, in light of the political discord surrounding its introduction as well as continuing (if waning) academic debate, subsidiarity probably accentuated rather than alleviated the concurrent powers conflict. And second, it is difficult to assess the extent to which the principle had or continues to have an impact in practical terms. Attempts to grapple with its potential torments have fallen somewhat out of fashion since the initial fluster in the aftermath of Maastricht; moreover, the codification of closer cooperation became the constitutional preoccupation after Amsterdam.

In Chapter 3, Article 151 EC was shown, on the one hand, to contain as many limitations on as possibilities for EC action in the cultural field. It was argued also, however, that its general objectives may be broad enough to encompass, potentially at least, a more ambitious policy agenda. Either way, to establish legal basis for the enactment of cultural measures, Community action has to be justified by reference to subsidiarity. An advanced cultural framework would have to go beyond the purely aesthetic concept of 'cultural heritage' that already dominates the application of Article 151, to address more coherently, for example, the linguistic imbalances generated by the operation of the internal market and related Community freedoms; and it was argued in Chapter 1 that responsibility for minority languages and their speakers in this context is probably even more acute. The imminent Commission proposals on the *Arcipelago-Archipel* multiannual programme will bring these issues to the fore of Community debate. Ironically, the application of subsidiarity will probably involve defensive reliance on the principle by both the EC *and* the Member States. What must be remembered is that the principle does not, and cannot, decide whether the EC or the Member States actually *have* competence in a given policy area; rather, where both levels of authority already have respective spheres of competence in the same area, subsidiarity determines which level of authority should *act*. The mistaken impression that the principle is some sort of tool by use of which EC competences can be clawed back is challenged throughout this Chapter; as the EC Treaty protocol on subsidiarity states quite clearly, "[t]he principle of subsidiarity does not call into question the powers conferred on the [EC] by the Treaty....[It] provides a guide as to how those powers are to be exercised...." The main question addressed here is whether, by applying Article 5 EC, the Community or the Member States emerge as the most appropriate actor for the development of minority language policy founded on Article 151. This theoretical question will have to be answered in real terms when substantive proposals for *Arcipelago-Archipel* are introduced. But it is first necessary, given the extent of disagreement on the latitude of the principle as codified in EC law, to try and establish what the term 'subsidiarity' is actually taken to represent.

2.   THE SCOPE OF ARTICLE 5 EC: 'WHICH PRINCIPLE'?

A.   The Codification of Subsidiarity in Community Law

Perhaps in the manner that flexibility provoked constitutional speculation in the wake of the Amsterdam Treaty, there is a wealth of thought-provoking literature on subsidiarity, tracing its origins in the Community context, and both predicting and assessing its influence as a general principle of EC law. This section does not attempt to deconstruct the subsidiarity debate in a substantive sense; rather, the character of the term as it is understood and applied here will be set out, directing the reader to more detailed academic sources where relevant, as well as to recent case law of the Court of Justice.

(i)   Before Maastricht

One of the most notable characteristics of subsidiarity in any context— whether specifically that of the Community, its ideological origins in the Aristotelian 'civic existence' ideal or its influence on Roman Catholic theology[2]—is its chameleon-like capacity for apparently supporting both sides of a division of powers argument. Essentially, the principle is drawn upon to ascertain the just exercise of competence in a power-sharing

---

[2]   For discussions on the history and ideologies of subsidiarity, see particularly, Deborah Z. Cass, "The word that saves Maastricht? The principle of subsidiarity and the division of powers within the European Community", (1992) vol. 26:6 *Common Market Law Review* 1107-1136; see also Andrew Beale and Roger Geary, "Subsidiarity comes of Age?", (1994) 144 *New Law Journal* 12-14 and Vlad Constantinesco, "Who's afraid of subsidiarity?", (1991) 11 *Yearbook of European Law* 33-55.

organisation or system, with the overall objective that each level of authority should perform its allocated tasks to optimum effectiveness. It is traditionally construed as ensuring that decisions and actions must be taken, where possible, at the level of authority closest to individual citizens; but equally, on the premise of effectiveness, subsidiarity can both justify and require action at higher levels of authority. This anomaly explains why the formal introduction of the doctrine into EC law had been supported by those who seek to justify the enlargement of Community powers as well as by those who are determined to curtail this tendency.[3] It is not quite clear when the ethos of subsidiarity can be said to have permeated the framework of EC law-making. In 1990, the *Common Market Law Review* remarked that the term was 'until recently almost unknown'.[4] But it has also been argued that subsidiarity has been a guiding, if implicit, principle throughout the evolution of Community law.[5] There was a hint of subsidiarity in Article 130r(4) EEC,[6] the environmental protection provision introduced by the SEA;[7] otherwise, references to the principle were confined more to the political domain. It is particularly illuminating, however, to sketch how its conceptual flexibility has long been exploited in this domain of political rhetoric. In the 1975 Commission Report on European Union, one of the first blueprints for the push towards an 'ever closer union among the peoples of Europe', subsidiarity was promoted as a mechanism for widening EEC

---

[3]   See Constantinesco, "Who's afraid of subsidiarity?", p. 35 and Cass, "The word that saves Maastricht?", p. 1112.

[4]   Editorial Comments, (1990) vol. 27:2 *Common Market Law Review*, 181-184 at 181. Similarly, Toth argues that the pre-TEU Community competence allocation structure would actually have precluded the application of the principle (A.G. Toth, "The principle of subsidiarity in the Maastricht Treaty", (1992) vol. 29:6 *Common Market Law Review* 1079-1105); this idea is discussed further below in the context of exclusive and concurrent powers.

[5]   See for example, Cass, "The word that saves Maastricht?", pp. 1110-1128, Constantin-esco, "Who's afraid of subsidiarity?", pp. 42-49 and G.A. Berman, "Taking subsidiarity seriously: Federalism in the European Community and the United States", (1994) 94 *Columbia Law Review*, 331-456 at 342.

[6]   Now Article 174(4) EC.

[7]   It has also been argued that there were tacit references to subsidiarity in the Treaty of Rome: see note 5. Article 130r(4) EEC provided that "[t]he Community shall take action relating to the environment to the extent to which the objectives referred to in [this provision] can be attained better at Community level than at the level of the individual Member States...." This paragraph was not retained in Article 130r (now 174) EC as amended by the TEU; the phrase '[w]ithin their respective spheres of competence' is used in Article 174(4), on the development of cooperation with third countries and competent international organisations.

competence.[8] This can be better appreciated against the background of then prevailing Christian Democratic ideology which, adapting the tenets of Catholic philosophy, focused on the auxiliary role of higher authorities in the specific context of the welfare state. One of the primary characteristics of the Christian Democratic view of subsidiarity was the temporary duration of its legitimate application: Community intervention was seen a dynamic concept, valid but ephemeral. In terms of taking decisions 'close' to the citizen, Christian Democratic ideology focuses on assisting the weaker groups in society and, significantly, on the achievement and maintenance of a pluralist or diverse society. The 1975 Report delimited the competence of an envisaged new entity—a 'European Union'—in accordance with a *principe de subsidiarité*. It was envisaged that the 'union' would act as lawmaker only where individual Member State action would not yield optimum efficiency, or where centralised policies were necessary to ensure cohesion. The architecture of the proposed union differed from Christian Democratic theory in one crucial respect: subsidiarity, as outlined in the Report, was not envisaged as a dynamic or guiding concept, but was presented as a more static formula applicable only at the initial allocation of union/Member State competence. This divergence reflects the influence of federal theory, particularly German federalism. The German approach to subsidiarity is more acutely concerned with the idea that decisions be taken at lower levels of authority where appropriate. More specifically, the German *Länder* feared that the autonomy of sub-national authorities would not respected within new European developments.[9] While a strict application of the German construction would not have been appropriate given the inherently dynamic character of European integration, certain characteristics of the proposed union did reflect that approach. It was intended, for example, that a new treaty would ratify an 'Act of Constitution' as the legal basis of the union.[10] Union competence could be exclusive, concurrent or potential and, crucially, would be specified as such in the Act. The principle of subsidiarity would be relevant to concurrent competence *i.e.* where both the union and the Member States had competence to act, but the union would actually act in accordance with subsidiarity where collective intervention was deemed more efficient or appropriate in light of the objectives to be achieved. It should be stressed that whether an area of competence was exclusive or concurrent would

---

[8] EC Bulletin Supp. 5/75, especially pp. 10-11.

[9] The relevant provisions of the Basic Law of Germany are Articles 72-74, which set out the legislative competence of the *Länder* and *Bund* respectively; in particular, Article 72GG outlines limits on the legislative capacity of the *Bund*.

[10] See Toth, "The principle of subsidiarity", pp. 1088-9.

already have been set out in the proposed treaty, in line with a federal application of subsidiarity. Thus, competing ideologies had been shrewdly incorporated into the Community perspective on the principle *ab initio*, confirming the elasticity already exhibited in its philosophical and religious origins. This evolution continued with the European Parliament's Draft Treaty on European Union, in 1984.[11] But by now, earlier emphasis on the principle's 'widening' capacity had shifted rather subtly towards its alternative 'limiting' facility, setting hurdles to centralised policy-making. Once again, the Draft Treaty viewed the proposed union as an entirely new legal entity, replacing the existing Communities; again, it was envisaged that a constitutional act would set out precisely the competence of the union and of its Member States, and competence was classified as either exclusive or concurrent. But the Draft Treaty did not contain any 'lists' of powers, as intended in the 1975 Report; instead, the nature of competence was clearly and individually outlined for each area of legislative activity identified therein. The first explicit reference to subsidiarity is in the Preamble, where it was noted that the institutions of the Union would be attributed "...in accordance with the principle of subsidiarity, with those powers required to complete successfully the tasks they may carry out more successfully than the states acting independently." Article 12 then provided as follows:

> Where this Treaty confers exclusive competence on the Union ...national authorities may only legislate to the extent laid down by the law of the Union.... The Union shall only act to carry out those tasks which may be undertaken more effectively in common than by the Member States acting separately, in particular those whose execution requires action by the Union because their dimension or effects extend beyond national frontiers. A law which initiates or extends common action in a field where action has not been taken hitherto by the Union or by the Communities must be adopted in accordance with the procedure for organic laws.

Thus, Article 12 codified specific guidelines for the application of subsidiarity in the new union, including 'effectiveness' and 'dimension or effects' tests. In many ways, however, Article 12 raised more questions than it answered. Who exactly would determine these criteria? Would the principle be justiciable? Moreover, the previously central 'close to the citizen' benchmark was not prioritised. Sub-national authorities were not mentioned,

---

[11]   Adopted 14 February 1984, [1984] OJ C77/33.

initiating the assumption that in the new union, the entities 'closest' to citizens were the Member States. This interpretation is at variance with the intentions of those who had proposed the codification of subsidiarity in the first place, yet had been anticipated and challenged by the *Common Market Law Review* in 1990:

> In the discussions between Brussels and the capitals of the [Member States], the question is usually whether a given matter should be governed by Community or national legislation. It is always implicitly assumed in this respect that governmental rules and regulations are in fact necessary. However, this is by no means always clearly the case. It must first be asked whether a given matter cannot be left to the private sphere *i.e.* to the individual, the family, firms, trade unions, associations and co-operatives.[12]

The Draft Treaty was, of course, never ratified; as seen in Chapter 1, the Member States were simply not ready for such a drastic acceleration in the process of European integration. At that time, a reformulated version of neo-functionalist integration theory was dominant; significantly, this coincides to a large extent with the supremacy of a third ideology of subsidiarity *i.e.* as a counter-centralist theory, usually associated with British Conservatism. This approach differs from that of the German federalists in that it does not focus on sub-national authorities versus *any* higher authority level, but on the sovereignty of Member States in the Community institutional context; any assumption of inevitable or automatic integration not founded on a negotiated treaty framework is anathema and EC intervention is justifiable only where efficiency and transnational or cross-border concerns clearly merit collective action (essentially, measures based on the traditional 'four freedoms' of the internal market).

Thus, diverse ideological bases have shaped the origins of subsidiarity in Community law. The notion that subsidiarity can mean all things to all people had become entrenched in EC relations so it is hardly surprising that it holds a reputation as a 'double-edged sword'.[13] In any event, the frame-work documents noted (1975 Commission Report, 1984 Draft Treaty) had contemplated an entirely different model of integration than that which has been achieved in practice. In that sense, it is misleading to think of Article 5 EC as the culmination of a coherent process. The inherent ambiguity of the

---

[12] (1990) Editorial Comments, p. 182.

[13] See Theodor Schilling, "A new dimension of subsidiarity: Subsidiarity as a rule and a principle", (1994) 14 *Yearbook of European Law*, 203-256 at 205.

principle paved the way for an arguably lowest common denominator settlement at Maastricht, a sort of consolation prize to reassure Member States that their sovereignty was not being swallowed up by the fact of enhanced integration. Even before this, however, the association of subsidiarity with environmental policy in the SEA established a potentially ominous precedent, with Member States retaining a substantial degree of control over controversial Community competences *after* the fact of their incorporation into the treaty framework. This holds true perhaps even more for the 'new' TEU policy domains, including culture. Finally, two further characteristics of 'Community subsidiarity' can be traced to the 'better attainment' test enunciated originally in Article 130r(4) EEC: first, establishing this criterion is necessarily a value judgment not always susceptible to objective review and, second, its application to environmental policy *per se* implies a strong presumption of a transnational or cross-boundary justification for Community action.

(ii)   Subsidiarity and the EC Treaty

The Conclusions of the 1992 Edinburgh summit describe subsidiarity as a 'basic principle of the European Union'.[14] This was first codified in Community law via the Maastricht Treaty. The preamble to the TEU characterises the Union as "…[continuing] the process of creating an ever closer union among the peoples of Europe, in which decisions are taken as closely as possible to the citizen in accordance with the principle of subsidiarity…." This objective is reiterated in Article 1 (formerly A) TEU, while Article 2 (formerly B) provides that "[t]he objectives of the Union shall be achieved as provided in this Treaty and in accordance with the conditions and the timetable set out therein while respecting the principle of subsidiarity as defined in Article 5 of the [EC Treaty]."[15] The construction of

---

[14]   European Council, *Conclusions of the Presidency*, (Edinburgh Summit, December 1992), (hereafter 'Edinburgh Conclusions'), Annex 1, Part A, Bull.EC 12-1992, p. 3.

[15]   Article 5 deals with the respective competence of the *Community* and the Member States; it is unlikely that it applies in the Union context. Article 2 TEU is more likely intended as a statement of principle more than one of practice (but see Toth, "The principle of subsidiarity", pp. 1086-7). Furthermore, Article 46 (formerly L) TEU provides that the jurisdiction of the Court of Justice does not extend to the TEU preamble, or *inter alia* to Title I TEU, supporting the conclusion that the TEU references to subsidiarity are declarations of principle rather than clear legal statements (although as tools of interpretation, constitutional principles of this nature can have indirect legal significance—see Nicolas Bernard, "The future of European economic law in light of the principle of subsidiarity", (1996) vol. 33:4 *Common Market Law Review*, 633-666 at 634).

'close to the citizen' does not necessarily imply that decisions should be taken by sub-national authorities where possible, as advocated within federal ideology. Instead, as traced above, the phrase has, rightly or wrongly, become equated with the Member States. This was arguably confirmed by the European Council, concluding that "[subsidiarity] contributes to the respect for the *national* identities of Member States and safeguards their powers."[16] Article 5 EC is the key exponent of subsidiarity in Community law and provides as follows:

> The Community shall act within the limits of the powers conferred upon it by this Treaty and of the objectives assigned to it therein.

> In areas which do not fall within its exclusive competence, the Community shall take action, in accordance with the principle of subsidiarity, only if and in so far as the objectives of the proposed action cannot be sufficiently achieved by the Member States and can, therefore, by reason of the scale or effects of the proposed action, be better achieved by the Community.

> Any action by the Community shall not go beyond what is necessary to achieve the objectives of this Treaty.

This provision is generally assumed to reflect a deliberately intended bias towards Member State action where there is uncertainty over EC/Member State capacity to act. The fact that specific criteria are outlined, such as 'scale or effects', implies that the Community must justify any intended action for policy areas in which it does not have exclusive competence; in turn, this implies that Member State action is *prima facie* legitimate. But this too is open to interpretation. And despite underlying intentions, Article 5 may in fact *require* as well as permit Community intervention where certain criteria are met. These ambiguities reinforce the perception of subsidiarity as

---

[16]   Edinburgh Conclusions, p. 1 (emphasis added); but see Chapters 1 and 3 on the possibility of more teleological interpretations of 'national' in this context. Regarding minority languages specifically, Temple summarises that "[a]lthough subsidiarity taken to its logical conclusion might have helped some regional languages, the interpretation favoured by the British Government (that is, the 'devolution' of power to Member State governments) and which is no doubt supported by...other...governments, could have serious consequences for the languages spoken in states...where the government is not particularly sympathetic to their lot." (Rosalind M. Temple, "Great expectations? Hopes and fears about the implications of political developments in Western Europe for the future of France's regional languages", in M.M. Parry, W.V. Davies and R.A.M. Temple, *The Changing Voice of Europe*, (Cardiff: University of Wales Press, 1994), 191-211 at 204. This theme is discussed in more detail below.

an ideologically interchangeable concept, with both centralising and decentralising potential. These divergent views are even more apparent when legal and political interpretations of the principle are contrasted. Essentially, politicians have steadfastly promoted subsidiarity as a legal norm, while lawyers have been far less convinced of its capacity as such. In the political context, subsidiarity has been associated with Article 6(3) TEU, as an additional safeguard for national identity. The difficulty with this approach is that it contradicts the ethos of Community intervention in the first place, which strives to transcend national boundaries. Obviously, collective action should be undertaken taken only where warranted and subsidiarity has a feasible role to play in this context; but artificial or regressive manipulation of principles can only serve to weaken their effect, especially where such orchestration is based primarily on an attempt to evade the legitimate effects of Community law more generally.[17] The legal construction accorded to subsidiarity is set out below, but first, it is necessary to break down Article 5 EC because, in addition to an expression of subsidiarity, the provision contains two other—distinct—general principles of Community law: the attribution of powers and the principle of proportionality.[18] The first sentence of Article 5 provides that '[t]he Community shall act within the limits of the powers conferred upon it by this Treaty and of the objectives assigned to it therein', expressing one version of a circular argument: alternatively, it could be stated that if an objective has been assigned to the Community, then the Community must have the requisite power to achieve it. Thus, 'power' refers to a treaty-based sanction for EC action. In practice, however, the attribution of powers is somewhat more complicated. This can be ascribed to the nature of Community law generally and to the diversity of substance in treaty provisions, which are not drafted in as precise a manner as those of, for example, federal constitutions. The distinction between exclusive and concurrent competences is discussed further below, and for present purposes, it is sufficient to distinguish between the attribution of powers and the principle of subsidiarity. Articles 2 and 3 EC contain lists of activities for the Community but these provisions do not of themselves constitute legal bases

---

[17] Note, for example, the tone of this extract from *The Economist*, (11 July 1992): "[t]he true worth of the principle [of subsidiarity] will be known only once some busybody Directive has been challenged in the European Court and the judges have ruled on where Brussels stops and nations are to be left alone." (quoted in Nicholas Emiliou, "Subsidiarity: Panacea or fig leaf?" in David O'Keeffe and Patrick Twomey (eds.), *Legal Issues of the Maastricht Treaty of the Maastricht Treaty*, (London: Chancery, 1994), 65-83 at 77).

[18] On the general principles of EC law generally, see Takis Tridimas, *The General Principles of EC Law*, (Oxford: Clarendon Press, 1999) and John A. Usher, *General Principles of EC Law*, (London: Longman, 1998).

for EC action; legal basis is ascertained from subsequent, more detailed treaty provisions. In practical terms, the Community institutions are required to assess draft legislative measures against the boundaries of Community powers and this examination "...should establish the objective to be achieved and whether it can be justified in relation to an objective of the Treaty and that the necessary legal basis for its adoption exists."[19] In accordance with Article 253 EC, measures adopted must set out 'the reasons on which they are based'; moreover, the Court of Justice has the power to annul a measure where an inadequate explanation of its legal basis has been given. Two further Treaty provisions are relevant to the attribution of Community powers. First, Article 10 EC provides that:

> Member States shall take all appropriate measures, whether general or particular, to ensure fulfilment of the obligations arising out of this Treaty or resulting from action taken by the institutions of the Community. They shall facilitate the achievement of the Community's tasks.

> They shall abstain from any measure which could jeopardise the attainment of the objectives of this Treaty.

Member State duties that have been grounded in this provision include the obligation on Member States to give full effect to Community law, to implement Community objectives, to co-operate with Community institutions to this end and to co-operate with the other Member States.[20] The European Council has declared that Member State duties under Article 10 EC cannot be called into question by the principle of subsidiarity.[21] Thus, even where Community action is precluded by Article 5, the Member States themselves are still required to fulfil the Treaty obligation in question, a dictum reinforced in the EC Treaty protocol. Second, as introduced in Chapter 3, Article 308 EC provides as follows:

> If action by the Community should prove necessary to attain, in the course of the operation of the common market, one of the objectives of the Community and this Treaty has not provided the necessary powers, the Council shall, acting unanimously on a proposal from the Commission and after consulting the European Parliament, take the appropriate measures.

---

[19] Edinburgh Conclusions, p. 6.

[20] See John Temple Lang. "Community constitutional law: Article 5 EEC Treaty", (1990) vol. 27:4 *Common Market Law Review* 645-681.

[21] Edinburgh Conclusions, p. 4.

But Article 308, referring only to powers required specifically for the achievement of the common market, addresses the need to sanction *additional* Community competence, while subsidiarity is concerned with the power to act where competence *already* exists. The provision does highlight procedures for the attribution of competence more generally within the EC structure, however; essentially, the Member States retain the power of Treaty amendment and, in this way, govern the ultimate direction of Community policy. Against this background, fears that the Community (or perhaps more specifically, the Commission) has taken on a policy-making life of its own are not quite so straightforward. In practice, it must be conceded that EC policies have often been tacked to ambiguous legal bases, legitimised by Treaty amendments 'after the fact'. Consequently, the initial impetus of co-operation has been somewhat eroded and a feeling of competitiveness between the Member States and their own dynamic creation has surfaced. Indeed, this tension was primarily responsible for the inclusion of subsidiarity in the EC Treaty in the first place.

The third indent of Article 5—'any action by the Community shall not go beyond what is necessary to achieve the objectives of this Treaty'—expresses the principle of proportionality. Once again, the concern here is to differentiate subsidiarity (which relates to the allocation of power to act) from proportionality, which concerns the way in which that power is actually exercised. Furthermore, proportionality applies across the entire range of Community competences and is not confined, like subsidiarity, to concurrent competence only. It is a ubiquitous, long-established and objective Community benchmark, deployed to assess whether measures enacted (or related actions taken) are lawful or excessive, in accordance with other Treaty provisions or principles.[22] Subsidiarity, on the other hand, is an arguably more subjective judgment, in terms of appropriateness and relative efficiency, as to which level of authority should take the action in the first place. Finally, proportionality is largely operative in the sphere of claims made by natural or legal persons, while subsidiarity pertains more inevitably to relations between the Member States and the EC. The 1992 Edinburgh guidelines on the application of both proportionality and subsidiarity have now been effectively reincarnated as a Protocol to the EC Treaty.[23] The

---

[22] See, for example, Case 15/83 *Denkavit* [1984] ECR 2171 at 2175, para. 25: "[b]y virtue of the principle of proportionality, according to well established case law of the Court, measures adopted by Community institutions must not exceed what is appropriate and necessary to attain the objective pursued."

[23] See Edinburgh Conclusions, pp. 8-10; see also, the EC Treaty Protocol on the Application of the Principles of Subsidiarity and Proportionality.

Protocol establishes that burdens (whether financial or administrative) associated with the implementation of Community law should be minimised, and must be proportionate to the objective to be achieved (paragraph 8). Furthermore, Community measures should 'leave as much scope for national decision as possible, consistent with securing the aim of the measure and observing the requirements of the Treaty', by providing Member States 'with alternative ways to achieve the objectives of the measures' (paragraph 7). The Protocol advocates the use of directives over regulations, and framework directives instead of detailed measures, where appropriate.[24] These guidelines demonstrate the fine line between proportionality and subsidiarity.[25] But it is important to bear in mind while the three principles contained in Article 5 EC are obviously interrelated, their application relates to fundamentally distinct aspects of both the allocation and exercise of competence.

Prior to the adoption of the Maastricht Treaty, an Interim Report on behalf of the Committee for Institutional Affairs noted that "...clarity with regard to the division of competences...of the Union [is] dependent on subsidiarity."[26] But it is really more correct to say that the application of subsidiarity is dependent on clarity in respect of competence division. And there exists considerable disagreement over this fundamental point of Community law. In any case, the principle of subsidiarity is contained in the second indent of Article 5: "[i]n areas which do not fall within its exclusive competence, the Community shall take action, in accordance with the principle of subsidiarity, only if and in so far as the objectives of the proposed action cannot be sufficiently achieved by the Member States and can, therefore, by reason of the scale or effects of the proposed action, be better achieved by the Community." This phrase generates an assumption that Community powers are distinguishable as being either exclusive or non-exclusive/concurrent. But an explicit distinction to this effect is not set out in *any* provision of the EC Treaty. The resulting debate on the exact nature of Community competence is thus both conflicting and persistent. As noted earlier, subsidiarity is usually associated with allocating competence in a federal system where the division of powers is clearly outlined in a written

---

[24] The role of the Community had been characterised by the European Council in terms of 'encouragement' and 'coordination', 'complementing' and 'supporting' Member State action (Edinburgh Conclusions, p. 9).

[25] Toth goes so far as to say that the European Council had itself confused the two principles (A.G. Toth, "A legal analysis of subsidiarity", in O'Keeffe and Twomey (eds.), *Legal Issues of the Maastricht Treaty*, 37-48 at 38.)

[26] PE Doc. A3-163/90, 22 June 1990, para. 6.

constitution or similar legal act. The desirability of adopting an act of that kind in the Community context has been called into question, since its rigidity might "...tie the hands of the Community unduly."[27] As noted, however, a 'more precise' delimitation of competence has been put on the agenda for IGC 2004.

As stressed throughout, subsidiarity neither extends nor restricts *competence*; rather, it determines the distribution of functions. So, in reality, a preliminary concern must be to define exclusive/concurrent competence; the appropriate actor can then be determined either independently (exclusive competence) or by means of (concurrent competence) the tests outlined in Article 5. Academic opinion on the character of exclusive competence is divided. Does it refer to competences granted to the EC by the original Treaty of Rome?[28] Was Article 130r(4) EEC the first example of concurrent competence? There is a basic level of agreement that core EC policy areas generate exclusive Community competence *i.e.* where centralised responsibility for collective action is essential to the implementation of common laws and standards. Although not defined in the Treaty as such, the exclusive character of Community competence is generally determined by the wording of the relevant provisions and, more precisely, by the type of legal measures which the Community institutions may adopt (where specified). The doctrine of exhaustiveness is also relevant here; it is a distinct concept but its effects are similar from the Member State perspective. Exhaustiveness means that even where treaty provisions have not implied exclusive Community competence, the EC legislation actually enacted leaves no room for any further regulation, by either the Member States *or* the Community.[29] Exhaustiveness is not, therefore, concerned with which level of authority *may* act: rather, it hinges on the fact that, in practical terms, neither level *can* act. A related issue is the sphere of exclusive Member State competence *i.e.* where matters are strictly internal and have

---

[27] Temple Lang, "What powers should the European Community have?" (1995) vol. 1:1 *European Public Law*, 97-116 at 103; conversely, Peterson notes that in more typical or traditional federal structures, such as Germany and the United States, "[t]he balance of power between the states and the centre...has never been static, predetermined or uncontroversial...[B]oth countries have been marked by far more concerns about the proper division of powers between the states and the centre than exists in Europe today...." (John Peterson, "Subsidiarity: A definition to suit any vision?", (1994) vol. 47:1 *Parliamentary Affairs*, 116-132 at 127.)

[28] See Toth, "The Principle of Subsidiarity", p. 1081 *et seq*; Schilling argues to the contrary (see "A new dimension", p. 219 *et seq.*)

[29] See Case 237/82 *Jongeneel Kaas*, [1984] ECR 483 at 515-517, paras. 12-16 (opinion of the Advocate General).

not been brought within Community competence, or where competence for implementing a Community objective has been allocated expressly and exclusively to the Member States. In this context, there are fears that Community law is systematically eroding internal policy fields, coupled with hopes that subsidiarity will somehow defend and preserve the realm of national competence;[30] this aspiration is, however, based on a fundamental misunderstanding of *when* subsidiarity is relevant in the competence division process. The phrase 'concurrent competence', on the other hand, is itself somewhat misleading, as it implies that the Community and the Member States are free to act simultaneously and with equal authority.[31] In any case, it is perhaps more widely agreed that the Maastricht provisions outlining 'new' EC policy areas—including Article 151 EC—are certainly intended instances of 'concurrent' or shared EC/Member State competence, to which the principle of subsidiarity can be applied. The substantive issues raised as a result will now be set out.

B.   Applying Article 5: Tests and Criteria

Article 5 EC establishes that for any policy area to which it applies (*i.e.* excepting areas of exclusive competence), Community action is justifiable where 'the objectives of the proposed action cannot be sufficiently achieved by the Member States and can, therefore, by reason of the scale or effects of the proposed action, be better achieved by the Community.' It has been argued that the wording of the paragraph ('...therefore...by reason of...') indicates that the 'sufficiently achieved' and 'scale or effects' criteria are cumulative.[32] This means that whether or not Community action is required by reason of necessity can only be established by first judging whether the objective can or cannot be sufficiently achieved by the Member States. If it

---

[30]   Schilling has referred to subsidiarity as "...an additional exit possibility..." ("A new dimension", p. 232).

[31]   For a range of views on the extent to which Member States may act in an area of 'concurrent competence', contrast Temple Lang, "What powers?", p. 99 and Nicholas Emiliou, "Subsidiarity: Panacea or fig leaf?" in O'Keeffe and Twomey (eds.), *Legal Issues of the Maastricht Treaty of the Maastricht Treaty*, 65-83 at 68, with Jo Steiner, "Subsidiarity under the Maastricht Treaty", in O'Keeffe and Twomey (eds.), *Legal Issues of the Maastricht Treaty of the Maastricht Treaty*, 49-64 at 58. The principle of the 'occupied field' or doctrine of pre-emption is relevant also here; see Case 20/70 *Commission v. Council* [1971] ECR 263 at 275.

[32]   See Virginia Harrison, "Subsidiarity in Article 3b of the EC Treaty: Gobbledegook or justiciable principle?", (1996) vol. 45:2 *International and Comparative Law Quarterly*, 431-439 at 433.

cannot, then the 'scale or effects' test comes into play. The priorities of the Member States and of the Community are often graded as competing interests. Conflicting views on whether stated objectives can be 'sufficiently achieved' at one level of authority or the other are thus inevitable, and far from objective. The 'scale or effects' condition is usually taken to imply that an objective must have a cross-border or transnational dimension before Community action can be justified. But even then, it cannot be assumed that EC legislation is *automatically* warranted; it must first be shown that Member State action cannot 'sufficiently achieve' the objective in question. It may be significant that the phrase does not read '*has* not sufficiently achieved'; the fact that Member States have not already attained the objective in question could not (arguably) be used to justify Community intervention, so that potential as well as proven capacity might determine the necessity test from the Member State perspective. Accordingly, even where an objective has a transnational dimension, the tests outlined in Article 5 still produce a clear bias in favour of Member State action. And if these two strands are problematic even on an individual basis, their combined effect will not always produce a logical result.[33] The European Council attempted to provide some clarity in this context and, as noted, the conclusions arrived at now form the basis of a protocol to the EC Treaty; the guidelines contained therein are considered below, in respect of the specific application of subsidiarity to Article 151 EC.

The extent to which subsidiarity was intended to be justiciable was not clear initially: did the Court of Justice have jurisdiction to strike down a measure of Community law on the grounds that the measure infringed Article 5 EC?[34] The principal objection here was that this would necessarily involve the Court in overtly political assessments, a function more correctly left to the legislative institutions. This view is typified by the following

---

[33] Toth has devised a pragmatic example to illustrate this point, showing that there can be different answers to the 'sufficiently achieved' and 'scale or effects' tests where Community action would be justifiable in terms of effectiveness and enforcement, but the scale of the problem is negligible in the broader European context: see "The principle of subsidiarity", p. 1098.

[34] Subsidiarity could be referred to in the existing procedures for judicial review of Community acts *i.e.* direct actions initiated in the Court of Justice and preliminary rulings via Article 234 (formerly 177) EC. A direct action based on Article 230 (formerly 173) EC involves the annulment of a measure on the grounds that it exceeds the Community's powers, subject to limitations on standing. Other possibilities include actions for damages under Articles 235 and 288(2) (formerly (178 and 215(2)) EC. An action may also be taken against a Member State by the Commission (Article 226 (formerly 169) EC) or by another Member State (Article 227 (formerly 170) EC).

extract from a 1990 report of the House of Lords Select Committee on the European Communities:

> [S]ubsidiarity [cannot] be used as a precise measure against which to judge legislation. The test of subsidiarity can never be wholly objective or consistent over time—different people regard collective action as more effective than individual action in different circumstances...[T]o leave legislation open to annulment or revision by the European Court on such subjective grounds would lead to immense confusion and uncertainty in Community law...The principle [should] be kept clearly in the minds of those who formulate Community legislation. But this should not be done so as to open the way to pointless litigation after the Council or the Commission have acted.[35]

Others had argued, however, that presumptions of this kind underestimated both the capacity and credibility of the Court in the application of general principles of Community law.[36] An intermediate proposition was that the Court should confine its analysis of EC measures in this context to assessing whether an issue fell within exclusive Community competence or not.[37] In any case, the European Council guidelines stated unambiguously that "...interpretation of the principle, as well as review of compliance with it by the Community institutions are subject to control by the Court of Justice, as far as matters falling within the [EC Treaty] are concerned."[38] The EC Treaty protocol, while reaffirming that the Edinburgh guidelines continue to apply,

---

[35] House of Lords Select Committee on the European Communities, *Report on Economic & Monetary and Political Union*, Session 1989-90, 27th Report (London: HMSO, 1990), p. 55.

[36] See for example, Steiner, "Subsidiarity under the Maastricht Treaty", p. 62; Leon Brittan, "Institutional development of the European Community", (1992) *Public Law*, 567-579 at 569; Dominik Lasok, "Subsidiarity and the occupied field", (1992) 142 *New Law Journal*, 1228-1230 at 1229. On the principle of subsidiarity and the Court of Justice more generally, see Gráinne de Búrca, "The principle of subsidiarity and the Court of Justice as an institutional actor", (1998) vol. 36:2 *Journal of Common Market Studies* 217-235, who argues (at 217) that "...the Court is regularly confronted, in its decision-making capacity, with interpretative choices which have considerable policy implications, and that while its role is not to be equated with that of the other political institutions, it is an EU actor with a significant degree of normative influence and autonomy...."

[37] See for example, Toth, "The principle of subsidiarity", p. 1102; see also Toth, "Is subsidiarity justiciable?", (1994) 19 *European Law Review* 268-285.

[38] Edinburgh Conclusions, p. 4; the European Parliament had observed that "[j]udicial guarantees must be given with regard to respect for the principle of subsidiarity." (Resolution on the Principle of Subsidiarity, 12 July 1990, [1990] OJ C231/163).

states simply (at paragraph 13) that "[c]ompliance with the principle of subsidiarity shall be reviewed in accordance with the rules laid down by the Treaty." It has been suggested that the cases to date in which subsidiarity has been raised indicate that the Court "...will not lightly overturn Community action on the ground that it does not comply with Article 5."[39] The European Council envisaged roles for all of the institutions in the practical implementation of subsidiarity, but foresaw a 'crucial role' for the Commission in particular, given its power of initiative regarding EC legislation.[40] It is difficult to quantify the effect subsidiarity has actually had on policy initiative in practice. It is often felt that the principle has generated more hot air than anything else, and that its impact in reality is negligible. The Commission's annual report to the European Council on "Better Lawmaking" does not really provide much clarity;[41] the Commission has asserted here that it 'endeavours to apply scrupulously the principles of subsidiarity and proportionality', yet while it refers to the codification of the principles via the Amsterdam Protocol, it urges that both should 'remain evolutionary and dynamic principles, flexible to apply and pragmatic'. But 'flexibility' of interpretation introduces the risk that subsidiarity could be employed arbitrarily; this is discussed further below, and in Chapter 6 regarding the self-censorship undertaken by the Commission on the ambit of its minority language initiatives.

C.   Conclusion

Article 5 has been associated with confusion far more than it has with clarity and it is invariably tempting to write subsidiarity off as an ongoing storm in a political teacup. Perhaps the principal misconception is that it could somehow have solved the political dilemma which caused its introduction into EC law in the first place. The elasticity of the concept lends itself to multiple interpretations, and the holders of every view are wholly convinced that the principle will protect their interests above all competing concerns. Even the Commission has acknowledged the obscurity of the doctrine, stating in plain terms that subsidiarity may not work in practice simply

---

[39]   Paul Craig and Gráinne de Búrca, *EU Law: Text, Cases and Materials*, 2nd ed., (Oxford: OUP, 1998), p. 129, referring to Case C-233/94 *Germany v. European Parliament and Council* [1997] ECR I-2405 and Case C-84/94 *United Kingdom v. Council* [1996] ECR I-5755; see also de Búrca, "The principle of subsidiarity".

[40]   See Edinburgh Conclusions, Annex I, Part III.

[41]   See in particular, *Better Lawmaking 1998: A shared responsibility*, (1998) COM (98) 715 (previous reports are cited in footnote 1 therein).

because each Member State has its own entrenched view of what the principle actually means.[42] It is difficult to gauge its impact in reality, given that its bearing is most likely to be felt at the (not readily quantifiable) stages of negotiation and deliberation. Nonetheless, the very fact of its existence in the EC Treaty means that its potential cannot be ignored and so subsidiarity is something of a looming spectre in EC law. This concern is particularly apt in the context of minority language policy—given the enduring political sensitivity associated with language issues generally, it is entirely possible that the manipulation of subsidiarity will prove crucial here. The following paragraphs introduce the types of questions that will have to be asked where Article 151 EC is used as a legal basis for enhanced Community action in this field, a possibility not only likely but, in light of *Arcipelago-Archipel*, necessary at the behest of the Commission itself.

3.   ARTICLE 151 AND THE APPLICATION OF SUBSIDIARITY

It has always been recognised, not least by the EC institutions, that the application of subsidiarity requires the determination of vague and ambiguous criteria. In response, various guidelines—official and otherwise —have been published over the years. This section details some of these frameworks, and tests the development of language policy under Article 151 against the various standards cited. The overriding limitations identified in Chapter 3 apply throughout, however: first, language policy is being considered equally as an aspect of the general objectives outlined in Article 151(1), since Article 151(2) may be prohibitively narrow; second, the role of the Community is limited to that of 'contributor'; and finally, only incentive measures and recommendations may be enacted.

A.   Early Predictions

In 1990, before the adoption of the Maastricht Treaty, the *Common Market Law Review* anticipated the formal introduction of subsidiarity into Community law.[43] The analysis put forward was based on a traditional, ecclesiastical interpretation of the principle, as well as on Article 12 of the 1984 Draft Treaty and Article 130r(4) EEC. Pooling these sources, a

---

[42]   See Gráinne de Búrca, "The quest for legitimacy in the European Union", (1996) vol. 59:3 *Modern Law Review*, 349-376 at 366.

[43]   Editorial Comments, (1990) vol. 27:2 *Common Market Law Review* 181-184.

sequence for the application of subsidiarity was suggested. The first step was ascertaining whether the objective in question should be dealt with by the private or public sector. It was advocated that 'maximum leeway' be given to the private sphere; issues should be tackled by public authorities only where absolutely necessary. Where the need for government action *was* established, the appropriate level of authority had then to be resolved—local, regional or central government within a state, Community intervention where greater efficiency was at issue. Where domestic action was justified, the level of authority should be chosen in accordance with national rules, without any external interference. Action taken at Community level should be minimal, leaving the 'maximum amount of room to manoeuvre to the Member States'.[44] On the whole, this approach is faithful to the ecclesiastical notion of subsidiarity. It does not presume that official action is desirable. And even where this can be established, a broad interpretation of 'official' is applied, identifying the many strands of authority on hand. From the perspective of language policy, it is likely that this would have been welcomed by minority language groups, since it attributes to them a degree of responsibility for their own fate. In practice, however, it has been more usual to supplant national government or EC measures instead of allocating competence to subsidiary groups and regional bodies. Besides, the range of action that may be taken at regional level is usually determined by higher levels of authority in the first place; and if a national government is unreceptive to minority language claims at any rate, it not likely to grant far-reaching powers to regional bodies to this end. The Community may yet play an enabling role here, establishing minimum but effective policy guidelines that take due account of national *and* sub-national diversity; the express recognition of regional as well as national cultures in Article 151(1) lends credence to this assertion. Focusing on incentive measures of this kind also fits with Article 151(5). But it must be borne in mind that the *Common Market Law Review* comments were not actually based on Article 5 EC, and that the role of sub-national authorities has been of far less (legal) significance in reality. Finally, the recently evolving and somewhat controversial stance of the Court of Justice on regional language arrangements, discussed in Chapter 6, will need to be borne in mind here.

---

[44]   *ibid.*, p. 183.

B.   Official Guidelines: The Edinburgh Summit and Amsterdam Protocol

Even after the content of Article 5 was settled, possible difficulties with its implementation were already foreseen at the Lisbon Summit, in June 1992. The European Council called on the Commission and Council to provide clarification, and to report at the Edinburgh Summit in December of that year. As noted above, the Edinburgh Conclusions set out the basic characteristics of Community subsidiarity, detailing both its legal significance and likely impact on the workings of the institutions. The idea of taking decisions 'as closely as possible to the citizens' was mentioned briefly, in conjunction with what was then Article A (now 1) TEU, but the document dealt almost exclusively with the concepts enshrined in Article 5 EC. It was stated that the Council must be satisfied that *both* aspects of the subsidiarity test are fulfilled *i.e.* that 'the objectives of the proposed action cannot be sufficiently achieved by Member State action', and that they can *therefore* be better achieved by the Community.[45] In order to determine precisely when EC intervention is justifiable, three alternative but complementary benchmarks were outlined:

- the issue has transnational aspects that cannot be regulated satisfactorily by the Member States, and/or,

- Member State action alone, or the absence of Community action, would conflict with Treaty requirements or otherwise 'significantly damage' Member State interests, and/or,

- the Council is satisfied that Community action would produce clear benefits, in light of the scale or effects of the proposed action, compared to what could be accomplished by Member State action alone.

It was stipulated that the 'better achieved' test should be substantiated by qualitative and, where possible, quantitative indicators. Finally, a preference for minimum harmonisation was stressed. As already noted, the spirit—and more often than not, the letter—of the Edinburgh guidelines was codified as a Protocol to the EC Treaty, appended via the Amsterdam Treaty.

It cannot be taken for granted that EC intervention is the automatic response where Member State action is perceived to be inadequate. It was noted above that Article 5 creates a significant presumption in favour of Member State measures; as a result, action aiming towards a Community

---

[45]   Edinburgh Conclusions, Part II, pp. 6-7.

solution even to the *Community* dimension of language shift needs to be advanced to rebut this presumption. The dynamics of European integration have affected and will continue to affect language patterns throughout the Member States. It has been argued that there is an economic as well as moral significance to language issues; so quite apart from the implications for concepts like fundamental rights and citizenship, even practical and economic concerns mean that language matters cannot be managed sufficiently by national action alone. The three guidelines developed at Edinburgh are reproduced in the Protocol but without the 'and/or' formulation, giving the impression that now, all three must be fulfilled collectively. The existence of minority language groups throughout the Member States satisfies the requirement that a proposed measure must have a transnational aspect and, in some cases, there are cross-border elements also (*e.g.* Basque speakers in both France and Spain; Irish speakers in Ireland and in Northern Ireland). Again, it cannot be assumed that transnational and/or cross-border concerns *must* be regulated by the Community. But minority languages are rarely a priority on the domestic political agenda. The indifference of the majority of Member States to the Charter for Regional or Minority Languages—which outlines entitlements for speakers yet ensures that ample discretion remains with the signatory states—supports this contention. The second test is especially ambiguous, containing two alternative yet distinct standards. Community action is justifiable where its absence would either conflict with the requirements of the Treaty *or* significantly damage Member State interests. The Protocol provides examples of 'Treaty requirements'—the 'need to correct distortion of competition or avoid disguised restrictions on trade or strengthen economic and social cohesion'. The second consideration, that of significant damage to Member State interests, is more elusive. At face value, it seems erroneous that Community action in pursuit of an objective incorporated into the Treaty by the Member States themselves would in turn be employed to 'damage' Member State interests. Why would the Member States sanction a Treaty objective without ever intending that Community action could be undertaken in consequence? This scenario feeds into a deceptive image of the Community as an autonomous polity entirely free of restraints which, in the context of culture, basically ignores the stringent unanimity requirement in Article 151(5). The concept of 'significant damage' is grounded in the cautionary ideology of subsidiarity itself; its resolution involves a subjective, political assessment that cannot be determined categorically. A danger exists, therefore, that otherwise legitimate Community action could be dismissed on an indeterminate basis. This is particularly plausible in sensitive policy spheres, such as culture and language. On the one hand, a palpable degree of Member State hostility is directed, often defensibly, at Community intrusion into what are regarded as domestic concerns; and this is especially evident when the issue is closely linked to national identity. Member States can also manipulate sovereignty concerns, however, and thus shirk from their own responsibilities as the engineers of the EC Treaty. Certainly, it cannot be denied that the momentum of 'Community' policy-making has taken on, to some extent, an organic momentum of its own; the ongoing and in-depth academic enquiries into supranational integration and intergovernmental decision-making, introduced in Chapter 1, prove conclusive here. The Commission is usually tagged as the 'guilty party' in this context, more often than not assisted ably by the Court of Justice. But, ultimately, the Community does not chart its own course. It is misguided to think otherwise. This idea is explored further in Chapter 5, which charts the eventful evolution of Community fundamental rights protection. In the specific context of language, it could be argued that all linguistic matters are domestic, so that Community action in this field would 'significantly damage' Member State interests from the perspective of national identity, or using the 'closer to the citizen' criterion. The contrary view highlights the Community dimension of language concerns, however, and projects a more realistic vision of contemporary language patterns and interactions.

The concerns raised here tie in, somewhat ironically, with the last test *i.e.* whether Community action would produce clear benefits in consideration of scale and effects. Assessing benefits of this kind is where the application of qualitative and quantitative analysis seems most feasible. But the Council consists of Member State representatives. And if a proposal is perceived to damage Member State interests, it is unlikely that the Council will be prepared to adopt it. If one Member State or a minority of Member States have an objection to proposed measures, they lose out where qualified majority voting is practised. But for Article 151, all Council decisions must be taken unanimously. This proviso is an in-built and arguably legitimate safeguard, but one that should not be used as an incentive to misapply subsidiarity. Interestingly, the proviso that the Council must be satisfied that action at Community level would produce 'clear benefits' has been dropped from the Protocol; although in reality, such decisions do lie, in due course, with that institution. The relationship between the three tests outlined is thus clearly an interdependent one. By developing this sequence of questions, an impression that the application of subsidiarity is a logical, step-by-step procedure has been created. Specifying the desirability of employing quantitative as well as qualitative analysis compounds the illusion. But the answers to the questions posed are more likely to be arrived at by political than practical reflections. Subsidiarity is not a straightforward concept, especially where it is introduced as an ambiguous compromise between fundamentally contentious interests. As in the Community, where the principle is applied on a recurring basis outwith a structure of clearly delimited competences, each and every application will have to be considered on its own facts. That is not the problem here. In reality, it is likely that very little emphasis will be placed on 'facts'. No attempt was made, for example, to define the key phrases, such as 'sufficiently achieved', 'significant damage' or 'clear benefits', or to suggest the issues that ought to be considered in these contexts, leaving remarkable scope for subjectivity, and not a little obscurity.

C.   Elaboration of the EC Criteria: Academic Commentary

The Protocol on the application of subsidiarity animates Article 5 EC to some extent; but there remains ample scope for further clarification. Just what kind of questions should be considered when contemplating, for example, whether the Community or Member States can 'better achieve' a given objective? In contrast to the relatively minimalist guidelines favoured by the European Council, a detailed framework for the application of subsidiarity was later developed by John Temple Lang.[46] His pragmatic approach remains uniquely comprehensive and pragmatic, notwithstanding the vast wealth of literature on subsidiarity referred to throughout this Chapter, and is therefore used as a yardstick here. He does not really address the relative capacity of the Member States to achieve Treaty objectives, but focuses instead on the idea that Community action is 'better' where it:

(1) can go further in the direction desired than national measures could go;

(2) is more efficient or effective;

(3) can do something which states could not achieve at all;

(4) is a necessary basis for common policies;

(5) provides co-ordination of otherwise uncoordinated national measures, where lack of co-ordination would be undesirable;

(6) is needed to facilitate or make possible Community measures on some other point, or to offset the inconvenient effects of

---

[46]   Temple Lang, "What powers?", pp. 110-112.

> Community measures in some way (*e.g.* a cohesion fund is needed to offset ill effects on peripheral regions).[47]

The requirement that Community action must be a 'necessary' basis for common policies reinforces the idea that EC measures are not the inevitable means of implementing Treaty objectives. In the context of culture, encouraging co-ordination to the extent anticipated here may actually contradict the express prohibition on harmonisation in Article 151(5). But co-ordination can also be interpreted broadly—as developed in the context of environmental policy, for example—where the co-ordinated adoption of (initially) basic, minimum standards meant not only that the ensuing obligations were not prohibitive from the Member State perspective but also, that national measures detailing more intensive protection were entirely permissible. Finally, the idea that the EC should develop policies to offset the effects of Community measures on peripheral regions is particularly significant from the perspective of minority language policy.

Temple Lang goes on to formulate eleven questions to determine comprehensively whether Community or Member State action is required. He does not attempt to evade the necessarily subjective nature of subsidiarity, stating plainly that the criteria are of a practical and political rather than legal character. These questions will now be considered individually, in the context of language policy development.

(i) Is the scale of the problem so large that it needs to be tackled by the EC?

In political terms, language rights are rarely a priority, apart from situations that degenerate to more widespread, even militant, disruption. In national terms, the number of speakers of a minority language can range from a limited scattering to millions. But in aggregate terms, more than fifty million European citizens are estimated to speak a language other than those officially recognised by the EC. In addition, the increasing utility of just one or two languages in the Community institutions has accentuated government concern in respect of the 'smaller' official languages. It is surely arguable, then, that in the Community context, the preservation and promotion of minority and other languages, and attending to the corollary needs of their speakers, is a large-scale problem.

---

[47] *ibid.*, p. 110.

(ii)   Is there a substantial impact on cross-border situations and policies?

No EC Member State is classified as absolutely monolingual.[48] And language issues can have cross-border implications. The Court of Justice has assessed the language policy measures of various Member States, for example, in the context of free movement for workers and discrimination against non-nationals.[49] On a more literal interpretation, several language groups span Member State borders. The role of the EC in foreign language teaching programmes and in education more generally is also relevant here, but notwithstanding the promotion of multilingualism as the key to Community movement, this policy area might not always be considered 'substantial' except by those involved directly in language education.

(iii)   Would differences between Member States be inherently inconsistent with the objective?

Article 151 EC provides that the Community must respect the national and regional diversity of its Member States. Differences between Member State policies are not only legitimate, but necessary to secure the effective implementation of language rights; initiatives to promote Gaelic in Scotland, for example, are not going to be comparable with those suitable in respect of the Catalan language. The application of diverse solutions is enhanced by the exclusion of harmonisation in Article 151(5). But the ideology of accepting these differences could inadvertently condone the absence of a basic standard of respect for language rights; the Treaty commitment to respect for cultural diversity could provide some redress in this context.

(iv)   How important economically is the distortion of competition, or the barrier to trade or other problem, which it is intended to eliminate? Will its importance increase or diminish?

While minority language issues do have an economic dimension, the impact on aggregate EC trade is, in a literal sense, arguably negligible. But the various impacts of trade laws are far broader that those which can be

---

[48]   See Appendix II; see also, Alpha Connelly, "The European Convention on Human Rights and the protection of linguistic minorities", (1993) vol. 2:2 *Irish Journal of European Law* 277-293.

[49]   See Chapters 2 and 6.

denominated in monetary terms only. In any event, the existing economic dimension of language policy is certain to increase rather than diminish, in light of the accelerating spread of languages of wider communication. This has two principal effects: first, an increased demand for education and services in the predominant languages and second, a counter-attempt to bolster and promote all other languages, both official and non-official.

(v)   What ill effects will result if no action is taken? Will the ill effects increase over time if not prevented?

To date, the Community has not taken steps to implement the more comprehensive measures in favour of minority languages long proposed by the European Parliament. Recognition of the value of minority languages is freely given, but this usually stops short of taking more substantive action. *Culture 2000* and the expected *Arcipelago-Archipel* programme will govern policy direction for the foreseeable future; both are firmly grounded in consolidation, both of funding and organisation. But the ambitions of and motivations behind EC language policy that have been influential to date will need to be reconsidered. The predominance of one or two languages within the Community institutions and, increasingly, in European society more generally, has accentuated nationalist tensions in the EC power structure. This has often dissuaded Member States from approaching European issues from a European perspective, so they strive instead to cultivate a separatist defence of national integrity. In turn, this has encouraged an ethos of 'us' and 'it' in the Member State/Community context, which weakens the impetus for supranational co-operation in the first place and which inevitably permeates, even erodes, the various layers of EC achievement. It is inevitable that these ill effects, left unchecked, will increase rather than diminish over time. The fraught counter-promotion of an artificial common European identity, discussed in Chapter 3, has had little effect in reality and is questioned increasingly, even by its (once) chief proponents; a continued, even perceived, promotion of assimilation in this way will simply alienate Member States and their citizens, causing them to retreat further into the creed of national interest and jeopardising the foundations of European integration in a more critical way than an appreciation of diversity ever could.

*(vi)   Can the objective be achieved by minimum standards or by
        mutual recognition rather than by comprehensive rules?*

(vii)   Is a regulation or a directive more appropriate?

These issues relate more correctly to the principle of proportionality but do
raise important considerations for the application of subsidiarity. Article
151(5) excludes the harmonisation of rules in the sphere of cultural policy; it
specifies 'incentive measures' and recommendations as the appropriate acts
of implementation. Ultimately, the Court of Justice may have to determine
the extent to which Article 151's guiding principles of 'co-operation' and
'contribution' can encompass the introduction of minimum standards by the
EC; in the meantime, implementation rests, in practical terms, within the
discretion of the Member States acting through the Council. As noted above,
the adoption of minimum standards allows more stringent measures to be
sanctioned at national level. It is a system that has been readily applied to
environmental protection and may yet prove advantageous for language
policy, since the needs of language groups across Europe are as diverse as
the languages themselves. But 'minimum standards' should never be equated
with minimum effectiveness or enforcement. In the context of international
protection for fundamental rights more generally, a parallel dilemma exists.
Given that the protection of rights varies considerably in different countries,
finding a common standard can be a politically contentious struggle. This is
exacerbated when the rights in question are considered not to be as
'fundamental' as others; the debate on the implementation of economic and
social rights is particularly illustrative here. As a compromise, minimum
standards are often declared, along with an aspiration that they will be
implemented gradually and in consideration of practical exigencies. It is
generally maintained that settling for minimum standards ensures that, at
least, rights are being recognised at some level rather than not being
protected at all. The most common enforcement mechanism applied here is
the procedure of state reporting; but this leaves an appreciable level of
discretion to states and does not provide independent redress for the individual. It is unfortunately significant that, in the context of language policy,
most European states have not yet been prepared to accept even the
discretionary obligations outlined in the Charter for Regional or Minority
Languages. But minimum standards can work, if accompanied by a commitment to maximum effectiveness. In view of the structure of Article 151 and
the application of subsidiarity, this commitment can only be made by the
Member States themselves.

(viii) Can the objective be achieved by providing funds rather than by rule making, or by co-ordination of national policies rather than by a Community measure?

Moneys allocated to language groups can be used in numerous ways: funding co-ordinating bodies, setting up and maintaining minority language education structures, developing enterprise in associated regions, as well as encouraging and sponsoring cultural activities and exchanges through the medium of the language(s) in question. The EC cultural programmes devised to date are hinged primarily on this premise. What remains crucial, however, is that the provision of these funds be guaranteed via a secure legal basis; and this in itself is subject to the application of subsidiarity. At present, the security of EC funding for minority language projects is far from assured, as discussed in Chapter 6. And legal certainty demands that this must be rectified. It is also worth noting here that providing funds does not span the reach of language policy in any case; it does not confront the use of minority languages within public bodies, for example, whether national or supra-national. Thus, while the provision of funds is critical, it is not sufficient. What must be asked, however, is whether the EC has a role to play beyond the provision of funds; and if so, what limits can be attached to this realistically? These questions move into the realm of the EC as a governing public body and are discussed in Chapter 5. It is not really clear what Temple Lang intended the second phrase to mean, since is difficult to see how national policies can be co-ordinated *without* a Community impetus. In any case, Article 151(5) explicitly commits the EC to adopting 'incentive measures' for the purpose of encouraging cooperation in the cultural field.

(ix) If the aim can be achieved in several different ways, could the Community measure allow Member States to choose one of several options?

In reality, an EC minority language policy would *only* be effective if framed in this manner, for several reasons. At present, national regimes for the protection of language rights vary considerably across the Community. But, as stressed throughout, different language groups have very different needs. In any event, Article 151 prohibits the harmonisation of national laws. From the political perspective, it is unlikely that the Member States would concede authority to the Community to this extent *without* having a number of choices or options but again, the danger exists that political compromises and the enjoyment of inordinate discretion could lead to ineffectiveness;

there is a fine line between flexibility and detrimental freedom of choice. This question is explored in more detail in Chapter 5, in the context of the Charter for Regional or Minority languages.

(x)   Would Community measures to achieve the aim in question be an objectively reasonable quid pro quo for a significant number of Member States to seek in response to some other Community measures?

Decision-making in the Council is unavoidably political, since the Member State representatives are balancing national as well as Community interests; so it is inevitable that political bargaining can secure support for or rejection of proposed measures, often on a *quid pro quo* basis. Drawing Article 5 into this equation is a bluntly candid assessment of the decision-making process. It would be naïve to think that subsidiarity is immune from Council haggling, but this makes more real also the idea that political horse-trading contains ample potential for abuse of the principle, which can only diminish its legitimacy in practice.

(xi)   If a Community measure were adopted, should it contain provisions for the special problems of particular regions?

In terms of cultural policy generally, this is recognised expressly in Article 151(1); in respect of minority languages, it is inevitable. But caution must also be taken not to classify language rights inherently as 'special problems', or to associate minority languages exclusively with the regions; this argument has been raised already in Chapters 1 and 3.

4.   CONCLUSION

The preceding paragraphs detail an attempt to identify specific questions that may arise when justifying EC intervention on the basis of subsidiarity. There are no exact rules or procedures; indeed, Community measures are typically framed to deal with diverse circumstances. In addition, their impact on national law varies greatly, in terms of both practical effect and political significance. Temple Lang has at least grappled with criteria which may be determining factors in the application of the European Council and Amsterdam Protocol guidelines. Subsidiarity is an obscure and subjective concept, capable of manipulation by both the Community institutions and the Member States. The analytical spotlight may now have turned more to flexibility and closer co-operation, but it would be a mistake to dismiss subsidiarity; it retains substantial power as a political weapon and may well come to the fore as the development of sensitive policy areas, including culture and language, comes more directly onto the EC agenda. Article 151 is a provision of limited application, containing a number of internal restrictions; but within Article 151(1) surely lies the potential for more comprehensive language policy than has been conceived to date. Subsidiarity will—rightly—curb improper ambitions. But there is a real danger that policy making won't get that far, that an indeterminate allusion to the sweeping omnipotence of Article 5 will be accepted as sufficient; that this may already have occurred is questioned in Chapter 6. Restrictions and difficulties do exist, but clear possibilities for Community action in the cultural, and especially linguistic, sector, have also been shown to conform with both the express limitations of Article 151 and the application of the principle of subsidiarity: a role for the Community in minority language issues can be justified when considering at least eight of the preceding eleven questions. EC involvement in minority language issues is not primarily therefore a question of competence at all; it is more a question of willingness, on all sides. Even taking into account the explicit boundaries of Article 151, and allowing for the application of subsidiarity, more comprehensive language programmes that face up to contemporary language issues are, at the very least, possible; but to date, the subtle political battle of sovereignty takes precedence, with subsidiarity as the chief weapon deployed, ironically, by all sides. Discussion of Commission proposals for the *Arcipelago-Archipel* programme will bring about more honest contemplation of the kinds of issues identified in this Chapter; and whether Article 151 can be used successfully as its legal basis will, of course, depend on the nature of the proposals put forth. The programme is likely, however, to seek to place funding arrangements accorded fairly tenuously in the past on a more concrete legal and organisational footing and in that case, the scope of Article 151 should be sufficient, taking full account of subsidiarity. Thus, the role of the EC in language policy as regards its cultural aspects is likely to be assured, from a legal perspective at least. Beyond culture, however, is there a role for the EC in the determination and protection of language rights in a more general (and enforceable) sense? This question has significant implications for EC fundamental rights protection and citizenship, as well as for current understanding on what the Community should and should not do, and is considered in Chapter 5.

Language, Rights and Citizenship: An EC Equation?

1. INTRODUCTION

The realisation of EC fundamental rights protection is a controversial cornerstone in the realisation of European integration more generally, permeating seasoned debates on democracy, legitimacy and citizenship. At the Nice Summit in December 2000, the proclamation of an EU Charter of Fundamental Rights marked the latest chapter of an eventful legal and political process. Dissension abounds as to what exactly the status of this instrument might (or should) yet be, reflecting broader uncertainty as to the character and purpose of the Community itself. But in light of current political priorities—intensifying monetary union, enlargement of the Union (including the attendant institutional reform), the feasibility of 'two-speed' integration, and the Union's external borders—fundamental rights protection has taken on a sharper significance. How successfully to date has the EC enforced this jurisdiction? And what does it mean, in real terms, from the perspective of individuals? Attention has been focused on the rights recognised by the Court of Justice thus far, on the extent to which Community rights interact with standards of protection provided for elsewhere (both nationally and internationally), and on the relationship (if any) between fundamental rights protection and the concept of European citizenship. There is considerable pressure on the Community to clarify, at least, its position on these points; and there is also an awareness that its achievements to date cannot remain static. At present, Member State authorities are obliged to take 'Community' fundamental rights into account, but only where the implementation of EC law is at issue; in other words, the principle of non-interference in domestic affairs takes precedence in the fundamental rights context as in any other. But the Charter preparatory phase has called the retention of this proviso into question: should the Community actually have a broader rights protection remit? It has also been acknowledged that the development of EC human rights policy must take into account the rising significance of non-discrimination and the rights of minorities,[1] a trend that, if pursued, would have obvious implications for the recognition of language rights. The position of the Court of Justice on this point is not really clear; it has never, for example, classified language rights expressly as 'fundamental' rights; and yet, it has arguably been favourably disposed to such reasoning in the specific context of minority languages.[2] In Chapters 3 and 4, it was argued that cultural policy, on its own, cannot secure the introduction of more comprehensive language policy measures, especially regarding the public or official use of language. This chapter introduces the existing fundamental rights jurisdiction of the EC and questions the extent to which more coherent protection for (minority) language rights could be incorporated therein; how that jurisdiction might yet evolve will then be assessed. But it must first be established that language rights can be legitimately categorised as 'fundamental' rights; in other words, what does having the 'right' to speak a particular language actually mean?

2.   LANGUAGE MATTERS? LANGUAGE RIGHTS AS FUNDAMENTAL RIGHTS

Writing in the Canadian context, Réaume has observed that "[l]anguage policy making has for too long been conducted solely as an aspect of power politics. The result has been a singular inattention to the development of a principled theoretical grounding as an important aspect of human rights."[3] The basic question to be addressed here is whether the right to use a particular language for either official or non-official purposes is a fundamental human right, as opposed to an administrative or legal claim. What difference does this make either way? And even if we can speak in terms of 'rights', what pragmatic limitations can legitimately be placed on the exercise of language choice? These questions are obviously not peculiar to

---

[1]   See, for example, the human rights agenda adopted in 1998 by a *Comité des Sages, Leading by Example: A Human Rights Agenda for the European Union for the Year 2000*, reproduced in Philip Alston (ed.), with Mara Bustelo and James Heenan, *The EU and Human Rights*, (Oxford: OUP, 1999), 919-927 at 923, paras. 11-12.

[2]   Contrast, for example, the position of the Court in competition law cases involving breaches of Regulation 1/58 (discussed in Chapter 1) with its stance in Case 137/84 *Ministère Public v. Mutsch* [1985] ECR 2681 (Chapter 2) and Case C-274/96 *Criminal Proceedings against Bickel and Franz* [1998] ECR I-7637 (Chapter 6).

[3]   Denise G. Réaume, "The constitutional protection of language: Survival or security?", in David Schneiderman (ed.), *Language and the State: The Law and Politic of Identity*, (Quebec: Les Éditions Yvon Blais, 1989), 37-57 at 57.

language rights protection; they reflect ongoing uncertainties within fundamental rights discourse more generally. But, as Réaume has indicated, theoretical frameworks are rarely constructed in the language rights context specifically—a conceptual deficit that weakens many claims in favour of language choice, given that governing entities are obviously affected—and not always receptive—where duties of implementation can be found to exist.

Classification of language rights as fundamental rights hinges ultimately on whether or not the term 'fundamental' can encompass degrees of rights: are some rights inherently (and thus justifiably) 'more fundamental' than others? This construction would allow for a priority of rights that might run from, for example, abolishing the death penalty, to securing due process in criminal proceedings, to the enjoyment of social and cultural rights. Are rights divisible in this manner? Listing claims in this way necessarily implies a priority of order, which cannot always be determined objectively and thus brings the issue of value judgments into play. A related consideration is that different rights invariably clash with each other; balancing conflicting rights is a task undertaken in both legal and political realms on a continual basis but it is inevitably one that, again, hinges on the notion of priority. Rights are also balanced against other (often relatively abstract) interests, usually societal—*e.g.* the requirements of the common good or of public policy—but also economic and political. Ultimately, who should decide which interests will take precedence? It is a basic truth that rights evolve from common aims, from the eradication of tyranny and the achievement of justice. And there is a real danger that differentiating between 'types' of rights could lead to varying commitments in terms of enforcement and implementation, or even to the belief that norms at the 'lower' end of the scale do not really constitute rights at all. A conclusive definition of rights is thus elusive, and often subjective; bearing this in mind, the degree to which the international community has absorbed external standards for human rights protection is extraordinary. Taking that view, the absence of conclusive definitions does not seem fatal to the realisation of rights protection. Yet equally, ascertaining whether or not a given claim is a 'genuine' fundamental or human right can be decisive when striving to determine either the existence or extent of a corollary duty of enforcement. How can this quandary be solved? Both the historical development of international rights protection and contemporary theoretical paradigms are relevant here; and both are introduced in the following paragraphs from the particular perspective of language claims.

A.   International Standards on the Protection of Language Rights: Historical Origins

Contemporary human rights law envisages that participating states surrender a considerable degree of sovereignty and thus stands in marked contrast to the original inter-state system. Language rights, as an aspect of minority rights more generally, constitute one of the three typically acknowledged sources of international human rights law, along with humanitarian intervention and the abolition of slavery.[4] It is helpful to identify attitudinal trends that characterised the early stages of international cooperation in this field, since they reflect the historical interaction between minority claims and fundamental rights more generally. Protection of minority rights derived initially from tolerance of religious diversity, followed by the granting of more positive rights to religious freedom. This ethos was expanded to take in other minority claims, such as national origin (which, more often than not, would involve language differences). In the nineteenth century, very few countries gave purely internal legislative consideration to the protection of minorities within their territories.[5] But a number of international or inter-state treaties were concluded at this time, primarily in an effort to quell potentially unsettling nationalism among minority groups, and based on fears of secession.[6] After the First World War, the redrawing of national boundaries meant that national minorities were often displaced on the 'wrong' side of new state frontiers. This was of considerable importance at both domestic and international levels, not owing especially to a desire to develop tenets of human rights law, but because of the more pragmatic need to establish and maintain political stability. A more elaborate inter-state

---

[4]   See, for example, A.H. Robertson and J.G. Merrills, *Human Rights in the World: An Introduction to the Study of the International Protection of Human Rights*, 4th ed., (Manchester: Manchester University Press, 1996), Chapter 1. For a historical overview of international law and language rights more specifically, see Fernand de Varennes, *Language, Minorities and Human Rights*, (The Hague: Martinus Nijhoff, 1996), Chapter 1.

[5]   Capotorti, as Special Rapporteur for the United Nations, has noted that Austria, Switzerland, Hungary and Belgium made some provision for minorities, particularly in respect of the official use of languages (Francesco Capotorti, *Study on the Rights of Persons belonging to Ethnic, Religious and Linguistic Minorities*, (New York: United Nations, 1979), p. 3, para. 18.

[6]   de Varennes traces provision for language differences in earlier international agreements, back to the fourteenth century, but mainly discusses nineteenth century treaties: see Fernand de Varennes, *To Speak or Not To Speak: The Rights of Persons belonging to Linguistic Minorities*, (Working Paper prepared for the UN Sub-Committee on the rights of minorities, 21 March 1997, published at http://www.unesco.org/most/ln2pol3.htm), p. 2 *et seq.*

treaty system was devised under the supervision of the League of Nations, whereby states undertook to ensure that members of ethnic, religious or linguistic minorities enjoyed civil and political rights on an equal footing with the rest of the population. But these minorities treaties were designed to be situation-specific; they did not guarantee minority rights in a universal sense. In any case, the demise of the League itself necessarily resulted in the demise of the treaties. It is usually acknowledged that the system was not a satisfactory one in practice, but a number of ideas still subscribed to were developed at this time. In particular, the Permanent Court of International Justice issued a number of advisory opinions on minority rights, stressing that equality in law was futile without a commitment on the part of state authorities to the realisation of equality in fact.[7] In the context of language rights, it was intended that the right to speak a particular language should be enforced irrespective of whether or not an individual understood the official language of the state, with any related costs to be borne by the state.[8] Ironically, a change in attitude towards minority rights can be linked to the foundation of both the United Nations and the Council of Europe. In the aftermath of the Second World War, the international community sought to emphasise the dignity and equality of all human beings as the source of fundamental rights. In this way, the principles of equality and non-discrimination were generalised and universalised; 'special' protection for minority groups was no longer a priority. Consequently, international human rights instruments drafted at this time do not contain provisions that deal expressly with minority rights although, as outlined later, numerous provisions therein are likely to affect language choice both directly and indirectly. On the whole, the philosophy that had been promoted via the inter-state treaties and the League of Nations was that political stability could be achieved by according rights to displaced minority groups; but thinking at the time of the foundation of the UN deemed minority rights themselves a threat to national unity and, therefore, to economic and political stability. In recent years, the grim reality of minority rights denial has been manifested repeatedly, at its most extreme (and therefore most publicised) in the violent breakdown of multiethnic states and unions, perhaps forcing some rethinking on minority issues back onto the international political agenda. For present purposes, what is most noticeable is the shift over time from the idea that minority rights protection necessitated something 'extra'

---

[7] See in particular, the opinion delivered in the *Minority Schools in Albania Case*, (1935) [PCIJ] Ser. A/B, No. 64.

[8] This is actually a stronger standard of protection than that now provided for under the European Convention of Human Rights, discussed below.

towards their derivation from universal or 'general' human rights, including in particular the concepts of freedom of expression and non-discrimination.

B.   Language Rights as Fundamental Rights: Competing Theories?

The dimension of language policy looked at in this chapter relates primarily to aspects of the official use of language—*i.e.* choice of language for administrative purposes, for the business of government (whether dealing with a state or with an entity such as the EC), in the courts, and so on. Within that context, we return to the questions asked at the outset: is the right to speak a particular language in these particular circumstances a 'fundamental' or human right, and if so (or indeed, if not), what does that mean? This must be placed equally in the realm of minority rights, picking up the legal threads of socio-cultural, economic and political debates introduced in Chapter 1. It may be recalled that, as established in Chapter 1, there is no universally recognised definition of a 'minority' in human rights theory. But prevailing criteria of assessment, both objective and subjective, were identified; and it was also observed that the absence of a universal definition has not precluded the creation of legally binding rights in various legal strata. Declarations on the value of linguistic diversity are reaffirmed continuously in a wide variety of perspectives and theories—cultural, historical, anthropological and sociological. But what now falls for consideration is whether these arguably abstract claims can be advanced to the *legal* realm of fundamental rights discourse.[9] Perhaps the least contentious starting point is that embodied in the European Convention on Human Rights (ECHR). Discussed more fully below, it is sufficient at this point to note that language 'rights' protected therein are grounded in the philosophy of natural justice. In its legal context, this refers to basic language rights acquired by virtue of not understanding a certain language or languages. Interpreters would only be introduced into court proceedings, for example, where the accused or a witness does not understand the language through which the proceedings are being conducted; the underlying rationale is that it would be unjust if restrictions on someone's liberty or property could be determined where s/he was not be able to follow the proceedings. But it is becoming increasingly rare that speakers of minority languages are not

---

[9]   Skutnabb-Kangas and Phillipson have characterised this process as "...an attempt to harness fundamental principles and practices from the field of human rights to the task of rectifying some linguistic wrongs...." ("Linguistic rights and wrongs", (1995) vol. 16:4 *Applied Linguistics*, 483-504 at 483).

additionally competent in one or more languages of wider communication; thus, the broader question of allowing individuals to use the language of their *choice* in a majority/minority language situation arises. In this scenario, it is irrelevant that an individual seeking to use a minority language for official purposes is competent in the majority language through which the court (or other authority) normally functions. The right to choice of language would accommodate the preference of the individual, with any costs of interpretation or translation falling on the state or other governing entity involved. A further contention exists within the linguistic choice thesis itself *i.e.* whether the right to choice of language would protect mother tongues only or should also cover languages acquired voluntarily. MacMillan, for example, restricts the scope of language rights to "...a right to one's mother tongue or native language...not simply a right to speak a language *per se* but rather the language of one's heritage."[10] It must be acknowledged that the vast majority of those who claim the right to speak a minority language *are* native speakers of the particular language in question. But it is not clear why the language choice concept should exclude those who have acquired a minority language at a later stage in their lives and choose voluntarily to communicate through the medium of that language. The Canadian Supreme Court pronounced on this question in *Attorney General of Quebec v. Nancy Forget*, holding that "[t]he concept of language is not limited to the mother tongue but also includes the language of use or habitual communication.... There is no reason to adopt a narrow interpretation which does not take into account the possibility that the mother tongue and the language of use may differ."[11] In this vein, language choice has been compared to choice of religion, which is also mutable yet steadfastly protected.[12] Realistic minority language 'rights' must be capable of covering linguistic choice as well as natural justice arguments; it is not an absolute right, however, and the extent to which it may be curtailed legitimately is returned to below, in the context of limitations and viability.

When we move beyond the need to secure natural justice, we must then establish just why someone's interest in using a minority language on the

---

[10] C. Michael MacMillan, "Linking theory to practice: Comments on the 'Constitutional protection of language'", in Schneiderman (ed.), *Language and the State*, 59-68 at 61.

[11] [1988] 2 SCR 90 at 100. The Irish High and Supreme Courts have also long taken this view: see Niamh Nic Shuibhne, "The Constitution, the courts and the Irish language", in Tim Murphy and Patrick Twomey (eds.), *Ireland's Evolving Constitution 1937-1997: Collected Essays*, (Oxford: Hart Publishing, 1998), 253-263.

[12] See Bill Piatt, "Toward domestic recognition of a human right to language", (1986) 23 *Houston Law Review*, 885-906 at 901.

premise of language choice can be called a 'right', and what the implications of that classification might be for states (or, for our purposes, for the EC). After all, people have a multitude of varied—and worthy—interests that do not come within the discourse of rights. In one of the few studies examining these issues, Green outlines the key questions as follows: "[a]re language rights legal rights only, justiciable in court but without deeper moral foundation? Or are they on a footing with the more familiar fundamental rights...? If so, [a]re they perhaps derivatively related to other fundamental rights, for example, freedom of expression?"[13] Schools of thought on these questions reflect, on a simplistic interpretation, the dichotomy evidenced above in the historical evolution of language rights. A theoretical model developed by Green and Réaume—which hinges on the notion that human rights generally cannot encompass minority claims (and more particularly, on the idea that non-discrimination and freedom of expression are essentially part of a negative—and thus insufficient—rights approach[14]) has been superseded to some extent by more recent work, primarily that of de Varennes.[15] The primary advantage of establishing that language rights are fundamental rights, by whatever theoretical means, is that it aids the entrenchment of protection for related claims, taking them outside the discretionary arena of administrative policy; more particularly, their recognition and implementation would not be so dependent on the potentially inconstant priorities of policy makers. The significance of this distinction cannot be overstated, given that a supportive political environment is frequently elusive. Rickard elaborates on this submission as follows:

> [If] protection...is a mere policy option to be adopted or not, depending on the social climate of the day, it is itself subject to the very conditions that generate and entrench minority disadvantage. The democratic processes that guide policy are essentially majoritarian in nature, and there is no assurance that

---

[13] Leslie Green, "Are language rights fundamental?", (1987) 25 *Osgoode Hall Law Journal*, 639-669 at 640.

[14] Green, "Are language rights fundamental?", p. 660 *et seq.*; Réaume, "The constitutional protection of language", p. 50 *et seq.* The notion that approaching language rights from the perspective of non-discrimination *etc.* effects only 'negative' protection—in the sense of non-interference and tolerance—is widespread in language rights literature; see, for example, Tove Skutnabb-Kangas and Robert Phillipson, "Linguistic human rights, past and present", in Skutnabb-Kangas and Phillipson (eds.), *Linguistic Human Rights: Overcoming Linguistic Discrimination*, (Berlin; New York: Mouton de Gruyter, 1994), 71-110 at 79-80.

[15] See de Varennes, *Language, Minorities and Human Rights*, especially Chapters 3 and 4.

mainstream interests will not dominate in those decisions. Policies that advantage minorities at the apparent expense of the majority are likely to be unpopular and have low priority...A regime of protection...would [need] to be deep enough to extend into the basic institutional structure where the problem has its roots.[16]

What must now be considered is whether language rights are autonomous claims in and of themselves, human rights *sui generis*; or whether they are derivative, premised on (and no more than a subset of) 'other' human rights principles like non-discrimination. To outline current thinking first, de Varennes maintains that language rights are effectively 'covered' by general human rights standards—in the context of the official use of language, typically non-discrimination.[17] Green has suggested that these principles govern language use under 'normal conditions' only *i.e.* 'where there is no need for distinctive rights protecting interests in a particular language'.[18] 'Normal conditions' can be taken to imply the use of majority languages, in that the language rights of speakers here can typically be taken for granted. The situation is quite different for speakers of a minority language, who cannot use that language in the same range of domains or outlets as their counterpart majority language speakers. Crucially, and in contrast to earlier work, de Varennes works with an interpretation of non-discrimination that *can* encompass a positive as well as negative rights framework.[19] The basic premise here is that when a state employs one or more languages for various functions, it is not acting neutrally; those individuals who are fluent in the languages selected are automatically favoured and those outside are potentially within the arena of discrimination, since they are not being

---

[16] Maurice Rickard, "Liberalism, multiculturalism and minority protection", (1994) vol. 20:2 *Social Theory and Practice*, 143-170 at 154/6.

[17] In the context of freedom of expression, de Varennes distinguishes between the use of language for private activities—a domain covered by an individual's freedom of expression, in the negative sense of non-intervention—and the use of language for official purposes, which necessarily involves the response or reaction of the state and is, therefore, something beyond the scope of an individual's freedom of expression: see *Language, Minorities and Human Rights*, Chapter 3 (see in particular, the summary on p. 53). This is reflected in decisions relating to the ECHR, discussed further below. Moreover, it must be remembered that freedom of expression is a right enjoyed by *all* and cannot be used to hoist one language group above or ahead of another: on this point, see the UN Human Rights Committee decision in *Ballantyne, Davidson and McIntyre v. Canada*, CCPR/C/47/D/ 359/1989 and 385/1989 (31 March 1993).

[18] Green, "Are language rights fundamental?", p. 641.

[19] de Varennes, *Language, Minorities and Human Rights*, especially at Chapter 4.

treated equally (although the notion of legitimate limits on language policy—or on what a governing entity can actually be expected to provide—is a valid one, discussed in more detail below). What must also be addressed here is whether non-discrimination not only allows for differentiation but can sometimes justify active assistance towards its maintenance—fuelling the creation of 'real' or substantive equality, within reason—a position at odds with many understandings of non-discrimination and language policy, even though it is traceable back to the stance of the PCIJ outlined above. Where an administrative practice of the state is found to contravene the principle of equal treatment, then it may be obliged to take positive measures to remedy this on the basis of correcting discriminatory treatment, in a more complete contemplation of equality. But the state may equally choose to withdraw completely its provision of the service in question—in other words, there is no inevitable or inherent presumption in favour of the state taking positive measures; there is no duty that imposes *only* a positive course of action. There exists an 'out-clause'. Of course, it is highly unlikely—and indeed, in the context of due process, impossible—in practical terms that a state would choose not to allow anyone to speak in the courts, for example; but there remains a theoretical possibility against taking positive measures towards language rights implementation. This leaves a conceptual deficit at the very least, and one biased in favour of the state to the extent that it detracts from the logic of rights in the first place. This is one critical example of the difficulties associated with the notion that non-discrimination encompasses positive action. It can do so—and while this is an aspect of the principle's scope that tends mistakenly to be overlooked in language theory generally, it is not necessarily a sufficient grounding for all positive claims involving minority interests. If non-discrimination on its own was enough, then why, for example, was Article 27—an explicit provision on the rights of minorities specifically—included in the UN International Covenant on Civil and Political Rights (ICCPR, discussed below)? Recent developments in the sphere of EC gender equality have preferred to spell out both the possibility for and scope of positive measures rather than to assume their inclusion in declarations of non-discrimination.[20] The extent of and limitations to positive action programmes in the first place is yet another theoretical maelstrom, however, returned to below. But it should be noted also that non-discrimination may be more appropriate for inherent or immutable characteristics; in

---

[20]   See, for example, Article 141(4) EC, inserted via the Amsterdam Treaty; see also Article 23 of the Charter of Fundamental Rights. Prior to this, see the somewhat controversial decisions in Case C-450/93 *Kalanke v. Bremen* [1995] ECR I-3051 and Case C-409/95 *Marschall v. Land Nordrhein-Westfalen* [1997] ECR I-6363.

other words, it may not cover the concept of language *choice*. For present purposes, there is a further reason why adopting a derivative rights framework only may not be sufficient. When writing on the scope of non-discrimination in relation to language rights, de Varennes is dealing exclusively with consequences for states; because even when writing on non-discrimination in international law, it is in terms of the resultant impact on states and their citizens. In other words, when looking at the ambit of non-discrimination, public authorities are equated with state authorities. But the EC is not a state. Nor is it an international organisation in the more typical understanding of what that means. In the context of language rights, it exhibits something of a dual role that draws from both. As a governing entity, the relationship between the Community and those affected by Community law must be explored; and as an international entity, it does impose duties and standards on its Member States, but not in the way that this occurs more typically in international law. To examine the place of language rights in both of these EC guises, we need to bear in mind a framework that goes beyond the traditional 'individual-state' and 'state-international law' relationships.

For these reasons, and notwithstanding the argument that language rights may be covered by 'universal' human rights, it remains valid to look at the possibility of language rights as autonomous rather than derived interests that can impose duties of implementation in a broader sense. To this end, Green and Réaume had applied theories based on the correlativity of rights and duties.[21] The underlying idea here, drawn primarily from the work of Joseph Raz, is that a legal right is a fundamental right only where it protects some moral right. This line of thought does not require the use of variable concepts like natural law to establish what constitutes a moral right; as Green states bluntly, "[w]e need not seek timeless, transcendental proofs of the existence of fundamental rights, and it is just as well since we will not find them."[22] Green uses an alternative 'interest → duty = right' formulation *i.e.* if some person's interest in realising their linguistic choices in official language domains is sufficient reason for holding others, whether private individuals or collective entities, to be under a duty to provide or secure that

---

[21] Green, "Are language rights fundamental?", p. 647 *et seq*. There is a vast wealth of academic literature on the relationship between rights and duties, but see especially Joseph Raz, *The Morality of Freedom*, (Oxford: Clarendon Press, 1986); another, more formalistic, strand of theoretical debate hinges on the work of Wesley Newcomb Hohfeld; see in particular, his *Fundamental Legal Conceptions*, (Westport: Greenwood Press, 1964).

[22] Green, "Are language rights fundamental?", p. 648.

interest, then language claims can be termed language 'rights'. Whether rights or duties are considered as 'prior' here is not really the point for present purposes; what remains is a common emphasis on the inter-relationship between the two. While rights can be ascribed to or said to inhere in the basic yet abstract notions of humanity, dignity and freedom, the plain fact is that they are virtually meaningless without corresponding recognition and implementation. What is most relevant for present purposes is that the concept of duty takes 'fundamental' rights beyond the often discretionary administrative or legal rights domain. Two further aspects of the rights-duties thesis can be noted here: first, the idea that if duties are seen as obligations, then the operation of legal sanctions can be justified when the duties or obligations are breached;[23] and second, as discussed further below, the rights-duties construction does not preclude the recognition of collective rights as fundamental rights in certain instances.[24] Green has also argued that the application of Raz's theory does *not* require that all fundamental rights are equal or even of great importance: "[t]hus, one source of scepticism about language rights is immediately defused."[25] This brings to mind the controversial discourse on priorities *within* rights, introduced earlier, which has particular implications for how we limit their recognition and implementation, an idea explored more fully below.

The next step then is to determine when an interest in speaking a particular language will be sufficient to generate a duty of implementation. Because as noted above, a myriad of human interests might be very nice or worthy indeed, but that does not in itself generate legitimacy for the placing of related obligations on others. In order to satisfy Raz's interest/duty/right formula, Green classifies interests in language as falling within two categories, linguistic survival and linguistic security. Even for those who argue that language rights do not need to be put through this theoretical testing—above and beyond their source in 'general' human rights principles —in the first place, the survival/security distinction is a useful paradigm either way. Furthermore, it reflects the way in which the EC has actually approached minority language claims, being reminiscent of the reasoning of Advocate General Darmon in *Groener*, where he derived a state duty to

---

[23]   On the application of this concept in the specific domain of language, see Joseph G. Turi, "Typology of language legislation", in Skutnabb-Kangas and Phillipson (eds.), *Linguistic Human Rights: Overcoming Linguistic Discrimination*, (Berlin; New York: Mouton de Gruyter, 1994), 111-119 at 116.

[24]   See, for example, Michael Freeman, "Are there collective human rights?", (1995) 43 *Political Studies*, 25-40 at 30.

[25]   Green, "Are language rights fundamental?", p. 647.

provide education through the medium of the Irish language from its constitutional recognition.[26] Linguistic survival is the broader of the two concepts, referring to the survival of language groups over time. Thus, it is a goal of indefinite scope, in terms of both ambition and time, which seeks to combat the extinction of a particular language or languages. It is usually based on a desire for continuity, linguistic continuity specifically and cultural continuity more generally. Green defines linguistic survival as an abstract, aesthetic concept, which "...evinces a concern for languages as things in themselves rather than for their speakers."[27] On this point, Réaume asserts bluntly that "[i]t is not languages that have rights, but people."[28] Arguments advanced in favour of minority language support are wedded frequently to the theme of linguistic survival. It is proposed almost invariably, for example, that linguistic diversity is a valuable attribute, both for individual speakers and for its contribution to the 'rich texture of human society'.[29] Moreover, the historical circumstances that have impacted on the status or use of a language are often recited to justify the contemporary and future allocation of resources for the maintenance, or even revival, of that language. Neither Green nor Réaume seek to detract from the legitimacy of these arguments as absolutely valid concerns in themselves. But they do not accept that reasoning founded on linguistic survival can justify sufficiently the classification of language rights as fundamental or *human* rights. As Réaume surmises:

> [t]he interest in linguistic continuity would undoubtedly be sufficient to motivate people to teach their children their language and participate in cultural events which help improve the chances that the language will survive. But I am doubtful that it is sufficiently strong to justify imposing duties on others who may have different and competing cultural ambitions....[30]

Transferring this logic to the EC context, and to the cultural challenges triggered by the specific (if not unique) phenomenon of European integration, where does this leave interests based on the inherent value of linguistic diversity? How can the maintenance of even limited language

---

[26] Case 379/87 *Groener v. Minister for Education and the Dublin Vocational Education Committee*, [1989] ECR 3967, Opinion of Advocate General Darmon, especially at pp. 3982-3, paras. 21-24; see Chapter 2.

[27] Green, "Are language rights fundamental?", p. 656.

[28] Réaume, "The constitutional protection of language", p. 39.

[29] *ibid.*, p. 41.

[30] *ibid.*, p. 44.

measures based on EC cultural policy, for example, be justified under the ideology of 'duty'? The key here is to look at who actually benefits from EC language policy, to go beyond languages *per se* and to focus instead on language speakers. This alternative interest in language is described by Green as the achievement of linguistic security, a present-oriented concept based on the premise 'that one may use one's language with dignity'.[31] Essentially, it is at this point that arguments grounded in freedom of expression, in non-discrimination and in the make-up of human identity come into play; but viewing things in this way, linguistic security is more than just the sum of its parts.

As well as an individual interest in language, linguistic security can encompass a social interest, based on interactions through a shared linguistic medium that represent an expression of the speaker's identity as a member of a language community. Social and individual considerations are thus interrelated, since linguistic security strives above all to ensure that 'speaking a certain language should not be a ground of social liability'.[32] The crucial distinction is that language interests in communication and identity are grounded in the present, in contrast to both the prospective and historical aspects of language survival.[33] Applying his thesis to linguistic security, Green legitimates both the negative, tolerance-based approach to language claims and the positive duty of proactive protection, to ensure that language use is facilitated effectively for both private *and* public functions. He asserts that "[t]he duties which this places on governments may make little difference to the long-term prospects of survival, but they will make an immediate and palpable difference to linguistic security."[34] Reaffirming the view that minority language rights are not special privileges, Réaume describes speakers of majority languages as already having '*de facto* linguistic security'.[35] Another key difference between survival and security is that linguistic security places responsibility for the fate of minority languages on,

---

[31]   Green, "Are language rights fundamental?", p. 658.

[32]   *ibid.*

[33]   Brett argues, however, that the notions of survival and security cannot be separated so definitely, suggesting that a perceived threat to the future survival of a language constitutes a threat that affects *present* speakers, and thus impinges on their linguistic security: Nathan Brett, "Language laws and collective rights", (1991) vol. 4:2 *Canadian Journal of Law and Jurisprudence*, 347-360 at 351.

[34]   Green, "Are language rights fundamental?", p. 663 (but again, see Brett, *ibid.*).

[35]   Réaume, "The constitutional protection of language", p. 46.

in the first instance, their speakers.[36] But, "[while] the ultimate fate of a language community is up to its members...they should be protected from unfair or coercive pressures distorting normal practices of language use and transmission."[37] This is probably the most basic yet significant argument that justifies language planning and intervention in the first place. Minority languages cannot compete equally on an open linguistic market. And as regards the distortion of normal language practices, the effects of EC integration on language use and transmission generate corresponding EC responsibilities towards language communities. The central premise of linguistic security is dignity, as it relates to identity and individual choice. On this basis, language rights certainly share a common foundation with the vast majority of more widely acknowledged fundamental rights based on the equality of all individuals. But again, whether it is enough simply to leave the matter there forms the crux of the Green/de Varennes divergence.

In a similar vein, an argument often levelled against the recognition of language rights is their alleged breach of the tenet of universality. Addressing Réaume's thesis directly, MacMillan reasons that the very fact that certain members of society are necessarily excluded from minority language rights (given that only individuals in particular social contexts can claim them) violates the condition of universality which is, he argues, a central premise of human rights theory;[38] he cites the exclusion of tourists and immigrants as examples. But using this logic to detract from the status of language rights as fundamental rights is not sustainable. To take the second example first, the language rights of immigrants constitute in reality one of the primary motivations behind contemporary language planning; as explained in Chapter 1, the in-depth exploration that this question deserves is not within the scope of the present text but it should be restated that concentration here on indigenous or autochthonous languages should *not* be interpreted as an implicit rejection of other language rights. Linguistic security, on the contrary, is an innately universal ambition that relates just as much to majority populations as to minority ones; there are no inherent reasons why the rights-duties thesis applies only in static (and thus largely unrealistic) situations. This approach contrasts somewhat with the ambit of the European Charter on Regional or Minority Languages, introduced in

---

[36] In this context, Raz has argued that "...public policies can only serve to facilitate developments desired by the population, not to force cultural activities down the throats of an indifferent population." (Joseph Raz, "Multiculturalism: A liberal perspective", (1994) *Dissent*, 67-79 at 78)

[37] Réaume, "The constitutional protection of language", p. 47.

[38] MacMillan, "Linking theory to practice", pp. 61-2.

Chapter 1 and discussed in detail below. In truth, the key question on the language rights of immigrants, as for all rights issues, is *how* they can best be recognised and protected. The notions of setting acceptable limits, and of balancing rights and priorities come into play once again here, a balance that the EC has already tried to strike regarding education policy for the children of migrant workers, for example, outlined in Chapter 1. Tourists, on the other hand, are generally—and legitimately—excluded from an array of host-state fundamental rights, such as the right to vote; in any case, basic standards of language protection that apply equally in such cases of temporary dislocation are guaranteed in international rights instruments— including the ECHR—and are summarised below. In terms of exclusion on grounds of social context, a full-time worker does not generally have the right, for example, to claim concurrent social welfare benefits. Individuals who speak majority languages already *have* their language rights secured, so the exclusion of which MacMillan speaks is predominantly minority-based. And it must be stressed once again in response that minority language rights strive to redress an imbalance rather than to create an additional privilege. This, essentially, is why the implementation of minority language rights arises in the first place, a view epitomised by the derivative rights thesis. What is perhaps not so clear-cut is the way in which the universal ambition of linguistic security requires to be implemented in different ways for different language groups. This introduces yet again the difference between the origin of rights and their realisation. In a related sense, women's rights and children's rights would, using the non-discrimination argument, be derivative rights. But like minority language rights, they are not strictly uni- versal in terms of realisation; and so arguably by definition, men do not have women's rights, adults do not have children's rights, and majority language speakers do not benefit from *minority* language rights. So while the ultimate goal might be the achievement of a universal standard of treatment, the means by which this can be achieved—or in other words, the rights in which we can ground corollary duties of implementation—arguably substantiate further the need for exploring the 'non-universal' or *sui generis* theoretical paradigm.

If interests in speaking a minority language for official purposes *can* be held to legitimate the imposition of duty, using arguments based on dignity and equality outlined throughout, how then is that concept of duty discharged? The typical responses to language rights claims—by states, within international human rights instruments and by other governing entities such as the EC—have been charted by Skutnabb-Kangas and Phillipson; the spectrum ranges from the assimilation-oriented extreme of prohibition, to tolerance, non-discrimination (although, bearing in mind here the differences of opinion on its scope, outlined above), permission and finally, the maintenance-centred strategy of proactive promotion.[39] Tolerance is the most basic manifestation of minority language rights, "...[extending] just barely beyond what civility already requires."[40] A policy or programme grounded solely in this value of non-intervention will not achieve substant-ive equality between speakers of majority and minority languages; but as a starting point, tolerance is an obvious prerequisite to any language policy regime. It is derived from democratic principles such as freedom of expression and communication, non-discrimination and the ethos of natural justice. Tolerance is associated primarily with the private or non-official use of languages; it prescribes, for example, against prohibiting language groups from organising their own cultural events or educational structures.[41] To go beyond creating a climate of tolerance, consideration must be given to the adoption of positive measures which are designed to place speakers of majority and minority languages on an equal footing (so far as possible) in respect of the public or official use of languages—and this conclusion is arrived at irrespective of which of the two theoretical approaches discussed in this chapter is adopted. Governments usually formulate such measures within the framework of an official languages regime, grounded in consti-tutional or legislative provisions, or involving both; examples include providing for language choice beyond the requirements of natural justice in the courts, government services, legislature, state education facilities, and so on.[42] The imposition of language duties in the public sphere is justified by Réaume on the reasoning that policy formulation on the official use of languages is firmly within the control of the government itself.[43] Conversely, participation in political institutions is an essential feature of all democratic communities; inclusive participation by *all* citizens should thus be secured.

---

[39] Tove Skutnabb-Kangas and Robert Phillipson, "Linguistic human rights, past and present", Skutnabb-Kangas and Phillipson (eds.), *Linguistic Human Rights*, 71-110 at 79-80.

[40] Green, "Are language rights fundamental?", p. 660.

[41] On the non-official use of language, see de Varennes, *To Speak or Not to Speak*, p. 13 *et seq.*

[42] Advocate General Darmon clearly advocated a proactive approach in *Groener*, stating that "...since [Irish] is a minority language, [it] cannot be preserved without the adoption of voluntary and obligatory measures. *Any minority phenomenon, in whatever field, cannot usually survive if appropriate measures are not taken.*" (Case 379/87 *Groener v. Minister for Education and the Dublin Vocational Education Committee*, [1989] ECR 3967 at 3982, para. 18 (emphasis added).)

[43] Réaume, "The constitutional protection of language", p. 53.

The political theorist Will Kymlicka has been especially critical of any application of non-discrimination that does not involve the adoption of complementary positive measures, arguing that "...the ideal of benign neglect is not in fact benign.... [T]rue equality requires not identical treatment, but rather differential treatment in order to accommodate differential needs."[44] This extract recalls the controversial debate introduced above, which explores the legitimacy of positive measures and seeks to identify a legitimate cut-off point beyond which they are no longer justifiable. 'Affirmative action' programmes have increasingly become subject to criticism and derision, particularly in the United States. The primary objection to affirmative action policy is that it can amount, in effect, to discrimination against a contemporary majority for historical offences against various minority groups. But minority language rights do not demand the creation of special privileges; they strive instead to achieve the enjoyment of the same rights already taken for granted by the speakers of majority languages. Using a historical or future oriented justification for language rights has already been called into question in consideration of linguistic survival; emphasis was placed instead on the linguistic security of contemporary speakers. Moreover, it was stressed that the primary responsibility for the viability of a language group lies with the members of the group themselves. Government policy can facilitate language choices but it should not seek to impose them arbitrarily. And the implementation of language rights should not involve the involuntary imposition of language choices on *unwilling* citizens.[45] There is an admittedly fine line between acceptable and unacceptable positive action geared towards the implementation of language rights, but this is a difficulty associated with most fundamental rights concerns. Any abstract declaration of rights without a commitment to their implementation is a meaningless exercise, just as non-discrimination clauses without the introduction of policies actively to eliminate existing discrimination and to facilitate substantive equality—which may involve differential treatment—will remain a hollow ideal. The key here is identifying where the boundaries should be set. And so, the duty aspect of the rights-duties thesis requires hard decisions to be taken: on whom may enforceable duties be legitimately placed? The extent to which duties in respect of language rights can reach into the private sector is a significant contemporary issue, given the general tendency towards privatisation and deregulation of formerly state-controlled services and interests.

---

[44] Will Kymlicka, *Multicultural Citizenship: A Liberal Theory of Minority Rights*, (Oxford: Clarendon Press, 1995), pp. 110-3.

[45] On this point, see Réaume, "The constitutional protection of language", p. 54 *et seq.*

Within the framework of market integration, this is an obvious concern in the EC context. MacMillan has questioned the appropriateness of placing correlative obligations even on public authorities.[46] He has reservations, for example, in respect of hiring bilingual staff to provide bilingual or unilingual services. But requirements of this kind are commonplace throughout the EC Member States, and indeed EC institutions, and significantly, have been challenged before but upheld by the European Court of Justice.[47] Overall, however, the idea that imposing duties on the state (or other entities) must be grounded in something that goes beyond mere 'interest' becomes all the more evident. And what we must now address is the fact that even where duty can be established, it is by no means an unlimited concept—an idea that flows equally from the work of de Varennes, in terms of legitimate constraints on the implementation of equality.

One of the most obvious questions to be settled when devising a language policy framework is that of which languages will be recognised for official purposes in a given political structure. Even where it is accepted that language claims come within the realm of fundamental rights, there are pragmatic choices to be made. The distinction between languages understood—on the natural justice criterion—and the doctrine of linguistic choice has already been introduced, and it has been argued that in contemporary terms, minority language claims do tend to go beyond those that could be grounded in natural justice. Numerous other factors are relevant when selecting the languages to be used for official purposes within a political entity. As well as ideological and legal arguments, practicality and economics are obviously prevalent.[48] As is the case for fundamental rights protection more generally, the declaration of rights is not especially difficult but their implementation often is. Political entities have to make pragmatic choices; so the question is not whether rights are limited or not, but whether inevitable limitations are legitimate. How are these choices made in the language domain? How significant, for example, is the (relative) size of a language group in determining the extent to which public support is either

---

[46] MacMillan, "Linking theory to practice", pp. 61 *et seq.*

[47] *See* for example, Case 379/87 *Groener v. Minister for Education and the Dublin Vocational Education Committee*, [1989] ECR 3967, discussed in Chapter 2, and more recently, Case C-281/98 *Angonese v. Cassa di Risparmio di Bolzano SpA*, judgment of 6 June 2000, not yet reported (see Chapter 6).

[48] Ó Riagáin and Nic Shuibhne write, for example, that "[c]onceptually, the question of minority language rights can be located within the classic debates about the balancing of liberal freedom with the demands of a capitalist economy, of equity and efficiency." [Pádraig Ó Riagáin and Niamh Nic Shuibhne, "Minority language rights", (1997) 17 *Annual Review of Applied Linguistics*, 11-29 at 12].

warranted or feasible? Or is the criterion of viability decisive? Réaume, for example, refers to 'currently viable language communities, each able to sustain for its members a reasonably full cultural life'.[49] She qualifies this condition by adding that "[t]he argument that a language group deserves special protection is not based on the fact that other groups have it, but that this group needs it and can make use of it."[50] It is important to restate for these purposes the distinction between the existence of language rights and their implementation in practical terms: this is especially relevant as regards arguments made both for and against the existence of group rights. Under classic, liberal-democratic theory, fundamental rights inhere organically and equally in every individual by virtue of his/her humanity. By focusing on individuals as the bearers of rights, the protection of groups *per se* is excluded. It is not collective rights and duties as such—as they might apply to associations and corporations, for example—that have engendered debate; rather, it is the specific concept of collective *human* rights. The principal objections to the latter proposition can be summarised as follows: the promotion of group rights would be used to justify the denial of individual human rights; they constitute a threat to national stability, leading to secession and other forms of autonomy; there would be attempted justifications of cultural or religious practices that are generally regarded as unacceptable; states could not afford to bear the costs of providing special facilities for minority groups; and finally, positive action in favour of minorities constitutes discrimination against the rest of the population.[51] Notwithstanding the very real concerns raised here, it is significant (as Triggs observes) that most of the arguments listed were once used to thwart the development of fundamental rights in general. The primary justification for restricting minority rights to individuals is to avoid the 'institutionalisation of minorities';[52] in other words, every member of a minority group should have a choice as to whether s/he wishes to remain in the distinctive group or assimilate into the majority population. There is no reason why the rights-duties thesis cannot apply to groups at the level of theory, in that it is surely arguable that a group interest can be sufficiently fundamental so as to place others under a correlative duty of implementation. Rather than viewing the harmonisation of individual and group rights as an attempt to reconcile

---

[49]   Réaume, "The constitutional protection of language", p. 54.

[50]   *ibid.*, p. 56.

[51]   See Gillian Triggs, "The rights of peoples and individual rights: Conflict or harmony?", in James Crawford (ed.), *The Rights of Peoples*, (Oxford: Clarendon Press, 1992), 141-157.

[52]   Francesco Capotorti, "The protection of minorities under multilateral agreements on human rights", (1976) 2 *Italian Yearbook of International Law*, 3-32 at 19.

two inherently discordant concepts, theorists now strive to stress the compatibility of their coexistence. Freeman asserts that "[c]ollective human rights are rights the bearers of which are collectivities, which are not reducible to but are consistent with individual human rights...."[53] Here again, the distinction between the implementation and origin of rights is relevant. Réaume locates group rights within the social dimension of language practices, writing that "...the group protected by [language] rights requires a community [large enough to warrant them], yet it is possible, for enforcement purposes, legally to define the right-holder in individualistic terms."[54] Using this definition, the extent of correlative duty applicable is reinforced by the collective strength of minority language speakers as a group. This construction fits neatly with the UN solution in this context, as incorporated within Article 27 of the ICCPR ('persons...shall not be denied the right, in community with the other members of their group', discussed below); this gives to a language group the benefits derived from claims made as a collectivity, yet avoids the difficult and controversial debate surrounding the origin of the rights. Thus, Freeman talks about collective rights occupying a 'third space', "...recognising the value of both individual autonomy and collective solidarity, reconciling liberal universalism and cultural pluralism."[55] A related question is whether language rights enforcement applies irrespective of geographical factors (the personality principle, which is attuned more to language rights in an individual sense) or is conditioned by specific geographical boundaries (the territorial principle, as practised in *e.g.* Belgium, which fits better with the concept of group rights). Strict or absolute compliance with the territorial principle would seem to go against the grain of minority language rights, by compelling linguistic choices on individuals by virtue of where they happen to be in a geographical or physical sense. In reality, however, the idea of pragmatism comes to the fore here once again; in accordance with the principles of feasibility and demand, there must be some limitations placed on the extent to which language services can be provided, an objective formula that links territorial/personality arguments with numerical/viability criteria and that is taken into account in virtually all language planning structures. And this illustrates yet again the material distinction in practice between the declaration and implementation of rights.

---

[53] Freeman, "Are there collective human rights?", p. 38.

[54] Réaume, "The constitutional protection of language", p. 49.

[55] Freeman, "Are there collective human rights?", p. 40.

There are no hard and fast rules to assist in the determination of the matters raised in the preceding paragraphs; yet it is probably true (if perhaps unsatisfactory) that notwithstanding this multitude of uncertainties, the recognition and protection of language rights has nonetheless taken root in both international law and in the majority of EC Member States—with varying degrees of intensity and success. Can the rights-duties thesis be applied to the protection of language rights at Community level? When minority rights groups assert claims against the EC, what do they actually mean? And perhaps more cogently, what *can* they mean? In Chapters 3 and 4, it was argued that programmes grounded in Article 151 EC which might go beyond the more aesthetic aspects of culture could not come about without a fundamental change in the perspectives of the Community institutions and, perhaps more especially, of the Member States. The cultural aspect of language policy, which is linked more to the value of linguistic survival, is both valid in itself and vital to the maintenance and flourishing of any language group. But bracketing language issues as an exclusively cultural concern does not other practical difficulties faced by speakers on a daily basis that stem from the narrow range of domains in which they may use their languages. A distinction has been drawn here between the 'rights of languages', which include guarantees on education and cultural concerns, and fundamental 'language rights'.[56] Language policy rooted in the cultural realm is especially relevant to the rights of languages *i.e.* to linguistic survival, but this on its own does not fulfil critical aspects of the fundamental right to linguistic security, most markedly as regards both communicative and functional interaction between the public and private sectors. Primary responsibility lies clearly with national and regional government, however, so the most difficult question here is the extent to which the EC has a role to play, if any, above and beyond its contribution in the sphere of cultural policy. In other words, if individuals can be said to have language rights in their capacity as EU citizens, then what are the corollary Community duties? And it must be borne in mind equally that EC fundamental rights standards can be imposed on the Member States in certain circumstances; is there any scope for the development of EC language rights in this sense? The following sections look first at the protection of fundamental rights by the EC in a general sense, tracing both the origins of this jurisdiction and its

---

[56] On this point, see also Elisabetta Zuanelli, "Italian in the European Community: An educational perspective on the national language and new language minorities", in Florian Coulmas (ed.), *A Language Policy for the European Community: Prospects and Quandaries*, (Berlin; New York: Mouton de Gruyter, 1991), 291-300 at 297.

likely future directions. Then, language claims—both current and potential —can be assessed against this background.

3. FUNDAMENTAL RIGHTS AND THE EUROPEAN COMMUNITY

It is somewhat paradoxical that despite the seemingly extensive protection of human rights now codified at both national and international levels, "...the legal landscape is presently littered with craters so that citizens may often find themselves without adequate legal protection...."[57] Minority rights can be all too illustrative of this observation. On the one hand, there is an evident, and indeed fashionable, trend in recent times towards renewed interest in minority rights as an independent concern, complementary to but distinct from more 'traditional' fundamental rights; but this has not been achieved without a considerable degree of controversy and inconsistency. Language rights have been raised both as a subset of non-discrimination and as an autonomous category of duty-imposing rights in themselves. The ambiguities that typify minority rights protection generally, along with the perceived inconsequence (even frivolity) of linguistic choice claims have meant that language rights are rarely a priority and thus exemplify the 'crater' analogy outlined above. On the other hand, intervention via international standards is an intensely sensitive matter, given the particular link between languages and identity, and thus sovereignty. It is fair to say that the EC might be considered an unlikely champion in this regard. The gradual recognition and protection of fundamental rights by the EC institutions is consistent with an acceptance by states more generally of external limits on public power, but the fundamental rights jurisdiction developed by the ECJ relates specifically to the dominion of EC law and policy. The breadth of 'Community rights' stems from the fact that they do not just guide the EC institutions; they also impinge upon the Member States. But this applies only when Member States (or more appropriately, emanations of the Member States) are administering EC law or restricting Community freedoms. This means that the EC does not, at present, have a general or complete human rights jurisdiction. If language rights are to be recognised at all, the claim must first be linked in some way to the implementation of Community law. Moreover, the sources of rights protected by the Community legal order are obviously relevant here.

---

[57] Andrew Clapham, "A human rights policy for the European Community", (1990) 10 *Yearbook of European Law*, 309-366 at 344.

A.   The EC and Fundamental Rights: Tracking a Jurisdiction[58]

In reality, the protection of fundamental rights by the EC amounts to the fulfilment of a historical ambition more than the genesis of a contemporary innovation. Proposals for the creation of a European organisation to regulate political as well as economic activities fell by the wayside in the early 1950s; essentially, states were not yet prepared to cede national sovereignty to such an extent.[59] Fundamental rights did not feature explicitly in the Treaty of Rome,[60] but this is not surprising given the limited scope of the original EEC —at least in terms of the extent to which Member States had committed on paper—and the fragility of inter-state relations at that time. It is widely submitted that judicial activism in the Court of Justice was primarily responsible for introducing fundamental rights norms into the EC arena, but the Court's choices must be checked against the political impasse with which it was confronted. Initially, the ECJ resisted arguments put before it that were based on human rights principles.[61] This led to acute tension between the Community and Member States (notably Germany and Italy) concerned that a legal system which was establishing supremacy over domestic law[62] was not accountable in terms of fundamental rights, thus effectively flouting basic principles of democratic legitimacy. The response of the ECJ is well

---

[58]   The following paragraphs refer almost exclusively to the *internal* fundamental rights jurisdiction/policy of the EC and EU. On this and on other (external) aspects of EU fundamental rights protection, see the comprehensive collection in Alston (ed.), *The EU and Human Rights*.

[59]   The Treaty establishing the European Defence Community (EDC) was signed in 1952; proposals for the creation of the European Political Community (EPC), a transnational organisation with policies of considerably broad application, were put forward in 1953. The EDC Treaty was never ratified, however, leading to the abortion of contingent plans for the EPC also.

[60]   Although Dauses identifies a number of quasi-rights provisions, such as the prohibition of discrimination on grounds of nationality (Article 7 EEC (now 12 EC)) and the principle of equal pay for equal work irrespective of gender (Article 119 EEC (now 141 EC)): Manfred A. Dauses, "The protection of fundamental rights in the Community legal order", (1985) *European Law Review*, 398-419 at 398-9.

[61]   Case 1/58 *Stork v. High Authority* [1959] ECR 17; Cases 36-38, 40/59 *Geitling v. High Authority of the ECSC* [1960] ECR 523; Case 40/64 *Sgarlata v. Commission of the EEC* [1965] ECR 215. The Court did not, as is often claimed, reject fundamental rights *per se* in any of these decisions; rather, it refused to accept that 'imported' constitutional principles, as *national* legal concepts, could prevail over EC law (see the phrasing used by the Court in *Stork*, p. 26; *Geitling*, p. 438; *Sgarlata*, p. 227).

[62]   See the landmark decisions in Case 26/62 *Van Gend en Loos v. Nederlandse Administratie der Belastingen* [1963] ECR 1 and Case 6/64 *Costa v. ENEL* [1964] ECR 585.

documented. In *Stauder v. City of Ulm*, the judgment refers tersely (and arguably *obiter dictum*) to "...the fundamental human rights enshrined in the general principles of Community law and protected by the Court."[63] The Court did not elaborate on either the nature or scope of these rights in that decision but proceeded tenuously to weave a more complete rights jurisprudence in a series of subsequent judgments. It was confirmed that an independent rights protection regime existed in the Community legal order, drawn from and inspired by the protection of rights as a feature of the common constitutional traditions of the Member States,[64] as well as the fundamental rights protected by international treaties, with particular emphasis on the European Convention on Human Rights (ECHR).[65] The basic premise was that Community measures contravening fundamental rights recognised by the Court would be struck down. Along with supremacy and direct effect, the consequences of fundamental rights protection in the Community legal order were thus designed by the Court of Justice. But its approach was endorsed explicitly by a Joint Declaration of the Parliament, the Council (and thus by inference, the Member States) and the Commission, issued on 5 April 1977,[66] and endorsed by the Member States more directly via the European Council in 1978. So the Court did not act alone. It was obliged initially to react to what was effectively a constitutional dispute, in the absence of contemporaneous solutions from the 'political' institutions; the Joint Declaration represents retrospective complicity, at the very least.[67]

Rights recognised to date can broadly be categorised as follows: first, rights at national level in respect of the application of Community law; second, rights in the context of action by Community institutions or agents; and, finally, rights granted by the Community itself, such as social rights and

---

[63] Case 29/69 *Stauder v. City of Ulm* [1969] ECR 419 at 419, para. 7. De Búrca has argued that the introduction of rights terminology into the jurisprudence of the ECJ (and thus into the Community legal order) served broader purposes also, however, and discusses especially the ideas of legitimation and integration: see Gráinne de Búrca, "The language of rights and European integration", in Jo Shaw and Gillian More (eds.), *New Legal Dynamics of European Union*, (Oxford: Clarendon Press, 1995), 29-54 at 39 *et seq.*

[64] Case 11/70 *Internationale Handelsgesellschaft* [1970] ECR 1125.

[65] See Case 4/73 *Nold v. Commission* [1974] ECR 491; Case 44/79 *Hauer v. Land Rheinland-Pfalz* [1979] ECR 3727.

[66] [1977] OJ C103/1.

[67] The tensions between the ECJ and domestic courts did not, however, end neatly with *Stauder*; see especially, the decisions of the German Constitutional Court in *Solange I* [1974] 2 CMLR 540, *Solange II* [1987] 3 CMLR 225 and *Brunner v. European Union Treaty* (Cases 2 BvR 2134/02 & 2159/92) [1994] 1 CMLR 57.

citizenship rights.[68] As noted above, the ECJ identified more or less *ab initio* the two broad sources from which it would draw 'Community rights'; these sources will now be looked at in more detail. In *Nold v. Commission*, the Court declared that "...international treaties for the protection of human rights, on which the Member States have collaborated or of which they are signatories, can supply guidelines which should be followed within the framework of Community law."[69] In reality, the international instrument to which the Court refers almost exclusively is the ECHR,[70] although instruments with universal international application have been mentioned occasionally, most notably the UN International Covenant on Civil and Political Rights.[71] The paucity of references to other international treaties which the Member States have ratified is purely a matter of practice and not a legal preclusion. International treaties in general are not referred to in Article 6(2) (formerly F(2)) TEU, which mentions the ECHR exclusively. But this relates to fundamental rights protection within the Union only and does not disturb the *acquis communautaire* on rights protected by the EC legal order.

The ECHR was first mentioned specifically by the Court in *Rutili*.[72] Dauses distinguishes between the 'suprapositive principles of law incorporated in the Convention'—constituting an independent source of law that takes precedence over even primary Community law—and the Convention text itself as the embodiment of those principles, which is subordinate to the EC Treaties.[73] The realisation of this distinction in practice has enabled the Court of Justice sometimes to go beyond the extent of protection accorded to certain rights under the Convention; in other words, the interpretative

---

[68] See Clapham, "A human rights policy", pp. 317-8.

[69] Case 4/73 *Nold v. Commission* [1974] ECR 491 at 507, para. 13.

[70] In Cases 46/87 & 227/88 *Hoechst AG v. Commission* [1989] ECR 2859 the Court referred to the 'particular' significance it attaches to the ECHR (at 2923, para. 13.).

[71] See for example, Case 374/87 *Orkem v. Commission* [1989] ECR 3283, where the Court referred to Article 14(3)(g) of the UN International Covenant on Civil and Political Rights (on the right against self-incrimination). See also Joined Cases C-297/88 and C-197/89 *Dzodzi v. Belgian State* [1990] ECR I-3763, and Case C-249/96 *Grant v. South West Trains* [1998] ECR I-621. In Case C-274/96 *Criminal Proceedings against Bickel and Franz* [1998] ECR I-7637, Advocate General Jacobs discussed arguments related to the Covenant (Articles 14(3)(a) and (f) ICCPR) in the specific context of language rights (see Chapter 6).

[72] Case 36/75 *Rutili* [1975] ECR 1219. In Cases 60, 61/84 *Cinéthèque v. Fédération Nationale des Cinémas Français* [1985] ECR 2605, the ECJ confirmed that it had no power to assess the compatibility of domestic law with the ECHR in an area that fell solely within national jurisdiction

[73] Dauses, "The protection of fundamental rights", p. 412.

approach adopted by the Court has been to look at fundamental rights *principles* as distinct from the substantive *provisions* of the Convention. This development has engendered criticism, particularly regarding the risk of incoherence between the Community interpretation of a given right and that of the European Court of Human Rights—which is, after all, the primary interpreter of the Convention.[74] On the other hand, it is widely recognised in international human rights law that treaty provisions represent a compromise, mirroring the level of agreement achieved among (often) divided negotiating parties; domestic or other (*e.g.* regional) measures that give *additional* protection in fundamental rights matters are not only valid, but welcomed. In *Mutsch*, an ECJ decision dealing with language rights in criminal proceedings and discussed in Chapter 2, Advocate General Lenz claimed that "[i]t is not contrary to the [ECHR] for Community law to grant more extensive protection to individual rights. Indeed, the Court has held that Community law takes precedence over other agreements concluded within the framework of the Council of Europe *in so far as it is more favourable to individuals.*"[75] The continuing controversy that characterises the relationship between the Luxembourg and Strasbourg courts suggests that it is one of divisive, counterproductive tension. Obviously, there are legitimate issues at play here.[76] But the difficulties raised are not easy actually to quantify. How can this inter-organisational relationship best be channelled? It has been argued consistently that the EC should accede to the ECHR, thus establishing an interpretative hierarchy as regards the interpretation of the Convention and, in turn, enhancing the accountability of the Community itself. While persuasive in many respects, this solution does not really solve the specific issues raised here *i.e.* the interpretation of 'extra-Convention' principles, or the granting of additional protection over and above that codified in the Convention provisions. The ECJ's Opinion on accession thwarted the momentum of this debate still further. The Court held that such a step would only be possible following a Treaty amendment, given the constitutional significance attached to entering a 'distinct international institutional system'.[77] Although the Commission had not favoured

---

[74]   See, for example, Clapham, "A human rights policy", p. 338.

[75]   Opinion of Advocate General Lenz in Case 137/84 *Ministère Public v. Mutsch* [1985] ECR 2681 at 2690, citing Case 187/73 *Callemeyn v. Belgium* [1974] ECR 553 (emphasis added).

[76]   See Dean Spielman, "Human rights case law in the Strasbourg and Luxembourg courts: Conflicts, inconsistencies and complementarities", in Alston (ed.) *The EU and Human Rights*, 757-780.

[77]   Opinion 2/94, [1996] ECR I-1759 at 1789, para. 34.

accession initially,[78] its perspective changed gradually to that of actively recommending that the Convention should be ratified. In a 1979 memorandum, the Commission stressed that accession would portray a favourable image of the Community and acknowledged that it would ensure consistent and harmonious interpretation of the ECHR.[79] The Commission did not really examine the question from the perspective of fundamental rights protection for individual citizens, a miscalculation that has been criticised as portraying institutional self-interest in the Community context.[80] But the Commission's stance has evolved over the years; it argued in 1990, for example, that accession to the Convention would redress an imbalance (since the EC institutions are not themselves subject to the control mechanism of the Council of Europe) and would constitute an additional guarantee that human rights were being respected in the Community.[81] The accountability of the institutions is a habitually criticised and vulnerable link in the present edifice of EC rights protection; it is often perceived that the Court of Justice has been far more vigilant in its jurisdiction over Member States and their authorities than it has been with regard to alleged breaches involving the Community institutions. This anomaly is exacerbated by the fact that "[t]he individual's ability to challenge a measure on fundamental rights grounds is more restricted where the measure of taken by an EU institution than it is where it has been taken by a national authority."[82] In her commentary on the ECJ opinion, O'Leary summarised the advantages of accession in terms of democracy, legitimacy, valuable symbolism, consistency in the interpretation of the Convention and broadening the ambit of EC fundamental rights protection beyond the limited scope of the application of Community law.[83] She identified also some problematic aspects; for example, the ECHR provides only a basic, minimum standard of protection (then arguing in response that the Convention is not a static but an evolving instrument that

---

[78] See, for example, the Commission's response (EC Bull. Supp. 5/76) to the European Parliament ([1973] OJ C26/7) on how the fundamental rights of Member State citizens could best be protected; the Commission favoured protection via the case law of the Court of Justice rather than by accession to the ECHR.

[79] 6724/76 Bull. Supp. 2/79.

[80] See Clapham, "A human rights policy", pp. 361-2.

[81] Commission Communication on Accession to the ECHR, [1990] Bull.EC 11/1990.

[82] House of Lords Select Committee on European Union, *Report on the EC Draft Charter of Fundamental Rights*, Eighth Report, (London: The Stationery Office, 2000), para. 128; see also, paras. 129-133.

[83] Siofra O'Leary, "Accession by the EC to the ECHR: The Opinion of the European Court of Justice", (1996) 4 *European Human Rights Law Review*, 362-377 at 369.

has been interpreted by the European Court of Human Rights accordingly[84]). O'Leary points out that the ECHR should be viewed as 'the safety net but not the standard setter' and argues that should the Community accede, the Union—as distinct from the Community—could still supplement and improve on areas falling outside the remit of the Convention. But it is difficult to gauge why she has distinguished between the Community and the Union in this context. There is nothing to prevent *any* party to the Convention, whether a State or the Community if it should ever accede, from introducing measures that strive to implement *greater* protection that that offered by the Convention. The standards set by any international instrument represent a lowest common denominator, not the last word on the acceptable benchmark of rights protection; and this is expressly provided for in Article 53 ECHR.[85] Thus, the relationship between the EC and the Council of Europe is a peculiarly complex one, calling into question issues that simply do not arise in the context of state relations. The debate on accession has moved forward yet again in recent times, framed now by the EU Charter of Fundamental Rights, discussed below.[86] Regarding the ECJ's interpretative approach more generally then, the current position remains that it may draw inspiration from international treaties when developing the fundamental rights jurisdiction of the Community. The Court has not relied extensively on any instrument other than the ECHR, although this situation has resulted from practice rather than any legal prohibition. It has, on occasion, applied fundamental rights principles in a manner that appears inconsistent with their codification in the Convention (or more specifically, with the interpretation of these provisions by the European Court of Human Rights); while this has caused tension in terms of consistency of interpretation, it is typically beneficial from the perspective of individuals. On this point, Article 52(3) of the Charter—discussed in more detail below—embodies the advancement of individual protection in terms of establishing the ECHR (and its interpretation by the Strasbourg Court) as a minimum standard from which the ECJ may not detract, as well as providing explicitly for the possibility of more

---

[84] *ibid.*, pp. 370-2; the interpretative approach of the European Court of Human Rights is addressed below in the specific context of language rights under the Convention.

[85] Article 53 ECHR provides that "[n]othing in this Convention shall be construed as limiting or derogating from any of the human rights and fundamental freedoms which may be ensured under the laws of any High Contracting Party or under any other agreement to which it is a Party."

[86] For analysis of the arguments for and against accession in light of the Charter, see the House of Lords Select Committee, Eighth Report, especially at paras. 15-17, 104-112 and 139-143.

extensive EU protection. Aside from the tensions sparked by differing Court of Justice/Court of Human Rights interpretations, perhaps a more serious issue here, again from the perspective of individuals, was the unpredictability that resulted from the ECJ's *ad hoc* interpretative approach, which raises concerns in the domain of legal certainty and legitimate expectations. This was especially relevant when a 'new' fundamental right is raised in the EC context, even more so where that right was protected already under the Convention. The inevitable level of doubt generated here is yet another reason why the possibility of a specific catalogue of 'EC rights' needed to be taken on board, returned to in more depth below.

Defining the second source of 'Community' fundamental rights—the common constitutional traditions of the Member States—is even more complicated. All EC Member States guarantee the protection of fundamental rights at national level.[87] As is the case for international treaties, the Court of Justice can draw from the principles enshrined in national constitutions, but it will interpret and prioritise these concepts to formulate 'Community rights', against the background of other Treaty objectives. In *Internationale Handelsgesellschaft*, Advocate General Dutheillet de Lamothe concluded that fundamental legal principles drawn from national legal orders "...contribute to forming that philosophical, political and legal substratum common to the Member States from which through the case-law an unwritten Community law emerges."[88] In this way, once again, the supremacy of EC law is thus secured. The main difficulty with constitutional traditions as a source of Community rights is the presupposition that a 'common' standard can be distilled in the first place. Dauses has argued that "...although all the Member States are conscious of certain intellectual and political traditions...they go their own ways as regards method, structure, normative rank and definition of the scope of individual guarantees".[89] This is especially true for social and economic rights (rendering constitutional principles particularly problematic as a source of fundamental rights in the

---

[87] The constitutions of thirteen Member States (excluding France and the United Kingdom) contain references to the protection of fundamental rights. The preamble to the French Constitution does, however, proclaim its 'dedication' to the 1789 Declaration of the Rights of Man. The UK does not have a written Constitution, but the UK government has provided recently for the incorporation of elements of the ECHR into domestic law (via the 1998 Human Rights Act).

[88] Case11/70 *Internationale Handelsgesellschaft*, [1970] ECR 1125, Opinion of Advocate General Dutheillet de Lamothe, pp. 1146-7.

[89] Dauses, "The protection of fundamental rights", p. 407; see also, O'Leary, "Accession by the EC to the ECHR", pp. 373-4 and Bruno de Witte, "Community law and national constitutional values", (1991-2) *Legal Issues of European Integration* 1-22.

context of Community law) and becomes still more complex where particular rights are either protected weakly by, or excluded altogether from, one or a number of Member State constitutions. So reliance by the Court on often anomalous Member State understandings of various rights as a source of inspiration for uniform Community interpretation seems potentially ineffective and politically divisive, given the inevitable selection process that will ensue. This reconciling of various domestic expressions of protection has long been an issue of controversy in the Court's case law and in related academic commentary. A Commission communication issued in 1976 recommended that where standards of protection differed in Member State constitutions, the constitutional provision that offered the greatest level of protection for the individual should be drawn from as the basis in EC law of the fundamental right in question.[90] Linking the delineation of rights to national provisions to this extent arguably challenges the legitimacy of the autonomous Community legal order. Moreover, attempting to extract a common position from discordant provisions presents the converse danger that the Court might apply what it has gleaned to be the *lowest* standard of protection.[91] A related issue is whether a certain minimum number of constitutions must protect a fundamental right before it will be recognised at all in the Community context. Advocate General Warner, in the *IRCA* decision, considered that protection of a fundamental right by just one Member State constitution was sufficient to trigger its incorporation into Community law.[92] It has been argued that this submission was ignored in subsequent decisions of the Court;[93] it has also been asserted that the Advocate General's stance was rejected implicitly in *Hauer*, where the view that infringement of fundamental rights in the Community context can only be assessed by reference to Community, not national, law was reaffirmed.[94] This question, then, remains unsettled.

---

[90] EC Bull. Supp. 5/76, p. 16.

[91] For a discussion on the fluctuating jurisprudence of the Court in this regard, see Lars Bondo Krogsgaard, "Fundamental rights in the EC after Maastricht", (1993) *Legal Issues of European Integration*, 99-113 at 105-107.

[92] Case 7/76 *IRCA v. Amministrazione delle Finanze dello Stato* [1976] ECR 1213; see the Opinion of Advocate General Warner, p. 1237.

[93] Jason Coppel and Aidan O'Neill, The European Court of Justice: Taking rights seriously?", (1992) 29 *Common Market Law Review*, 669-692 at 685.

[94] J.H.H. Weiler and Nicolas J.S. Lockhart, "'Taking rights seriously' seriously: The European Court of Justice and its fundamental rights jurisprudence", (1995) vol. 32:1; vol. 32:2 *Common Market Law Review* 51-94; 579-627 (at Part II, p. 596); Case 44/79 *Hauer v. Land Rheinland-Pfalz* [1979] ECR 3727. The matter is not resolved, however; Phelan, for example, refers to authority for the proposition that the *IRCA* position remains valid:

As noted at the beginning of this chapter, balancing and prioritising fundamental rights—against both other fundamental rights and competing values of a different order—is an acutely sensitive issue in fundamental rights discourse generally, but it takes on heightened significance in the EC context. Essentially, this is because conflicts that have arisen between Community and Member State interpretations have often reflected the collision of moral and economic values. When it is considered that a given claim must have a Community law element before 'Community' fundamental rights will kick in, it could logically be presumed that the ECJ will find itself involved only peripherally with a limited catalogue of (primarily) economic and social rights, engaging in economic analysis and sheltered from more politically volatile moral questions. This position seems cushioned when a core rule of interpretation is recalled: the ECJ will balance fundamental rights claims against limits set by the overall objectives of the EC Treaty but must ensure that the substance of the right in question is not impaired.[95] The Court restated this principle most recently in *Karlsson*:

> [I]t is well established in the case law of the Court that restrictions may be imposed on the exercise of fundamental rights, in particular in the context of a common organisation of the market, provided that those restrictions in fact correspond to objectives of general interest pursued by the Community and do not constitute, with regard to the aim pursued, disproportionate and unreasonable interference undermining the very substance of those rights.[96]

But examination of the Court's case law demonstrates that while the Court focused initially on economic and social rights, a broader agenda encompassing civil and political rights has evolved, in keeping with the gradual extension of Community competence, the expansion of Community objectives and an emphasis on administrative and procedural fairness that characterises the majority of contemporary claims invoking EC law

---

Diarmuid Rossa Phelan, "Right to life of the unborn v. promotion of trade in services: The ECJ and the normative shaping of the European Union", (1992) vol. 55:5 *Modern Law Review*, 670-689 at 674 (footnote 23).

[95] See Case 4/73 *Nold v. Commission* [1974] ECR 491 at 508, para. 14 ("...these rights should, if necessary be subject to certain limits justified by the overall objectives pursued by the Community, on condition that the substance of these rights is left untouched.") This approach is exemplified the Court's analysis in Case 44/79 *Hauer v. Land Rheinland-Pfalz* [1979] ECR 3727 (see especially p. 3750, para. 32).

[96] Case C-292/97 *Karlsson and others*, judgment of 13 April 2000, not yet reported, para. 45.

arguments.[97] A pragmatic view outlined by Phelan observes that "[w]hen numerous judges from [the diverse] legal systems [of the Member States]...are obliged to decide cases in widely disparate fields under a new and complex legal system which each Member State, in addition to private parties, is trying to influence in its own favour, it is not surprising that they should give general objectives such prominence."[98] More contentiously, the perceived subordination of nuclear constitutional values has sparked virulent debate among academic commentators, characterised most notably the accusation that the Court of Justice does not take its fundamental rights jurisdiction seriously.[99] The Court's decision in *Grogan* is a strikingly apt example of where morals and economics collide, and has spawned a wealth of intense, often biting, analysis.[100] This debate reflects the ongoing deliberation on EC/Member State competence boundaries, complicated by the overt clash of values as well as legal and political structures. Phelan has recommended modification of the 'exceptionless supremacy doctrine', giving precedence to adjudications by national constitutional courts on 'basic principles concerning life, liberty, religion and the family' while maintaining the primacy of EC law for economic and social rights.[101] He considers that this teleological approach conforms especially well with the principle of subsidiarity, enshrined in the EC Treaty. But his solution fails to appreciate the very problem epitomised in *Grogan*, that the severance of values into neatly distinct constitutional and economic categories is just not always possible. The gulf that exists between according competences to the EC and accepting their implementation at supranational level, discussed in Chapter 4, reflects a simmering uneasiness that is also relevant here, given the clash

---

[97] O'Neill traces the protection of a number of political rights protected by the Court, including the rights to privacy, freedom of expression, fair hearing and due process: Michael O'Neill, "Fundamental rights and the European Union", in Gerard Quinn (ed.), *Irish Yearbook of Human Rights*, (Dublin: Round Hall Sweet and Maxwell, 1995), 67-95 at 68-9. See also the list of rights given on the European Parliament Factsheet at http://www.europarl.eu.int/dg4/factsheets/en/2_1_0.htm.

[98] Phelan, "Right to life of the unborn", p. 686.

[99] Coppel and O'Neill, "The European Court of Justice"; responded to by Weiler and Lockhart, "'Taking rights seriously' seriously"; Phelan, in "Right to life of the unborn", refers to a 'chasm' that exists between EC and Member State perceptions of fundamental rights and values (pp. 680-1).

[100] Case C-159/90 *S.P.U.C. v. Grogan* [1991] ECR I-4685; see Phelan, "Right to life of the unborn" and Gráinne de Búrca, "Fundamental rights and the reach of EC law", (1993) 13 *Oxford Journal of Legal Studies* 283-319. See also, Coppel and O'Neill, pp. 685-689, and Weiler and Lockhart, pp. 597-605.

[101] Phelan, "Right to life of the unborn", pp. 688-9.

of deeply rooted national values with fledgling 'Community' versions, the contingent threat to national sovereignty, the uncertain scope of fundamental rights within the Community legal order and the inevitable reaction of mainly civil law Member States to what is perceived as bald judicial activism, associated more usually with the common law tradition. The resulting impression of Community/Member State competition is, however, misplaced. As Weiler and Lockhart have expressed succinctly, "...human rights issues do not necessarily pit the Community against Member States: human rights issues typically will pit the individual against public authorities [rendering] artificial in many instances the notions of Member States v. Community institutions."[102]

Language rights empower the individual against public authorities in exactly this sense. The consequences of dealing with language claims out-with the domain of fundamental rights is especially evident in the conflicting decisions of the ECJ on Regulation 1/58, analysed in Chapter 1. But the development of a more coherent EC perspective on language rights could become an unfortunate casualty of a broader reluctance to submit to Community jurisdiction at the controversial fringes of the fundamental rights domain. To alleviate Member State discomfort with judicial activism and to strengthen the position of the individual, it had been long been suggested that the Community should draw up a catalogue of enumerated fundamental rights.[103] It was anticipated that a Community 'bill of rights' might settle Member State anxieties to a greater extent and would also, more importantly, provide clarity for individuals as to what level of protection for which rights can reasonably be expected in the context of EC law. Concern had been voiced regarding the difficulties inherent in achieving consensus on both the scope and content of a bill of rights but finally, as an offshoot of IGC 2000 on institutional reform, an EU Charter of Fundamental Rights was prepared, giving the Member States a chance to shape more conclusively at the political level the course of EU fundamental rights protection.[104] The drafting process was not without controversy and notwithstanding the 'proclamation' of the Charter at the Nice Summit in December 2000, its eventual status and impact are far from clear, as discussed below. The way in which Community competence in the fundamental rights domain evolves in the future is of crucial importance in contexts such as language rights, since they are not

---

[102] Weiler and Lockhart, "'Taking rights seriously' seriously", p. 621.

[103] Within the EC institutions, this call was taken up primarily by the European Parliament: see especially, its resolution of 16 May 1989 [1989] OJ C120/51.

[104] Charte 4487/00, Brussels, 28 September 2000; see the European Union website at http://europa.eu.int/comm/justice_home/unit/charte/index_en.html.

typically linked to the more traditional applications of EC law. At this point, before considering the likely evolution of fundamental rights protection within the Community legal order, the extent to which language rights are protected within international legal instruments and the constitutional traditions of the Member States will be outlined; both of these sources currently inform the divination of rights by the ECJ and furthermore, as the raw materials of the *acquis* in this field, their influence on the Charter is obviously considerable. If the ECJ is going to recognise language rights at all, then their protection at national and international levels is the inevitable starting point.

C. The Protection of Language Rights: Sourcing International and National Standards[105]

(i) *International Foundations: The United Nations*[106]

As noted earlier, the principle of universal application, based on the dignity and equality of each individual person, was the value upon which early United Nations human rights instruments hinged (in contrast to the more 'specific' protection of minority groups that had been undertaken by the League of Nations). From the outset, key UN rights instruments included language in their non-discrimination clauses *e.g.* Article 1(3) of the UN Charter (1945), Article 2 of the Universal Declaration on Human Rights (UDHR–1948) and Article 2(1) of the International Covenant on Civil and Political Rights (ICCPR), adopted in 1966 and in force ten years later. The UDHR provisions on equality before the law (Article 7), freedom of expression (Article 19), education (Article 26) and freedom of participation in cultural life (Article 27) are also relevant to language issues. In addition,

---

[105] For a comprehensive guide to international and national legal instruments that refer to language rights, see de Varennes, *Language, Minorities and Human Rights*, pp. 279-459.

[106] Given that this work focuses solely on language rights in the EC context, the international sources of language rights referred to in the following paragraphs will be limited to instruments from which the ECJ either has or is likely to derive Community rights. For this reason, UN standards in this area will be considered briefly, with concentration given to the work of the Council of Europe. In particular, the work of the Organisation for Security and Cooperation in Europe (OSCE)—though considerable—will not be discussed. For information on the scope of the OSCE and its work on minority languages, see Jane Wright, "The OSCE and the protection of minority rights", (1996) vol. 18:1 *Human Rights Quarterly* 190-205. For the text of and information on the OSCE Oslo Recommendations on the Linguistic Rights of National Minorities, see http://www.unesco.org/most/ln2pol7.htm.

the UN Commission on Human Rights established its Sub-Commission on the Prevention of Discrimination and the Protection of Minorities in 1946.[107] Focusing more specifically on the official use of language, the principal UN mechanism for protecting minority rights is contained in Article 27 ICCPR, which provides that "[i]n those states in which ethnic, religious or linguistic minorities exist, persons belonging to such minorities shall not be denied the right, in community with the other members of their group, to enjoy their own culture, to profess and practise their own religion, or to use their own language." Article 27 represents a hybrid of group and individual rights, in that the rights are bestowed on individuals but exercised 'in community' with other group members. As suggested above, this apparent fudging may actually represent a very workable compromise in the individual/group rights debate. The provision has been interpreted as placing reciprocal duties of implementation on signatory states, although the nature and extent of this assertion are far from settled.[108] The increasing concern of the international community over minority rights violations was confirmed resolutely in the UN General Assembly's Declaration on the Rights of Persons belonging to National or Ethnic, Religious and Linguistic Minorities, issued in 1992.[109] Notably, the Declaration refers expressly, in Article 1(2), to the positive obligation on states to provide legislatively and otherwise for the promotion of ethnic, cultural, religious and linguistic identities. In addition, the Declaration is framed in more positive terms than Article 27 ICCPR, employing the phrase 'has the right' instead of 'shall not be denied the right'.

In terms of redress, the ICCPR provides for both individual petition (based on an Optional Protocol to the Covenant) and state reporting, although it is widely acknowledged that neither mechanism can protect individual rights very effectively: the former is dependant on the relevant state having acceded to the Protocol, while the latter relies on a state's own representations of the domestic human rights situation. In reality, the protection of language rights by the UN (particularly a lower priority fundamental right such as the right to choice of language) is seen as a fairly remote option from the perspective of individual claimants, given the multitude and extent of human rights atrocities with which the UN Human

---

[107] *See* Asbjørn Eide, "The Sub-Commission on the Prevention of Discrimination and the Protection of Minorities", in Philip Alston (ed.), *The United Nations and Human Rights*, (Oxford: Clarendon Press, 1992), 211-264.

[108] See Capotorti Report, *Study on the Rights of Persons*, p. 37 and the Decision of the Human Rights Committee in *Kitok v. Sweden*, Comm. No. 197/1985, 27 July 1985. But see also, de Varennes, *Language, Minorities and Human Rights*, p. 150 *et seq.*

[109] Res. 47/135, adopted 18 December 1992.

Rights Committee is preoccupied on an ongoing basis, and the virtually innate extraordinariness attached to pursuing a claim at this level. The work of the UN in the realm of establishing norms and standards of international human rights law cannot be overestimated; the influence of UN standards on international and national action shaped the legal landscape of the twentieth century to a profound degree and this legacy, thankfully, strives to endure. The pace of its development may not yet meet the needs of the international community but the system continues to mature, challenging continuously the conventional shelter of state sovereignty where appropriate. To increase its effectiveness as an institution, the UN must develop its role in the implementation and enforcement of human rights law, as well as maintaining its traditional strength as a standard setter; otherwise, non-binding instruments such as the 1992 Declaration will amount to nothing more than a collection of aspirations. Obviously, political will is crucial here and in truth, this is beyond the control of the United Nations which, like the EC, is not an autonomous creature. But the UN has begun to grapple tentatively with the enduring question of minority rights in a contemporary context. This alone should signal to states, other political entities and individuals that minority rights matter. As a subset of minority rights, language rights—as fundamental rights, however so derived—have been shown to warrant the imposition of effective corollary obligations and duties on governing entities. The influence of United Nations standards—especially those set by Article 27 ICCPR—is critically relevant here; as a basic international yardstick, extracted from treaties to which the EC Member States are signatories, this ethos can certainly be drawn from by the Court of Justice where appropriate.

(ii)   Regional Adaptation: The Council of Europe

The extent to which states have submitted to the jurisdiction of the Council of Europe—or more specifically, to that of the European Court of Human Rights—illustrates the efficacy of international cooperation at regional level. Regional human rights organisations do not set out to impede standards established on the basis of universalism; they seek instead to apply and build on these principles, given that states are more likely to have confidence in an association founded by a group of like-minded states (relative to the immense diversity of state actors in the global international arena). Regional organisations are also more accessible—again, in relative terms—to individuals seeking to enforce international standards against their own states. The success of the European Convention on Human Rights (ECHR) as an enforceable source of rights and freedoms is unparalleled in the international community, not least because of the acceptance by all signatory states of the compulsory jurisdiction of the European Court of Human Rights.[110] As outlined, the ECJ has drawn extensively on provisions of the ECHR in establishing its own fundamental rights jurisprudence; but it has not restricted itself absolutely to applying either the letter of the provisions themselves or relevant interpretations by the Court of Human Rights. Nonetheless, the content of the ECHR clearly establishes a basic level of rights protection by which the Court of Justice is greatly influenced; and the shadow of the Convention falls not lightly on most provisions of the EU Charter of Fundamental Rights.[111] In contrast to the initiatives on fundamental rights generally, the extent to which language rights are protected by the ECHR is essentially disappointing. Relevant provisions fall under two main headings—the use of language in the courts and the principle of non-discrimination. Articles 5 and 6 of the Convention relate to the deprivation of personal liberty and the right to a fair trial respectively. Both provide that information must be provided to anyone charged with a criminal offence in a language understood by them;[112] in addition, Article 6(3)(e) stipulates that the free assistance of an interpreter is to be provided if an accused cannot understand or speak the language used in court proceedings.[113] These provisions are grounded firmly in the principles of natural justice, relating only to instances where an individual cannot *understand* the language used by the relevant official authorities; they do not introduce any right to *choice* of language. The (now defunct) European Commission on Human Rights has refused relief to parties who understood the language used in domestic courts yet sought to have interpreters appointed so that they could speak another language of their choice, as members of minority language groups based in the states in question.[114] Article 14 ECHR outlines a general prohibition on

---

[110] The House of Lords Select Committee on European Union, for example, has described the Council of Europe as being 'universally recognised' as "the fount and guardian of [human] rights [at the wider European level]." (Eighth Report, para. 1).

[111] Moreover, the extent to which the ECJ is obliged to take into account the interpretations of the European Court of Human Rights may now have altered, in light of Article 52(3) of the EU Charter, discussed further below.

[112] See Articles 5(2) and 6(3)(a) ECHR.

[113] Similar rights can be found in Articles 14(3)(a) and (f) of the ICCPR (see also, note 71).

[114] See *K. v. France*, 7 December 1983, (1984) 35 Decisions and Reports 203; *Bideault v. France*, 6 December 1986, (1986) 48 Decisions and Reports 232; both relate to failed attempts to use the Breton language in French courts. Regarding the European Commission on Human Rights, which had issued preliminary decisions on the admissibility of claims, Protocol No. 11 to the Convention resulted in the restructuring of the Convention's institutional (or 'control') machinery and the establishment of a 'new' Court of

various forms of discriminatory treatment, including discrimination based on language. The provision is not, however, an independent guarantee of non-discrimination: its application is restricted to the contexts of other rights protected specifically by the Convention. Examples of rights that may be relevant to language choice include freedom of expression (Article 10)[115] and the right not to be denied education, set out in Article 2 of Protocol 1 to the Convention. Although the Commission on Human Rights had acknowledged the validity of cultural and linguistic pluralism in the context of the media,[116] it decided early on that Article 10 does not entitle individual citizens to communicate with public authorities in the language of their choice.[117] The most comprehensive discussion of linguistic minorities by the Court of Human Rights is contained in the complex *Belgian Linguistics Case*, decided in 1968.[118] The decision examined regional policies on the provision of state education, relating specifically to extensive legislative provisions made for unilingual regions. The Court held that unilingual policy measures were not discriminatory, notwithstanding the claims of minority language speakers who had sought to compel the Belgian state to provide education through the medium of French in officially delimited Dutch-speaking regions. The Court interpreted Article 2 of Protocol No. 1 narrowly, stating that it did not contain any provision dealing with languages of instruction and that only instruction in the national language(s) of a state was relevant to ensuring implementation of a genuine right to education.[119] In a subsequent decision, the Strasbourg Commission reiterated that the Convention does not contain any provisions that grant rights explicitly to speakers of minority

---

Human Rights; the Protocol (and therefore, the new Court) came into force on 31 October 1998, but the Commission continued on a transitional basis for one further year. For details on the present admissibility procedure, see http://www.echr.coe.int/default. htm.

[113] The ECJ has recognised freedom of expression, as embodied in Article 10 of the Convention, as a general principle of law in the EC context: see Case C-260/89 *Elliniki Radiophonia Tileorassi AE v. DEP* [1991] ECR I-2925 at 2964, para. 44; Case C-219/91 *Criminal Proceedings against Ter Voort* [1992] ECR I-5485 at 5513, paras. 34-35.

[116] App. no. 10746/84 *Verein Alternatives Lokalradio Bern and Another v. Switzerland*, 16 October 1986, 49 Decisions and Reports 126.

[117] App. no. 2333/64 *Inhabitants of Leeuw-St.Pierre v. Belgium* [1965] 8 YBECHR 338; see on this point, note 17 and accompanying text.

[118] Series A., No. 6, 23 July 1968, 1 EHRR 252.

[119] Decision of the Court, at para. 31; the Commission's report had been more favourable, accepting a broader interpretation of Article 2/Protocol 1 when read in conjunction with Article 14 ECHR, and finding that the Belgian legislation infringed this guarantee in a number of respects.

languages.[120] The evolving interpretation of the Convention is not, however, wedded exclusively to early decisions of the Court and Commission. Two arguments are relevant here. First, the Court of Human Rights has held repeatedly, since its decision in *Marckx* (1979), that despite the negative formulation of rights and freedoms therein, the Convention does place a positive obligation on states to remove any obstacles to the exercise of those rights.[121] The Court has thus developed more effective recognition for positive rights notwithstanding the limiting phraseology of the Convention itself. This fits also with the contemporary construction attributed to the scope of non-discrimination by de Varennes, outlined in Section 2. Second, the Court has veered noticeably towards teleological interpretation of the Convention, reading its provisions in the context of evolving European standards.[122] Harris, O'Boyle and Warbrick describe the nature of and limitations to this interpretative approach:

> [T]he Convention will not be interpreted to reflect change so as to introduce into it a right that was not intended to be included when the Convention was drafted…In this way, a line is sought to be drawn between judicial interpretation, which is permissible, and judicial legislation, which is not. [W]ith this

---

[120] App. No. 8142/78 *X. v. Austria* 10 October 1979, 18 Decisions and Reports 88. The Council of Europe's Framework Convention for the Protection of National Minorities was opened for signature on 1 February 1995 and, with the requisite twelve ratifications, entered into force exactly three years later; at the time of writing, it has been ratified by thirty three states in total. As a preliminary remark, it should be noted that there is no definition in the Convention as to what actually constitutes a 'national minority', meaning that its scope of application is uncertain. Language rights do feature in the Framework Convention, first, as an aspect of expressing the identity of national minorities, alongside religion, traditions and cultural heritage (see Article 5; see also Article 6), or as linked to *e.g.* freedom of expression in respect of language use outwith public domains (Article 9(1)). Articles 10-11 deal with public use of minority languages but in quite a limited sense; in Article 10(3), the right to be informed of criminal charges adopts the ECHR 'in a language which he or she understands' formula, which does not necessarily imply the use of a minority language. In general, public duties in this regard are limited by phrases such as 'as far as possible'; similar restrictions are set out in Articles 12-14 (education). Overall, then, the Convention does not go beyond the measures set out explicitly in the context of linguistic minorities in the European Charter for Regional or Minority Languages, discussed below, and is not, therefore, addressed in detail here.

[121] Series A, No. 31 *Marckx v. Belgium*, 13 June 1979, (1979-80) 2 EHRR 330; see D.J. Harris, M. O'Boyle and C. Warbrick, *Law of the European Convention on Human Rights*, (London: Butterworths, 1995), pp. 19-22. See most recently, on non-discrimination and positive obligations, *Thlimmenos v. Greece*, 9 BHRC 12 (ECHR).

[122] See in particular, Series A, No. 26 *Tyrer v. UK*, 25 April 1978, (1979-80) EHRR 1; Harris, O'Boyle and Warbrick, *Law of the European Convention*, pp. 7-11.

distinction in mind, the Court tends to emphasise incremental, rather than sudden change. However, as in national law, the line between judicial interpretation and legislation can be a difficult one to draw.... Decisions can be seen either as judicial creativity that move the Convention into distinct areas beyond its intended domain or as the elaboration of rights that are already protected.[123]

Given repeated declarations by the Commission on Human Rights that there was no right to choice of language under the Convention, it would seem unlikely that this could now be introduced judicially. But there are two further developments that must be considered here. First, in the domain of non-discrimination, a new Protocol (No. 12) to the ECHR provides for a general prohibition on non-discrimination independently of the rights guaranteed under the ECHR itself. The Protocol was adopted by the Committee of Ministers in June 2000, and was opened for signature in November of the same year.[124] Article 1 of the text provide as follows:

> 1. The enjoyment of any right set forth by law shall be secured without discrimination on any ground such as sex, race, colour, language, religion, political or other opinion, national or social origin, association with a national minority, property, birth or other status.
>
> 2. No one shall be discriminated against by any public authority on any ground such as those mentioned in paragraph 1.

A non-discrimination clause of this nature has the potential to add much to the scope of application of the ECHR, and language claims such as those formerly dismissed out of hand, outlined above, may have new arguments upon which to draw.

Second, and even more notably, the existence of an evolving or 'incremental' standard on minority language rights can be traced to the development of another instrument introduced by the Council of Europe *i.e.* the European Charter for Regional or Minority Languages. It is commonly

---

[123] Harris, O'Boyle and Warbrick, *Law of the European Convention*, p. 8; de Witte describes the Court's contemporary interpretation of the Convention as 'more sophisticated and probing': Bruno de Witte, "Surviving in Babel? Language rights and European integration", in Yoram Dinstein and Mala Tabory (eds.), *The Protection of Minorities and Human Rights*, (Dordrecht: Martinus Nijhoff, 1992), 277-300 at 280.

[124] To enter into force, the Protocol requires ratification by ten Member States; at the time of writing, the Protocol had been signed by 25 states, but not yet ratified by any.

acknowledged that the work of the European Parliament in the early 1980s, promoting the need for effective action in support of minority languages and their speakers, directly inspired the Council of Europe to address this specific domain of fundamental rights. Following a public hearing to consider the need for adoption of a legal instrument to defend and promote the rights of minority language speakers, the text of the draft Charter was completed by March 1988. The Charter was adopted by the Committee of Ministers in June 1992 and opened for signature in November of that year; with the requisite five ratifications in place, it entered into force on 1 March 1998. But state response has been tepid: at the time of writing, the Charter has been ratified by only eleven states.[125] Moreover, despite the impetus that characterised the public hearing and preparatory work, the Charter is framed in terms of state obligations rather than legally enforceable individual rights. This focus may have inadvertently contributed to the subsequent (and continuing) reluctance of states to ratify and implement it. If this is true, however, it is misguided, given the discretion accorded to states when selecting the degree of obligation to be assumed, as well as the numerous qualifications attached to most of the provisions; for example, a typical requirement is that the number of speakers must be 'sufficient' but the Charter does not supply any objective criteria itself for determining whether the number of speakers is sufficient or not, thereby leaving considerable discretion with the state parties. An instrument designed to apply to several language groups must necessarily be suitably flexible, so that each state can adapt its obligations to the diverse needs of each language group. But the Charter, in seeking to accomplish this difficult but essential task, has diluted state obligations to an inordinate extent. Perhaps even more damaging, however, is the Charter's grounding in languages and not language speakers. The explanatory report issued by the Council of Europe explains this choice as follows:

> The concept of language used in the charter focuses primarily
> on the cultural function of language. That is why it is not

---

[125] *i.e.* Croatia, Denmark, Finland, Germany, Hungary, Liechtenstein, the Netherlands, Norway, Slovenia, Sweden and Switzerland. In Appendix I, the languages specified by EC Member States that have ratified the Charter are listed. Liechtenstein attached a declaration to its ratification instrument, stating that there are no languages within the Principality that come within the Charter definition of regional or minority languages; in its first periodical report, it grounded its ratification in the 'high priority' Liechtenstein attaches to the 'preservation and cultivation of the cultural diversity of Europe' ((15 March 1999, MIN-LANG/PR (99) 1, p. 9). Thirteen other states—including the United Kingdom—have signed but not yet ratified the Charter.

defined subjectively in such a way as to consecrate an individual right, that is the right to speak "one's own language", it being left to each individual to define that language. Nor is reliance placed on a politico-social or ethnic definition by describing a language as the vehicle of a particular social or ethnic group. Consequently, the charter is able to refrain from defining the concept of linguistic minorities, since its aim is not to stipulate the rights of ethnic and/or cultural minority groups, but to protect and promote regional or minority languages as such.[126]

The arguments against protecting 'languages' in this way have been set out at the beginning of this chapter; in particular, it is inherently difficult to ground state obligations—the very linchpin of the Charter—in this thesis of linguistic survival. Furthermore, as set out in Chapter 3, while safeguarding the cultural aspects of language is a fundamental objective, this is not—on its own—sufficient; moreover, if any aspect of language policy can be said to be better protected than others already, it is surely the cultural dimension. The Charter is the only international instrument devoted to regional and minority language issues yet it has ruled out the application of language rights. This is a serious anomaly, calling into question its rationale in the first place. It is arguable, as something of a compromise, that the spirit if not the phrasing of language rights does colour many of the Charter's provisions, especially those on language use before and/or within judicial and administrative authorities. But this is certainly a weaker, second-best route.

The Charter is designed in a 'pick and choose' format: a state must select at least three provisions each from Articles 8 (education) and 12 (cultural activities and facilities), and one provision each from Articles 9 (judicial authorities), 10 (administrative authorities), 11 (media) and 13 (cultural and social life). With this design, obligations that require more substantive administrative and monetary input on the part of signatory states have been relegated to the latter grouping. Furthermore, a state can choose the most innocuous sub-paragraph over more comprehensive measures at its own discretion. This weakens the position of individual minority language speakers significantly; states could legitimately comply with commitments assumed under the Charter, yet to such a minimal degree as to render the obligations ineffectual in practice. For example, states are required to adopt only one

---

[126] Council of Europe, *European Charter for Regional or Minority Languages and explanatory report*, (European Treaty Series No. 148, Council of Europe Publishing, Strasbourg, 1993), p. 7.

sub-paragraph from Article 10(1), which deals with the use of regional or minority languages for both oral and written communications with public authorities. Options within the provision range from publishing official texts and documents in minority language versions (a potentially comprehensive requirement) to allowing an individual to use the minority language version of his/her name, which is little more than a manifestation of good manners. Furthermore, a general (and fairly woolly) qualification—'as far as this is reasonably possible'—has been attached to all sub-paragraphs of Article 10(1). Essentially, then, effective implementation of the Charter depends excessively on the goodwill of the signatory states. The main difficulty with this premise is, of course, that states possessing the requisite goodwill towards speakers of minority languages in the first place have *already* adopted measures similar to and beyond those available in the Charter. A state that has consciously refused to provide for minority language use in public domains is unlikely to select the more comprehensive obligations (that is, of course, if it even agrees to ratify the Charter in the first place).[127] There is no doubt that the Council of Europe had to encompass and encourage flexibility, but it must also be vigilant in preventing abuse of these same concepts. This idea is borne out further when it is considered that implementation of the Charter is supervised by the submission of periodic state reports.[128] International instruments that introduce relatively new or controversial rights usually adopt this mechanism, to defuse counter-productive pressures on reluctant signatories in order that state responsibilities might be realised progressively (which is obviously better than their not being realised at all). As an enforcement mechanism, however, the short-comings of the state reporting system are well documented. It may be a valuable way of ensuring that state signatories assess their achievements continually and it thus enables a certain momentum to be maintained after

---

[127] There had been considerable optimism among France's regional and/or minority language groups when it signed the Charter on 7 May 1999, given the staunch resistance against the promotion of linguistic diversity encountered traditionally. These hopes were thwarted, however, by a decision of the Constitutional Council declaring that ratification of the Charter would contravene Article 2 of the French Constitution, which states simply that '[t]he language of the Republic is French' (see Chapter 1).

[128] At the time of writing, seven of the nine states that have ratified the Charter had presented, in accordance with Article 15 of the Charter, their initial reports: Liechtenstein (15 March 1999, MIN-LANG/PR (99) 1); The Netherlands (15 March 1999, MIN-LANG/PR (99) 2); Croatia (29 March 1999, MIN-LANG/PR (99) 3); Finland (12 April 1999, MIN-LANG/PR (99) 4); Norway (31 May 1999, MIN-LANG/PR (99) 5); Hungary (7 September 1999, MIN-LANG/PR (99) 6); and Switzerland (30 November 1999, MIN-LANG/PR (99) 7).

the initial enthusiasm of ratification; but, crucially, it fails to incorporate a redress mechanism for the individual. Connelly has argued that the establishment of complaints procedures, whether based on inter-state or individual petition measures, would have strengthened the position of minority language speakers to a far greater extent.[129] The Charter must therefore be interpreted as a beginning rather than an end. Skutnabb-Kangas and Phillipson recognise the dilemma that faced the drafters but warn against complacency in terms of implementation and enforcement: "[w]hile the Charter demonstrates how difficult it is to write binding formulations that are sensitive to local conditions, it permits a reluctant state to meet the requirements in a minimalist way which it can legitimate by claiming that a provision was not 'possible' or…numbers were not 'sufficient'…."[130] If the Charter succeeds in persuading states traditionally opposed to the recognition of language rights to enact even minimal safeguards for the speakers of minority languages, it will have achieved a significant breakthrough. For now, the potentially fatal degree of confidence placed in state discretion can be interpreted more favourably as the incorporation of flexibility.[131] But the Council of Europe must continue to strive towards conferring *enforceable* language rights on individuals as a corollary of its work in the realm of state duty. Significantly, the Charter is not confined to situations where individuals do not speak or understand the national or official language(s) of the state signatories. On this point, it has clearly surpassed the natural justice philosophy underlying the language provisions of the ECHR and is firmly attuned to the realities of contemporary language acquisition and language use, which are grounded in considerations of language choice. And this in itself is a valuable advance.

When the preceding paragraphs are taken together, it is clear that there is emerging in international law a perceptible ethos of recognition and protection for language rights. Instruments of both global and regional application have sought to reflect this; and although there are inevitable problems, the developments charted above have underpinned the validity of claims that might otherwise have been discounted as peripheral or idealistic. Significantly, this force of influence cannot be discounted when it is remembered that the ECJ draws inspiration not necessarily from specific

---

[129] Alpha Connelly, "The European Convention on Human Rights and the protection of linguistic minorities", (1993) vol. 2:2 *Irish Journal of European Law*, 281- 293 at 293.

[130] Skutnabb Kangas and Phillipson, "Linguistic human rights", p. 91.

[131] In this vein, see Ferdinando Albanese, "Ethnic and linguistic minorities in Europe", (1991) 2 *Yearbook of European Law*, 313-338 at 332-8.

provisions, but precisely from these 'suprapositive principles' of international law.

(iii)   National Provisions: Language and the Member State Constitutions

The constitutional provisions enacted by the EC Member States in respect of minority languages, along with references to key legislative acts, are listed in Appendix I. The various degrees of protection that have been codified can be placed within the Skutnabb-Kangas and Phillipson paradigm of state responses to language rights claims, set out at the beginning of this chapter. These range from tolerance/non-interference (essentially, tolerance of the private use of language but no provision for official use *e.g.* France), to non-discrimination and permission (*e.g.* the United Kingdom in respect of Welsh), and maintenance-oriented promotion (*e.g.* Belgium, for Dutch, French and German).[132] Significantly, Capotorti, as UN Special Rapporteur on Article 27 ICCPR, argued that international protection of minority rights is *not* contingent on their domestic recognition.[133] Thus, while the EC *may* draw from national constitutional principles on the recognition of language rights, the absence of appropriate provisions would not be inherently fatal to the development of a Community perspective on this issue. Moreover, this interpretation fits with the ECJ's interpretative approach to fundamental rights generally, as derived from the supremacy of Community law.

In any case, notwithstanding the diversity of measures listed in Appendix I, virtually all EC Member States have made some provision for the recognition of linguistic minorities based within their territories. Fishman observes that the number of languages officially recognised world-wide increased from thirty to three hundred in the twentieth century alone, and this alongside, ironically, the rapid spread of English as a world-wide *lingua franca* for 'econotechnical, political, diplomatic, educational and touristic

---

[132] A more elaborate model of state response to language policy was developed by Ostrower *i.e.* (1) legal equality of national languages for all practical and official purposes; (2) legal equality of all national languages, some of which are designated as official; (3) formal equality of national languages conditioned upon doctrinal considerations and changing official policies; (4) supremacy of the language of the dominant national grouping, the official state language, within a system of constitutional protection of linguistic minorities; (5) recognition of a foreign language as an auxiliary official language and (6) designation of one or more native tongues as the official form of state expression: Alexander Ostrower, *Language, Law and Diplomacy*, (Philadelphia, Oxford: University Press, 1965), p. 597 *et seq.*

[133] Capotorti, *Study on the Rights of Persons*, p. 121, para. 61.

purposes'.[134] The drafting of national and international provisions on language rights is something of a circular process, with both sources feeding into each other. On the one hand, securing the implementation of domestic measures is acutely essential to the enforcement of effective and relevant language rights, since their exercise (especially in the context of the official use of language) relates primarily to communications with national authorities. The development of concurrent language rights for citizens dealing with the EC institutions is explored below. In turn, the chief advantage of international instruments from the perspective of individuals is that standards set externally can influence—both directly and indirectly—internal state practice, persuading states to undertake obligations that they might not have assumed independently.

(iv)   Conclusion

Drawing together the two main sources of fundamental rights in Community law, it is fair to conclude that there exists a basic level of respect, both nationally and internationally, for language rights. Substantive provisions differ in both content and emphasis, and there are many unsettled issues regarding the rationale behind and enforcement of language rights. Significantly, however, the underlying premise of language choice does appear to be displacing the more traditional—and restrictive—natural justice model. To date, the Court of Justice has never been faced directly with having to make a decision on whether language rights constitute fundamental rights in the Community legal order. In cases related to the language regimes of Member States, some encouraging soundings have been made; that much is clear from many of the cases discussed in Chapters 2 and 6.[135] But cases involving breaches of Regulation 1/58 demonstrate that the Court has not always dealt with language issues on the basis of rights. The discretionary distinction that appears to have been created in that context was challenged in Chapter 1, providing a patent example of how language claims can be manipulated when addressed as administrative or procedural but not fundamental rights. If, in an appropriate case, the ECJ decided to root language claims in a more substantive theoretical framework, there is ample support to be gleaned both from theoretical doctrine, and from national and international legal instruments. At present, it seems as if the Court has not

---

[134] Joshua A. Fishman, *Language and Ethnicity in Minority Sociolinguistic Perspective*, (Clevedon: Multilingual Matters Ltd., 1989), p. 220.

[135] See especially Case C-274/96 *Criminal Proceedings against Bickel and Franz* [1998] ECR I-7637, discussed in Chapter 6.

made up its mind either way. Whether it will yet recognise language rights as fundamental rights depends on any number of factors, including political and economic concerns, but it also depends on a more generic question *i.e.* the evolution of the EC perspective on fundamental rights protection more generally, which is what remains now to be explored.

4.   WHERE TO FROM HERE? THE EVOLVING PROTECTION OF RIGHTS IN THE COMMUNITY LEGAL ORDER

The phrase 'fundamental rights' embodies an array of rights, duties and protection mechanisms, varying in both content and degree. This is reflected in the case law of the ECJ; and it is clear that the Court's traditional concentration on a limited type and range of rights has evolved over time. The diverse commentary discussed throughout this Chapter converges on one central point at least—that the motivation behind EC involvement in the recognition and protection of rights should be anchored in the protection of the individual. The EC institutions have made concerted efforts in recent years to demystify the Community, stressing its relevance to individuals, projecting an image of accessibility and striving to emphasise the wide-ranging benefits of EC membership. It is difficult to surmount the cynical proposition that these declarations amount to little more than rhetoric, a demystification in the abstract rather than one of meaningful substance. But if the Community fails to evolve in accordance with the benevolent image it has designed for itself, there will be a high price to pay in terms of legitimacy and credibility. It is not easy therefore to ascertain the true priority accorded to fundamental rights protection in the Community legal order, especially outwith the jurisprudence of the ECJ. The Preamble to the Single European Act referred to both the ECHR and the European Social Charter, but a more definite legal basis for action in the human rights sphere was not established until the enactment of the Maastricht Treaty. Article F(2) (now 6(2)) TEU confirmed that the Union must respect fundamental rights derived from the sources established by the Court of Justice; but the Court was not deemed to have jurisdiction over the implementation of this obligation. Fundamental rights within the *Community* did, however, remain under the jurisdiction of the Court. Krogsgaard notes that Article F(2) did not merit high priority on the Maastricht agenda.[136] This is not surprising, given that the new provision added little to the existing *acquis communautaire* and the

---

[136] Krogsgaard, "Fundamental rights in the EC", p. 105.

already troubled state of the negotiations in a political sense. The Amsterdam Treaty consolidated the existing regime of protection and introduced a number of further initiatives, including a procedure for suspension of an EU Member State in cases of serious and persistent breaches of fundamental rights (Article 7 TEU) and the expansion of the jurisdiction of the Court of Justice in fundamental rights issues.[137] Article 13 EC, which creates competence for the Community to combat discrimination in a number of guises, is also relevant here; it does not, however, include linguistic discrimination. This is both surprising and disappointing, in light of the supposed commitment of the EC to linguistic pluralism and the existence of other international standards on language rights, outlined above.

While it could be said that the fundamental rights commitment of the EC (and EU) has been strengthened by each of the Treaty provisions outlined above, all managed to avoid the enumeration of the rights actually protected; but now, the Charter of Fundamental Rights has taken centre stage in this debate. Alongside the fundamental rights thread that links together the various reforming treaties, the significance of EU citizenship has also been quietly evolving. In addition, as the House of Lords Select Committee has observed, one of the Treaty objectives introduced at Amsterdam—the maintenance and development of the Union as an area of freedom, security and justice—creates "...greater scope than hitherto for EU actions and policies to impinge on individual rights and freedoms."[138] Clearly, then, fundamental rights protection within the EC has never been a static concept. And its importance as a Community and Union concern continues to intensify. In the following paragraphs, the key issues identified above are assessed in terms of the likely implications they hold in the quest for recognition of language rights as fundamental rights. It has been established that the EC has undoubtedly woven fundamental rights protection into its legal order, however imperfectly; it has also been argued that there is no reason why language rights cannot be considered as legitimate fundamental rights, and that this is, in fact, reflected in both national and international rights instruments. But a key question remains unanswered: should language

---

[137] See Anthony Whelan, "Fundamental rights", in Ben Tonra (ed.), *Amsterdam: What the Treaty Means*, (Dublin: Institute of European Affairs, 1997), 147-158, and Dominic McGoldrick, "The European Union after Amsterdam: An organisation with general human rights competence?", in David O'Keeffe and Patrick Twomey (eds.), *Legal Issues of the Amsterdam Treaty*, (Oxford: Hart Publishing, 1999), 249-270.

[138] House of Lords Select Committee, Eighth Report, para. 25; see Article 2 TEU, the new Title IV EC and Title VI TEU. See also, Patrick Twomey, "Constructing a secure space", in O'Keeffe and Twomey (eds.), *Legal Issues of the Amsterdam Treaty*, 351-374.

rights be recognised within the *Community* legal order? As de Búrca has observed, "[to refer to] 'excluded categories' is not necessarily to argue that they should be considered as fundamental rights within Community law."[139] To locate this challenge in a suitable framework, the first three sections below—on Article 13 EC, the Charter of Fundamental Rights and EU citizenship respectively—relate predominantly to language rights in the context of dealing with the Community as a governing entity. The final section introduces the 'aspirational' dimension of Community rights protection, asking how, or indeed, whether, the Community does or should influence the (internal) fundamental rights practices of its Member States.

A.   'Combating' Discrimination? Article 13 EC

Article 13 EC, introduced via the Amsterdam Treaty, received a fairly mixed welcome. What is now Article 13(1) provides as follows:

> Without prejudice to the other provisions of this Treaty and within the limits of the powers conferred by it upon the Community, the Council, acting unanimously on a proposal from the Commission and after consulting the European Parliament, may take appropriate action to combat discrimination based on sex, racial or ethnic origin, religion or belief, disability, age or sexual orientation.[140]

Some aspects of this provision are relatively straightforward. For example, it is the first time that discrimination beyond that based on nationality (or within certain circumstances, gender) has been addressed in the EC Treaty. Article 13 does not itself constitute a ban on discrimination for any of the grounds listed, but provides a legal basis for 'appropriate' action that the Council 'may' take in this regard. Reflecting the political consequences of the new competence, Council decisions must be unanimous and within the limits of the Community's powers, and the role of the European Parliament is (generally) limited to that of consultation.[141] As to its likely impact,

---

[139] de Búrca, "The language of rights", p. 38.

[140] For an overview of the (political) background to the provision, see Leo Flynn, "The implications of Article 13 EC—After Amsterdam, will some forms of discrimination be more equal than others?", (1999) vol. 36:6 *Common Market Law Review* 1127-1152.

[141] The progress report on IGC 2000, prepared for the Feira European Council (CONFER 4750/00, Brussels, 14 June 2000) had listed Article 13 EC as one of the provisions to be considered for a switch to qualified majority voting without substantive amendment (see Annex 3.1, p. 74) but this did not come to pass. The provision had not originally been

commentators are, in the main, cautiously optimistic while adopting a 'wait and see' approach.[142] In June 2000, the Council took its first steps in this field, enacting Directive 2000/43 to implement the principle of equal treatment between persons irrespective of racial or ethnic origin.[143] This success of this fledgling Community competence cannot really be judged until after the date for implementation of the Directive by the Member States—19 July 2003—has passed. But it can be noted at this stage that the Council has certainly not been shy in its ambitions. For example, the scope of application of the Directive has been set to include both the public *and* private sectors (Article 3(1)); while its scope in a substantive sense is obviously limited to the employment and social spheres, education has been included. Article 5 contains an express endorsement of positive action to 'compensate for disadvantages linked to racial or ethnic origin'; and in addition to provisions on remedies and enforcement, the Directive compels the Member States to designate a body or bodies for the promotion of equal treatment (Article 13).

For present purposes, however, Article 13 is incomplete. McGoldrick has argued that the provision is wider than its counterparts in the ECHR (Article

---

considered in respect of extension of the co-decision procedure (see Annex 4.3, p. 94), but via the Nice Treaty, a new Article 13(2) was attached, which provides:

> By way of derogation from paragraph 1, when the Council adopts Community incentive measures, excluding any harmonisation of the laws and regulations of the Member States, to support action taken by the Member States in order to contribute to the achievement of the objectives referred to in paragraph 1, it shall act in accordance with the procedure referred to in Article 251.

[142] In O'Keeffe and Twomey (eds.), *Legal Issues of the Amsterdam Treaty*, for example, Hervey argues that the very inclusion of Article 13 in the EC Treaty is highly significant, despite its apparently limited scope (Tamara K. Hervey, "Putting Europe's house in order: Racism, race discrimination and xenophobia after the Treaty of Amsterdam", 329-349) while Arnull points out that the express reservation of power to the Council via Article 13 may act as a restraint on the Court of Justice (Anthony Arnull, "Taming the beast? The Treaty of Amsterdam and the Court of Justice", 109-121 at 111); this latter argument can be contrasted somewhat with the Court's dynamic approach to Article 12 EC (non-discrimination on grounds of nationality) in Case C-85/96 *Martínez Sala v. Freistaat Bayern* [1998] ECR I-2691 (see Sybilla Fries and Jo Shaw, "Citizenship of the Union: First steps in the European Court of Justice", (1998) vol. 4:4 *European Public Law* 533-559; Siofra O'Leary, "Putting flesh on the bones of European Union citizenship", (1999) vol. 24:1 *European Law Review* 68-79). In the same volume, Barnard suggests that the use of the phrase 'combat' may yet enable the Council to be progressively proactive in areas requiring positive discrimination (Catherine Barnard, "Article 13: Through the looking glass of Union citizenship", 375-394 at 387 *et seq.*); see also, Arnull "Taming the beast?", 109-121 at 109-110. On positive action, see below with regard to Directive 2000/43.

[143] [2000] OJ L180/22

14) and the ICCPR (Article 26).[144] But in both of those provisions, language is included as a ground upon which discrimination can occur. In Article 13 EC, it is not. And it is unlikely that the grounds listed expressly in the provision could be interpreted in any way other than as being exhaustive.[145] Does this omission imply that, within the Community legal order, language claims are seen as an administrative issue outwith the ambit of fundamental rights? Such a conclusion is arguably mirrored in other areas of Community activity. For example, in the draft *Code of Good Administrative Behaviour*, drawn up by the European Ombudsman as a model for consideration by the EC institutions,[146] Article 5(1) sets down a principle for equality of treatment regarding communications from and decisions affecting members of the public. Article 5(3) provides that Community officials should 'in particular avoid any unjustified discrimination between members of the public based on nationality, sex, racial or ethnic origin, religion or belief, disability, age, or sexual orientation'—which aside from the inclusion here of 'nationality', is virtually identical to Article 13 EC. It is arguable that language could come within the general principle of equal treatment, and that the phrase 'in particular' means that consideration of additional grounds is not precluded. In a more specific sense, Article 13 of the Code deals with letters received from citizens of the Union or any member of the public written in one of the Treaty languages, stipulating that letters of this kind must be responded to in the language in which they have been written. This reflects the linguistic equality concept codified in Regulation 1/58, as well as more specific provisions on EU citizenship, discussed below. So it is not that language has been ignored; but it has characterised independently of non-discrimination. Thus, the content of Article 13 EC has filtered through to other Community practices; while the maintenance of linguistic diversity is espoused

---

[144] Dominic McGoldrick, "The European Union after Amsterdam", p. 253.

[145] See Flynn, "The implications of Article 13 EC", 1149-1151, who refers to the purposive approach evident in the jurisprudence of the Canadian courts on Section 15 of the Canadian Charter of Fundamental Rights and Freedoms, but concludes that "[u]nlike equivalent provisions in national and international instruments on discrimination which use phrases such as 'including' or 'amongst other grounds', [Article 13 EC] sets out its six statuses in an apparently exhaustive fashion. The Court of Justice may not find it easy to respond…in a fashion similar to that of the Canadian courts." (at 1150).

[146] See the Special Report from the European Ombudsman to the European Parliament following the own-initiative inquiry into the existence and public accessibility, in the various Community institutions and bodies, of a Code of Good Administrative Behaviour (OI/1/98/OV); the Code was first sent as a draft recommendation to the Commission on 28 July 1999, and to the Parliament and Council on 29 July 1999. For details on the responses received, see the European Ombudsman website at http://www.euro-ombudsman. eu.int/recommen/en/oi980001.htm.

continuously as a political salve, the corresponding concerns of speakers are not prioritised to the same extent. This situation is simply not tenable. Not only does it contrast with ideas emerging in the Court of Justice's treatment of language issues,[147] it stands apart from more typical international standards on non-discrimination. Non-discrimination is, of course, just one aspect of the complex package that moulds language policy; but it is—as already established—a pivotal one. Significantly, the 'equivalent' provision in the Charter of Fundamental Rights—Article 21, discussed further below —contains an expanded list of grounds upon which discrimination 'shall be prohibited', and this includes language. Article 13 EC is not, then, the definitive Community word on this matter.

B.   The Way Forward? The EU Charter of Fundamental Rights

At the Cologne Summit in June 1999, the European Council declared that "[t]here appears to be a need, at the present stage of the Union's development, to establish a Charter of fundamental rights in order to make their overriding importance and relevance more visible to the Union's citizens."[148] As noted earlier, the need for a catalogue of rights of this nature had long been mooted. But the key point regarding the present momentum has been expressed succinctly by the House of Lords Select Committee on European Union: "[t]he difference, this time, is that the initiative has been endorsed at the highest political level and machinery has been established to take it forward."[149] The European Council proposed that the charter should cover civil and political rights, economic and social rights, and rights associated with Union citizenship. It then assigned the drafting task to a specially constituted body—confusingly, dubbed 'the Convention'— composed of fifteen representatives of heads of state of government, sixteen members of the European Parliament, thirty members of national parliaments and a Commissioner representing the President of the Commission. Following some months of debate and discussion that generated various partial and complete drafts, as well as the receipt and consideration of

---

[147] Contrast, for example, the language used in Case 137/84 *Ministère Public v. Mutsch* [1985] ECR 2681 with that in Case C-274/96 *Criminal Proceedings against Bickel and Franz* [1998] ECR I-7637, discussed in Chapters 2 and 6 respectively.

[148] Conclusions of the European Council in Cologne, 4 June 1999, Annex IV.

[149] House of Lords Select Committee, Eighth Report, para. 2.

submissions from an array of organisations and individuals,[150] the final version of the Charter was published on 28 September 2000.[151] It is difficult, however, to avoid feeling that the most challenging work has not yet begun. The Charter is organised into seven 'chapters': dignity (Articles 1-5, including the right to life and prohibitions on torture and slavery); freedoms (Articles 6-19, setting out a range of civil and political rights such as privacy, freedom of expression, education, property and asylum); equality (Articles 20-26, which contain provisions on non-discrimination, equality between men and women and the integration of persons with disabilities); solidarity (Articles 27-38, outlining a range of social rights), citizenship (Articles 39-46, reiterating mainly the citizenship rights set out in the EC Treaty), justice (Articles 47-50, dealing primarily with the right to a fair trial) and general provisions (Articles 51-54, dealing with the scope of the Charter and its relationship to rights and freedoms recognised in both national and international law). Indeed, one of the Charter's outstanding innovations is this enunciation of civil, political, social and economic rights in a single instrument.

A detailed analysis of the substantive provisions of the Charter lies outwith the scope of this work, but some general points should be noted. Although there is now a definitive text, it is still not clear what status or legal effect the Charter will ultimately have; it was 'proclaimed' by the European Parliament, the Commission and the Council on 7 December 2000, having been approved by the European Council at the Nice Summit, but more concrete decisions have been put off until IGC 2004. The outcome of this particular debate is obviously crucial to the Charter's effectiveness but it is likely to be an arduous process, having already ignited a fractious debate on sovereignty and relative competences in some Member States. In so far as the Charter restates the *acquis communautaire* on fundamental rights protection, it can only codify, and thus clarify, an already effective (although unwritten) legal standard. This seems to have been the purpose of the Charter as envisaged at Cologne but equally, the Charter cannot be

---

[150] For a complete list of the submissions received by the Convention, as well as various reports and other documents relevant to the drafting procedure, see the website of the Council at http://db.consilium.eu.int/df/default.asp?lang=en.

[151] Charte 4487/00, Brussels, 28 September 2000. The Draft Charter was presented for consideration by the Biarritz European Council in October 2000 and proclaimed by the Parliament, Council and Commission on 7 December 2000 after European Council approval at the Nice Summit. Decisions as to its future status have been postponed as a matter for the agenda of IGC 2004. For diverging views on the composition and procedures of the Convention, see the House of Lords Select Committee, Eighth Report, especially at paras. 32-38.

dismissed as a modest reproduction of the ECJ's jurisprudence to date.[152] The first deliberation on the Charter by an Advocate General of the Court of Justice can be found in *BECTU v. Secretary of State for Trade and Industry*.[153] Discussing entitlement to paid annual leave as a fundamental (social) right, Advocate General Tizzano described the current status of the Charter and its interaction with the *acquis* as follows:

> Admittedly...the Charter of Fundamental Rights of the European Union has not been recognised as having genuine legislative scope in the strict sense. In other words, formally, it is not in itself binding. However, without wishing to participate here in the wide-ranging debate now going on as to the effects which, on other forms and by other means, the Charter may nevertheless produce, the fact remains that it includes statements which appear in large measure to reaffirm rights which are enshrined in other instruments...I think therefore that, *in proceedings concerned with the nature and scope of a fundamental right, the relevant statements of the Charter cannot be ignored*; in particular, we cannot ignore its clear purpose of serving, where its provisions so allow, as *a substantive point of reference* for all those involved—Member States, institutions, natural and legal persons—in the Community context. Accordingly, I consider that *the Charter provides us with the most reliable and definitive confirmation* of the fact that the right to paid annual leave constitutes a fundamental right.[154]

In any event, whatever the ultimate legal effect that is accorded (politically) to the Charter, there are important limitations as to scope set down expressly in the text itself. In Article 51(1), it is made clear that "[t]he provisions of

---

[152] This is borne out by both the range of rights included in the Charter (especially regarding its provisions on social rights) and by the way in which the enumeration of rights has been updated (see for example, the innovative and contemporary expression of the right to the integrity of the human person (Article 3 of the Charter), which is based on principles set out in the Council of Europe's 1997 Convention on Human Rights and Biomedicine).

[153] Case C-173/99 *Broadcasting, Entertainment, Cinematographic and Theatre Union (BECTU) v. Secretary of State for Trade and Industry*, Opinion of Advocate General Tizzano, delivered on 8 February 2001, not yet reported. The CFI was invited but declined to consider the impact of the Charter in Case T-112/98 *Mannesmannröhren-Werke v. Commission*, judgment of 20 February 2001, not yet reported, given that the events at issue had taken place prior to the proclamation of the Charter (see para. 76 of the judgment).

[154] *BECTU*, paras. 27-8 (emphasis added).

this Charter are addressed to the institutions and bodies of the Union with due regard for the principle of subsidiarity and to the Member States *only when they are implementing Union law.*"[155] As if to drive this point home, it is stated outright in Article 51(2) that the Charter "...does not establish any new power or task for the Community or the Union, or modify powers and tasks defined by the Treaties." Thus, if it had been anticipated that the Charter might cause EC standards on fundamental rights protection to seep beyond the reach of EC law, this ambition has been dispelled explicitly. Significantly, however, the Preamble confirms that the majority of rights set out in the Charter are guaranteed to 'each person' rather than to EU citizens only (aside from the rights specified in Articles 39-46 and other instances where 'citizens' are mentioned explicitly[156]); this has considerable implications for the inclusion/exclusion debate and is discussed in more detail below, in the context of citizenship rights. Two further points should also be noted. First, limitations on the rights and freedoms recognised by the Charter are to be provided for 'by law [and] subject to the principle of proportionality...may be made only if they are necessary and genuinely meet objectives of general interest recognised by the Union or the need to protect the rights and freedoms of others' (Article 52(1)), arguably shifting this task in effect from the Court of Justice. The ECJ rule of construction that limitations must 'respect the essence of those rights and freedoms' is enshrined also.[157] Second, while it is clarified that the standards set down in the ECHR are not to be 'adversely affected' by interpretation of the Charter (Article 53), Article 52(3) confirms that "[t]his provision shall not prevent Union law providing more extensive protection." One aspect of the complex relationship between the EC and the Council of Europe has thus been clarified, but perhaps not in the way that might have been expected by those who have long argued that the Court of Justice should defer routinely to the Court of Human Rights. Interestingly, the penultimate draft of the Charter had stated that 'greater or more extensive protection' must be derived from 'the Charter' as opposed to the now codified—and potentially broader—

---

[155] Emphasis added.

[156] *i.e.* Articles 12(2), 15(2) (but see Article 15(3)), and 39-46 (but not Article 41, and see Article 45(2)).

[157] Although this aspect of Article 52(1) has something of a chequered history. In line with the Court's test as outlined in *Hauer* and *Karlsson* (discussed above, see notes 95, 96 and accompanying text), a draft text of 16 May 2000 provided that "[t]he actual substance of those rights and freedoms must be respected.' (see Article 47 of Charte 4316/00); however, in the penultimate version of the Charter, nothing to this effect was included in the relevant provision (Article 50 of Charte 4422/00, 28 July 2000).

'Union law'; it is certainly arguable that the earlier version would have amounted to something of a limitation on the interpretative approach developed by the Court of Justice in this context.[158] Finally, it can be implied from Article 52(3) that limitations on rights cannot exceed those established under the ECHR; again, this had been stated expressly in an earlier draft of the Charter.[159] Furthermore, by stating that the 'meaning and scope' of rights guaranteed by the Convention shall be 'the same as those laid down in the said Convention', the Charter has arguably introduced indirect deference to relevant interpretations of the European Court of Human Rights.

To what extent, then, do the provisions of the Charter support the idea that (minority) language rights are fundamental rights? Or more specifically, and bearing in mind the overall rider on its unsettled character, is there anything in the Charter to suggest that language rights should be protected within the Community legal order? Some conceptual—but admittedly abstract—support can be gleaned from the tenor of rights protection established by the Preamble, where the principles of dignity, democracy and the rule of law are restated; perhaps more specifically, the Union is committed once again to respecting 'diversity of the cultures and traditions of the peoples of Europe as well as the national identities of the Member States'. Some of the substantive provisions of the Charter are potentially relevant to language rights. Article 11 sets out the right to freedom of expression and information in terms similar to those of Article 10 ECHR. It has already been noted, however, that a right to linguistic choice when dealing with public authorities has *not* been implied into the ECHR provision; moreover, the relevance of freedom of expression in terms of the official use of language is inherently limited.[160] The right to education is set out in Article 14 of the Charter; Article 14(3) contains a statement on the religious and philosophical convictions of parents that echoes Article 1 of Protocol 2 to the ECHR. Here, however, there is an interesting addition. Article 14(3) requires respect also for the *pedagogical* convictions of parents, which might render a more favourable interpretation on language education than that delivered by the Court of Human Rights in the *Belgian Linguistics Case*, discussed above. As already noted, Article 21 of the Charter, on equality and non-discrimination, contains a comprehensive list of grounds upon which discrimination 'shall be prohibited' that goes beyond both Article 13 EC and

---

[158] See Article 50(3) of Charte 4422/00, 28 July 2000.

[159] See Article 47 of Charte 4316/00, Brussels, 16 May 2000.

[160] See note 17 and accompanying text.

Article 14 ECHR. Crucially, language is included.[161] This brings the Community stance on non-discrimination into line with international standards more generally and locates language claims more within the spectrum of fundamental rights than in that of administration. In Chapter V of the Charter (citizenship rights), Article 41 codifies the right to good administration; Article 41(4) expresses the right of every person who writes to the institutions of the Union 'in one of the languages of the Treaties' to have an answer in the same language. This principle reflects Article 21 EC, and is discussed in more detail below. Chapter VI of the Charter sets out the right to a fair trial and specifies basic minimum rights of defence. Article 47 provides that '[e]veryone shall have the possibility of being advised, defended and represented' but makes no reference to language in that context; similarly, Article 48(2) promises that '[r]espect for the right of defence of anyone who has been charged shall be guaranteed' without elaborating on what constitutes the 'right of defence' in the first place. In an earlier draft, the statement of reasons explained that "[g]iven the decision taken in favour of concise drafting, it was not thought necessary to include [Article 6 ECHR] in full, but in accordance with Article 6 of the TEU these provisions, which clarify the principles set out in the Article of the Charter, are applicable in Community law."[162] It can be assumed that this reasoning applies also to the finalised Charter; but as established above, the language rights related to defence as set out under the ECHR are premised on the natural justice standard of 'understanding' a language and do not confer any right to language choice.

To this point, then, the Charter has fairly limited impact on the recognition of language rights as fundamental rights within the Community. Aside from the inclusion of language as a ground upon which discrimination can occur (and the potential impact of adding 'pedagogical convictions' regarding the right to education), the relevant provisions add nothing that is not already recognised by either the ECHR or the EC Treaty to date. Vague anticipation that a provision on the protection of minority rights in a general sense would be included in the Charter has not been realised,[163] although membership of a national minority has been included in the non-discrimination clause. Regarding language rights specifically, both the

---

[161] The other grounds not included in Article 13 EC but specified here are colour, genetic features, political or any other opinion, membership of a national minority (which may also be relevant to certain language claims), property and birth.

[162] See the notes accompanying Article 9 of Charte 4316/00.

[163] See, for example, the recommendations in "Leading by Example", reproduced in Alston (ed.), *The EU and Human Rights*, 921-927 at 923.

European Parliament[164] and the European Bureau for Lesser Used Languages had called for a clause on language rights to be included in the Charter. EBLUL phrased their initial recommendations in the vein of citizenship, arguing that:

> [t]he Charter will be a further step in the process of European integration. It is highly significant because it signals a move away from mostly economic matters which have been at the centre of European attention in recent years towards a more comprehensive understanding of European citizenship, incorporating the notion of fundamental rights. Cultural and linguistic diversity in Europe lies at the heart of fundamental rights for its citizens as the integration process advances. An essential part of this diversity are the regional and minority languages traditionally spoken by linguistic communities within the EU member states.[165]

The Bureau submitted that the Charter should provide 'at least a minimum standard of protection of regional and minority languages which will become a fundamental basis in this field for the European Union itself and for its current and future member states'. In April 2000, framing its submission finally in terms of non-discrimination, freedom of expression and respect for cultural diversity, EBLUL presented the following provision for inclusion in the Charter:

> 1. European citizens have the right to maintain and develop their own language and culture, in community with the other

---

[164] In its Resolution on the Drafting of a European Union Charter of Fundamental Rights (A5-0064/2000, 16 March 2000), the European Parliament submitted that "...it is important that, while respecting the role of every national language, the European Union and its Member States attend to the protection of the diversity of the languages and cultures of Europe, especially regional and minority languages and cultures, and to this end guarantee to the citizens of the Union, through appropriate means of support, that they can maintain and develop their own languages and cultures in the public and private domain...." (at paragraph P of the Resolution)

[165] Submission from EBLUL on the Draft Charter of Fundamental Rights of the European Union, Charte 4143/00, Brussels, 29 February 2000, Contrib. 33. EBLUL referred to the European Charter for Regional or Minority Languages in support of its stance, and also to standards on minority rights established by the OSCE. EBLUL reiterated this submission in Charte 4166/00, Brussels, 16 March 2000, Contrib. 50. See also, the submission of the working group on EU citizenship, fundamental rights and cultural diversity of the federalist group at the European institutions (UEF-EU), Charte 4348/00, Brussels, 4 July 2000, Contrib. 212.

members of their group, as an expression of the cultural and linguistic diversity that is a common heritage of Europe.

2. Within its spheres of competence, the European Union shall promote the effective exercise of this right.

3. No policies and measures of the European Union shall be adopted or applied in ways that are detrimental to the linguistic diversity of Europe.[166]

In some ways, this is quite a modest proposal, echoing and expanding on the general commitment of the Union to respect the diversity and national identities of the Member States, rather than introducing contextual—and enforceable—language rights. EBLUL was careful also to recognise the implications of its proposal for the determination and exercise of Union/ Member State competence. What was ultimately enacted, however, falls well short even of the EBLUL draft: Article 22 of the Charter states simply that "[t]he Union shall respect cultural, religious and linguistic identity." This very basic statement—included only in the final version of the Charter— contains little more, in cultural and linguistic terms, than an additional expression of Article 6(3) TEU and Article 151(4) EC. It is not, at least, confined to *national* identities; moreover, it makes the linguistic aspect of broader cultural policy more explicit. It is doubtful, however, that any binding, justiciable duty could be read into this short statement. At least the provision was included, and the significance of this in itself is not inconsiderable, given its late appearance as part of the Charter at all.

Given that there is no provision in the Charter on minority rights more generally, it is not really surprising that protection of minority language rights does not feature independently, beyond what might be implied from the provisions already listed above. Equally, there is no specific protection for language rights outwith the minority context apart from the limited right related to written contact with the institutions under the ambit of citizenship. And the limitations of Article 22 are obvious. On the one hand, then, the Charter neither detracts from nor extends the recognition already accorded to language within the Community context. But if maintaining the *status quo* is itself viewed as an omission, the consequences will not be apparent until the status of the Charter and, more crucially, the prospective extent of its 'ownership' of fundamental rights protection within the Union are decided finally. The Charter is a critical step in the narrative of EC rights protection. But it is not a cure-all. There are several outstanding issues that simply have

---

[166]   Charte 4237/00, Brussels, 18 April 2000, Contrib. 110.

not been addressed. The remedies available for individuals at EC level (especially, in terms of standing for Article 230 EC judicial review proceedings) have not been revised. The Charter is silent as to the need for additional institutional support in the human rights domain.[167] The relationship between the EC and the Council of Europe has been clarified at certain junctures but has not been tackled in a comprehensive sense. A parallel judgment can be drawn on the question of language rights; they have not been looked at expressly as a discrete aspect of fundamental rights, but they have been enveloped in the mesh of non-discrimination. This leaves us with two issues still to consider. First, given that language claims have been mentioned explicitly in both the EC Treaty and Charter of Fundamental Rights as an element of EU citizenship, to what extent can it be said that citizenship rights encompass *minority* language claims? And second, are future developments in the EC human rights jurisdiction likely to elevate the protection of language rights therein? These questions are now dealt with respectively in the remaining sections of this chapter.

C.   Citizenship of the Union: Evolving Rights and Duties

The 'true' nature of citizenship of the European Union has been debated since its inception via the Maastricht Treaty; the rationale behind it can be linked to democratic legitimacy in the relations between a political entity and the individuals governed thereby, but the motivation is habitually disputed: is EU citizenship a virtually useless, symbolic palliative or a genuine (if embryonic) stage in the evolution of the supranational legal order? Even if citizenship is tagged primarily as a strategic political move, it must at least be acknowledged that, motives aside, its introduction does have the potential to enhance the rights of the individual at EU level. Definitions of citizenship vary, depending on the nature of the political entity in question, but its central theme relates almost invariably to the role (based on both rights and duties) of the individual within a polity. Preuß outlines the historical development of citizenship, tracing its evolution from the passive submission of governed individuals to the more inclusive and participatory version

---

[167] See Philip Alston and J.H.H. Weiler, "An 'ever closer union' in need of a human rights policy: The European Union and human rights", in Alston (ed.) *The EU and Human Rights*, 3-66, on suggested reforms to present EU human rights policy; on the role of the ECJ in particular, see, in the same volume, Bruno de Witte, "The past and future role of the European Court of Justice in the protection of human rights", 859-897.

embodied in democratic theory, developed in the last two hundred years.[168] The idea of 'European citizenship' can be traced from early discussions in the Tindemans Report on European Union to its eventual codification in Articles 17-22 (formerly 8) EC, introduced by the TEU.[169] The initially predominant view among academic commentators was that the EC Treaty provisions on citizenship grouped together a number of existing, movement-oriented rights but did not introduce anything particularly new to the Community legal order, or at least, anything particularly tangible.[170] This seems to have been recognised equally by the drafters of the Maastricht Treaty given the dynamic nature of Article 22, which empowers the Council to strengthen or add to (but not detract from) the rights already laid down.[171] Crucially, EU citizenship rights are dependent on an individual 'holding the nationality of a Member State' (Article 17(1) EC), the determination of which remains outwith Community or Union competence, a point returned to below. The Amsterdam Treaty did not change the citizenship provisions very drastically; but a key addition to Article 21 from the perspective of language rights is discussed below. Otherwise, aside from an explicit confirmation that EU citizenship 'shall complement and not replace national citizenship' (inserted into Article 17), the provisions remained unchanged. But debate on the meaning of EU citizenship and on what that entails has not remained so

---

[168] Ulrich K. Preuß, "Problems of a concept of European citizenship", (1995) vol. 1:3 *European Law Journal*, 267-281 at 268-9.

[169] See Carlos Closa, "The concept of citizenship in the Treaty on European Union", (1992) 29 *Common Market Law Review*, 1137-1169 at 1141-1153; see also, David O'Keeffe, "Union citizenship", in O'Keeffe and Twomey (eds.), *Legal Issues of the Maastricht Treaty*, 87-107 at 87-89.

[170] See Michelle Everson, "The legacy of the market citizen", in Shaw and More (eds.), *New Legal Dynamics*, 71-90.

[171] D'Oliveira, however, has interpreted this facility as a front for lack of coherence within the citizenship provisions: Hans Ulrich Jessurun D'Oliveira, "European citizenship: Its meaning, its potential", in Renaud Dehousse (ed.), *Europe After Maastricht: An Ever Closer Union?*, (Munich: Law Books in Europe, 1994), 126-148. The Nice Treaty provides for substantive amendment to Article 18, with a revised second and new third paragraph to provide as follows:

> 2. If action by the Community should prove necessary to attain this objective and this Treaty has not provided the necessary powers, the Council may adopt provisions with a view to facilitating the exercise of the rights referred to in paragraph 1. The Council shall act in accordance with the procedure referred to in Article 251.
>
> 3. Paragraph 2 shall not apply to provisions on passports, identity cards, residence permits or any other such document or to provisions on social security or social protection.

static. As the objectives of the Union have evolved, so too have corollary expectations on both the role and protection of the individual. The extent to which citizenship changes the parameters of free movement and non-discrimination, for example, has been explored by the ECJ in a series of cases beginning with *Martínez Sala*;[172] and, as heightened by the Amsterdam Treaty, the creation of the 'area of freedom, security and justice' has particular implications for the individuals within that zone.[173] In other words, as the political aspirations set down in the EC Treaty and TEU come more distinctly to the fore, the impact on both the nature and substance of EU citizenship will have to be honed correspondingly, causing us all perhaps to think more carefully about what citizenship at the supranational level actually means.[174] Whether citizenship should be framed more openly in terms of fundamental rights protection is an ongoing consideration, long proposed and reassessed more specifically at present as a result of the EU Charter of Fundamental Rights;[175] this and the concurrent situation of *non-EU* citizens resident in the Member States are discussed more fully below.

As the provisions stand currently, however, it is noteworthy for present purposes that some features of citizenship were never linked inherently to free movement but relate instead to the relationship of government. Article

---

[172] Case C-85/96 *Martínez Sala v. Freistaat Bayern* [1998] ECR I-2691; for case comment and analysis, see Fries and Shaw, and O'Leary (as note 142); see generally, Jo Shaw, "The many pasts and futures of citizenship in the European Union", (1997) 22 *European Law Review* 554-572. See also, the earlier analysis of Advocate General Jacobs in Case C-168/91 *Konstantinidis v. Stadt Altensteig, Standesamt, & Landratsamt Calw, Ordnungsamt* [1993] ECR I-1191, especially at 1211-1212, para. 46, and the decisions in Case C-274/96 *Criminal Proceedings against Bickel and Franz* [1998] ECR I-7637 (see Chapter 6) and Case C-378/97 *Criminal Proceedings against Wijsenbeek*, judgment of 21 September 1999, not yet reported. Flynn argues that through its decisions in *Martínez Sala* and *Bickel and Franz*, "...the Court of Justice has already confounded those who considered that Union citizenship was itself an empty vessel...." (Flynn, "The implications of Article 13 EC", p. 1151.)

[173] See Title IV of the EC Treaty (Articles 61-69), discussed in Twomey, "Constructing a secure space", especially at 372-374.

[174] For an interpretation of 'membership' in the evolving context of EU citizenship, see Jo Shaw, "The problem of membership in European Union citizenship", in Zenon Bankowski and Andrew Scott (eds.), *The European Union and its Order: The Legal Theory of European Integration*, (Oxford: Blackwell Publishers, 2000), 65-89; see also, in the same volume, Carole Lyons, "The limits of European Union citizenship", 149-167.

[175] For the background to this debate, see Shaw, "The many pasts and futures"; Siofra O'Leary, "The relationship between Community citizenship and the protection of fundamental rights in Community law", (1995) 32 *Common Market Law Review* 519-554; Peter Neussl, "European citizenship and human rights: An interactive European concept", (1997) vol. 24:2 *Legal Issues of European Integration* 47-66.

21 EC outlines the right of EU citizens to petition the European Parliament, and the European Ombudsman established by Article 195.[176] A third paragraph was added to Article 21 by the Amsterdam Treaty, providing that "[e]very citizen of the Union may write to any of the institutions or bodies referred to in this Article or in Article 7 in one of the languages mentioned in Article 314 and have an answer in the same language." Thus, an EU citizen may communicate in writing with the European Parliament, Council, Commission, Court of Justice, Court of Auditors, Economic and Social Committee, Committee of the Regions (Article 7) and Ombudsman (Article 21) in any of the Treaty languages (thus, the eleven official languages *and* Irish). This is not a novel concept. Article 2 of Regulation 1/58 established a similar right for Member States and persons 'subject to their jurisdiction' (which is inevitably broader than the cohort covered by EU citizenship); differing phraseology in the Regulation excluded Irish, however. What is primarily different is the elevation of this procedure to that of a 'right' via the channel of EU citizenship. Two other formulations of the mechanism are worth noting in support of this claim. Article 13 of the Ombudsman's *Code of Good Administrative Behaviour* is virtually identical in scope to the third paragraph of Article 21 EC, although it extends the procedure to 'any member of the public' who writes to an EC institution in one of the Treaty languages; and the equivalent provision of the Charter on Fundamental Rights similarly refers to 'any person' (Article 41(4)). Before addressing the implications of the Treaty/official language distinction, the extent to which language rights are (or should be) reserved for citizens should be raised. The application of Article 21 EC is confined to EU citizens only; as noted, designation of EU citizenship is a Member State matter given the requirement of Member State nationality.[177] But the Charter of Fundamental Rights and the Ombudsman's *Code* both extend this right to 'any person' and 'any member of the public' respectively (as, indeed, did Regulation 1/58 itself), notwithstanding the location of the relevant Charter provision in the title on citizenship rights. The exclusion of non-Community nationals legally resident in the Member States from rights associated with citizenship of the Union—not to mention the application of most Community law rights more

---

[176] Note, however, that the European Parliament had submitted on its own initiative since 1953 to the individual's right to petition.

[177] On this point, see Hans Ulrich Jessurun D'Oliveira, "Nationality and the European Union after Amsterdam", in O'Keeffe and Twomey (eds.), *Legal Issues of the Amsterdam Treaty*, 395-412

generally—has long been a source of heated argument.[178] The contention is not that the attachment of rights to citizenship is an invalid concept *per se*, but that a considerable sector of the population of the Union is unjustly excluded from the resulting framework. Citizenship rights should not detract from the universality and indivisibility of fundamental rights protection; rights accorded exclusively to citizens should relate to the specific relationship of government, and a basic threshold of fundamental rights and principles must still apply without distinction where relevant. The difference between language rights granted on the premise of linguistic choice—more usually associated with the official use of language within a domestic polity —and those derived from the universally applicable principles of natural justice is illustrative here. On the whole, the phrasing of the provisions of the Charter of Fundamental Rights—where the vast majority of rights are recognised as being inherent in 'every person' rather than 'every citizen' marks a significant advance in the treatment of third country nationals within the EU; the extent to which the Charter will impact in practice remains, of course, to be seen; but the shift in attitude conveyed even at the level of the terminology used can only be welcomed.

The variable references to Treaty/official languages in the different provisions mentioned above probably reflects a presumption that both categories are identical, rendering the inclusion of Irish surely accidental where 'Treaty languages' has been the preferred formulation. And nowhere have the language choices of EU citizens (or others) who speak other minority languages been considered. The result of this anomaly is that Irish has become something of an official EC language by stealth; yet the overall position of other minority languages remains unchanged. The European Parliament has sought status similar to that of Irish for Catalan but, as yet, to no avail.[179] There are some other scattered instances in EC law of language choice rights acquired 'by accident'. For example, as mentioned in Chapter 1, Article 48(1) of Regulation 574/72 provides that a claimant of certain social security benefits is entitled to have any decisions of the authorities, *both Community and national*, notified to him 'in his own language':

---

[178] See specifically, Patrick M. Twomey, "European citizenship and human rights: Actual situation and future perspectives", in Epaminondas A. Marias (ed.), *European Citizenship*, (Maastricht: European Institute of Public Affairs, 1994), 119-133; Carlos Closa, "Citizenship of the Union and nationality of Member States", in O'Keeffe and Twomey (eds.), *Legal Issues of the Maastricht Treaty*, 109-119; Martin Hedemann-Robinson, "Third country nationals, European Union citizenship, and free movement of persons: A time for bridges rather than divisions", (1996) 16 *Yearbook of European Law* 321-362.

[179] See, for example, European Parliament Resolution on Languages in the Community and the Situation of Catalan, 11 December 1990, A-169/90, [1991] OJ C19/42.

significantly, there is no express restriction to the official Community languages.[180] It is arguable, therefore, that a migrant worker who speaks a minority language is entitled to receive notice in that language, given the absence of any requirement to the contrary. De Witte points out that the application of this EC procedure would in turn affect practices in the public authorities of Member States.[181] But again, the expansion of language rights in this way has hardly been by design. And, as put forward in Chapter 1, it is probably arguable that Regulation 1/58 (or perhaps more correctly, the Treaty) establishes an overriding ceiling on languages that may be used in the Community context, and a ceiling that can be implied into any ambiguous Community provisions or measures.

The way in which the market ideology of the Community seems unable to meet the human needs of the migrant worker has been called into question.[182] Thus the scope of what exactly can be demanded as an aspect of citizenship has been thrown into focus. Taking the framework of language rights generally, the EC has put in place an official languages regime, and an undeniably ambitious one at that. In Chapter 1, the necessity of publishing legislation in a language that can be understood by those affected was stressed, on the premise of democracy and legal certainty. According to citizens the right to communicate with the EC institutions in any one of the Treaty languages is a logical extension of those arguments. But immediately, the question of legitimate limitations must be raised. Article 21 EC covers written communications only, for example: is this as much as can reasonably

---

[180] [1972] OJ L74/1 (emphasis added).

[181] De Witte, "The scope of Community powers in education and culture in the light of subsequent practice", in Roland Bieber and Georg Ress (eds.), *Die Dynamik des Europäischen Gemeinschaftsrechts*, (Baden-Baden: Nomos, 1987), 261-278 at 266; see also Chapter 1, on Case 66/74 *Farrauto v. Bau-Berufsgenossenschaft* [1975] ECR 157, especially at 162, para. 6. Similarly, Directive 77/486 ([1977] OJ L199/32) requires that Member States should take appropriate measures to ensure that children of migrant workers are educated in the languages of both the host state and the state of origin; on this point, de Witte argues that "…granting the right to mother-tongue education to children of Community workers may well put under pressure those states that deny the same right to their own national minorities." He observes that such policies have particular effect on states with regional-unilingual language arrangements, *e.g.* Belgium. But Cullen has argued that difficulties of implementation have rendered the Directive virtually ineffective in practice: Holly Cullen, "From migrants to citizens? European Community policy on intercultural education", (1996) 45 *International and Comparative Law Quarterly*, 109-129 at 121-125.

[182] See Tamara K. Hervey, "Migrant workers and their families in the European Union: The pervasive market ideology of Community law", in Shaw and More (eds.), *New Legal Dynamics*, 91-110.

be expected, given the sheer number of languages involved? In an earlier version of Article 41(4) of the Charter of Fundamental Rights, it had been stated simply—and perhaps more ambiguously—that every person 'may address' the institutions in one of their official languages.[183] Moving into the spectrum of minority language rights, the arguments on limitations exist at a more fundamental level; is it acceptable that EU citizens who speak languages other than the Treaty languages cannot exercise a more complete linguistic choice when communicating with the EC institutions, over and above selecting the Treaty language with which they are most familiar? The official use of language has been addressed by Réaume in the context of the linguistic security thesis.[184] She considers, on the one hand, that most people rarely, if ever, come into contact with a court or legislature; this can be applied equally to the even lower probability that citizens will write to any of the EC institutions or be involved directly in litigation before the Community courts. Viewed in these terms, based solely on the frequency of occurrence or usage, Réaume concludes that the inability to carry out such functions in one's own language is hardly a threat to linguistic security. But taking another view, in the context of language rights as fundamental rights, the official use of language has deeper implications. It is a domain over which the governments of states or the institutions of other entities have absolute authority, where the principle of linguistic choice is implemented to both practical and symbolic effect. De Witte expresses the argument in bald financial terms, arguing that the provision from public money of official services in the majority language means that "…the money of the members of a linguistic minority contributes to providing a service which is culturally optimal for the majority alone."[185] Moreover, a considerable proportion of the case law of the Court of Justice relates to administrative and procedural issues, demonstrating the practical relevance of such matters to litigants; as an example of this, the perplexing distinctions that have been drawn by the CFI and ECJ in cases involving Regulation 1/58 were charted in Chapter 1.

Essentially, over fifty million EU citizens are excluded from the full potential of the procedure outlined in Article 21 EC; so what demands to be considered is whether that exclusion can be justified objectively. The implementation of language rights as an aspect of citizenship constitutes a more proactive and individual-oriented approach than the more typically

---

[183] See Article 27(3) of Charte 4284/00, Brussels, 5 May 2000.

[184] Réaume, , "The constitutional protection of language", pp. 51-4.

[185] Bruno de Witte, "Le principe d'égalité et la pluralité linguistique", in Henri Giordan (ed.), *Les Minorités en Europe: Droits Linguistiques et Droits de l'Homme*, (Paris: Éditions Kimé, 1992), 52-64 at 57-8.

incidental, reactive protection of fundamental rights undertaken to date by the Community. Also relevant here is the argument, introduced above, that the evolution of citizenship at EU level in substantive terms is inevitably coloured by the realisation of other objectives set down in the Treaties. The consistent Treaty references to diversity and identity thus form part of the mould of EU citizenship; and this has been consolidated by Article 22 of the Charter of Fundamental Rights. Well before this, the Intergroup on Minority Languages in the European Parliament succeeded, for example, in having a reference to lesser used languages included in the Parliament's Report on Union Citizenship, prepared for the Maastricht Intergovernmental Conference.[186] It is also evident from the Draft Text on Union Citizenship submitted by the Commission to the Maastricht IGC that the Community is aware of the direction in which it may need to go in the future. The Commission had proposed the inclusion of the following article into the TEU: "[e]very Union citizen shall have the right to cultural expression and the obligation to respect cultural expression by others."[187] The explanatory memorandum accompanying the draft article stated that the right to cultural expression was a corollary of Community competence in the field of culture, outlined in Article 151 EC, and was grounded in the dignity and diversity of individuals. Encouraging this dimension of citizenship still further has been advocated strongly by Jessurun D'Oliveira:

> It is a clear indication of a phenomenon which is also to be observed in the component parts of the European Community: that the Member States have to a large extent become multi-cultural and multiethnic societies which may be bound together not by a set of common values, but the development of a competence to deal with their differences; indeed the re-definition of political institutions in Europe reflects this mutation. It is this competence to deal with differences which may be the nucleus of modern active citizenship, and European citizenship may be useful as a laboratory for this procedural concept of proto-cosmopolitan citizenship.[188]

Imminent EU enlargement recasts this view as a necessary inevitability rather than a merely desirable aspiration. The views expounded by Jessurun D'Oliveira reflect the revisitation of democratic theory to encompass the

---

[186] See (1994) vol. 11/12 *Contact Bulletin* 1.

[187] Bull. EC Supp. 2/91, 85-88 at 86.

[188] D'Oliveira, "European citizenship", pp. 147-8.

representation of minorities, in view of the fact that traditional liberal democratic structures "...treat minorities as sets of outvoted individuals."[189] This is further exhibited by the gradual displacement of a benign concept of tolerance in favour of a more proactive approach to non-discrimination, involving the implementation of corrective measures where appropriate and justifiable. The nation-state model of governance has certainly been eroded somewhat as a result—but not really because of the rejection of nationalist philosophy, as predicted by proponents of European integration. In fact, phenomena such as attachment and identity, usually associated with nationalism, are clearly apparent in contemporary society. What has been displaced is the primacy of the nation-state as the polity best positioned to embody attachment and identity; in any case, nation-states have always tended to encapsulate a largely artificial sense of homogeneity. On moral arguments, even on fundamental rights arguments, the rules and procedures governing language use for communicating with the Community institutions should in theory be extended so as to apply equally to speakers of minority languages, as an expression of respect by the EC for the language choices of its citizens. This proposition would fit within the model for language policy reform set out in Chapter 1, in which a more streamlined approach was recommended for the internal administration of the institutions but not for procedures with external application (such as the translation of EC legislation). But this assertion also demands consideration of the extent to which the language rights of individual citizens can be compromised—legitimately—on the basis of efficiency. On the one hand, the relative infrequency of communications between citizens and the EC institutions would not necessarily generate prohibitive costs; furthermore, translation and interpretation could be undertaken by associate service providers, instead of requiring personnel for every minority language on stand-by in a centralised office. Not every minority language spoken in the EC Member States would qualify for inclusion into the scheme *e.g.* languages with a prohibitively low number of speakers could be legitimately excluded. Clear and objective guidelines would have to be devised; the European Bureau for Lesser Used Languages, for example, would be ideally placed to contribute here, preferably on a consultative basis with the language communities themselves. But even if these arrangements could be sustained at present—and that is itself a matter of some doubt— could they really survive EU enlargement, which will cause a significant increase in both the number of languages and speakers involved? Fishman sets out the acceptability of limits in any linguistic regime, although he does

---

[189] Freeman, "Are there collective human rights?", p. 26.

express the concern that "[t]hose who wield greater power are particularly likely to have a disproportionate say in the establishing of such limits."[190] The language rights and duties that can be imposed in the EU context are no less valid in theory than those implemented at the level of domestic governance, but they are less tenable, mainly for reasons of pragmatism. Communication with the institutions of the EU may thus be an instance where the principles of natural justice rather than full linguistic choice may be more appropriate. If this situation can be said to satisfy the tenets of realism, there is still a lingering unease, because "[w]hen a substantial minority of a population is denied full effective citizenship because of the language they speak, then language and language rights matter."[191] All of this implies that while the objectives of the Treaties impinge increasingly on the lives of individuals throughout the Member States, the extent to which a fully representational EU citizenship can match that encroachment is skewed. We are thus faced not only with trying to establish an objective justification for rights limitation, but with the limitations of citizenship more generally, or with the constraints of supranational citizenship more specifically. And in the sphere of language, this holds true notwithstanding the delineation of language choice as a fundamental as well as citizenship right.

D.   EC Influence on Member State Policy: 'Aspiration Rights'

The protection of fundamental rights at EC level aptly symbolises the complex relationship between the Community and its Member States, reflecting a more acutely paradoxical arrangement of powers than is usually evident in structures founded on international cooperation. Member States are ultimately both the architects and subjects of Community law; but this simplistic construct fails to appreciate the intricate temporal and political synergy that has created (and feeds still) the Community legal order. It is fair to say that the Member States remain in charge, although of what is not exactly sure, and of what in the future perhaps even less so. The identification of matters 'purely internal' to the Member States is relevant here also. This concept establishes a boundary beyond which the reach of EC law should not intrude and it has been seen that this applies in the realm of fundamental rights protection as much as in any other aspect of Community law; indeed, as noted, the Charter of Fundamental Rights takes care to reaffirm rather than erode this principle. But the *acquis communautaire* is a

---

[190] Fishman, "On the limits of ethnolinguistic democracy", in Skutnabb-Kangas and Phillipson (eds.), *Linguistic Human Rights*, 49-61 at 51.

[191] Ó Riagáin and Nic Shuibhne, "Minority language rights", p. 12.

sum of its parts. Treaty amendments that extend EC law, while obviously of fundamental significance, do not represent the complete equation. Developments forged through the case law of the Court of Justice have shifted the margins of EC law, sometimes subtly, sometimes less so, and principally via the doctrine of direct effect and the rules on indistinctly applicable measures.[192] The reserve of what remains 'purely internal' to a Member State has shrunk accordingly. And this renders the distinction between situations triggering the application of 'Community rights' and those that do not both more fuzzy and less tenable. The decision of the ECJ in *Bickel and Franz*, analysed in Chapter 6, is illustrative of this phenomenon in the domain of language rights, ostensibly regulated by national (and in this case, regional) legislative arrangements. Using the EC Treaty provisions on EU citizenship and freedom of movement, the Court of Justice deemed instead that Community law granted language rights to EU citizens who had exercised the right to free movement over and above the rules enacted at domestic level (and as such, rules applicable to situations that were purely internal). This raises the question of 'reverse' discrimination against nationals of the state in question who lose out because they have not, in basic terms, moved anywhere, and thus have not activated Community rights. How these gaps in the protection of the individual should be addressed is a question that will increase in importance over time, as the 'purely internal' reserve ebbs further still.[193] It is persuasively arguable that while gaps in protection might be highlighted via cases involving Community law, it is the Member States themselves that should look more carefully, then, at their domestic rules. But the catalytic influence of the EC on this process is remarkable in itself; moreover, it skirts around the difficult sovereignty questions necessarily associated with attempts to manipulate Member State protection mechanisms

---

[192] For example, see Case C-281/98 *Angonese v. Cassa di Risparmio di Bolzano SpA*, judgment of 6 June 2000, not yet reported, at para. 39, in which the ECJ has declared that Article 39 EC applies to private as well as public employment relationships. On the impact of the decision generally, and regarding the erosion of the 'purely internal' principle specifically, see Robert Lane and Niamh Nic Shuibhne, (case comment) 2000 vol. 37:6 *Common Market Law Review* 1237-1247. On the rules regarding indistinctly applicable measures, see in particular the line of authority beginning with Case 120/78 *Rewe-Zentrale AG v. Bundesmonopolverwaltung für Branntwein (Cassis de Dijon)* [1979] ECR 649 (free movement of goods); see also Case C-415/93 *Union Royale Belge des Sociétés de Football Association ASBL v. Jean-Marc Bosman* [1995] ECR I-4921 at 5070 (free movement of workers).

[193] See Niamh Nic Shuibhne, "The European Union and fundamental rights: Well in spirit but considerably rumpled in body?", in Paul Beaumont, Carole Lyons and Neil Walker (eds.), *Convergence and Divergence in European Public Law*, (Oxford: Hart Publishing, forthcoming, 2001).

more directly. The model that best incorporates the possible development of EC rights protection in this way is that devised by Lenaerts almost a decade ago, grounded in the thesis that "[t]he central protection of fundamental rights in a composite legal order should shield the citizens not only in their relationship with the institutions of that legal order itself, but also in their relationship with its component entities."[194] This is, in a sense, the inverse of the citizenship rights idea, which focuses precisely on 'the relationship with the institutions of that legal order'. Lenaerts first asserted that the application of the ECHR in areas of residual Member State power should be guaranteed, free from EC interference; on this point, his model is entirely in keeping with the ethos of the Charter of Fundamental Rights. But he then argued that the EC should claim "...some specific responsibilities for the protection of fundamental rights which are not enumerated in the ECHR, even if those rights somehow related to the residual powers of the Member States."[195] He acknowledged that this could only take place as a result of "...a deliberate political choice during the process of making or amending the Community constitution."[196] For this reason, the advocated development of EC competence is purely an aspiration, forming the outer layer of his 'concentric circles' framework—where the nucleus of rights protection is constituted by implementation of the ECHR, leading outwards to general principles of law, rights based on Union citizenship and, finally, 'aspirational' fundamental rights, particularly social and cultural rights.[197] Lenaerts stressed that the integrity of the ECHR system must be guaranteed, but he also acknowledged the aim of securing higher standards of protection where possible. As a starting point, rights related to culture, social and economic policy, the environment and consumer issues were grouped together on the basis that their enumeration is meaningless without proactive intervention by public authorities.[198] Lenaerts then argued that effective protection of rights within this category requires the express division of competence among competing public authorities since, in the EC/Member State context, "...silence about the respective responsibilities of the Community and the Member States...leads to a black hole in the Community's constitution."[199] In terms

---

[194] Koen Lenaerts "Fundamental rights to be included in a Community catalogue", (1991) vol. 16:5 *European Law Review*, 367-390 at 368.

[195] *ibid.*, p. 375.

[196] *ibid.*, p. 376.

[197] *ibid.*

[198] *ibid.*, p. 386.

[199] *ibid.*

of the rights of minority language speakers, primary responsibility for implementation lies with national authorities, given that these authorities control the administration of domestic courts, the civil service, state education structures, and so on. But Lenaerts combined state responsibility with the development of a new competence for the EC, as "...the supervisory structure for the protection of fundamental rights in areas which substantively continue to belong to the sphere of powers of the Member States (and without the Community itself having any specific normative power in this respect)."[200] This latter aspect of aspirational rights conforms favourably with the tenor of more recent Treaty provisions, including Article 151 EC, which envisage the EC as a co-ordinator rather than lawmaker. The fact that substantive policies would not necessarily emanate from centralised institutions also lessens the need for controversial balancing by the Court of Justice of an EC policy *per se* against competing domestic versions. Clapham has elaborated on possibilities for practical implementation, referring to "...imaginative solutions such as Community-wide collective agreements...and provisions which are adaptable to the various different legal systems...[that] go beyond attempts to harmonise or searches for convergence."[201] Non-harmonisation accommodates suitably the very different needs of different language groups; moreover, Member States would not be able to plead the corrosion of cultural diversity in an attempt to evade consequential responsibilities. This accords with the increasing prevalence of minimum standards in Community decision-making more generally, examined in Chapters 3 and 4; and, in truth, it merely restates the main characteristics of international rights protection, placing the Community in a more central, albeit supervisory, role—a development justified by the unique impact of EC law and integration on both Member States and their residents. The envisaged structure has considerable advantages from the perspective of individuals, given that primary responsibility is correctly placed on national authorities (meaning more tangible results at national level), although Lenaerts does not really address the extent to which the Community as supervisor could provide an external mechanism for redress, the absence of which is a key weakness in other structures of international supervision. What is clear, however, is that the relationship between individuals and the EC is a multifaceted one in the context of fundamental rights. The rhetoric of the institutions—including the Court of Justice—is rooted firmly in the protection of the individual,

---

[200] *ibid.*, p. 389.

[201] Clapham, "A human rights policy", p. 365.

although the extent to which this holds true in practice is impossible to determine accurately. The concentric circles model adds two aspects in particular to this debate; first, it challenges our understanding of a purely bilateral conception of EU citizenship, given that the Member States (and not just the EC institutions) are located in Lenaerts' parallel construction, and second, it generates a more fluid vision of fundamental rights protection—although alongside and *not* in place of the existing *acquis communautaire* and evolving developments such as the EU Charter—that could work especially well in subject areas that are politically sensitive, and/or claims the realisation of which is both demanding of resources and inherently subject to localised variation. In keeping with arguments made at the beginning of this chapter, assigning rights to this 'outer' circle or layer of protection does not diminish their character as fundamental rights, but seeks to overcome real problems associated habitually with their implementation. And more particularly, it perhaps offers a compromise that recognises the limits as well as the potential of supranational government, in accordance with the tenets of subsidiarity. A defined catalytic function for the EC in this way demands more than an amended legal framework, however; it would be erroneous to underestimate the need for a corresponding shift in political culture. Bearing this in mind, Lenaerts chose the label of 'aspiration' most wisely.

5.   CONCLUSION

Clapham has written that "[o]ne cannot simply dismiss the concerns of states over the future of their language…as disguised protectionism. More satisfactory answers and attention could be given to such questions if the impoverished status of human rights in the Community legal order were improved."[202] Language rights are legitimate fundamental rights that impose enforceable correlative duties on public authorities (and, some would argue, on private bodies also in certain circumstances). Transferring this to the Community milieu, the delineation of language rights at EC level is not, as a matter of theory, problematic; it can be supported by international instruments and constitutional provisions (both recognised as sources of fundamental rights by the Court of Justice), by the manifestation of EU citizenship, as already recognised tentatively via Article 21 EC, and by the increasingly visible value placed on diversity and identity within the Union more generally. But setting pragmatic yet justifiable limits to EC language

---

[202] Clapham, "A human rights policy", p. 359.

rights renders this conclusion less straightforward. This becomes even more complex when the premise switches to the paradigm of *minority* language rights. At one level, the ratification of EC language rights would both codify and underpin existing trends, and could legitimately take in many of the aspects of the EC official languages regime outlined in Chapter 1. Multilingual publication of EC legislation (as an element of legal certainty) and written communication between individuals and the EC institutions (and other administrative bodies) are clear examples of this 'codification' idea. The need for a clearer expression of the terms of Regulation 1/58 in the idiom of rights exhibits the complementary advantage of underpinning an embryonic inclination towards language rights, and would go some way towards sorting out the interpretative discrepancies evident in the case law of the Court of Justice, discussed in Chapter 1. The expectations of consumers regarding product information could also be clarified more rationally. In these ways, at least, EC language policy could clearly be reconstituted more coherently to express the value of language rights as fundamental rights. But is there scope for the extension of these rights to speakers of minority languages? On the one hand, denying minority language speakers the right to linguistic choice at Community level serves to deepen further the inequity that sprouts from a base of sheer numerical difference. Stretching the already precarious EC language structure (still beyond the changes that will be wrought in any case by EU enlargement) seems, however, to be a disproportionate and misplaced response to minority language needs, as well as a logistic impossibility. This might be interpreted as a dejected resignation to a two-tiered level of protection (and also, a parallel (down)grading within citizenship); and the need even to consider differentiation reflects further the inherent limitations on supranational government at the level of the individual. But it also causes us to contemplate more honestly our expectations of that same concept. Framing minority language rights at EC level remains possible. But their content will necessarily be different from what is actually feasible within the official languages regime: just as within a domestic polity, not all languages can be recognised in the same way, but this is not itself a denial of the basic legitimacy of language claims. There are two main ways in which the EC can contribute here. First, minority language rights should feature in policies developed to counterbalance the negative impact of integration where appropriate, as discussed in Chapter 1. Anchoring this ambition in linguistic security rather than in the more open-ended value of linguistic survival is essential here, from the perspective of both identifying and enforcing the precise nature of EC responsibility; outwith the ambit of 'rights', however, complementary 'survival' or language-oriented support—

already the main thrust of Community measures directed towards minority language claims and open to development via an enhanced interpretation of legal basis under cultural policy—should continue. Second, minority language rights are relevant within the general framework of free movement rights; the advanced reasoning apparent in *Bickel and Franz*, when compared with that employed previously in *Mutsch* (see Chapters 6 and 2 respectively), indicates that the Court of Justice has already taken this on board. The claims of minority language speakers regarding the official use of their languages are thus left at the level of government most competent to address them, that of the Member State (taking internal government structures into account also), but are incorporated into the Community ethos of non-discrimination and equal treatment where movement rights have been exercised. And finally, a projected evolution of fundamental rights protection at EC level includes the possibility that the Community could have a role in highlighting gaps in the protection of individuals at national level, which obviously holds further potential for the recognition and realisation of minority language rights. The enhanced competence of the Community to combat discrimination—particularly as derived from its more comprehensive basis in the EU Charter of Fundamental Rights—is perhaps the glue that could hold together all of the aspects of language rights development summarised here, both minority and otherwise. It would be facile to suppose that the Community can do either nothing or everything in this regard. But, overall, what remains imperative is that it must do something.

Chapter 6

Minority Language Policy and the EC Institutions:
The Emerging Ethos

1. INTRODUCTION

Throughout the 1980s, the EC institutions began tentatively to explore the margins of Community law at its intersection with the language policies of both the EC itself and its Member States, as chronicled in Chapter 2. The interim changes to Community law and competences have been charted primarily from the standpoints of culture, fundamental rights and citizenship; taken together, the altered legal and political terrain that has since been fashioned arguably generates an enhanced capacity for the EC to participate in the formation and implementation of minority language policy. In particular, the following preliminary conclusions have come to the fore:

- the codification of subsidiarity in the EC Treaty reflected fundamental concerns in respect of the shifting borders between EC and Member State competence; but even under a restrictive interpretation of the principle, there are certain instances where the EC is the most appropriate actor in the language policy context, especially in order to redress the detrimental impact on language use patterns of intensified European integration;

- Article 151 EC is a provision of mixed potential; on the one hand, its structure seems more attuned to a literal and limited definition of culture; but equally, while the cultural aspect of language reflected in Article 151(2) is a necessary component of any language policy (and the provision has, at least, placed cultural issues more firmly on the Community agenda), the broader ambit of Article 151(1) could arguably be drawn upon independently; significantly, the balance in Article 151 is fixed firmly in favour of promoting the diversity of cultures, as strengthened expressly by the Amsterdam Treaty;

- the recognition and protection of language rights as fundamental rights is an underdeveloped facet of EC language policy, causing a deficit that should be remedied; in addition to the fact that language rights are already embedded in national and international rights ideology, considerations of legal certainty, identity and the realisation of representational citizenship add potency to the argument that the Community should express more openly in the language of rights standards that, on the whole, it has accepted already.

An overall stipulation is that both the rights and duties associated with language claims are not the same in all instances. A distinction between language rights and minority language rights is thrown into focus most clearly when attention turns to effective implementation; but this holds true for political entities as a rule and should not be interpreted as an 'out' clause for the Community. The scope of these rights and duties may be different, but the expectation that they should be fulfilled is undiminished.

When looking at the pre-Maastricht era, it was argued that the EC institutions, though evidently sympathetic, did not have the requisite legal competence to act more decisively on minority language issues. The current position, summarised above, is radically different. But have any of these possibilities actually been taken on board? The following paragraphs seek to find out.

2. DEVELOPMENTS IN THE INSTITUTIONS: THE PARLIAMENT AND THE COMMISSION

A.   Killilea Report (1994)

Resolution on Linguistic and Cultural Minorities in the European Community[1]

(i)   Background

In Chapter 2, the European Parliament emerged as something of an institutional champion in the domain of minority language rights. And here, its early work was consolidated. Prior to the enactment of the TEU, the Parliament's Committee on Culture, Youth, Education and the Media commissioned a report on minority languages. Mr. Killilea, charged with this responsibility, advanced three reasons to explain why yet another study on lesser used languages was necessary: first, the resurgence (in a political

---

[1]   [1994] OJ C061/110; text in Appendix II.

sense) of smaller nations and repressed communities in central and eastern Europe; second, the adoption of the Maastricht Treaty, which included a new Community competence in cultural affairs; and finally, the adoption of the Charter for Regional or Minority Languages by the Council of Europe.[2] In the vein of the Commission's 1986 report (see Chapter 2), a questionnaire format was devised; information was received not only from Member State governments but also from regional and local authorities, research institutes and language associations. The completed Report was adopted in the European Parliament on 9 February 1994, by a virtually unanimous majority.[3]

(ii)   Content and Commentary

The lengthy Preamble recalls both the Arfé and Kuijpers Resolutions, as well as referring to interim developments in the Council of Europe and OSCE on minority language protection. But somewhat surprisingly, it does not draw on Article 151 EC as a legal basis *per se*; rather, it speaks of the Parliament's taking 'encouragement' from the commitment to national and regional diversity espoused therein. This 'commitment' is later rephrased, however, as a Community 'responsibility' (paragraph G). The Preamble goes on to set out the role of the EC in terms far stronger than those employed in any of the previous resolutions. In paragraph L, for example, Parliament restates the importance of financial contributions from the Community, but it refers also to *legal* protection at the supranational level; paragraph N represents an effort to placate political sensibilities while setting out Member State obligations, recognising that 'while the duty of every Member State government to protect and promote its official language(s) must be fully respected, it must not be exercised to the detriment of the lesser used languages and the people for whom they are the natural cultural vehicle'.[4] On the whole, the Parliament constructed a pragmatic justification for language policy, in line with arguments advanced here in Chapter 1, arguing that 'European integration must make the use of the most widespread

---

[2]   (1994) vol. 11:1 *Contact Bulletin*, 1-4 at 2.

[3]   The total number of votes cast was 325, which broke down as 318 in favour, one against and six abstentions; Dónall Ó Riagáin (then Secretary General of the European Bureau for Lesser Used Languages) noted, however, that "[t]he size of the majority should not belie the fact that there had been stiff opposition to the report at various stages." (*Contact Bulletin, ibid.*, p. 2).

[4]   Interestingly, the vote against the Resolution and the majority of abstaining votes were cast by French MEP's: as outlined in Appendix I, policies to promote the French language do operate to the detriment of France's minority languages, which are not officially recognised at domestic level.

languages as a way of communicating across the present internal borders compatible with protecting and safeguarding the less widespread languages in regional or transregional contexts' (paragraph K). On this point, the Parliament drew expressly from the process of democratisation in central and eastern Europe, where cultural and linguistic rights have acute significance. But while the Resolution went further (in terms of philosophical basis and the explicit allocation of responsibility to both the Community and the Member States) than any of its predecessors, there was no real attempt to establish a definitive EC competence for language policy development.

The main body of the Resolution commenced with a call for full implementation of the Arfé and Kuijpers Resolutions; it proceeded to restate the need for official and practical recognition of minority languages by the Member States, in the domains of education, justice and public administration, the media and other sectors of public and cultural life (Article 4). The Parliament declared support for the Council of Europe's Charter for Regional or Minority Languages (Article 6) and called on EC Member States to ratify the Charter 'as a matter of urgency...choosing at all times to apply those paragraphs best suited to the needs and aspirations of the linguistic communities in question' (Article 7). In Article 10, Parliament called on the Commission to take a number of positive steps; essentially, this section restated similar provisions from the earlier resolutions, including the far-reaching request that the Commission take the needs of minority language speakers into account when working out Community policy generally, which conforms with the cultural policy integration clause set out in Article 151(4) EC (discussed in Chapter 3). Articles 10(c) and (d) reflect technological innovations, calling on the Commission to provide assistance for minority language projects in the context of digital television. Article 11(g) asked the Commission to 'encourage the publication of the Treaties ...and other basic provisions and information on the European Community and its activities in the Union's lesser used languages'. This measure contemplates both retrospective and prospective language rights that relate most obviously to citizenship and to the principle of legal certainty, amounting in effect to a partial extension of the official languages regime to include minority languages. There is no doubt that an extension to that effect can be justified in theory; but, as argued in Chapter 5, the inevitably extensive impact on resources demands that the setting of realistic limitations must equally be considered. It certainly seems both acceptable and logical that the Treaties, for example, could (and should) be published in the 'Union's lesser used languages'; but after that, the cut-off point becomes more and more arbitrary: what exactly constitutes 'other basic provisions and information'? And who would decide? Minority languages could perhaps be endowed with a legal status similar to that of Irish, as 'Treaty' languages; but the way in which the consequences of status as a Treaty language have since been extended, via Article 21 EC for example, shifts the location of legitimate limitations—and the potential for uncertainty—still further.

In one sense, in its reiteration of established goals and policies, the Killilea Report did not add anything new to the earlier resolutions. This might be considered disappointing, in view of the fact that it was the first Resolution grounded in the extended competences of the amended EC Treaty. But two points should be noted. First, preparation of the Report coincided with preparation of the Charter for Regional or Minority Languages by the Council of Europe; Mr. Killilea decided that more detailed proposals should be omitted from his Report and that the Parliament should instead use the opportunity to support fully the work of the Council.[5] Second, while the Resolution did not, therefore, contain especially innovative or detailed recommendations, the tone of the Preamble is quite different from the pre-Maastricht initiatives. The objective of securing Community/Member State cooperation in the overall best interests of linguistic minorities has been stated more clearly than in any previous text. This concept of power-sharing is plainly compatible with the objectives of Article 151 EC, with the principle of subsidiarity and with an evolving philosophy of coexisting competence more generally.

B. Communications from the Commission

Call for Proposals for European Commission Backing involving Actions in favour of Promoting and Safeguarding Regional or Minority Languages and Cultures (1995)[6]
Support from the European Commission for measures to promote and safeguard regional and minority languages and cultures (2000)[7]

The work of the Commission on regional and minority languages relates primarily to the implementation of cultural and education policy, and as such is discussed mainly in Chapter 3; but these Communications have been selected for inclusion here since they provide some insight into whether or

---

[5]   As footnote 2.

[6]   [1995] OJ C322/34, 2 December 1995.

[7]   [2000] OJ C266/07, 16 September 2000.

not the Commission has been receptive to the initiatives of the European Parliament over the past decade or so. The 1995 'call for proposals' reflects the coordination necessary so that EC funding for various minority language projects can be channelled effectively. The Commission confirmed at the outset that it is the institution with responsibility for the implementation of any action in favour of regional or minority languages (which are defined as 'autochthonous languages traditionally spoken by part of the population of a European Union Member State [excluding] both immigrants' languages and artificially created languages'). It then fenced its own boundaries quite abruptly: '[c]onsidering the competences of the Member States and in respect of the principle of subsidiarity, any activity with a political or statutory impact will be excluded'. This pithy and disappointing interpretation shut off a significant range of EC action *ab initio*, resulting in a clear—and somewhat worrying—example of how the Commission can raise the subjective shield of subsidiarity without actually explaining its full implications in objective, qualitative terms. The Commission *is* restricted in this field, not least by the prohibition against harmonisation in Article 151(5) EC; furthermore, the introduction of measures with direct statutory effect would challenge the express edict for limited legal measures in that provision. But it has been argued here that the principle of subsidiarity may actually *require* rather than prevent Community action in certain circumstances, particularly in respect of the impact of EC policy and integration on language use patterns. It is difficult even to isolate action having 'political' effect in the first place. And it is rarely possible to contain competences along definite or absolute Community/Member State lines. It could be possible to interpret the 'political effect' concept very broadly in order to oppose, for 'political' reasons, even objectively innocuous measures. The cautious approach adopted fits with the 'self-censorship' thesis put forward by Philip, who suggests that the Commission "...has been chastened by the difficulty of getting public approval of the [Maastricht] Treaty and is signalling that it intends to exercise its rights of initiative more modestly ...even if the scope of the Community's competence has been significantly widened."[8] Almost a decade after ratification of the TEU, however, the Commission continued to confine itself to a narrow range of initiatives in the field of culture.[9] It identified projects related to education, the media and

---

[8]   Alan Butt Philip, "Old policies, new competencies" in Andrew Duff, John Pinder and Roy Pryce, *Maastricht and Beyond: Building the New Europe*, (London: Routledge, 1994), 123-139 at 129.

[9]   See the work programme outlined by Joachin Fronia (representing what was then DGXXII), "The future role of the European Commission in respect of lesser used

culture as the priority areas for its allocation of financial assistance; but by not addressing language issues from the underlying premise of the equality of all language *speakers*, the Commission's mandate is, at best, incomplete.

At present, the future allocation of finance for even culturally-rooted language projects is at risk. Budget line B3-1006, dedicated to the provision of funds for these and other minority language initiatives (*e.g.* funding the European Bureau for Lesser Used Languages) was established in 1982, as a direct consequence of the first Arfé Resolution. It was not, however, authorised by a legislative act; and it is difficult to locate a Treaty provision in which the Commission could have grounded the allocation at that time. The security of this arrangement has never been taken for granted; the reduction of the budget line for the first time in 1997 was considered to highlight its precarious foundation.[10] But the most serious threat to its continued existence was brought about by the ECJ decision in *United Kingdom and others v. Commission*, where the Court of Justice held that every 'significant' EC expenditure must be grounded in the prior adoption of a legislative act.[11] A representative of (the then) DGXXII had predicted that while the discretionary budget line on minority languages was temporarily endangered, it would be reinstated on a more correct basis, in accordance with the Court's decision.[12] But the proposed *Arcipelago-Archipel* minority languages programme has not yet materialised, and EC funding (for EBLUL, for example) hangs presently on a precarious year by year basis (on the grounds, presumably, that more short-term funding of this kind does not constitute 'significant' expenditure). It now appears unlikely that the Commission will act more decisively before Autumn 2001, at the very earliest. It had been anticipated that the programme would be presented by the Commission in late 1999; and the apparent reason behind its ongoing suspension is that the Commission's legal services had advised that a programme of this kind

---

languages", in Comhdháil Náisiúnta na Gaeilge, *International Conference on Language Legislation: Conference Proceedings*, (Dublin: Comhdháil Náisiúnta na Gaeilge, 1999), 69-74; see also Chapter 3, on (past and projected) cultural initiatives in the field of language.

10 See (1997) vol. 14:1 *Contact Bulletin* 6-7.

11 Case C-106/96 *United Kingdom and others v. Commission* [1998] ECR I-2729 at 2755, para. 26; the Court did not, however, provide definitive guidelines on what constitutes a 'significant' Community expenditure, and what does not; it did state, however, that 'significant' Community action *can* entail limited expenditure or have effects for only a limited period; furthermore, 'the degree of coordination to which action is subject at Community level' does not determine whether it is significant or not (see p. 2758, para. 36).

12 Fronia, "The future role of the European Commission", p. 71.

should be considered under Article 151 (culture) as well as Article 149 EC (education).[13] The significance of this distinction is that Article 151 requires unanimity of the Member States for decision-making, whereas Article 149 is administered via qualified majority voting. But it is incredulous and somewhat shambolic to suppose that contemplation of Article 151 in this regard arose so late in the day. It is obviously a priority that arrangements for the allocation of finance are enacted on a solid—and correct—footing as soon as possible. And there is no reason, from a legal perspective, why Article 151 cannot be deployed, as contended in Chapters 3 and 4; moreover, while the real difficulties associated with achieving unanimity cannot be disregarded, it is arguable that it is, all things considered, a favourable decision-making option here in any case, also set out in Chapter 3. Other reasons given for the setback include limitations on the resources of the Education and Culture Directorate-General at a time that has seen a considerable number of resource-consuming initiatives (including *Culture 2000*), and the need to await the outcome of IGC 2000 as to whether or not the requirement of unanimity in Article 151 might be changed to qualified majority.[14] But the Commission must also face up to the often illusory constraints it had placed on its own power of initiative more generally. In the context of shared yet non-delimited competence, the Commission is more or less pitted against the Member States, given that it is has the power of legislative initiative. In sensitive domains, the Commission is likely to play down the scope of this power, so as not to transgress Member State relations. This may be advisable in a political sense but it necessarily curtails policy development in whatever the area concerned, and on far from objectively justifiable grounds. Community law has moved forward, but the Commission arguably prefers to prioritise more long-standing, less legal considerations in the field of language policy. Confusingly, there are signs elsewhere of how the double-edged capacity of subsidiarity has been used to bolster Community involvement where deemed necessary; for example, the seventh recital of the measure under dispute in *Parliament v. Council*, discussed in Chapter 3 (on the adoption of a multiannual programme to promote the linguistic diversity of the Community in the information society), states that while language policies are a matter for the Member States (taking account of Community law), "...promoting the development of modern language-processing tools and their use is a field of activity in

---

[13]   See (2000) vol. 16:2 *Contact Bulletin* 1.

[14]   *ibid.*, p. 4; the implications of switching from unanimity to qualified majority voting in respect of Article 151 EC are addressed in Chapter 3; it was noted, moreover, that the unanimity requirement in Article 151 has been retained.

which Community action is necessary in order to achieve substantial economies of scale and cohesion between the various areas;...the measures to be taken at Community level must be commensurate with the objectives to be attained and concern only those fields which are likely to produce an added value for the Community."[15] The 'call for proposals' issued by the Commission in 2000 demonstrates something of an advance from the 1995 version; the traditional focus on 'saving' languages is evident ('...helping these languages to survive and flourish...'), but alongside an expression of linguistic and cultural identity as an 'essential feature of European citizenship'. There is no reference to subsidiarity at all in the document, indicating a less constrained approach than that evident five years earlier. A fairly narrow list of 'fields of action' to which projects applying for funding must relate implies something of a similar 'non-political' proviso; and the need to consider the 'competences of the Member States' has been maintained as a clear message on the relevant page of the Commission's website ('[t]aking into account the responsibilities of the Member States themselves and in full respect of the principle of subsidiarity, any activity having a political or statutory impact is ruled out').[16] This subtle rewording places a more appropriate slant on the Commission's rationale, although it is still far from clear why 'any activity having a political or statutory impact' is considered to be automatically 'ruled out'. So while it does seem, on the one hand, that the Commission has become more active with time in minority language protection, the lack of coherence that characterises EC policy in this domain generally may well find its roots here.

---

[15] Council Decision 96/664, [1996] OJ L306/40; see Case C-42/97 *European Parliament v. Council of the European Union* [1999] ECR I-869.

[16] As published on the Commission's website at http://europa.eu.int/comm/education/langmin.html.

C.   The Euromosaic Report (1996)

The Production and Reproduction of the Minority Language Groups in the European Union[17]

(i)   *Background*

Euromosaic was prepared by four selected language centres on behalf of the Commission (at that time, for DGXXII specifically), to collect "...the necessary background information on each of these linguistic communities that will facilitate applying the resources that are devoted to them...".[18] The Report is based on the premise that EC support for minority languages is "...a direct result of increasing demands from the European Parliament and other organisations which point to the need for public authorities to actively compensate for the negative effects of economic and political integration".[19] Empirical analysis was undertaken to ascertain the potential for the production and reproduction of various language groups, as opposed to the (re)production of their languages *per se*, when confronted by 'an accelerated economic restructuring process'.[20] The ethos of the report is thus firmly rooted in the concept of linguistic security.

(ii)   *Findings and Commentary*

Euromosaic is the first Community publication to grapple directly with the economic dimension of language policy; in particular, the employment of social sciences theory and methodology distinguishes its base from the purely political (and arguably aspirational) assessments contained in the resolutions of the Parliament. The Report first provides a comprehensive account of the methodology deployed in the study and then publishes an analysis of the data collected. The results are sited in the context of emerging social and political discourses *i.e.* the contemporary, neo-liberal shift in emphasis from financial to human capital, the role of diversity in economic development, and the nature and process of European integration itself. It is

---

[17] European Commission, *Euromosaic: The Production and Reproduction of the Minority Language Groups in the European Union*, (Luxembourg: Office for Official Publications of the European Communities, 1996).

[18] *ibid.*, Executive Summary, para. 1.

[19] *ibid.*

[20] *ibid.*, para. 7.

concluded that language groups are centrally involved in these discourses and that "...a re-evaluation of their importance is already in place, albeit that it has yet to feed through into a self-evident social policy."[21] In particular, it is noted that the data collected "...highlights the shift in thinking about the value of diversity for economic development and European integration. It argues that language is a central component of diversity, and that if diversity is the cornerstone of innovative development then attention must be given to sustaining the existing pool of diversity within the EU."[22] Significantly, the Report identifies that "...those language groups which are in a position to sustain themselves are those which receive considerable state support which activates and promotes the production and reproduction processes operating within civil society... [T]he demographic size of a language group is no guarantee of the group's viability capacity, with the existence of some of Europe's largest language groups being threatened."[23]

The authors argue that the need for a programme of action to promote minority language groups, as a source of the diversity that derives from language and culture, cannot be over-emphasised:

> In many respects this is not a new insight, with one after another of the various reports presented to the Commission making similar suggestions. What is different in this Report is that whereas previous suggestions have conceived of minority language groups in emotive terms associated with the 'traditional' activities which are the emotional converse of rational 'modernity', concerned with the poetic, the literary or the musical, but never with the economic and the political, our argument involves the need to develop such action, not for the benefit of the various language groups as a European heritage, but for the economic advantage of the entire Community.[24]

The heritage aspect of culture, and its contribution to diversity, should not be discounted completely just because of the invocation of emotive (and thus generally uncomfortably vague) dialogue; but it has been stressed, in Chapters 1 and 4, that policies focused solely on the aesthetic aspect of language will not redress the contemporary difficulties faced by speakers of minority languages; furthermore, the heritage dimension is not, as

---

[21] *ibid.*, p. 45.

[22] *ibid.*, para. 10 (Executive Summary).

[23] *ibid.*, paras. 8/9.

[24] *ibid.*, p. 60.

established in Chapter 5, a legitimate basis for the recognition of language rights as fundamental rights. What is abundantly clear is that the Commission must continue but also move beyond its sponsorship of education and socialisation projects, more towards pro-active planning than non-directional intervention.[25] The *Euromosaic* study confirms the shift in contemporary legal and political thought, which has begun to accommodate provision for diverse social groups in its philosophies. The role of the EC in this process is then derived as follows:

> [H]istory tells us that the goal of the state has nearly always involved the integration of civil society through homogenisation of cultural and linguistic elements. It is our claim that the future, in contrast, must involve a reorientation of that integration within the context of diversity and that the emergence of the supra-state affords an important opportunity to realise this goal.[26]

Euromosaic is without doubt the most theoretically sophisticated study on minority languages undertaken by the Community to date. Its empirical, scientific approach contrasts sharply with the work initiated by the Parliament; but *all* of these studies have contributed in different ways to the body of data now accessible for the Community institutions. If the Commission takes on board the recommendations made to it, employing a more considered understanding of subsidiarity as well as the Community's evolving philosophy on fundamental rights protection, then it would have the tools to devise a more effective and influential language policy, taking full account of the particular situation of minority languages. In light of monetary union, EU enlargement and intensifying (political) integration more generally, there is perhaps a heightened responsibility on the Commission finally to embrace this challenge.

---

[25]   *ibid.*, pp. 60-1.

[26]   *ibid.*, p. 13.

3.   JURISPRUDENCE OF THE COURT OF JUSTICE

A.   *Commission* v. *Luxembourg*[27]

(i)   *Facts and Judgment of the Court*

In this case, the maintenance of a nationality requirement for access to civil service positions in Luxembourg (in the public sectors of research, teaching, health, inland transport, posts and telecommunications, and utilities) was challenged by the Commission using Community law principles on the free movement of workers.[28] The initiation of these proceedings (under Article 226 EC) marked the culmination of almost three years of communication with the Luxembourg Government in respect of its policy; in fact, the lengthy duration of the pre-litigation procedure was one of the main reasons why the Government's preliminary argument of inadmissibility failed before the Court of Justice.[29] The Court's decision (and the Opinion of Advocate General Léger) focused primarily on the interpretation of the public service exception in Article 39(4) EC. The Court's existing case law on strict and uniform interpretation of this derogation was confirmed: only civil service posts that necessitate a special relationship of allegiance with the state in question, or functions intended to safeguard the general interests of the state, can be considered to come within the ambit of the public service proviso.[30] Aside from arguments based on the interpretation of Article 39(4), the Luxembourg Government raised the question of the protection of its national identity and argued as follows, in the specific context of teachers:

> [T]he fact that teachers have Luxembourg nationality guarantees that traditional values are passed on and, for a small

---

[27]   Case C-473/93 *Commission v. Luxembourg* [1995] ECR I-3207.

[28]   *i.e.* Article 39 EC; Articles 1 and 7 of Regulation (EEC) No. 1612/68 ([1968] OJ Special English Edition, L257/2, p. 475). In particular, the Commission acted in accordance with Communication 88/C 72/02 [[1988] OJ C72/2] on the elimination of restrictions on grounds of nationality that hinder access of workers from other Member States to certain posts in the public service.

[29]   *Commission v. Luxembourg*, p. 3254, paras. 17-24; the other reason for the failure of the inadmissibility contention was that the Luxembourg Government had been allowed four months to comply with the Commission's reasoned opinions, more than twice the time period usually allowed by the Commission.

[30]   *ibid.*, p. 3255, paras. 26 *et seq.*, especially para. 31.

country, it is essential in order to safeguard national identity...
[I]t is difficult to imagine that a primary school teacher coming
from abroad would be sufficiently familiar with the atmosphere
in which Luxembourg children have spent the first few years of
their life, that he would know the national customs, songs,
poems and all the other elements forming part of the national
psychological outlook which play a role in teaching at that
level. Even in secondary education, a teacher's work cannot be
regarded simply as an economic activity whereby knowledge is
imparted in return for remuneration. The transmission of natural
culture continues at that level too.[31]

This extract is reminiscent of arguments made and accepted in *Groener* on
the nature of the teaching function.[32] The Luxembourg Government went
further in this case, however, extending the reasoning developed in the
context of language policy to a more exclusive concept of identity based on
nationality. But while the ECJ did not accept the extended argument, it did
confirm the legitimacy of employing language policies to this end. The
Court first referred to earlier case law, confirming that teaching positions do
not come within the public service exception in Article 39(4) EC.[33] It then
continued as follows:

This conclusion cannot be shaken by considerations relating to
the preservation of national identity in a demographic situation
as specific as that prevailing in...Luxembourg. Whilst the preservation of the Member States' national identities is a
legitimate aim respected by the Community legal order (as is
indeed acknowledged in Article [6(3)] of the Treaty on
European Union), the interest pleaded by the Grand Duchy can,
even in such particularly sensitive areas as education, still be
effectively safeguarded otherwise than by a general exclusion of
nationals from other Member States. As the Advocate General
points out...nationals of other Member States must, like
Luxembourg nationals, still fulfil all the conditions required for

---

[31] *ibid.*, p. 3232, para. 130; other issues raised here included the special demographic
position of Luxembourg and the application of other international instruments, such as the
European Convention on Establishment (1955).

[32] Case C-379/87 *Groener v. Minister for Education and the Dublin Vocational Education
Committee* [1989] ECR 3967; see Chapter 2.

[33] *Commission v. Luxembourg*, p. 3257, para. 33, referring to Case 66/85 *Lawrie-Blum*
[1986] ECR 2121 and Case 33/88 *Allué and Coonan* [1989] ECR 1591.

recruitment, in particular those relating to training, experience and language knowledge. Consequently, the protection of national identity cannot justify exclusion of nationals of other Member States from all the posts in an area such as education, with the exception of those involving direct or indirect participation in the exercise of powers conferred by public law and duties designed to safeguard the general interests of the State or other public authorities.[34]

Accordingly, the legislation implementing the policies of the Luxembourg Government was found to contravene Article 39 EC and Article 1 of Regulation 1612/68.

(ii) Commentary

The decision in this case confirms the Court's position in *Groener* to the extent that Member States may impose a linguistic competence requirement as a precondition to employment, so long as the linguistic knowledge required relates to the nature of the post to be filled, the policy applies to nationals as well as non-nationals and is proportionate in respect of the aim to be achieved. Advocate General Léger discussed this aspect of the protection of identity in his Opinion, stating, for example, that "...access to posts which by their nature involve contact with the public may be in particular made subject to conditions regarding the knowledge of [official languages]."[35] The Advocate General then proceeded, however, to adopt quite a peculiar reasoning, stating that "[i]n my view, the linguistic requirements to which access to numerous posts in the sectors concerned may be lawfully made subject should therefore in most cases allow only citizens born or long established in Luxembourg to respond to offers of employment or to participate in competitions conducted for recruitment purposes."[36] This ambiguous paragraph seems to offer some sort of consolation for the Luxembourg Government, arguably suggesting that its language policies might have the indirect effect of achieving what the original nationality requirement could not be allowed to continue overtly. But such an interpretation goes absolutely against the principle that both direct *and* indirect discrimination are prohibited by Community law. It also contrasts sharply with the Court's decision in *Groener*, where it was considered essential that,

---

[34]   *ibid.*, p. 3258, paras. 35-6.

[35]   *ibid.*, Opinion Advocate General Léger, p. 3243, para. 204.

[36]   *ibid.*, p. 3244, para. 207.

to justify the Irish Government's language policy, the required standard of competence must be attainable for non-nationals (a principle confirmed (implicitly) most recently in *Angonese*, discussed below. The reasoning employed by Advocate General Léger here can only be described as a statement as curious as it is careless. Neither the Advocate General nor the Court discussed language as a distinct marker of identity in any detail; the distinction between language and the other elements of identity put forward by the Luxembourg Government, for example, was not explained. This is regrettable, given that language was effectively singled out as a legitimate basis for differentiation within certain parameters, with the overriding stipulation that relevant measures must be proportionate. For present purposes, however, the status of Letzeburgesch as a national but *de facto* minority language was not discussed.[37]

B.   Criminal Proceedings against Bickel and Franz[38]

(i)   Facts

The facts of this case resemble the earlier decision of the Court in *Mutsch*, discussed in Chapter 2, but with one fundamental difference. The defendants here were Austrian and German nationals respectively, both of whom were charged with criminal offences while travelling through the Bolzano region of Italy, the first defendant being a lorry driver charged with driving while under the influence of alcohol and the second, a tourist found to be in possession of a knife of a type prohibited. In Bolzano, the German and Italian languages have the same official status; one practical effect of this policy is that Italian citizens who are residents of the region—but *not* Italian citizens generally—have the right to choose either Italian or German as the language of the case for criminal proceedings. The present case asked whether a similar right could be extended to the defendants by virtue of Community law. In both cases, pre-trial documents such as summonses and adjournment orders were issued in Italian. Both defendants declared that they did not have any knowledge of the Italian language and requested that the actual proceedings take place in German. In *Mutsch*, the defendant had been resident as a migrant worker in Belgium and it was decided that the right to choose the language of court proceedings (already granted to citizens

---

[37]   Letzeburgesch is a national but not official language of the Grand Duchy: see Chapter 1 and Appendix I.

[38]   Case C-274/96 *Criminal Proceedings against Bickel and Franz* [1998] ECR I-7637.

of the relevant region in Belgium) should be extended to migrant workers on the same conditions, on the premise of its constituting a 'social advantage' per Regulation 1612/68. But neither defendant in the present case could claim status as a relocated worker: both were merely passing through the region at the time of the alleged commission of the offences. The following question was, therefore, referred to the Court of Justice in respect of both cases:

> Do the principle of non-discrimination as laid down in the first paragraph of Article [12], the right of movement and residence for citizens of the Union as laid down in Article [18] and the freedom to provide services as laid down in Article [49] of the Treaty require that a citizen of the Union who is a national of a Member State and is present in another Member State be granted the right to call for criminal proceedings against him to be conducted in another language where nationals of that State in the same circumstances enjoy such a right?[39]

Interestingly, the referring court itself submitted that all Community citizens should be entitled to have criminal *and* civil proceedings conducted through German if they so wish, on the grounds that not to grant such a right would amount to "...a manifest breach of the principle of non-discrimination on grounds of nationality...."[40] The Advocate General identified two issues to be decided: "...first, whether the choice of language in the criminal proceedings before the referring court comes within the scope of the Treaty; and secondly, whether the Italian rules, if construed so as to deny [the defendants] the right to use German, would entail discrimination on grounds of nationality."[41] Significantly, he distinguished the Court's earlier decision in *Mutsch*, where language rights were conferred on non-nationals as a corollary of their status as migrant workers, rather than in the general contexts of freedom of movement (or European citizenship) *per se.*

(ii)   Judgment of the Court

The Court held that "...exercise of the right to move...freely in another Member State is enhanced if the citizens of the Union are able to use a given language to communicate with the administrative and judicial authorities of

---

[39]   *ibid.*, p. 7654, para. 11.

[40]   *ibid.*, Opinion of Advocate General Jacobs, p. 7641, para. 9.

[41]   *ibid.*, p. 7641, para. 10.

a State on the same footing as its nationals."[42] It acknowledged that establishing the rules of criminal procedure is generally within Member State competence, but stated that the fundamental principle of non-discrimination (Article 12 EC) and the overriding Community principles on freedom of movement set legitimate limits to these internal legislative procedures. The contention of the Italian Government that the aim of the rules was to protect the ethno-cultural minority residing in Bolzano was rejected. The Court confirmed that the protection of such a minority was a legitimate aim, but held that "…[i]t does not appear…that that aim would be undermined if the rules in issue were extended to cover German-speaking nationals of other Member States exercising their right to freedom of movement."[43] The Court did not, however, elaborate on this statement.

(iii)   Commentary

In *Bickel and Franz*, the Court delivered a judgment of fundamental significance on the free movement of persons and, more precisely, on the scope of EU citizenship. But the decision has clear and considerable implications for the determination of minority language policy also. Once again, the philosophical basis for this aspect of the decision can best be derived by drawing from the Opinion of the Advocate General. In the first instance, Advocate General Jacobs did not take the application of Article 12 EC quite so much for granted. In order for the provision to apply in the present case, the alleged discrimination would have to be seen as coming 'within the scope of application of the Treaty'. Having established only tenuous connections between the alleged offences and Community law,[44] the Advocate General introduced instead the general principle that "…criminal proceedings against a Community citizen based on alleged facts which occurred while that citizen exercised his right to free movement come within the scope of application of the Treaty and are therefore subject to the prohibition of discrimination on grounds of nationality."[45] He stressed that the extension of non-discrimination to cover criminal proceedings arising in the course of the exercise of free movement was particularly appropriate in

---

[42] *ibid.*, Judgment of the Court, p. 7655, para. 16.

[43] *ibid.*, p. 7658, para. 29.

[44] Opinion of Advocate General Jacobs, pp. 7642-3, paras. 13-16.

[45] *ibid.*, p. 7643, para. 15, relying on Case 186/87 *Cowan v. Trésor Public* [1989] ECR 195.

light of the concept of EU citizenship.[46] He declared that it was still open to Member States to justify advantages reserved to nationals on grounds unrelated to nationality, but that it was becoming "...increasingly difficult to see why Community law should accept any type of difference in treatment which is based purely on nationality, except in so far as the essential characteristics of nationality are at stake, such as access to a limited range of posts in the public service or the exercise of certain political rights."[47] This reflects the Court's earlier decision in *Commission v. Luxembourg*, discussed above. Having established that non-discrimination on grounds of nationality applied in respect of both applicants, the Advocate General went on to consider whether the Italian legislation discriminated against the two defendants. The Italian Government argued that the provision in question was *not* discriminatory on grounds of nationality, pointing out that even an Italian national not resident in Bolzano would not have been afforded the right to use German in this type of situation. It was argued alternatively that the rule came within the scope of the protection of linguistic minorities and not the rules of criminal defence. In this context, it was pointed out that the linguistic aspect of the rules of defence is already covered by the ECHR (outlined in Chapter 5). The Italian Government thus considered the legislation as a form of special constitutional protection, relating the right to use German in Bolzano to language choice rather than language competence. The Advocate General dismissed these arguments, however, on what can only be deemed pragmatic grounds:

> The argument advanced by the Commission and the Italian Government that Italian nationals not resident in Bolzano cannot choose German either is beside the point. Being Italian-speakers, the overwhelming majority of Italian residents will have no practical interest in choosing German. In other words, German and Austrian visitors are without exception denied an advantage granted to most Italian residents who actually want that advantage...[T]he advantage in the present case, although regional in form, is in reality directed at a general category of residents, namely German-speakers.[48]

---

[46]   The Advocate General made some especially strong remarks on the fundamental nature of Union citizenship and on the relevance of non-discrimination to citizenship at p. 7645, paras. 23-24.

[47]   *ibid.*, pp. 7645-6, para. 27.

[48]   *ibid.*, p. 7648, paras. 37-8.

Significantly, this construction is not quite the same as that decided by the Court in *Mutsch*, where all that was made clear was that the rights accorded to the defendant existed only "...if workers who are nationals of the host Member State have that right in the same circumstances."[49] The theme of citizenship is far more 'European' in the present case: the Advocate General established a linguistic connection between groups of EU citizens that transcends national borders and, in fact, distinguishes them from other nationals of the host Member State. Following on from this, he considered whether the Italian rule could be justified objectively on grounds other than nationality. He dismissed the possibility of justification on administrative grounds, pointing to an argument advanced by the defence—that the appointment of an interpreter so that the proceedings could take place in Italian would actually generate *extra* costs.[50] The Advocate General then responded to the argument that the Italian legislation was justifiable on the grounds of the protection of a linguistic minority:

> [It is not] possible, as the Italian Government suggests, to justify the rule on the ground that its purpose is to protect the German-speaking minority in Bolzano. I fully accept that the rule in question serves the *wholly legitimate aim of protecting a Member State's linguistic minority*, an aim unrelated to nationality. The difficulty, however, is that the exclusivity of the rule, that is to say, the denial of the advantage to visitors from other Member States, is neither a necessary nor an appropriate means of achieving that aim. In other words the rule is disproportionate. Refusing the use of German to visitors does not in any way serve that aim. If anything, it has the reverse effect: it reinforces Italian as the principal language even in the predominantly German-speaking region of Bolzano.[51]

Before examining the substance of the Advocate General's argument here, it is worth noting first that his outlook on the protection of a Member State's linguistic minority surpasses that enunciated by the Court in *Groener*, where the express status of Irish as a 'national' and 'official' language was employed. And the Court in *Bickel and Franz*, in turn, implied that it has

---

[49]   *Mutsch*, p. 2696, para. 18.

[50]   *Bickel and Franz*, Opinion of Advocate General Jacobs, p. 7648-9, para. 40; the Court also alluded briefly to this consideration, at. p. 7659, para. 30 of its judgment.

[51]   *ibid.*, p. 7649, para. 41 (emphasis added).

accepted this broader 'minority' basis, holding simply that protection of an 'ethno-cultural minority...may constitute a legitimate aim'.[52]

Again, it is significant that the Advocate General based his decision on transnational considerations, in terms of the German language and of European citizens, rather than national policy. This is a remarkable advance from *Mutsch*. The decision of the Court ultimately supports this even if it was not framed in such explicit, progressive language. This is, in itself, disappointing, in light of the relatively consistent approach of the Court over the past decade towards Member State minority language policies. The main difficulty lies in the perception that, in the absence of philosophical arguments, the decisions of the Court are concerned with fundamental Community principles over and above considerations of linguistic identity. What is often ignored in this context is that the limitations established by the Court, based on the application of non-discrimination and proportionality, are fundamental principles applied across the human rights law spectrum. This point relates back to some extent to broader criticisms that the Court of Justice engages in inappropriate balancing of values and objectives over and beyond legal rules, raised in Chapter 5 in the context of its fundamental rights judgments. The complex formula that is legal decision-making, however, cannot be ignored here. Because what court, in truth, considers cases in some sort of legal vacuum? It is not realistic to claim that, for any given case, there are no policy considerations, no values and objectives, no extraneous factors that influence the outcome. Acknowledgement and application of this fact is something of a contemporary legal trend, the impact that the Human Rights Act will have on UK decision-making being the most current domestic example at the time of writing. To pretend that the Court of Justice is any different denies both its character as a contemporary decision-making forum and the validity of its cumulative jurisprudence. And in any case, the consideration of values such as diversity, citizenship and regional identity has been factored into Community law expressly over the years via Treaty amendments. This point leads to another aspect of *Bickel and Franz* that is less difficult to reconcile, however. Leaving aside the objective argument that the result achieved here reinforced the use of German in Bolzano in actuality, the fact remains that regional language arrangements were effectively overridden by the ECJ in the interests of Community law, a position that has been sharply criticised.[53] Given that the

---

[52] *ibid.*, Judgment of the Court, p. 7658-9, para. 29.

[53] See for example, Karl Reiner, "Human rights and the protection of minorities in the independent province of Bolzano-Bozen", in Comhdháil Náisiúnta na Gaeilge, *International Conference on Language Legislation*, 83-89.

result in this case arguably made the most linguistic sense, it is difficult not to cast these criticisms more in the light of territorial than linguistic integrity; such an interpretation would, however, be as unhelpful as it is unfair. This incursion into regional integrity is thus discussed more fully below in the context of *Angonese* which, with *Bickel and Franz*, could be viewed as the Court's double strike against the autonomy of Bolzano.

C.   *Angonese* v. *Cassa di Risparmio di Bolzano SpA* [54]

(i)   *Facts and Judgment*

The question referred in *Angonese* presented to the Court of Justice a chance to consider openly what had been implied in *Groener*. In August 1997, Mr Angonese, an Italian national and resident of Bolzano, applied to enter into a competition for advertised posts with the defendants, a private banking undertaking in the province. The advertisement had required that candidates should possess a *patentino i.e.* a certificate of bilingualism in Italian and German issued solely by the public authorities in Bolzano, following successful completion of both oral and written stages of an examination (held four times annually at an examination centre in the province). Although residents of Bolzano tend to obtain the certificate routinely for purposes of employment, Mr. Angonese did not possess the *patentino* at the material time. His mother tongue was German and the national court had found that he was perfectly bilingual. He thus sought entry to the competition by submitting *inter alia* certificates relating to studies (through the medium of German) in English, Polish and Slovene at the University of Vienna from 1993 to 1997, although these studies had not led to the award of a degree. The *Cassa* refused to admit him to the competition purely on the grounds that he did not hold a *patentino*. The applicant went on to argue that the *Cassa's* precondition of possession of the *patentino* was unlawful in light of Community law on the free movement of workers, citing arguments based on Article 39 EC, and Articles 3(1), 7(1) and 7(4) of Regulation 1612/68. The national court referred the following question to the Court of Justice for a preliminary ruling under Article 234 EC:

> Is it compatible with Article [39](1), (2) and (3) of the EC Treaty and Articles 3(1) and 7(1) and (4) of Regulation (EEC) No 1612/68 to make the admission of candidates to a competi-

---

[54]   Case C-281/98, judgment of 6 June 2000, not yet reported.

tion organised to fill posts in a company governed by private law conditional on possession of the official certificate attesting to knowledge of local languages issued exclusively by a public authority of a Member State at a single examination centre (namely, Bolzano), on completion of a procedure of considerable duration (to be precise, of not less than 30 days, on account of the minimum lapse of time envisaged between the written and the oral test)?

In *Groener*, the Court had found that the linguistic competence requirement at issue could be justified 'by reason of the nature of the post to be filled' (in accordance with Article 3(1) of Regulation 1612/68) and was not, therefore, discriminatory; but it did caution that "...the principle of non-discrimination precludes the imposition of any requirement that the linguistic knowledge in question must have been acquired within the national territory."[55] The case in *Angonese* hinged upon this *dictum*. As in *Groener*, the right of the employer to require evidence of linguistic competence was not challenged; rather, it was contested that this requirement could be satisfied only by possession of a *patentino*.[56] And given that the *patentino* is held almost exclusively by residents of Bolzano, and so predominantly Italian nationals, its requirement could constitute indirect discrimination on grounds of nationality.

The Court dealt first with the question of the admissibility of the reference raised by the Italian Government and the *Cassa*, then determined that Regulation 1612/68 did not apply in the instant case.[57] It then issued the statement for which the judgment will undoubtedly continue to be evoked *i.e.* "...the prohibition of discrimination on grounds of nationality laid down in Article [39] of the Treaty must be regarded as applying to private persons as well."[58] Regarding the substance of the claim referred, the Court confirmed its position in *Groener*; whilst the requirement of linguistic knowledge and possession of a diploma attesting to it was *prima facie* legitimate, "...the fact that it is impossible to submit proof of the required linguistic knowledge by any other means, *in particular by equivalent qualifications obtained in other Member States*, must be considered disproportionate in

---

[55] *Groener*, p. 3994, para 23.

[56] The referring court had drawn attention also to the fact that the way in which the *patentino* examination stages were structured made it unlikely that a potential candidate who did not possess the certificate already could have obtained one before the closing date specified in the advertisement.

[57] For more detail on these aspects of the decision, see Robert Lane and Niamh Nic Shuibhne, (case comment) 2000 vol. 37:6 *Common Market Law Review* 1237-1247.

[58] *Angonese*, para. 36.

relation to the aim in view."[59] Accordingly, the Court held that "...Article [39] of the Treaty precludes an employer from requiring persons applying to take part in a recruitment competition to provide evidence of their linguistic knowledge exclusively by means of one particular diploma issued only in one particular province of a Member State."[60]

(ii)   Comment

Just as *Bickel and Franz* is likely to be remembered for its illumination of citizenship and freedom of movement, *Angonese* is similarly fated to be linked intrinsically to the declaration that Article 39 EC is directly effective for both public and private employment relationships. Moreover, the seemingly indiscriminate displacement of the 'purely internal' question will no doubt merit some debate, given that the Court addressed only cursorily the extent to which the applicant could establish a connecting factor with Community law.[61] But the judgment is analysed here from the perspective of its implications for language policy and regional autonomy. The substantive decision, as an assessment of indirect discrimination, can hardly (following on from *Groener*) be considered surprising. But after *Bickel and Franz*, the result is unlikely to be well received in Bolzano. On the first point, the ECJ confirmed that employers—both public and private—may require evidence of linguistic knowledge, subject to the Community principles of non-discrimination and proportionality. Given that the *Cassa* were prepared only to accept one specific diploma (the attainment of which outside Bolzano was impossible), the Court did not have to probe further in this case the extent to which an actual diploma or certificate of some sort can be required in the first place; in other words, would the presentation of evidence of linguistic knowledge by *other* means be a sufficient criterion for the assessment of that knowledge in situations even where a diploma had been required explicitly? Advocate General Fennelly gave considerable attention to this point. He referred to the 'linguistic regime in the province of Bolzano and the linguistic make-up of its population' as a justification for the requirement of bilingualism in the first place.[62] The referring court had established that the applicant was perfectly bilingual in German and Italian; furthermore, he had submitted certificates attesting to his studies in Vienna which, though not

---

[59]   *ibid.*, para. 44 (emphasis added).

[60]   *ibid.*, para. 46.

[61]   See Lane and Nic Shuibhne, Case Comment, p. 1240 *et seq.*

[62]   *Angonese*, Opinion of Advocate General Fennelly, para. 42.

resulting in the award of a degree at the material time, had been conducted through the medium of German. On this point, the focus of the Opinion was entirely different from the approach adopted ultimately by the Court of Justice, in that Advocate General Fennelly sought primarily to establish, from the perspective of the applicant, a connecting factor with Community law. He thus took as his starting point the reasoning derived from *Knoors* and subsequent jurisprudence *i.e.* that "...account can only be taken of time spent studying abroad in the exercise of Community-law rights if it results in a relevant diploma or recognised training—a condition not satisfied in the present case, as the applicant's studies in Vienna had no connection with banking...."[63] He went on to analyse subsequent decisions on the mutual recognition of qualifications, notably *Bouchoucha*[64] and *Kraus*[65]. In particular, he referred to the Court's decision in *Kraus* on the point that "...possession of a postgraduate academic title is not usually a prerequisite for access to a profession...[but] could improve its holder's chances relative to candidates who did not have such a supplementary qualification by attesting to the former's fitness for a particular post and, as the case may be, *his command of the language of the country where it was awarded.*[66] On the facts of the present case, the Advocate General concluded as follows:

> Leaving aside for the moment the fact that the applicant had not completed his studies, it is of primary importance, in my view, that while those studies can be characterised as a type of vocational training within the meaning of [Article 150 EC], they were, none the less, quite remote in content both from the banking post for which the applicant wished to be considered and from the certificate of bilingualism required of candidates for that post...[T]he facts as found by the national court do not suggest any link between the nature of those studies and the employment sought by him in Bolzano or the condition imposed for access to that employment."[67]

---

[63] *ibid.*, para. 9, relying on Case 115/78 *Knoors v. Secretary of State for Economic Affairs* [1979] ECR 399; see also Council Directive 64/427, 7 July 1964, [OJ Special English Edition, Series I, 1963-1964, p. 148], regarding recognition of periods of relevant work experience for certain trades.

[64] Case C-61/89 *Criminal Proceedings against Bouchoucha* [1990] ECR I-3551.

[65] Case C-19/92 *Kraus v Land Baden-Württemberg* [1993] ECR I-1663.

[66] *Angonese*, para. 20 of the Advocate General's Opinion (emphasis added).

[67] *ibid.*, para. 28.

But here the reasoning is arguably flawed, ignoring the submission of the applicant that the *patentino* itself had no particular relevance to banking terminology.[68] The 'condition imposed for access to that employment' was evidence of bilingualism in German and Italian, *not* knowledge of 'banking German'; and 'the facts as found by the national court' *did* suggest that the applicant was perfectly bilingual. Furthermore, the Advocate General sought to distinguish the passage from *Kraus* cited above, arguing that it "...is not directly material to the present applicant's case, as it refers to the assessment of the holder's fitness to engage in an economic activity related to the substantive subject-matter of the diploma."[69] Both cases, however, involved assessment of the candidates' qualifications at the point of *access* to employment. The Advocate General seemed prepared, on the one hand, to allow an extension of the general rules on mutual recognition: he stated openly that he had not attached 'particular importance' to the fact that the applicant had not completed his studies at the material time.[70] Once the requirement of *any* diploma or equivalent qualification is removed, it then becomes inevitably and materially difficult to gauge the substance of knowledge acquired; in an attempt to respond to this, the Advocate General attached the 'banking German' proviso. But it is submitted that this was not an entirely appropriate way of going about things in the present case, given that it places an additional burden on the applicant that possession of the *patentino* does not itself impose. As things panned out, the Court did not have to deal with this question in any case. But it is worth noting that if it had chosen to follow the reasoning of the Advocate General, it would have amounted to a significant advance in the jurisprudence on the mutual of recognition of qualifications more generally and not necessarily a welcome one, from the perspective of coherence.

Finally, the implications of the decision in *Angonese* for autonomous regional policy-making should be noted. The Court of Justice was no doubt keenly aware in *Groener* of the political consequences of its decision; in fact, the reasoning employed in that case is not altogether convincing from a legal perspective (see Chapter 2) although the result achieved makes good political sense. But in both *Bickel and Franz* and *Angonese*, the judgments do not reflect a similar degree of deference by the ECJ to the Member State's language policy arrangements. In truth, regional competence in this matter must still be traced to national rules, entrenched by the fact that

---

[68]   *ibid.*, para. 12.

[69]   *ibid.*, para. 30.

[70]   *ibid.*, para. 33.

representations in both cases needed to be made by the *Italian* government, as the EC Member State. But the fact that the implications of the decision strike actually at the regional level demonstrate a fundamental gap in the Community legal order: the channels through which sub-national authorities can participate in EC decision-making are effectively controlled by the internal constitutional structures of the Member States, yet the policies implemented by sub-national authorities are still subject to the application of Community law. How a state organises its internal administrative structure is seen properly and exclusively, on the one hand, as an internal constitutional matter. But the idea that a matter can be 'purely internal' does not emerge only at the level of the Member State. This does not seem even to have been acknowledged in either of the Bolzano language cases. It was argued above that the Court of Justice has to achieve a balanced decision in any given case, taking into account a myriad of competing claims and values. And perhaps the outcome of *Angonese* could not have been any different even had the regional autonomy question been addressed. But recognition, at least, of the anomaly raised here would have validated the legitimacy of regional decision-making structures in the Community context, and perhaps made the ECJ decisions just that bit easier to swallow for the Bolzano administration.

4.   CONCLUSION

The developments discussed in this Chapter could be said to indicate more the disclosure of rather than change in the attitude of the EC institutions on the question of linguistic diversity, as it relates to minority languages in particular. The *Euromosaic* report and the decisions of the ECJ in *Bickel and Franz* and *Angonese* reflect significant advances from the equivalent pre-Maastricht thinking set out in Chapter 2. And in comparison to other ECJ decisions on language matters—such as the cases on consumer protection and information, and those calling into question the status of Regulation 1/58—the jurisprudence on minority languages is easily the most speaker-friendly, in which the brand (if not always the letter) of language rights is both apparent and decisive. This strengthens the argument in favour of a more coherent expression of language rights at Community level in a wider sense. But it does not represent the complete picture. The more restricted approach adopted by the Commission and the clumsy reasoning evident in *Commission v. Luxembourg* exhibit lingering uncertainties, traceable most likely to the ongoing battle between Community and Member State competence. What can perhaps be noted as a common thread is that responsibility for the substantive implementation of minority language policy is considered almost invariably to reside at Member State level in the first instance (apart from Community duties arising especially from the momentum of integration, set out most lucidly in *Euromosaic*). But equally, the Court and Parliament in particular have made it clear that the EC still has a role to play. This accords fully with the revised interpretation of harmonisation apparent in Community law more generally, enunciated expressly in, for example, Article 151 EC. In real terms, this appears to have been manifested via the supervision of the Court of Justice where free movement principles are triggered, and in two main ways. First, the Court acts as something of a watchdog, assessing Member State minority language policy against the Community benchmarks of non-discrimination and proportionality. This is nothing new, established already since *Mutsch* and *Groener*. But there is an emerging second aspect, less discernible in the earlier decisions, in that the Court now seems more willing to examine the substantive issues raised from a Community perspective on free movement intermingled with minority language discourse. As it has happened, to date, the results of this venture have benefited the individuals concerned and have thus, even if indirectly, promoted the use of the minority languages at issue. Moreover, it is difficult to pin this advance on any one aspect of either the TEU or Amsterdam Treaty; rather, shifting views on culture and identity, on diversity, on competence, on fundamental rights and citizenship are arguably converging to elevate the human dimension of both the Community and Community law; and it is thus somehow appropriate that the decisions in *Bickel and Franz* and *Angonese* were vehicles for considerable advancement in the jurisprudence of the Court on citizenship and the free movement of workers respectively. How this sits with both national and regional decision-making autonomy, however, is quite another matter.

Chapter 7

Conclusion

Identity and diversity, rights and citizenship, legitimacy and democracy, non-discrimination and equal treatment: concepts that figure markedly in any articulation of a contemporary, EC lexicon. Language policy impinges inexorably on—or alternatively, is impinged on by—the achievement of all of these values. But at present, EC language policy can only be deciphered by piecing together a number of disparate canons; there is no coherent framework. As a starting point, the Community has committed itself repeatedly to the preservation of linguistic diversity; but what does 'linguistic diversity' actually mean? Or more specifically, what does it mean in the EC context? There are several aspects to distinguish here, treatment of official and non-official languages being especially germane. The present EC official languages regime is floundering and enlargement of the EU will impact on existing procedures more radically; this does not seem to have been taken into account to the degree necessary at IGC 2000. Although premised on the admirable concept of linguistic equality, the bolstering of state sovereignty seems to be the objective best served by absolute 'equality' as it is presently realised. An operative distinction between official and working languages is both justified and necessary; this would enable less languages to be used in certain instances, thus enhancing efficiency, but would maintain the equality of the official languages for other (primarily external) purposes in the interests of democracy and legal certainty. An express reformation of language policy in this vein is unlikely to be easily sold in a political sense; but the way in which the institutions and other EC bodies skirt around the system at present is probably, in reality, even more damaging.

It is not easy to assess the extent to which the value of linguistic diversity generates legitimate constraints on EC trade principles. For example, a fairly ambiguous 'cultural heritage' derogation (explored by Advocate General Van Gerven in *Fedicine*[1] but implicitly influential in *Groener*[2] some years

---

[1] Case C-17/92 *Federacion de Distribuidores Cinematográficos (Fedicine) v. Spanish State* [1993] ECR I-2239.

[2] Case C-379/87 *Groener v. Minister for Education and the Dublin Vocational Education Committee* [1989] ECR 3967.

earlier) seems to have taken root to some extent; but language policy more expressly falls below consumer protection in the hierarchy of priorities established by the ECJ. Apart from limited procedural rights now associated with EU citizenship, there is no real conception at EC level of fundamental language rights as a corollary of official language policy, and this has caused some (jurisprudential) inconsistency in the application of Regulation 1/58. This disparity should be addressed. Another matter usually overlooked is the extent to which language shift throughout the Member States has been—and continues to be—affected by the dynamics of European integration. Even at a purely economic level, creating and maintaining the internal market have resulted in the distortion of linguistic environments, in that the relative utility of many languages has been diminished by the spread of the languages of wider (market) communication. While language itself has an economic dimension, it is not an inherently economic concept; but this does not mean that forces of economic integration have no bearing on language use and the empirical results presented in the *Euromosaic* report point conspicuously to the contrary.[3] Acting on an individual basis, Member States cannot redress effectively the widespread and disruptive influence of intensifying integration on patterns of language use, undoubtedly heightened still further by monetary union. As the key economic actor, with ever more exclusive competence, the involvement of the Community here is not just a goodwill gesture; it is a responsibility. Moreover, EC law—both measures enacted primarily towards the fulfilment of economic objectives and those forming part of a swelling corpus on more general matters—encroaches continuously on seemingly unrelated aspects of domestic policy. These so-called peripheral policy domains are far from peripheral to the individuals involved and affected, who deserve to have their priorities secured within the supranational structure that (often) governs them yet still seems too remote. Community rhetoric, at least, has taken this agenda on board; whether this is purely a contrived ploy induced to reap credence and legitimacy remains to be seen.

Here, another deficiency in EC language policy comes to the fore. If the position of even the official EC languages merits concern, then how much more vulnerable are regional and minority languages? And to what extent can a corresponding EC responsibility be established here? Over fifty million EU citizens are estimated to speak languages other than those recognised officially by the Community. And these languages contribute equally

---

[3]   European Commission, *Euromosaic: The Production and Reproduction of the Minority Language Groups in the European Union*, (Luxembourg: Office for Official Publications of the European Communities, 1996).

to the linguistic diversity allegedly cherished by Member States and Community alike. The fate of all languages lies ultimately with their speakers and public authorities should not strive to fabricate the structures of linguistic behaviour; but societal conditions should be favourable to the exercise of genuine linguistic choice within reason. Primary responsibility here lies firmly, at first instance, with the Member States: no-one is asking the EC to 'save' minority languages single-handedly. But it does have a distinct part to play, as a governing public authority. Its actions to date on minority language matters arguably reveal that it has acknowledged this, at least at an elementary level, although there are enduring difficulties. Paradoxically, over-zealous promotion of national languages in the EC forum has probably operated against the recognition of non-official languages, contravening the very ethos of diversity in the first place.

It has been argued that there are two main ways in which the Community might exercise competence in the minority language domain *i.e.* action at EC level *per se* and, more tentatively, action as a coordinator of Member State policy. Although there are persuasive ideological and legal arguments for the inclusion of (certain) minority languages in the EC official languages regime, this would not be a particularly wise or sustainable move in terms either of efficiency or of actual benefit for the speakers concerned. But the distinct position of minority languages and their speakers should be incorporated into EC responsibility for checking the aggravation of language shift. In a somewhat related sense, the EC institutions have initiated over the years various programmes for the allocation of funding to minority language projects; the continuation, consolidation and expansion of this activity is imperative. At present, funding has been suspended for reasons related to legal basis;[4] yet there is no (legal) reason why the general objective on an EC contribution to cultural diversity enshrined in Article 151 EC cannot be employed in this context.

Sponsoring the cultural aspects of language policy, while crucially important, is not sufficient; but limitations as to competence feature more acutely in respect of an EC role as (potential) coordinator and supervisor of Member State language policy. In the soft law sphere, the European Parliament has prepared and adopted a number of studies and resolutions, gently (and sometimes less so) directing the Member States towards recognising the rights of minority language speakers within their jurisdictions. In more legally compelling terrain, the Court of Justice has taken something of a dual approach. First, it has consistently affirmed that Member State language

---

[4]   See Chapter 6 on Case C-106/96 *United Kingdom and others v. Commission* [1998] ECR I-2729.

policies are subject to review against Community law standards on non-discrimination and proportionality where relevant; but more recently, it has begun to assess domestic language policy more objectively against a meshed background of Community values on free movement and the discourse of minority rights. The Court's decision in *Groener*[5] epitomises the former approach, which wasn't so much about the EC being proactively supportive of language rights as not precluding a Member State from going about that business for itself. The judgments delivered more recently in *Bickel and Franz*[6] and (to a lesser extent) *Angonese*[7] reveal quite a different interpretative tactic. Significantly, the Court is far more amenable to rights ideology in the minority context than regarding (administrative) language claims more generally. Bearing this in mind, it is arguable that little more can be expected of the EC than what it has actually done already. What is vital, however, is that this somewhat tenuous base is substantiated more decisively in the edifice of fundamental rights, and citizenship where appropriate. The emerging competence of the Community on issues of discrimination beyond that based on nationality may yet be significant here, especially in light of the more comprehensive—and language-inclusive— remit specified in the Charter of Fundamental Rights (as opposed to that already established in Article 13 EC). On language policy as a whole, the EC certainly needs to put its own house in more coherent order. And although outwith the scope of this work, devising a framework that takes non-indigenous languages into account brings a whole other dimension to language policy; this is especially true in an environment grounded explicitly in the tenets of freedom of movement and, for the EC, this has obvious internal implications. In light of Title IV EC, it has considerable external significance also.

As a constituent of the Community language framework, minority language policy is arguably one of the better developed aspects to date— somewhat ironically, given that minority languages are not 'official' EC languages and are traditionally the least protected interest in the province of language policy and language rights. Is it closer to the truth to state that what minority language groups want, however, is for the EC somehow to bring about more substantive changes to language policy at domestic level? Probably. But this is not necessarily a legitimate objective for the Commun-

---

[5]   Case C-379/87 *Groener v. Minister for Education and the Dublin Vocational Education Committee* [1989] ECR 3967.

[6]   Case C-274/96 *Criminal Proceedings against Bickel and Franz* [1998] ECR I-7637.

[7]   Case C-281/98 *Angonese v. Cassa di Risparmio*, judgment of 6 June 2000, not yet reported.

ity actually to pursue. The EC is no longer, if it ever was, an organisation concerned solely with economic policy. That is not the decisive point here. What asks to be considered is the harder question of EC/Member State power-sharing. The often brittle relationship between the Member States and the Community which they have (in the main) created is characterised by insecurity; Member States flinch from the implications of EC action in so-called 'shared' or 'concurrent' policy areas, notwithstanding the fact that it is they themselves that have caused Community competences to be incorporated into the Treaty in the first place. In other words, the EC is not some abstract, autonomous entity that has somehow divined its powers by and for itself. Certainly, what is habitually perceived as a virtually autonomous momentum of integration cannot be dismissed out of hand, an argument shored up by the activist course taken by the 'more' supranational institutions at times. And while it becomes perhaps more and more difficult to reverse the force now in train, did the Member States *ever* really call a halt when it was arguably easier so to do? The 1979 Joint Declaration on Fundamental Rights, endorsed subsequently by the European Council and coming after the oft-criticised activism of the ECJ, is a good example of quiet *ex post facto* legitimation. Ultimately, the political map of the Community remains in the hands of the Member States; the EC does not control its own destiny. Dashwood has cautioned quite strikingly that "...there are too many people who suspect the Community of being a Triffid, quietly gaining strength in order to gobble up everything that gives substance to our sense of having separate national identities."[8] But Fishman's analysis is perhaps closer to the truth, arguing that "[s]uprastate organisations...are originally and basically the creatures of states. As such, these organisations are rarely, if ever, strong enough to impose their own will on the strongest of their own creators."[9]

As it stands, a more precise delineation of EC/Member State competence is shunned for being a step too far in the direction of federalism; yet ironically, the osmotic alternative that is favoured at present inevitably risks second-guessing and confusion all round. The principle of subsidiarity was hauled in primarily to work this out. But what effect does it really have in practice? The shared competences introduced by the TEU are usually still classed as 'new, but almost a decade has now passed. Why is EC

---

[8] Alan Dashwood, "The limits of European Community powers", (1996) 21 *European Law Review*, 113-128 at 113.

[9] Joshua A. Fishman, "On the limits of ethnolinguistic democracy", in Tove Skutnabb-Kangas and Robert Phillipson (eds.), *Linguistic Human Rights: Overcoming Linguistic Discrimination*, (Berlin; New York: Mouton de Gruyter, 1994), 49-61 at 51.

competence in cultural matters, for example, still regarded as novel and uncertain? In the specific context of language policy, the Commission has precluded itself from exploring a broader range of more substantive initiatives by setting down a sweeping assumption that any such measures are prohibited by subsidiarity. But they are not. When subjected to scrutiny, limitations attached to competence in the cultural and linguistic domains materialise in the political realm far more than in the legal one. The virtually mystic character of subsidiarity that has thus been encouraged is misleading and potentially damaging. It may well be part of a political stratagem, to reassure Member States that primary power in the areas of shared competence remains with them. But this causes the institutions to cede powers they actually, legitimately have, which might soothe political tensions from time to time but, in the long run, erodes the need for supranational government in the first place. As an extension of this, the consequences of clawing back powers retrospectively cannot be ignored. Subsidiarity could work. The political landscape is challenged concomitantly at present by what could be considered, on the one hand, as polar objectives of enhanced supranationalism at international level and an increasing inclination toward devolved government at national level. This is a widely espoused supposition. While the EU and its Member States are fashioned by these trends in quite an intense way, the phenomenon is a global one. On an inclusive view, the tensions depicted above as theoretical extremities are more two sides of the same coin, constituting a universal shift towards layered governance. The 'new legal order of law'[10] that is constituted by the Community is, from a historical perspective, a very recent creation. The doctrine of sovereignty has survived considerable battering as a result; but the mutation is as yet unfinished. The principle of subsidiarity may yet have a more objective impact on the division of EC/Member State competence in a climate of power-sharing more secure than that which has been experienced to date.[11] But it should, at least, be applied more lucidly in the interim.

The disjointed way in which EC involvement in language policy has evolved thus exemplifies quite impressively the complexities faced at the fusion of law and politics. Other issues that have been shown to affect the treatment of (especially minority) languages and their speakers reveal some clefts in the Community legal order of a similarly extensive nature. For example, although the Charter of Fundamental Rights is essentially an

---

[10]   See the line of authority starting with Case 26/62 *Van Gend en Loos v. Nederlandse Administratie der Belastingen* [1963] ECR 1.

[11]   And, as has been noted, a 'more precise delimitation' of Member State and Community competences has been placed on the agenda for IGC 2004.

exercise in consolidation, the fact remains that as the reach of EC law extends further into the preserve of national policy, the distinction between situations triggering EC rights and those that do not seems more vulnerable; the likely increase in instances of 'reverse' discrimination will make the exclusion of Community standards more difficult to sustain, and more difficult to explain to the individuals concerned also. That these gaps in protection should be filled by the EC is not necessarily the corollary deduction; but a re-examination of national standards on a whole plethora of issues (most likely in the domain of employment) seems inevitable and the catalytic role of the EC in this context is itself significant. Tracing this analogy to language rights, perhaps the claims of groups seeking a more invasive Community approach would be met indirectly in this way. Equally pertinent is how individuals can expect to be treated by EC institutions, particularly as an aspect of citizenship; just what are the limits to supra-national government from this perspective? How can a pragmatic yet effective balance be struck between the fact that while the EC, as a regulatory entity, shapes national policy to a profound degree, it manifests an inherent remoteness from the individual? This reflects the enduring debate on the democratic legitimacy of the Union, typified, for example, by the fact that judicial review at EC level of Community acts can rarely be instigated by an individual, even an EU citizen.

On a related theme, concentration on the Member States as the embodi-ment of national democratic legitimacy leaves insufficient scope for the inclusive involvement of regional and devolved government. The extent to which these administrations are involved in EC issues is viewed as a matter governed by internal constitutional arrangements; but as decisions of the ECJ on language policy exhibit, regional authorities are subject to the application of Community law. Somewhat paradoxically, the mobilisation of regional and other sub-national groups across the Community—organised more on a thematic than nationality basis—continues to thrive. Sub-national groups tend to focus on lobbying at the supranational level where it is perceived that states either have not or cannot serve their needs efficiently and/or objectively. Taking both standpoints into account, there is a clear representative divergence here that does not sit easily with either national constitutional democracy or the emphasis placed at EC level on the contribution of the regions, or indeed, on the philosophy of subsidiarity and governing 'closer' to the citizen wherever possible.

Language as an EC policy issue thus reflects broader ideological quan-daries that test the realisation of multilevel governance; and taking language specifically, two things in particular appear to have been sacrificed in consequence—coherence and direction. Neither formative groundwork nor the potential for development are lacking at EC level, thus underlining the need for coherence; and regarding direction, the rationale that supports the development of more comprehensive and inclusive language policy—from the perspective mainly of linguistic security for individuals, then groups; and respecting the pedagogic, aesthetic and emotive aspects of language preservation and linguistic diversity—seems to have been lost somewhere along the way. Responsibility for changing this lies at many levels; but without doubt, the Community is included here.

Relevant Constitutional Provisions of the
EC Member States

1. AUSTRIA

Principal minority languages: Croat, Czech, Hungarian, Slovak, Slovenian and Rom.

Constitution of the Austrian Republic (1929/modified 1970)

Article 8

Without prejudice to the rights provided by federal law for linguistic minorities, German is the official language of the Republic.

Austria has signed but not yet ratified the European Charter for Regional or Minority Languages.

2. BELGIUM

Principal minority languages: Dutch, French and German.

Co-ordinated Constitution of the Belgian Kingdom (1831/modified 1980; 1989)

Article 3b

Belgium comprises four linguistic regions: the French language region, the Dutch language region, the bilingual region of Brussels-Capital, and the German language region.

Every commune in the Kingdom belongs to one of these linguistic regions.

The boundaries of the four regions may only be altered or amended by an act of Parliament passed on a majority vote in each linguistic group of each of the Houses, on condition that the majority of the members of each group are present and that the total voters in favour within two linguistic groups attain two thirds of the votes cast.

Article 3c

Belgium comprises three communities: the French community, the Flemish community, and the German-speaking community.

Each community enjoys the powers invested in it by the Constitution or such legislation as shall be enacted in terms thereof.

Article 23

The use of the languages spoken in Belgium is optional; it may only be regulated by law and only in the case of acts by public authorities and of legal matters.

Article 32b

For those cases prescribed in the Constitution, the elected members of each House are divided into a French language group and a Dutch language group in such manner as is laid down by law.

Article 38b

Except in the case of budgets and laws requiring a special majority, a reasoned motion signed by at least three quarters of the members of one of the linguistic groups and introduced after the report has been tabled and before the final voting in public session may declare that the provisions of a draft or proposed bill which it specifies are of such a nature as to have a serious effect on relations between the communities.

In such cases, parliamentary procedure is suspended and the motion is referred back to the Cabinet which, within a period of thirty days, gives its reasoned findings on the motion and invites the House to reach a decision either on those findings or on the draft or proposed bill in such form as it may have been amended.

This procedure may only be applied once by the members of a linguistic group in respect of one and the same draft or proposed bill.

Article 59b

1. There is a Council and an Executive for the French Community and a Council and an Executive for the Flemish Community whose composition and functioning are determined by law. Representatives of both Councils are elected.

...

3. Furthermore, the Community Councils, each in its own sphere, shall determine by decree, to the exclusion of the Legislative, the use of languages for:

(1) administrative matters;

(2) the education provided in establishments which are set up, subsidised or recognised by the public authorities;

(3) industrial relations between employers and their staff together with such business instruments and documents as are laid down by the law and regulations.

4. Such decrees...shall have the force of law respectively in the French language region and in the Dutch language region and also in respect of institutions established in the bilingual region of Brussels-Capital which, by virtue of their activities must be considered as belonging exclusively to one or other of the Communities.

Such decrees...shall have the force of law respectively in the French language region and in the Dutch language region except as regards:
- such communes or groups of communes which are adjacent to another linguistic region where the law lays down or permits the use of a language other than that of the region in which they are located;
- departments whose activities extend beyond the linguistic region in which they are established;
- national and international institutions referred to in legislation whose activity is common to more than one community. ...

Article 59c

There is a council and an executive for the German language community whose composition and functioning are determined by law.... Its decrees shall have the force of law in the German language region. ...

Article 86b

With the possible exception of the Prime Minister, the Cabinet comprises an equal number of French-speaking and Dutch-speaking ministers.

Article 108c

2. For those cases laid down in the Constitution and by legislation, the members of the urban area council are divided into a French language group and a Dutch language group in the manner prescribed by law. ...

4. In the urban area there is a French committee for culture and a Dutch committee for culture which are composed of an equal number of members elected respectively by the French language group and by the Dutch language group in the urban area council.

Each has the same powers in respect of its community as the other organising authorities:

(1) in pre-schooling, post-educational and cultural matters;

(2) in education.

Article 140

The text of the Constitution is drawn up in French and in Dutch.

3. DENMARK

Principal minority languages: German.

No constitutional provisions dealing with language.

Denmark has signed and ratified the European Charter for Regional or Minority Languages, with respect to German.

4. FINLAND

Principal minority languages: Swedish and Saami.

Constitution of the Finnish Republic (1919)

Article 14

Finnish and Swedish shall be the national languages of the Republic.

The right of Finnish citizens to use their mother tongue, whether Finnish or Swedish, before the courts and the administrative authorities, and to obtain from them documents in these languages, shall be guaranteed by law; care shall be taken that the rights of the Finnish speaking population and the rights of the Swedish speaking population of the country shall be promoted by the state upon an identical basis.

The state shall provide for the intellectual and economic needs of the Finnish speaking and the Swedish speaking populations upon a similar basis.

Article 22

Laws and decrees as well as bills submitted by the Government to Parliament and the replies, recommendations, and other documents addressed by Parliament to the Government shall be drawn up in the Finnish and Swedish languages.

Article 50

For the purpose of general administration Finland shall remain divided into provinces, circuits and communes. ...

In redrawing the boundaries of the administrative districts, it is to be observed that these shall, as far as circumstances permit, be so constituted as to contain populations speaking only one language, Finnish or Swedish, or to make the language minorities as small as possible.

Article 75

Every Finnish citizen must take part in, or make his contribution tom the defence of the country as prescribed by law.

Every conscript, unless he otherwise desires, shall if possible be enrolled in a military unit of which the rank and file speak his own mother tongue (Finnish or Swedish) and shall receive his training in that language. Finnish shall be the language of command of the Armed Forces.

Finland has signed and ratified the European Charter for Regional or Minority Languages, with respect to Saami and Swedish.

5. FRANCE

Principal minority languages: German/Alsatian, Basque, Breton, Catalan, Corsican, Francique/Luxembourgesch, Dutch/Flemish and Occitan.

Constitution of the French Republic (1958/modified 1992)

Article 2

The language of the Republic is French.

This provision has been implemented by legislative acts (e.g. Constitutional Law No. 94-665 (4 August 1994) which allow for the recognition and promotion of the French language only.

France has signed but not yet ratified the European Charter for Regional or Minority Languages.

6. GERMANY

Principal minority languages: Danish, Frisian, Sorbian and Romanès.

Basic Law of Germany (1949/amended 1990)

Article 3

No one may be prejudiced or favoured because of his sex, his parentage, his race, his language, his homeland and origin, his faith or his religious or political opinions.

Germany has signed and ratified the European Charter for Regional or Minority Languages, with respect to Danish, Upper Sorbian, Lower Sorbian, North Frisian, Sater Frisian, 'the Romany language of the German Sinti and Roma' and Low German.

7. GREECE

Principal minority languages: Albanian/Arvanite, Aroumanian, Pomak, Slav-Macedonian and Turkish.

Constitution of the Greek Republic (1975)

Article 3

The text of the Holy Scriptures shall be maintained unaltered. Official translation of the text into any other form of language, without prior sanction by the Autocephalous Church of Greece and the Great Church of Christ in Constantinople is prohibited.

Article 5

All persons living within the Greek territory shall enjoy full protection of their life, their honour and freedom, irrespective of nationality, race or language and of religious or political beliefs. Exceptions shall be permitted only in cases provided for in international law.

8. IRELAND

Principal minority language: Irish

The Irish Constitution (1937)

Article 8

1. The Irish language as the national language is the first official language.

2. The English language is recognised as a second official language.

3. Provision may, however, be made by law for the exclusive use of either of the said languages for any one or more official purposes, either throughout the State or in any part thereof.

Article 25.4.3°

Every bill shall be signed by the President in the text in which it was passed...by both Houses of the *Oireachtas*, and if a bill is so passed...in both the official languages, the President shall sign the text of the bill in each of those languages.

Article 25.4.4°

Where the President signs the text of a bill in one only of the official languages, an official translation shall be issued in the other official language.

Article 25.4.6°

In case of conflict between the texts of a law enrolled under this section in both the official languages, the text in the national language shall prevail.

Article 25.5.4°

In case of conflict between the texts of any copy of this Constitution...the text in the national language shall prevail.

A Language Act is currently being drafted by the Irish Government.

9. ITALY

Principal minority languages: Albanian/Arbërishtja Catalan, Croat, French/ Francoprovençal, Friulan, German (and variants), Greek, Ladin, Occitan, Roma, Sard and Slovenian.

Constitution of the Italian Republic (1948)

Article 3

All citizens are invested with equal social status and are equal before the law, without prejudice as to sex, race, language, religion, political opinions and personal or social conditions.

Article 6

The Republic shall safeguard linguistic minorities by means of special provisions.

Recognition and status of minority languages vary from region to region within Italy.

Italy has signed but not yet ratified the European Charter for Regional or Minority Languages.

10. LUXEMBOURG

Principal Minority Language Community: Letzebergish/Lëtzebuergesch.

Constitution of the Grand Duchy of Luxembourg (1868)

Article 29

The law will determine the use of languages in administrative and judicial matters.

The Law on the Linguistic Regime (24 February 1984) establishes that Luxembourgish is the national language of Luxembourg, French is the legislative language and French, German and Luxembourgish may be used in administrative and judicial matters.

Luxembourg has signed but not yet ratified the European Charter for Regional or Minority Languages.

11. THE NETHERLANDS

Principal Minority Language Community: Frisian.

No Constitutional Provisions dealing with language.

The Netherlands has signed and ratified the European Charter for Regional for Minority Languages, with respect to Frisian, Lower Saxon languages, Yiddish and Romanes languages.

12. PORTUGAL

No indigenous minority languages.

Constitution of the Republic of Portugal (1976/amended 1987

Article 13

No one may be privileged, benefited, damaged, deprived of any right or exempt from any responsibility by virtue of influence, sex, race, language, territory of origin, religion, political or ideological convictions, education, economic or social status.

Article 74

3. In the implementation of an educational policy, the state is obliged...

(h) to provide instruction in the Portuguese language and access to Portuguese culture to the children of immigrants.

13. SPAIN

Principal minority languages: Aragonese, Aranese, Asturian, Basque, Catalan and Galician.

Constitution of the Kingdom of Spain (1978)

Article 3

1. Castilian is the official Spanish language of the state. All Spaniards have the duty to know it and the right to use it.

2. The other languages of Spain will also be official in the respective autonomous communities, in accordance with their statutes.

3. The richness of the linguistic modalities of Spain is a cultural patrimony which will be the object of special respect and protection.

Article 148

The Autonomous Communities may assume jurisdiction in the following matters...

(17) assistance to culture, research and, as the case may be, for the teaching of the language of the Autonomous Community.

The respective Statutes of Autonomy for the Basque Country, Catalonia and Gallicia were enacted in 1979.

Spain has signed but not yet ratified the European Charter for Regional or Minority Languages.

14. SWEDEN

Principal minority languages: Finnish and Saami.

Constitution of the Swedish Republic (1975)

Article 8

In the exercise of their functions the courts and administrative authorities shall maintain objectivity and impartiality. They may not without legal grounds treat persons differently by reason of their personal conditions such as faith, opinions, race, skin colour, origin, sex, age, nationality, language, social status, or financial circumstances.

Sweden has signed and ratified the European Charter for Regional or Minority Languages, with respect to Sami, Finnish, Meänkieli (Tornedal Finnish), Romani Chib and Yiddish

15. THE UNITED KINGDOM

Principal minority languages: Cornish, Gaelic/Gàidhlig, Irish/Gaeilge, Scots and Welsh.

The United Kingdom does not have a written constitution.

The Welsh Language Act was enacted in 1993.

The United Kingdom has signed but not yet ratified European Charter for Regional or Minority Languages.

Appendix II

Text of the Resolutions of the European Parliament

1. Arfé Resolution (1981)

Resolution on a Community Charter of Regional Languages and Cultures and on a Charter of Rights of Ethnic Minorities

16 October 1981, [1984] OJ C287/106.

THE EUROPEAN PARLIAMENT,

- having regard to the resurgence of special movements by ethnic and linguistic minorities aimed at bringing about a deeper understanding and recognition of their historical identity,

- recognising the revival of regional languages and cultures associated with these movements as a source of enrichment for European civilisation and as an indication of its vitality,

- having regard to the declarations of principle made by the most representative and authoritative international organisations, from the UN to the Council of Europe, and to the most recent and widely accepted political, legal and anthropological theories,

- referring to Resolution No 1 of the Oslo Conference (1976) of the European Ministers responsible for cultural affairs,

- considering that all governments in the Community have acknowledged in principle the right of such groups to freely express themselves and their culture and have, in most cases, drawn up legislation in this specific field and begun co-ordinated programmes of action,

- considering that a cultural identity is today one of the most important non-material psychological needs,

- considering that autonomy must not be regarded as an alternative to the integration of peoples and different traditions, but as a means of guiding the process necessary for increasing intercommunication,

- considering therefore that linguistic and cultural heritage cannot be safeguarded unless the right conditions are created for their cultural and economic development,

- determined to bring about a closer union among the peoples of Europe and to preserve their living languages, drawing on their diversity in order to enrich and diversify their common cultural heritage,

- having regard to motions for resolutions Docs. 1-371/79, 1-436/79 and 1-790/79,

- having regard to the report of the Committee on Youth, Culture, Education, Information and Sport and to the opinion of the Committee on Regional Policy and Regional Planning (Doc. 1-965/80),

1. Requests National Governments and regional and local authorities, despite the wide differences in their situations and having due regard to the degree of independence which they enjoy, to implement a policy in this field inspired by and designed to achieve the same objectives, and calls on them:

(a) in the field of education:

- to allow and promote the teaching of regional languages and cultures in official curricula right through from nursery school to university;

- to allow and provide for, in response to needs expressed by the population, teaching in schools of all levels and grades to be carried out in regional languages, with particular emphasis being placed on nursery school teaching so as to ensure that the child is able to speak its mother tongue;

- to allow teaching of the literature and history of the communities concerned to be included in all curricula;

(b) in the field of mass communications:

- to allow and take steps to ensure access to local radio and television in a way that guarantees consistent and effective community communication and to encourage the training of specialist regional presenters;

- to ensure that minority groups receive organisational and financial assistance for their cultural events equivalent to that received by the majority groups;

(c) in the field of public life and social affairs:

- to assign in accordance with the Bordeaux declaration of the Council of Europe Conference of Local Authorities, a direct responsibility to the local authorities in this manner;

- to promote as far as possible a correspondence between cultural regions and the geographical boundaries of the local authorities;

- to ensure that individuals are allowed to use their own language in the field of public life and social affairs in their dealings with official bodies and in the courts;

2. Requests the Commission to provide, as soon as possible, recent, accurate and comparable data on the attitudes and behaviour of the public in the Member States towards regional languages and cultures in their various countries;

3. Calls on the Commission to set up pilot projects in the language teaching sector to try out methods of multilingual education capable of ensuring both the survival of the individual cultures and their openness to the outside world;

4. Recommends that the Regional Fund provide financial assistance for projects designed to support regional and folk cultures and calls upon the Commission to include measures in its educational and cultural programmes to promote a European cultural policy which takes account of the aspirations and expectations of all its ethnic and linguistic minorities who are looking towards Europe and its institutions with confidence and hope;

5. Recommends that the Regional Fund should contribute to the financing of regional economic projects since the cultural identity of a region can only exist if the population are able to live and work in their own area;

6. Calls on the Commission to review all Community legislation or practices which discriminate against minority languages;

7. Instructs its President to forward this resolution to the Council and the Commission, to the governments and regional authorities of the Member States and to the Council of Europe.

2. Arfé Resolution (2) (1983)

Resolution on Measures in favour of Minority Languages and Cultures

11 February 1983, [1983] OJ C68/103

THE EUROPEAN PARLIAMENT,

- Considering that some 30 million Community citizens have as their mother tongue a regional language or a little-spoken language,
- Aware of the resurgence of special movements by ethnic and linguistic minorities aimed at bringing about a deeper understanding and recognition of their historical identity,
- Having regard to its own resolution of 16 October 1981 on the subject,

1. Calls on the Commission:

- to continue to intensify its efforts in this area, particularly in relation to establishing pilot projects and studies,
- to review all Community and national legislation and practices which discriminate against minority languages, and prepare appropriate Community instruments for ending such discrimination,
- to report to Parliament by the end of 1983 on the outcome of action taken on the two points above;

2. Calls on the Commission to report to Parliament on the practical measures taken or due to be taken in the near future to encourage regional and folk cultures and cultural policy in the context of media and culture programmes and to finance regional economic projects under the Regional Fund within the meaning of paragraphs 4 and 5 of the resolution of 16 October 1981;

3. Calls on the Council to ensure that the principles of Parliament's resolution are respected in practice;

4. Believes that Parliament should continue to monitor progress in this area at Community level, and that the appropriate parliamentary committees should hold a joint meeting to consider how best this should be done;

5. Instructs its President to forward this resolution to the Commission, Council, Council of Europe and the governments of the Member States.

3. Kuijpers Resolution (1987)

Resolution on the Languages and Cultures of Regional and Ethnic Minorities in the European Community

30 October 1987, Doc. A 2-150/87

THE EUROPEAN PARLIAMENT

- having regard to the motion for a resolution by Mr. Columbu and others on linguistic rights in Northern Catalonia (Doc. 2-1259/84),

- having regard to the motion for a resolution by Mr. Kuijpers and Mr. Vandemeulebroucke on the protection and promotion of regional languages and cultures in the Community (Doc. B2-76/85),

- having regard to the motion for a resolution by Mr. Rossetti and others on the recognition of the rights of minorities and the full recognition of their cultures (Doc. B2-321/85),

- having regard to the motion for a resolution by Mr. Vandemeulebroucke and Mr. Kuijpers on the Commission's failure to implement the European Parliament's resolution on a Community charter of regional languages and cultures and a charter of rights of ethnic minorities (Doc. B2-1514/85),

- having regard to the motion for a resolution by Mr. Kuijpers and Mr. Vandemeulebroucke on the recognition of free radio stations (Doc. B2-1532/85),

- having regard to the motion for a resolution by Mr. Vandemeulebroucke and others on a Frisian television service in Friesland (Doc. B2-31/86),

- having regard to the motion for a resolution by Mr. Kuijpers and Mr. Vandemeulebroucke on the projected withdrawal of the grant from the Netherlands Ministry of Welfare, Health and Cultural Affairs for the Association for the Promotion of Standard Dutch and the detrimental consequences thereof for transfrontier co-operation in the field of culture (Doc. B2-890/86),

- having regard to the motion for a resolution by Mr. Columbu and others on the establishment of institutes for the study of minority languages (Doc. B2-1015/86),

- having regard to the motion for a resolution by Mr. Rubert de Ventós on the obstacles to the use of Catalan in the universities and on television (Doc. B2-1323/86),

- having regard to the motion for a resolution by Mr. Mizzau and others on support for institutions and associations for the study of minority languages (Doc. B2-1346/86),

- having regard to the motion for a resolution by Mr. Kuijpers and others on the integration of the bilingual Basque-French schools run by the SEASKA association (Doc. B2-149/87),

- having regard to the motion for a resolution by Mr. Colom i Naval on improving the position of minority languages within the EEC (Doc. B2-291/87),

- having regard to the Committee on Youth, Culture, Education, Information and Sport and the opinion of the Committee on Legal Affairs and Citizens' Rights (Doc. A2-150/87),

- having regard to its resolution of 16 October 1981 on a Community charter of regional languages and cultures and on a charter of rights of ethnic minorities and its resolution of 11 February 1983 on measures in favour of minority languages and cultures,

- having regard to the basic principles regarding rights of minorities formulated and approved by the United Nations and the Council of Europe,

- regretting that so far, the Commission has not put forward any proposals to implement the above-mentioned resolutions which deal comprehensively with the problems of ethnic, linguistic and cultural minorities in the Community,

- whereas there are still many obstacles to the full development of the specific cultural and social identity among the national and linguistic minorities, and whereas attitudes towards these minorities and their problems frequently reveal a lack of appreciation and understanding and, in some cases, are based on discrimination,

- having regard to the final declaration of the European Community and its resolution of 13 April 1984 on the role of the regions in the construction of a democratic Europe and the outcome of the Conference of the Regions, in which it is noted that strengthening the autonomy of the regions in the Community and the creation of a politically more unified

European Community represent two complementary and convergent aspects of a political development which is essential to cope effectively with the future tasks of the Community,

- noting that regional economic conditions determine the prospects for the expression and development of the local culture so that appropriate measures should therefore be worked out within a balanced European regional policy that starts from a regional basis and is designed to counteract the exodus from outlying regions to the centre,

1. Calls for the principles and proposals set out in its above-mentioned resolutions of 16 October 1981 and 11 February 1983 to be fully applied;

2. Points out once again the need for the Member States to recognise their linguistic minorities in their laws and thus to create the basic condition for the preservation and development of regional and minority cultures and languages;

3. Calls on the Member States whose Constitutions already contain general principles concerning the protection of minorities to make timely provision on the basis of organic laws, for the implementation of those principles;

4. Supports the Council of Europe's efforts to draw up a European Charter of regional and minority languages;

5. Recommends to the Member States that they carry out educational measures including:

- arranging for pre-school to university education and continuing education to be officially conducted in the regional and minority languages in the language areas concerned, on an equal footing with instruction in the national languages,

- officially recognising courses, classes and schools set up by associations which arc authorised to teach, under the regulations in force in the country concerned, and which use a regional or minority language as the general teaching language,

- giving particular attention to the training of teaching staff in the regional or minority languages and making available the educational resources required to accomplish these measures,

- promoting information on educational opportunities in the regional and minority languages,

- making provision for the equivalence of diplomas, certificates, other qualifications and evidence of professional skills so that members of regional or minority groups in one Member State may have easier access to the labour market in culturally related communities in other Member States;

6. Recommends to the Member States that they carry out administrative and legal measures including:

- providing a direct legal basis for the use of regional and minority languages, in the first instance in the local authorities of area where a minority group does exist,

- reviewing national provisions and practices that discriminate against minority languages, as called for in Parliament's resolution of 16 January 1986 on the rise of fascism and racism in Europe,

- requiring decentralised central government services also to use national, regional and minority languages in the areas concerned,

- officially recognising surnames and place names expressed in a regional or minority language,

- accepting place names and indications on electoral lists in a regional or minority language;

7. Recommends to the Member States that they take measures in respect of the mass media, including:

- granting and making possible access to local, regional and central public and commercial broadcasting systems in such a way as to guarantee the continuity and effectiveness of broadcasts in regional and minority languages,

- ensuring that minority groups obtain organisational and financial support for their programmes commensurate with that available to the majority,

- support for the training of journalists and media staff required to implement these measures,

- putting the latest technology to the service of the regional and minority languages,

- taking account of the extra costs entailed by provision for special scripts, such as Cyrillic, Hebrew, Greek, etc.;

8. Recommends to the Member States that they take measures in respect of the cultural infrastructure including:

- ensuring that representatives of groups that use regional or minority languages are able to participate directly in cultural facilities and activities,

- the creation of foundations and institutes for the study of regional and minority languages, one of whose tasks would be to set up the educational machinery for the introduction of regional and minority languages in schools and draw up a "general inventory" of the regional and minority language concerned,

- the development of dubbing and subtitling techniques to encourage audio-visual productions in the regional and minority languages,

- provision of the necessary material and financial support for the implementation of these measures;

9. Recommends to the Member States that they take social and economic measures including:

- providing for the use of the regional and minority languages in public concerns (postal service, etc.),

- recognition of the use of the regional and minority languages in the payments sector (giro cheques and banking),

- providing for consumer information and product labelling in regional and minority languages,

- providing for the use of regional languages for road and other public signs and street names;

10. Recommends to the Member States that they take measures in respect of the regional and minority languages that are used in several Member States, particularly in frontier areas, including:

- providing for the appropriate cross-frontier co-operation machinery for cultural and linguistic policy,

- promotion of cross-frontier co-operation in accordance with the European Outline Convention on Transfrontier Co-operation between Communities or Territorial Authorities;

11. Calls on the Member States to encourage and support the European Bureau for Lesser Used Languages and its national committees in each of the Member States;

12. Calls on the Commission to:

- do all it can within its terms of reference to implement the measures set out in paragraphs 5 to 10,

- take account of the languages and cultures of regional and ethnic minorities in the Community when working out the various areas of Community policy, particularly with regard to Community measures in the field of cultural and educational policy,

- accord the European Bureau for Lesser Used Languages official consultative status,

- make provision for a system of mutual study visits to increase mutual knowledge of minorities,

- reserve the necessary broadcasting time for minority cultures in European television,

- give the necessary attention to linguistic minorities in the Community's information publications;

13. Calls on the Council and Commission to continue their support and encouragement for the European Bureau for Lesser Used Languages by

- ensuring adequate budgetary resources and the reinstatement of a separate budget line,

- proposing the necessary budget funds for the implementation of the measures set out above,

- allocating ERDF and ESF funds for programmes and projects on behalf of regional and popular cultures,

- reporting annually to Parliament on the situation of the Community's regional and minority languages and measures taken in this connection by the Member States and the Community;

14. Stresses its determination to ensure that adequate provision is made for action in favour of minority languages and that at least 1 million ECU is entered in the 1998 budget;

15. Stresses categorically that the recommendations contained in this resolution are not to be interpreted or implemented in such a way as to jeopardise the territorial integrity or public order of the Member States;

16. Instructs its appropriate committee to draw up separate reports on the languages and cultures of non-permanent Community citizens, Community citizens living in another Member State from that from which they come, migrants and overseas minorities and points out that each of these groups share many of the disadvantages of speakers of lesser used languages and that their specific problems deserve detailed and separate treatment;

17. Decides that the Intergroup on Lesser Used Languages shall be granted full status as an official Intergroup of the European Parliament;

18. Instructs its President to forward this resolution to the Commission, the Council, the national and regional governments of the Member States, the Consultative Assembly of the Council of Europe and the Standing Conference of Local and Regional Authorities of Europe.

4. Killilea Resolution (1994)

Resolution on Linguistic and Cultural Minorities in the European Community

9 February 1994, [1994] OJ C061/110

THE EUROPEAN PARLIAMENT

- having regard to its resolution of 16 October 1981 on a Community charter of regional languages and cultures and a charter of rights for ethnic minorities,

- having regard to its resolution of 11 February 1983 on measures in favour of minority languages and cultures,

- having regard to its resolution of 30 October 1987 on the languages and cultures of regional and ethnic minorities in the European Community,

- having regard to its resolution of 21 January 1993 on the Commission communication to the Council, the European Parliament and the Economic and Social Committee entitled "New Prospects for Community cultural action",

- having regard to the motions for resolutions by:
  Mr Hume and others on the minority languages (B3-0016/90);
  Mr. Gangoiti Llaguno on the promotion and use of regional and/or minority languages (B3-2113/90);
  Mr Bandrés Molet on granting broadcasting licences to Basque-language radio stations (B30523/91);
  Mrs Van Hemeldonck on the signing of the European Charter of regional and minority languages (B3-1351/92);

- having regard to the European Charter for Regional or Minority Languages, accorded the legal form of a European Convention by the Council of Europe, and opened for signature on 5 November 1992,

- having regard to the final document of the Copenhagen meeting of the CSCE Conference on the Human Dimension of the CSCE (5-29 June 1990) and in particular to Chapter IV of that document,

- having regard to the Charter of Paris for a New Europe (CSCE) adopted in Paris on 21 November 1991,

- having regard to rule 148 of its Rules of Procedure,

- having regard to the report of the Committee on Culture, Youth, Education and the Media and the opinion of the Committee on Legal Affairs and Citizens' Rights (A3-0042/94),

- encouraged by the commitment, contained in Article 128 of the EC Treaty, to the Community contributing to the flowering of the cultures of the Member States while respecting their national and regional diversity,

- declaring the need for a European linguistic culture and recognising that its scope also includes protection of the linguistic heritage, the overcoming of the language barrier, the promotion of lesser-used languages and the safeguarding of minority languages,

- encouraged by the process of democratisation in central and eastern Europe and in particular by the determination of recently democratised peoples to promote their own languages and cultures,

- whereas all peoples have the right to respect for their language ad culture and must therefore have the necessary legal means to protect and promote them,

- whereas the linguistic diversity of the European Union is a key element in the Union's cultural wealth,

- whereas the protection and promotion of the Union's linguistic diversity is a key factor in the creation of a peaceful and democratic Europe,

- whereas the Community has a responsibility to support the Member States in developing their cultures and protecting national and regional diversity, including the diversity of indigenous regional and minority languages,

- whereas the Community should encourage action by the Member States in cases where the protection of such languages and cultures is inadequate or non-existent,

- whereas the Community also has a duty in its relations with the governments of associated and third countries to draw attention to the rights of minorities and, if necessary, to support governments in finding ways of ensuring that these rights are safeguarded; whereas it must also condemn any deliberate denial of these rights,

- whereas the linguistic diversity of the European Union is a reflection of its cultural diversity and too often goes unrecognised,

- whereas language is an essential means of communication in the European Union now being created and whereas European integration must make the use of the most widespread languages as a way of communicating across the present internal borders compatible with protecting and safeguarding the less widespread languages in regional or transregional contexts,

- whereas the minority languages and cultures are also an integral part of the Union's culture and European heritage and whereas, from this point of view, the Community should provide them with legal protection and the appropriate financial resources to this end,

- whereas many lesser used languages are endangered, with a rapid drop in the number of speakers, and whereas this threatens the well-being of specific population groups and greatly diminishes Europe's creative potential as a whole,

- whereas, while the duty of every Member State government to protect and promote its official languages must be fully respected, it must not be exercised to the detriment of the lesser used languages and the people for whom they are the natural cultural vehicle,

- whereas, however, the term "minority languages and cultures" may embrace phenomena of differing characteristics and dimensions according to the Member State in question and may be understood as referring to certain languages which are already official in some Member States but which do not receive adequate dissemination or identical status in the neighbouring Member State or another Member State,

1. Calls for the principles and proposals set out in its afforementioned resolutions of 16 October 1981, 11 February 1983 and 30 October 1987 to be fully applied;

2. Points out again the need for Member States to recognise their linguistic minorities and to make the necessary legal and administrative provisions for them to create the basic conditions for the preservation and development of these languages;

3. Believes, furthermore, that all minority languages and cultures should also be protected by appropriate legal statute in the Member States;

4. Considers that this legal statute should at least cover the use and encouragement of such languages and cultures in the spheres of education, justice and public administration, the media, toponymics and other sectors of

public and cultural life without prejudice to the use of the most widespread languages, when required to ensure ease of communication within each of the Member States or in the Union as a whole;

5. Points out that the fact that a proportion of the citizens of a state use a language of have a culture which is different from the dominant one in that state or form the dominant one in a part of region of that state should not give rise to discrimination of any kind or, in particular, to any form of social marginalisation that would impede their access to, or continuance in, employment;

6. Supports the European Charter for Regional or Minority Languages, accorded the legal form of a European Convention as an effective yet flexible instrument for the protection ad promotion of lesser used languages;

7. Calls on the Member State governments which have not yet done so as a matter of urgency to sign and their parliaments to ratify the Convention choosing at all times to apply those paragraphs best suited to the needs and aspirations of the linguistic communities in question;

8. Calls on the Member State governments and on the local and regional authorities to encourage and support specialised associations, in particular the Member State Committees of the European Bureau for Lesser Used Languages so that the responsibilities of citizens and their organisations for the development of their language can be realised;

9. Urges the Member States and the relevant regions and local authorities to examine the possibility of concluding agreements to create trans-frontier linguistic institutions for any minority languages or cultures existing in two neighbouring countries or in several Member States simultaneously;

10. Calls on the Commission to:

(a) contribute, within its field of competence, to the implementation of the initiatives undertaken by Member States in this area;

(b) take account of the lesser used languages and their attendant cultures when working out various areas of Community policy, and make equivalent provision for the needs of speakers of lesser used languages, alongside the needs of speakers of the majority languages, in all educational and cultural programmes, *e.g.* YOUTH FOR EUROPE, ERASMUS, TEMPUS, European Dimension, Platform Europe, MEDIA, schemes for the translation of contemporary literary work;

(c) encourage the use of lesser used languages in the Community's audio-visual policy, for instance in respect of High Definition television and assist lesser used language producers and broadcasters to produce new programmes in 16:9 format;

(d) ensure that modern digital telecommunications technology, which allows for the compressing of satellite and cable broadcast transmissions, is used for carrying a greater number of minority languages;

(e) put in place as quickly as possible a programme inspired by LINGUA for lesser used languages such as the Mercator education network;

(f) facilitate the immediate publication, after corrections and additions, of the scientific map of lesser used language communities in the EC, prepared by the European Bureau for Lesser Used Languages;

(g) encourage the publication of the Treaties of the European Communities and other basic provisions and information on the European Community and its activities in the Union's lesser used languages;

11. Calls on the Council and Commission to:

(a) continue their support and encouragement for European organisations representing the lesser used languages, particularly the European Bureau for Lesser Used Languages, and to provide them with the necessary resources;

(b) ensure that adequate budgetary provision is made for the Community's programmes in favour of lesser used languages and their attendant cultures and propose a multiannual action programme in this field;

(c) take due account of the linguistic and cultural heritage of regions in the development of regional policy and in the allocation of funds from the ERDF by supporting integrated regional development projects which include measures to support regional languages and cultures, as well as in the development of social policy and in the allocation of funds from the ESF;

(d) take due account of the needs of speakers of lesser used languages in the countries of central and eastern Europe, when developing EC programmes for economic and social reconstruction, and in particular the PHARE programme;

(e) encourage the translation of books and literary works and the subtitling of films between minority languages or into Community languages;

(f) ensure that in encouraging minority languages, the European Community does not do so to the detriment of the main relevant national language and must, in turn, ensure that this in no way affects the teaching of that main language in schools;

12. Calls for the languages spoken on overseas territories belonging to the Member States to enjoy the same rights and provisions as mainland languages;

13. In relation to non-territorial autochthonous languages (*e.g.* the Roma and Sinti languages and Yiddish) calls on all relevant bodies to apply mutatis mutandis the recommendations set out in this resolution;

14. Stresses that the recommendations contained in this resolution are not such as to jeopardise the territorial integrity or public order of the Member States and furthermore, are not to be interpreted as implying the right to enter into any activity or carry out any action which contravenes the objectives of the United Nations or any other obligation laid down in international law;

15. Instructs its President to forward this resolution to the Commission, the Council, the central and regional governments of the Member States, the Parliamentary Assembly of the Council of Europe, the Standing Conference of Local and Regional Authorities of Europe, the Conference for Security and Co-operation in Europe, the United Nations and UNESCO.

Bibliography

Albanese, Ferdinando, "Ethnic and linguistic minorities in Europe", (1991) 11 *Yearbook of European Law* 313-338.

Alfredsson, Gudmundur, *Minority Rights and Democracy*, (Discussion Paper, 3rd Strasbourg Conference on Parliamentary Democracy, 1991).

Alston, Philip (ed.), The United Nations and Human Rights: A Critical Appraisal, (Oxford: Clarendon Press, 1992).

___, (ed.), with Bustelo, Mara and Heenan, James, *The EU and Human Rights*, (Oxford: OUP, 1999).

___ and Weiler, J.H.H., "An 'ever closer union' in need of a human rights policy: The European Union and human rights", in Alston (ed.) *The EU and Human Rights*, (Oxford: OUP, 1999), 3-66.

Anderson, Malcolm, den Boer, Monica and Miller, Gary, "European citizenship and co-operation in justice and home affairs", in Duff, Pinder and Pryce (eds.), *Maastricht and Beyond: Building the New Europe*, (London: Routledge, 1994), 104-122.

Anderson, Malcolm and Bort, Eberhard (eds.), *The Frontiers of Europe*, (London: Pinter, 1998).

Anon., "Language rights and the legal status of English-only laws in the public and private sector", (1992) 20 *North Carolina Central Law Journal* 65-91.

Argemi, Aureli, "European recognition for Catalan", (1991) vol. 8:1 *Contact Bulletin* 6.

Arington, Michele, "English-only laws and direct legislation: The battle in the States over language minority rights", (1991) 7 *Journal of Law and Politics* 325-352.

Arnull, Anthony, "Taming the beast? The Treaty of Amsterdam and the Court of Justice", in O'Keeffe and Twomey (eds.), *Legal Issues of the Amsterdam Treaty*, (Oxford: Hart Publishing, 1999),109-121.

Bankowski, Z and Scott, A. (eds.), *The European Union and its Order: The Legal Theory of European Integration*, (Oxford: Blackwell Publishers, 2000).

Barnard, Catherine, "Article 13: Through the looking glass of Union citizenship", in O'Keeffe and Twomey (eds.), *Legal Issues of the Amsterdam Treaty*, (Oxford: Hart Publishing, 1999), 375-394.

Beale, Andrew and Geary, Roger, "Subsidiarity comes of age?", (1994) 144 *New Law Journal* 12-14.

Beaumont, Paul, Lyons, Carole and Walker, Neil (eds.), *Convergence and Divergence in European Public Law*, (Oxford: Hart Publishing, forthcoming, 2001).

Berman, G.A., "Taking subsidiarity seriously: Federalism in the European Community and the United States", (1994) 94 *Columbia Law Review* 331-456.

Bernard, Nicolas, "The future of European economic law in the light of the principle of subsidiarity", (1996) vol. 33:4 *Common Market Law Review* 633-666.

___, "Discrimination and free movement in EC law", (1996) 45 *International and Comparative Law Quarterly* 82-108.

Bieber, Roland and Ress, Georg, (eds.), Dic Dynamic des Europäischen Gemeinschaftsrechts/The Dynamics of European Law, (Baden-Baden: Nomos, 1987).

Bilder, Richard B, "Can minorities treaties work?", in Dinstein and Tabory (eds.), *The Protection of Minorities and Human Rights*, (Dordrecht: Martinus Nijhoff, 1992), 59-82.

Boch, Christine, "Language protection and free trade: The triumph of the *Homo MacDonaldus*?", (1998) vol. 4:3 *European Public Law* 379-402.

Bondo Krogsgaard, Lars, "Fundamental rights in the European Community after Maastricht", (1993) *Legal Issues of European Integration* 99-113.

Brackeniers, Eduard, "Europe without frontiers and the language challenge", (1991) 3 *Target* I-II.

Bradley, Kieran and Sutton, Alistair, "European union and the Rule of Law", in Duff, Pinder and Pryce (eds.), *Maastricht and Beyond: Building the New Europe*, (London: Routledge, 1994), 229-266.

Breton, Roland, "L'approche géographique", in Truchot (ed.), *La Plurilinguisme Européene*, (Paris: Honoré Champion, 1994), 41-68.

Brett, Nathan, "Language laws and collective rights", (1991) vol. 4:2 *Canadian Journal of Law and Jurisprudence* 347-360.

Brittan, Leon, "Institutional development of the European Community", (1992) *Public Law* 567-579.

Brown, L. Neville, "The European Community: Some problems of interpretation and drafting of plurilingual law", (1988) vol. 13:1 *Holdsworth Law Review* 16-45.

Brugmans, H., "Five starting-points", in Rijksbaron, Roobol and Weisglas (eds.), *Europe from a Cultural Perspective*, (The Hague: Nijgh en Van Ditmar Universitair, 1987), 15-16.

de Búrca, Gráinne, "Fundamental rights and the reach of European Community law", (1993) 13 *Oxford Journal of Legal Studies* 283-319.

___, "The language of rights and European integration", in Shaw and More (eds.), *New Legal Dynamics of European Union*, (Oxford: Clarendon Press, 1995), 29-54.

___, "The quest for legitimacy in the European Union", (1996) vol. 59:3 *Modern Law Review* 349-376.

___, "The principle of subsidiarity and the Court of Justice as an institutional actor", (1998) vol. 36:2 *Journal of Common Market Studies* 217-235.

Capotorti, Francesco, "The protection of minorities under multilateral agreements on human rights", (1976) 2 *Italian Yearbook of International Law* 3-32.

___, Study on the Rights of Persons belonging to Ethnic, Religious and Linguistic Minorities, (New York: United Nations, 1979).

Cappelletti, Mauro, "Is the European Court of Justice running wild?", (1987) 12 *European Law Review* 3-17.

Carrel, Sylvia, "Linguistic minorities in the European Community", (1993) 140 *The Courier* 66-67.

Cass, Deborah Z., "The word that saves Maastricht? The principle of subsidiarity and the division of powers within the European Community", (1992) vol. 29:6 *Common Market Law Review* 1107-1136.

Chalmers, Damian, "Judicial preferences and the Community legal order", (1997) vol. 60:2 *Modern Law Review* 164-199.

Chartered Institute of Patent Agents, "Translations: Costs and compromise", (1996) vol. 25:3 *Chartered Institute of Patent Agents Journal* 177-190.

Church, Clive H. and Phinnemore, David, European Union and European Community: A Handbook and Commentary on the Post-Maastricht Treaties, (Hemel Hempstead: Harvester Wheatsheaf, 1994).

Clapham, Andrew, "A human rights policy for the European Community", (1990) 10 *Yearbook European Law*, 309-366.

Closa, Carlos, "The concept of citizenship in the Treaty on European Union", (1992) 29 *Common Market Law Review* 1137-1169.

___, "Citizenship of the Union and nationality of Member States", in O'Keeffe and Twomey (eds.), *Legal Issues of the Maastricht Treaty*, (London: Chancery, 1995), 109-119.

Comhdháil Náisiúnta na Gaeilge, *International Conference on Language Legislation: Conference Proceedings*, (Dublin: Comhdháil Náisiúnta na Gaeilge, 1999).

Commission of the European Communities, "Language engineering in the European Community", (1992) vol. 16:3 *Language Problems and Language Planning* 249-252.

___, Report on the Education of Migrants' Children in the European Union, COM(94) 80 Final.

___, Euromosaic: The Production and Reproduction of Minority Language Groups in the European Union, (Luxembourg: Office for Official Publications of the European Communities, 1996).

___, First Report on the Consideration of Cultural Aspects in European Community Action, (1996) COM(96) 160 Final.

___, Better Lawmaking 1998: A Shared Responsibility, (1998) COM(98) 715.

Connelly, Alpha, "The European Convention on Human Rights and the protection of linguistic minorities", (1993) vol. 2:2 *Irish Journal of European Law* 277-293.

Conradh na Gaeilge, "Stádas na Gaeilge san Aontas Eorpach", (1994-5) 12 *CNAG* 4-5.

Constantinesco, Vlad, "Who's afraid of subsidiarity?", (1991) 11 *Yearbook of European Law* 33-55.

Coppel, Jason, "Rights, duties and the end of *Marshall*", (1994) 57 *Modern Law Review* 859-879.

___, and O'Neill, Aidan, "The European Court of Justice: Taking rights seriously?", (1992) 29 *Common Market Law Review* 669-692.

Corbeil, Jean-Claude, "L'aménagement linguistique en europe", in Truchot (ed.), *La Plurilinguisme Européene*, (Paris: Honoré Champion, 1994), 311-315.

Cosgrove, C.A. and Twitchett, K.J. (eds.), The New International Actors: The United Nations and the European Economic Community, (London: Macmillan, 1970).

Coulmas, Florian (ed.), *A Language Policy for the European Community: Prospects and Quandaries*, (Berlin; New York: Mouton de Gruyter, 1991).

___, "European integration and the idea of the national language", in Coulmas (ed.), *A Language Policy for the European Community*, (Berlin; New York: Mouton de Gruyter, 1991), 1-44.

Craig, Paul and de Búrca, Gráinne, *EU Law: Text, Cases and Materials*, 2nd ed., (Oxford: OUP, 1998).

Crawford, James (ed.), *The Rights of Peoples*, (Oxford: Clarendon Press, 1992).

Cullen, Holly, "From migrants to citizens? European Community policy on intercultural education", (1996) 45 *International and Comparative Law Quarterly* 109-129.

Curtin, Deirdre, "The constitutional structure of the Union: A Europe of bits and pieces", (1993) vol. 30:1 *Common Market Law Review* 17-69.

Dankert, P., "Areas of cultural policy", in Rijksbaron, Roobol and Weisglas (eds.), *Europe from a Cultural Perspective*, (The Hague: Nijgh en Van Ditmar Universitair, 1987), 17-18.

Dashwood, Alan, "The limits of European Community powers", (1996) 21 *European Law Review* 113-128.

Dauses, Manfred A., "The protection of fundamental rights in the Community legal order", (1985) 10 *European Law Review* 398-419.

Dehousse, Renaud (ed.), *Europe After Maastricht: An Ever Closer Union?*, (München: Law Books in Europe, 1994).

___, "Community competences: Are there limits to growth?" in Dehousse (ed.) *Europe After Maastricht*, (München: Law Books in Europe, 1994), 103-125.

Demaret, Paul, "The Treaty framework", in O'Keeffe and Twomey (eds.), *Legal Issues of the Maastricht Treaty*, (London: Chancery, 1995), 3-11.

Dinan, Desmond, Ever Closer Union? An Introduction to the European Community, (London: Macmillan, 1994).

Dinstein, Yoram and Tabory, Mala (eds.), *The Protection of Minorities and Human Rights*, (Dordrecht: Martinus Nijhoff, 1992).

D'Oliveira, Hans Ulrich Jessurun, "European citizenship: Its meaning and potential" in Dehousse (ed.), *Europe After Maastricht: An Ever Closer Union?*, (München: Law Books in Europe, 1994), 126-148.

Dondelinger, Jean, "1992, Les relations de la communauté et de la culture" (1990) 334 *Revue du Marché Commun* 77-79.

Duff, Andrew, Pinder, John and Pryce, Roy (eds.), *Maastricht and Beyond: Building the New Europe*, (London: Routledge, 1994).

Duff, Andrew, "Ratification", in Duff, Pinder and Pryce (eds.), *Maastricht and Beyond: Building the New Europe*, (London: Routledge, 1994), 53-68.

Editorial Comments, "The subsidiarity principle", (1990) vol. 27:2 *Common Market Law Review* 181-184.

___, "Subsidiarity: Backing the right horse", (1993) vol. 30:2 *Common Market Law Review* 241-245.

Edward, D.A.O. and Lane, R., *European Community Law: An Introduction*, 2nd ed., (Edinburgh: Butterworths/Law Society of Scotland, 1995).

Edwards, John, "Language minorities and language maintenance", (1997) 17 *Annual Review of Applied Linguistics* 30-42.

Ehlich, Konrad, "Linguistic 'integration' and 'identity': The situation of migrant workers in the EC as a challenge and opportunity", in Coulmas (ed.), *A Language Policy for the European Community*, (Berlin; New York: Mouton de Gruyter, 1991), 195-214.

Eide, Asbjørn, "The Sub-Commission on the Prevention of Discrimination and the Protection of Minorities", in Alston (ed.), *The United Nations and Human Rights*, (Oxford: Clarendon Press, 1992), 211-264.

Emiliou, Nicholas, "Subsidiarity: An effective barrier against 'enterprises of ambition'?", (1992) 17 *European Law Review* 383-407.

___, "Subsidiarity: Panacea or fig leaf?", in O'Keeffe and Twomey (eds.), *Legal Issues of the Maastricht Treaty*, (London: Chancery, 1995), 65-83.

___, "The death of exclusive competence?", (1996) vol. 21:4 *European Law Review* 294-311.

European Bureau for Lesser Used Languages, Language Rights, Individual and Collective: The Use of Lesser Used Languages in Public Administration, (Dublin: European Bureau for Lesser Used Languages, 1994).

___, EBLUL TV Co-Production Advisory Group Final Report, (Dublin: European Bureau for Lesser Used Languages, 1994).

___, Vade-Mecum: Guide to Legal Documents, Support Structures and Action Programmes pertaining to the Lesser Used Languages of Europe, (Dublin: European Bureau for Lesser Used Languages, 1994).

___, *Key Words: A Step into the World of Lesser Used Languages*, (Dublin: European Bureau for Lesser Used Languages, 1995).

___, *Unity in Diversity*, 2nd ed., (Dublin: European Bureau for Lesser Used Languages, 1996).

European Council, *Conclusions of the Presidency*, (Edinburgh Summit, December 1992, Annex 1, Part A, Bull.EC 12-1992).

Everling, Ulrich, "Reflections on the structure of the European Union", (1992) vol. 29:6 *Common Market Law Review* 1053-1077.

Everson, Michelle, "The legacy of the market citizen", in Shaw and More (eds.), *New Legal Dynamics of European Union*, (Oxford: Clarendon Press, 1995), 71-90.

Extra, Gus and Vallen, Ton, "Migration and multilingualism in Western Europe: A case-study of the Netherlands", (1997) 17 *Annual Review of Applied Linguistics* 151-169.

Fettes, Mark, "Europe's Babylon: Towards a single European language", (1991) vol. 13:3 *History of European Ideas* 201-213.

Fishman, Joshua A., "Whorfianism of the third kind: Ethnolinguistic diversity as a world-wide societal asset", (1982) 11 *Language in Society* 1-14.

___, Language and Ethnicity in Minority Sociolinguistic Perspective, (Clevedon, Avon: Multilingual Matters Ltd, 1989).

___, "On the limits of ethnolinguistic democracy", in Skutnabb-Kangas and Phillipson (eds.), *Linguistic Human Rights: Overcoming Linguistic Discrimination*, (Berlin; New York: Mouton de Gruyter, 1994), 49-61.

Flynn, Leo, "The implications of Article 13 EC - After Amsterdam, will some forms of discrimination be more equal than others?", (1999) vol. 36:6 *Common Market Law Review* 1127-1152.

Forrest, A., "La dimension culturelle de la communauté européene: Les ministres de la culture explorent le terrain", (1987) 307 *Revue du Marché Commun* 326-332.

Freeman, Michael, "Are there collective human rights?", (1995) 43 *Political Studies* 25-40.

Fries, Sybilla and Shaw, Jo, "Citizenship of the Union: First steps in the European Court of Justice", (1998) vol. 4:4 *European Public Law* 533-559.

Fronia, Joachin, "The future role of the European Commission in respect of lesser used languages", in Comhdháil Náisiúnta na Gaeilge, *International Conference on Language Legislation: Conference Proceedings*, (Dublin: Comhdháil Náisiúnta na Gaeilge, 1999), 69-74.

Gardner-Chloros, Penelope and Gardner, Nick, "The legal protection of linguistic rights and of the mother tongue by the European institutions", (1986) 27 *Grazer Linguistiche Studien* 45-66.

Gibbons, John (ed.), *Language and the Law*, (London; New York: Longman, 1994).

___, "Language and disadvantage before the law", in Gibbons (ed.), *Language and the Law*, (London; New York: Longman, 1994), 195-198.

Gilbert, "The Council of Europe and Minority Rights", (1996) vol. 18:1 *Human Rights Quarterly* 160-189.

Giordan, Henri (ed.), Les Minorités en Europe: Droits Linguistiques et Droits de l'Homme, (Paris: Éditions Kimé, 1992).

Green, John N., "Language status and political aspirations: The case of Northern Spain", in Parry, M.M., Davies, W.V. and Temple, R.A.M. (eds.) *The Changing Voices of Europe*, (Cardiff: University of Wales Press, 1994), 155-172.

Green, Leslie, "Are language rights fundamental?", (1987) 25 *Osgoode Hall Law Journal* 639-669.

___, "Freedom of expression and choice of language", (1991) vol. 13:3 *Law and Policy* 215-229.

Grin, François, "European economic integration and the fate of lesser-used languages", (1993) vol. 17:2 *Language Problems and Language Planning* 101-116.

___, "Combining immigrant and autochthonous language rights: A territorial approach", in Skutnabb-Kangas and Phillipson (eds.), *Linguistic Human Rights: Overcoming Linguistic Discrimination*, (Berlin; New York: Mouton de Gruyter, 1994), 31-48.

___ and Vaillancourt, François, "The economics of multilingualism: Overview and analytical framework", (1997) 17 *Annual Review of Applied Linguistics* 43-65.

Gromacki, Joseph, "The protection of language rights in international human rights law: A proposed draft declaration of linguistic rights", (1992) 32 *Virginia Journal of International Law* 515-579.

Gurr, T.R., *Minorities at risk: A Global View of Ethnopolitical Conflicts*, (Washington DC: United States Institute of Peace Press, 1993).

Gutmann, Amy, "The challenge of multiculturalism in political ethics", (1993) vol. 22:3 *Philosophy and Public Affairs* 171-206.

Guy, Gregory R., "International perspectives on linguistic diversity and language rights", (1989) 13 *Language Problems and Language Planning* 45-53.

Haarmann, Harald, "Language politics and the new European identity", in Coulmas (ed.), *A Language Policy for the European Community*, (Berlin; New York: Mouton de Gruyter, 1991), 103-120.

___, "Monolingualism vs. selective multilingualism; On the future alternatives for Europe as it integrates in the 1990s", (1991) 5 *Sociolinguistica* 7-23.

Haberland, Hartmut, "Reflections about minority languages in the European Community", in Coulmas (ed.), *A Language Policy for the European Community*, (Berlin; New York: Mouton de Gruyter, 1991), 179-194.

Habermas, Jürgen, "Citizenship and national identity: Some reflections on the future of Europe", (1992) vol. 12:1 *Praxis International* 1-19.

___, "Struggles for recognition in constitutional states", (1993) vol. 1:2 *European Journal of Philosophy* 128-155.

Hailbronner, Kay, "The legal status of population groups in a multinational state under public international law", in Dinstein and Tabory (eds.), *The Protection of Minorities and Human Rights*, (Dordrecht: Martinus Nijhoff, 1992), 117-144.

Harris, D.J., O'Boyle, M. and Warbrick, C., *Law of the European Convention on Human Rights*, (London: Butterworths, 1995).

Harrison, Virginia, "Subsidiarity in Article 3b of the EC Treaty: Gobblede-gook or justiciable principle?", (1996) vol. 45:2 *International and Comparative Law Quarterly* 431-439.

Hedemann-Robinson, Martin, "Third country nationals, European Union citizenship, and free movement of persons: A time for bridges rather than divisions", (1996) 16 *Yearbook of European Law* 321-362.

Hervey, T.K., "Putting Europe's house in order: Racism, race discrimination and xenophobia after the Treaty of Amsterdam", in O'Keeffe and Twomey (eds.), *Legal Issues of the Amsterdam Treaty*, (Oxford: Hart Publishing, 1999), 329-349.

___, "Migrant workers and their families in the European Union: The pervasive market ideology of Community law", in Shaw and More (eds.), *New Legal Dynamics of European Union*, (Oxford: Clarendon Press, 1995), 91-110.

Hesse, Joachim Jens and Wright, Vincent (eds.), *Federalising Europe?*, (Oxford: Oxford University Press, 1996).

Hilson, Christopher, and Downes, T. Anthony, "Making sense of rights: Community rights in EC Law", (1999) vol. 24:2 *European Law Review* 121-138.

Hilson, Chris, "Discrimination in Community free movement law", (1999) vol. 24:5 *European Law Review* 445-462.

Hohfeld, Wesley Newcomb, *Fundamental Legal Conceptions*, (Westport: Greenwood Press, 1964).

Holland, Martin, *The Community Experience*, (London: Pinter, 1993).

House of Lords Select Committee on the European Communities, *Report on Monetary and Political Union*, 1989-90, 27th Report, (London: HMSO, 1990).

House of Lords Select Committee on European Union, *Report on the EC Draft Charter of Fundamental Rights*, Eighth Report, (London: The Stationery Office, 2000).

Howe, Paul, "A community of Europeans: The requisite underpinnings", (1995) vol. 33:1 *Journal of Common Market Studies* 27-46.

Hudson, R.A., *Sociolinguistics*, (Cambridge: Cambridge University Press, 1980).

Hunt, Alan, Explorations in Law and Society: Towards a Constitutive Theory of Law, (London: Routledge, 1993).

Huntington, Robert, "European unity and the tower of Babel", (1991) 9 *Boston University International Law Journal* 321-346.

Istituto della Enciclopedia Italiana/Commission of the European Communities, *Linguistic Minorities in Countries belonging to the European Community*, (Luxembourg: Office for Official Publications of the European Communities, 1986).

Kaiser, Joseph H., "Final conclusions", in Schwarze and Schermers (eds.), *Structures and Dimensions of European Community Policy*, (Baden-Baden: Nomos, 1988), 237-238.

Karydis, Georges, "Le juge communautaire et la preservation de l'identité culturelle nationale", *IIIèmes Journées d'Études Jean Monnet* 1-11.

Keatinge, Patrick (ed.), *Ireland and EC Membership Evaluated*, (London: Pinter, 1991).

Kelly, J.B., "National minorities in international law", (1973) 3 *Denver Journal of International Law and Politics* 253-273.

Keohane, Robert O. and Hoffman, Stanley, "Conclusions: Community politics and institutional changes", in Wallace (ed.), *The Dynamics of European Integration*, (London; New York: Pinter, 1990), 276-300.

Kerse, C.S., *EC Antitrust Procedure*, 4th ed., (London: Sweet & Maxwell, 1998).

Khubchandani, Lachman M., "'Minority' cultures and their communication rights", in Skutnabb-Kangas and Phillipson (eds.), *Linguistic Human Rights: Overcoming Linguistic Discrimination*, (Berlin; New York: Mouton de Gruyter, 1994), 305-315.

Koch, Harald, "Legal aspects of a language policy for the European Communities: Language risks, equal opportunities, and legislating a language", in Coulmas (ed.), *A Language Policy for the Community*, (Berlin; New York: Mouton de Gruyter, 1991), 147-162.

Kon, Stephen D., "Aspects of reverse discrimination in Community law", (1981) 6 *European Law Review* 75-101.

Kymlicka, Will, Multicultural Citizenship: A Liberal Theory of Minority Rights, (Oxford: Clarendon Press, 1995).

Labrie, Normand, "La dynamique du français dans la construction européene", in Truchot (ed.), *La Plurilinguisme Européene*, (Paris: Honoré Champion, 1994), 245-264.

Laffan, Brigid, "Introduction: Social, educational and cultural policy", in Keatinge (ed.), *Ireland and EC Membership Evaluated*, (London: Pinter, 1991), 235.

___, "The politics of identity and political order in Europe", (1996) vol. 34:1 *Journal of Common Market Studies* 81-102.

Lane, Robert, "New Community competences under the Maastricht Treaty", (1993) 30 *Common Market Law Review* 939-979.

___and Nic Shuibhne, Niamh, (case comment), Case C-281/98 *Angonese v. Cassa di Risparmio di Bolzano SpA*, judgment of 6 June 2000, not yet reported, (2000) vol.37:6 *Common Market Law Review* 1237-1247.

Laponce, J.A., "Reducing the tensions resulting from language contacts: Personal or territorial solutions?", in Schneiderman (ed.), *Language and the State: The Law and Politic of Identity*, (Quebec: Les Éditions Yvon Blais, 1989), 173-179.

Lasok, Dominik, "Subsidiarity and the occupied field", (1992) 142 *New Law Journal* 1228-1230.

Lee, J.J., *Ireland 1912-1985: Politics and Society*, (Cambridge: Cambridge University Press, 1989).

Leitner, Gerhard, "Europe 1992: A Language perspective", (1991) 15 *Language Problems and Language Planning* 282-296.

Lenaerts, Koen, "Fundamental rights to be included in a Community catalogue", (1991) vol. 16:5 *European Law Review* 367-390.

___and Arts, Dirk, *Procedural Law of the European Union*, (London: Sweet & Maxwell, 1999).

___ and Van Nuffel, Piet, *Constitutional Law of the European Union*, (London: Sweet & Maxwell, 1999).

Lepschy, Giulio, "How many languages does Europe need?", in Parry, M.M., Davies, W.V. and Temple, R.A.M. (eds.), *The Changing Voices of Europe*, (Cardiff: University of Wales Press, 1994), 1-21.

Lerner, Nathan, *Group Rights and Discrimination in International Law*, (Dordrecht: Martinus Nijhoff, 1991).

Leslie, Peter M., "The cultural dimension", in Hesse and Wright (eds.), *Federalising Europe?*, (Oxford: Oxford University Press, 1996), 121-163.

Loman, AnneMarie, Mortelmans, Kamiel, Post, Harry and Watson, Stewart, *Culture and Community Law: Before and After Maastricht*, (Deventer, Boston: Kluwer Law and Taxation Publishers, 1992).

Lonbay, Julian, (book review), *Education and Culture in European Community Law*, by Joseph A. McMahon, (1996) vol. 21:1 *European Law Review* 88-89.

Lowrey, Frank, "Through the looking glass: Linguistic separatism and national unity", (1992) 41 *Emory Law Journal* 223-319.

di Lusignano, Livio Missir, "Communauté et culture", (1994) 376 *Revue du Marché Commun* 181-194.

Lyons, Carole, "The limits of European Union citizenship", in Bankowski and Scott (eds.), *The European Union and its Order: The Legal Theory of European Integration*, (Oxford: Blackwell Publishers, 2000), 149-167.

Mac Eoin, Gearóid, Ahlqvist, Anders and Ó hAodha, Donncha (eds.), *Third International Conference on Minority Languages: General Papers*, (Clevedon, Avon: Multilingual Matters, 1987).

Mackey, William F., "Language diversity, language policy and the sovereign state", (1991) vol. 13:1-2 *History of European Ideas* 51-61.

MacMillan, C. Michael, "Linking theory to practice: Comments on 'The constitutional protection of language'", in Schneiderman (ed.), *Language and the State: The Law and Politic of Identity*, (Quebec: Les Éditions Yvon Blais, 1989), 59-68.

Maher, Imelda, "Legislative review by the EC Commission: Revision without radicalism", in Shaw and More (eds.), *New Legal Dynamics of European Union*, (Oxford: Clarendon Press, 1995), 235-251.

Maihofer, Werner, "Culture, politique et identité européene" in Schwarze and Schermers (eds.), *Structure and Dimensions of European Community Policy*, (Baden-Baden: Nomos, 1988), 215-228.

Mancini, Giuseppe Federico and Keeling, David T., "Language, culture and politics in the life of the European Court of Justice", (1995) 1 *Columbia Journal of European Law* 397-413

Marias, Epaminondas A., (ed.), *European Citizenship*, (Maastricht: European Institute of Public Administration, 1994).

___, "From Market citizen to Union citizen", in Marias (ed.), *European Citizenship*, (Maastricht: European Institute of Public Administration, 1994), 1-24.

___, "Le droit de pétition devant le Parlement européen", in Marias (ed.), *European Citizenship*, (Maastricht: European Institute of Public Administration, 1994), 81-102.

Marshall, David F. and Gonzalez, Roseann D., "Why we should be concerned about language rights: Language rights as human rights from an ecological perspective", in Schneiderman (ed.), *Language and the State: The Law and Politic of Identity*, (Quebec: Les Éditions Yvon Blais, 1989), 289-302.

Massart-Piérard, Françoise, "Limites et enjeux d'une politique culturelle pour la communauté européene", (1983) 293 *Revue du Marché Commun* 34-40.

McCarthy, Niamh and Mercer, Hugh, "Language as a barrier to trade: The Loi Toubon", (1996) vol. 17:5 *European Competition Law Review* 308-314.

McDougal, Myres S., Lasswell, Harold D. and Chen, Lung-chu, "Freedom from discrimination in choice of language and international law", (1976) 1 *Southern Illinois University Law Journal* 151-174.

McGoldrick, Dominic, "The European Union after Amsterdam: An organisation with general human rights competence?", in O'Keeffe and Twomey (eds.), *Legal Issues of the Amsterdam Treaty*, (Oxford: Hart Publishing, 1999), 249-270.

McMahon, Bryan, (case note), Groener v. Minister for Education, (1990) 27 Common Market Law Review 129-139.

McMahon, Joseph A., *Education and Culture in European Community Law*, (London; New Jersey: The Athlone Press, 1995).

McRae, Kenneth D., "Precepts for linguistic peace: The case of Switzerland", in Schneiderman (ed.), *Language and the State: The Law and Politic of Identity*, (Quebec: Les Éditions Yvon Blais, 1989), 167-172.

Meade, James Edward, The Building of the New Europe: National Diversity versus Continental Uniformity, (Edinburgh: The David Hume Institute, 1991).

Milian-Massana, Antoni, "Le régime linguistique de l'union européene: Le régime des institutions et l'incidence du droit communautaire sur la mosaique linguistique européene", (1995) 3 *Rivista di Dirritto Europeo* 485-512.

Miller, David, "In defence of nationality", (1993) vol. 10:1 *Journal of Applied Philosophy* 3-16.

Mitrany, David, "The functional approach to world organisation", in Cosgrove and Twitchett (eds.), *The New International Actors: The United Nations and the European Economic Community*, (London: Macmillan, 1970), 65-75.

Mourik, M., "European cultural co-operation" in Rijksbaron, Roobol and Weisglas (eds.), *Europe from a Cultural Perspective*, (The Hague: Nijgh en Van Ditmar Universitair, 1987), 19-21.

Münch, Richard, "Between nation-state, regionalism and world society: The European integration process", (1996) vol. 34:3 *Journal of Common Market Studies* 379-401.

Murphy, Tim and Twomey, Patrick (eds.), *Ireland's Evolving Constitution 1937-1997: Collected Essays*, (Oxford: Hart Publishing, 1998).

Mutimer, David, "1992 and the political integration of Europe: Neo-functionalism reconsidered", (1989-1991) vol. 13:1 *Journal of European Integration* 75-101.

Nelde, Peter Hans, "Language conflicts in multilingual Europe: Prospects for 1993", in Coulmas (ed.), *A Language Policy for the European Community*, (Berlin; New York: Mouton de Gruyter, 1991), 59-74.

Neussl, Peter, "European citizenship and human rights: An interactive European concept", (1997) vol. 24:2 *Legal Issues of European Integration* 47-66.

Nicoll, W. and Salmon, T.L., *Understanding the New European Community*, (New York; London: Harvester Wheatsheaf, 1994).

Nic Shuibhne, Niamh, "The impact of European law on linguistic diversity", (1996) vol. 5:1 *Irish Journal of European Law* 62-80.

___, "The Constitution, the courts and the Irish language", in Murphy and Twomey (eds.), *Ireland's Evolving Constitution 1937-1997: Collected Essays*, (Oxford: Hart Publishing, 1998), 253-263.

___, "Rethinking language policy: A legal perspective", (2000) 3 *Contemporary Issues in Irish Law and Politics*, 36-53.

___, "The European Union and fundamental rights protection: Well in spirit but considerably rumpled in body?", in Beaumont, Lyons and Walker, Neil (eds.), *Convergence and Divergence in European Public Law*, (Oxford: Hart Publishing, forthcoming, 2001).

Ó Cuív, Briain, (ed.), *A View of the Irish Language*, (Dublin: Stationery Office, 1969).

O'Keeffe, David , "Union citizenship", in O'Keeffe and Twomey (eds.), *Legal Issues of the Maastricht Treaty*, (London: Chancery, 1995), 87-107.

___, and Twomey, Patrick (eds.), *Legal Issues of the Maastricht Treaty*, (London: Chancery, 1995).

___, *Legal Issues of the Amsterdam Treaty*, (Oxford: Hart Publishing, 1999).

O'Leary, Siofra, "The relationship between Community citizenship and the protection of fundamental rights in Community law", (1995) 32 *Common Market Law Review* 519-554.

___, "Accession by the European Community to the European Convention on Human Rights: The opinion of the European Court of Justice", (1996) 4 *European Human Rights Law Review* 362-377.

___, "Putting flesh on the bones of European Union citizenship", (1999) vol. 24:1 *European Law Review* 68-79.

O'Neill, Michael, "Fundamental rights and the European Union", in Gerard Quinn (ed.), *Irish Yearbook of Human Rights,* (Dublin: Round Hall Sweet and Maxwell, 1995), 67-95.

Ó Riagáin, Dónall, "Framework Convention for the Protection of National Minorities", (1995) vol. 12:1 *Contact Bulletin* 1.

Ó Riagáin, Pádraig, "National and international dimensions of language policy when the minority language is a national language: The case of Irish in Ireland", in Coulmas (ed.), *A Language Policy for the European Community,* (Berlin; New York: Mouton de Gruyter, 1991), 255-278.

___and Nic Shuibhne, Niamh, "Minority language rights", (1997) 17 *Annual Review of Applied Linguistics* 11-29.

Ó Ruairc, M., *Ó Chomhmhargadh go hAontas,* (Dublin: Comhar Teoranta, 1994).

Ostrower, Alexander, *Language, Law and Diplomacy,* (Philadelphia, Oxford: Oxford University Press, 1965).

O'Toole, Fintan, "Culture and media policy", in Keatinge (ed.) *Ireland and EC Membership Evaluated,* (London: Pinter, 1991), 270-276.

Palacio González, José, "The principle of subsidiarity (A guide for lawyers with a particular Community orientation", (1995) 20 *European Law Review* 355-370.

Parry, M.M., Davies, W.V. and Temple, R.A.M. (eds.), *The Changing Voices of Europe: Social and Political Changes and their Linguistic Repercussions, Past, Present and Future,* (Cardiff: University of Wales Press, in conjunction with the Modern Humanities Research Association, 1994).

Pavlidou, Theodossia, "Linguistic nationalism and European unity: The case of Greece", in Coulmas (ed.), *A Language Policy for the European Community,* (Berlin; New York: Mouton de Gruyter, 1991), 279-290.

Petersmann, Ernst-Ulrich, "Proposals for a new constitution for the European Union: Building-blocks for a constitutional theory and constitutional law of the EU", (1995) vol. 32:5 *Common Market Law Review* 1123-1175.

Peterson, John, "Subsidiarity: A definition to suit any vision?", (1994) vol. 47:1 *Parliamentary Affairs* 116-132.

Phelan, Diarmuid Rossa, "Right to life of the unborn v. promotion of trade in services: The European Court of Justice and the normative shaping of the European Union", (1992) vol. 55:5 *Modern Law Review* 670-689.

Philip, A.B., "Old policies, new competencies", in Duff, Pinder and Pryce, (eds.), *Maastricht and Beyond*, (London: Routledge, 1994), 123-139.

Phillipson, Robert and Skutnabb-Kangas, Tove, "Linguistic rights and wrongs", (1995) vol. 16:4 *Applied Linguistics* 483-504.

Piatt, Bill, "Toward domestic recognition of a human right to language", (1986) 23 *Houston Law Review* 885-906.

Pinder, John, "Building the Union: Policy, reform, constitution", in Duff, Pinder and Pryce (eds.), *Maastricht and Beyond: Building the New Europe*, (London: Routledge, 1994), 269-285.

Posner, Rebecca, "Romania within a wider Europe: Conflict or cohesion?", in Parry, M.M., Davies, W.V. and Temple, R.A.M. (eds.), *The Changing Voices of Europe*, (Cardiff: University of Wales Press, 1994), 23-33.

Posner, Roland, "Society, civilisation, mentality: Prolegomena to a language policy for Europe", in Coulmas (ed.), *A Language Policy for the European Community*, (Berlin; New York: Mouton de Gruyter, 1991), 121-138.

Preuß, Ulrich K., "Problems of a concept of European Citizenship", (1995) vol. 1:3 *European Law Journal* 267-281.

Prott, Lyndel V., "Cultural rights as peoples' rights in international law", in Crawford (ed.), *The Rights of Peoples*, (Oxford: Clarendon Press, 1992), 93-106.

Pryce, Roy, "The Maastricht Treaty and the new Europe", in Duff, Pinder and Pryce (eds.), *Maastricht and Beyond: Building the New Europe*, (London: Routledge, 1994), 3-16.

___, "The Treaty negotiations", in Duff, Pinder and Pryce (eds.), *Maastricht and Beyond: Building the New Europe*, (London: Routledge, 1994), 36-52.

Quinn, Gerard (ed.), *Irish Yearbook of Human Rights*, (Dublin: Round Hall Sweet and Maxwell, 1995).

Rasmussen, Hjalte, On Law and Policy in the European Court of Justice, (Dordrecht: Nijhoff, 1986).

___, "Between self-restraint and activism: A judicial policy for the European Court", (1988) 13 *European Law Review* 28-38.

___, "Structures and dimensions of EC cultural policy" in Schwarze and Schermers (eds.), *Structure and Dimensions of European Community Policy*, (Baden-Baden: Nomos, 1988), 185-194.

Raz, Joseph, *The Morality of Freedom*, (Oxford: Clarendon Press, 1986).

___, "Multiculturalism", (1994) *Dissent* 67-79.

Réaume, Denise G., "The constitutional protection of language: survival or security?", in Schneiderman (ed.), *Language and the State: The Law and Politic of Identity*, (Quebec: Les Éditions Yvon Blais, 1989), 37-57.

Reich, N., "The 'November Revolution' of the Court of Justice: *Keck, Meng* and *Audi* revisited", (1994) 31 *Common Market Law Review* 459-471.

Reiner, Karl, "Human rights and the protection of minorities in the independent province of Bolzano-Bozen", in Comhdháil Náisiúnta na Gaeilge, *International Conference on Language Legislation*, (Dublin: Comhdháil Náisiúnta na Gaeilge, 1999), 83-89.

Reuter, Michael, "Summing up", in Mac Eoin, Ahlqvist and Ó hAodha (eds.), *Third International Conference on Minority Languages: General Papers*, (Clevedon, Avon: Multilingual Matters, 1987), 213-218.

Rickard, Maurice, "Liberalism, multiculturalism and minority protection", (1994) vol. 20:2 *Social Theory and Practice* 143-170.

Rijksbaron, A., Roobol, W.H., and Weisglas, M. (eds.), *Europe from a Cultural Perspective: Historiography and Perceptions*, (The Hague: Nijgh en Van Ditmar Universitair, 1987).

Roberts, Elizabeth L., "Cultural policy in the European Community: A case against extensive national retention", (1993) vol. 28:1 *Texas Journal of International Law* 191-228.

Robertson, A.H. and Merrills, J. G., Human Rights in the World: An Introduction to the Study of the International Protection of Human Rights, 4th ed., (Manchester: Manchester University Press, 1996).

Roche, Nick, "Multilingualism in European Community meetings: A pragmatic approach", in Coulmas (ed.), *A Language Policy for the European Community*, (Berlin; New York: Mouton de Gruyter, 1991), 139-146.

Rubin, Alfred P., "Are human rights legal?", in Dinstein and Tabory (eds.), *The Protection of Human Rights and Minorities*, (Dordrecht: Martinus Nijhoff, 1992), 33-58.

Scharpf, Fritz W., "Community and autonomy: Multi-level policy-making in the European Union", (1994) vol. 1:2 *Journal of European Public Policy* 219-242.

Schermers, Henry G., "Final conclusions" in Schwarze and Schermers (eds.), *Structure and Dimensions of European Community Policy*, (Baden-Baden: Nomos, 1988), 229-235.

Schilling, Theodor, "A new dimension of subsidiarity: Subsidiarity as a rule and a principle", (1994) 14 *Yearbook of European Law* 203-256.

Schneiderman, David (ed.), *Language and the State: The Law and Politic of Identity*, (Quebec: Les Éditions Yvon Blais, 1989).

Schwarze, Jürgen and Schermers, Henry G. (eds.), *Structure and Dimensions of European Community Policy*, (Baden-Baden: Nomos, 1988).

Scott, Dermott, "Education", in Keatinge (ed.), *Ireland and EC Membership Evaluated*, (London: Pinter, 1991), 260-269.

Seurin, Jean Louis, "Towards a European constitution? Problems of political integration", (1994) *Public Law* 625-636.

Seville, Catherine, (book review), *Education and Culture in European Community Law* by Joseph A. McMahon, (1995) vol. 54:3 *Cambridge Law Journal* 635-637.

Shaw, Jo, "Equality of treatment for teachers under European Community law", (1991) vol. 3:1 *Education and the Law* 35-38.

___, "Legal developments", (1995) 33 *Journal of Common Market Studies* 87-102.

___, "Legal developments", (1996) 34 *Journal of Common Market Studies* 85-101.

___, "The many pasts and futures of citizenship in the European Union", (1997) 22 *European Law Review* 554-572.

___, "The problem of membership in European Union citizenship", in Bankowski and Scott (eds.), *The European Union and its Order: The Legal Theory of European Integration*, (Oxford: Blackwell Publishers, 2000), 65-89.

___, and More, Gillian (eds.), *New Legal Dynamics of European Union*, (Oxford: Clarendon Press, 1995).

Shaw, Malcolm N., "The definition of minorities in international law", in Dinstein and Tabory (eds.), *The Protection of Minorities and Human Rights*, (Dordrecht: Martinus Nijhoff, 1992), 1-31.

Sigler, J.A., *Minority Rights: A Comparative Analysis*, (Westport, Connecticut: Greenwood Press, 1983).

Skutnabb-Kangas, Tove and Phillipson, Robert (eds.), *Linguistic Human Rights: Overcoming Linguistic Discrimination*, (Berlin; New York: Mouton de Gruyter, 1994).

___, "Introduction", in Skutnabb-Kangas and Phillipson (eds.), *Linguistic Human Rights: Overcoming Linguistic Discrimination*, (Berlin; New York: Mouton de Gruyter, 1994), 1-22.

___, "Linguistic human rights, past and present", in Skutnabb-Kangas and Phillipson (eds.), *Linguistic Human Rights: Overcoming Linguistic Discrimination*, (Berlin; New York: Mouton de Gruyter, 1994), 71-110.

Smith, Anthony D., "National identity and the idea of European unity", (1992) vol. 68:1 *International Affairs* 55-76.

Spielman, Dean, "Human rights case law in the Strasbourg and Luxembourg courts: Conflicts, inconsistencies and complementarities", in Alston (ed.) *The EU and Human Rights*, (Oxford: OUP, 1999), 757-780.

Squarci, Lorenza, "What are minorities? Some possible criteria", (1993) 140 *The Courier* 50-52.

van der Staay, Adriaan, "On the feasibility of a European cultural policy" in Rijksbaron, Roobol and Weisglas (eds.), *Europe from a Cultural Perspective*, (Baden-Baden: Nomos, 1987), 22-24.

Steiner, Jo, "Subsidiarity under the Maastricht Treaty", in O'Keeffe and Twomey (eds.), *Legal Issues of the Maastricht Treaty*, (London: Chancery, 1995), 49-64.

Strain, J. Frank, Integration, Federalism and Cohesion in the European Community - Lessons from Canada, (Dublin: The Economic and Social Research Institute, 1993).

Stubbs, Michael, "Educational language planning in England and Wales: Multicultural rhetoric and assimilationist assumptions", in Coulmas (ed.), *A Language Policy for the European Community*, (Berlin; New York: Mouton de Gruyter, 1991), 215-240.

Tabory, Maia, *Multilingualism in International Law and Institutions*, (Alphen ann den Rijn/Rockville, MA: Sijthoff and Noordhoff, 1980).

Tabouret-Keller, Andrée, "Factors of constraint and freedom in setting a language policy for the European Community", in Coulmas (ed.), *A Language Policy for the European Community*, (Berlin; New York: Mouton de Gruyter, 1991), 45-58.

Tebbe, Gerd, "Minorities in the European Community", (1993) 140 *The Courier* 62-63.

Temple, Rosalind M., "Great expectations? Hopes and fears about the implications of political developments in Western Europe for the future of France's regional languages", in Parry, M.M., Davies, W.V. and Temple, R.A.M. (eds.), *The Changing Voices of Europe*, (Cardiff: University of Wales Press, 1994), 191-211.

Temple Lang, John, "European Community constitutional law: The division of powers between the Community and Member States", (1988) vol. 39:2 *Northern Ireland Law Quarterly* 209-234.

___, "Community constitutional law: Article 5 of the EEC Treaty", (1990) vol. 27:4 *Common Market Law Review* 645-681.

___, "The sphere in which Member States are obliged to comply with the general principles of law and Community fundamental rights principles", (1991) *Legal Issues of European Integration* 23-35.

___, "What powers should the European Community have?", (1995) vol. 1:1 *European Public Law* 97-116.

Thompson, Ian, "Bibliographic Snapshot: The citizen and Europe", (1994) *European Access* 37-45.

Thornberry, Patrick, *International Law and the Rights of Minorities*, (Oxford: Clarendon Press, 1991).

___, "UN support for linguistic minorities", (1993) vol. 10:1 *Contact Bulletin* 1-2.

Tonra, Ben (ed.), *Amsterdam: What the Treaty Means*, (Dublin: Institute of European Affairs, 1997).

Toth, A.G., "The principle of subsidiarity in the Maastricht Treaty", (1992) vol. 29:6 *Common Market Law Review* 1079-1105.

___, "Is subsidiarity justiciable?", (1994) 19 *European Law Review* 268-285.

___, "A legal analysis of subsidiarity", in O'Keeffe and Twomey (eds.), *Legal Issues of the Maastricht Treaty*, (London: Chancery, 1995), 37-48.

Tovey, Hilary, Hannan, Damian and Abramson, Hal, *Why Irish? Irish Identity and the Irish Language*, (Dublin: Bord na Gaeilge, 1989).

Tridimas, T., "The Court of Justice and judicial activism", (1996) vol. 21(3) *European Law Review* 199-210.

___, *The General Principles of EC Law*, (Oxford: Clarendon Press, 1999).

Triggs, Gillian, "The rights of peoples and individual rights: Conflict or harmony?", in Crawford (ed.), *The Rights of Peoples*, (Oxford: Clarendon Press, 1992), 141-157.

Truchot, Claude (ed.), La Plurilinguisme Européene: Théories et Pratiques en Politique Linguistique, (Paris: Honoré Champion, 1994).

___, "En amont des politiques linguistiques en europe", in Truchot (ed.), *La Plurilinguisme Européene*, (Paris: Honoré Champion, 1994), 21-36.

Tucker, G. Richard, "Multilingualism and language contact", (1997) 17 *Annual Review of Applied Linguistics* 3-10.

Turi, Joseph G., "Typology of language legislation", in Skutnabb-Kangas and Phillipson (eds.), *Linguistic Human Rights: Overcoming Linguistic Discrimination*, (Berlin; New York: Mouton de Gruyter, 1994), 111-119.

Twomey, Patrick M., "European citizenship and human rights: Actual situation and future perspectives", in Marias (ed.), *European Citizenship*, (Maastricht: European Institute of Public Affairs, 1994), 119-133.

___, "The European Union: Three pillars without a foundation?", in O'Keeffe and Twomey (eds.), *Legal Issues of the Maastricht Treaty*, (London: Chancery, 1995), 121-132.

___, "Constructing a secure space", in O'Keeffe and Twomey (eds.), *Legal Issues of the Amsterdam Treaty*, (Oxford: Hart Publishing, 1999), 351-374.

Usher, John A., "Language and the European Court of Justice", (1981) *The International Contract: Law and Finance Review* 277-286.

___, "Principles derived from private law and the European Court of Justice", (1993) 1 *European review of Private Law* 109-136.

___, "Languages and the European Union", in Anderson and Bort (eds.), *The Frontiers of Europe*, (London: Pinter, 1998), 222-234.

___, *General Principles of EC Law*, (London: Longman, 1998).

Van Calster, Geert, "The EU's Tower of Babel - The interpretation by the European Court of Justice of equally authentic texts drafted in more than one official language", (1997) 17 *Yearbook of European Law* 363-393.

Van Kersbergen, Kees and Verbeek, Bertjan, "The politics of subsidiarity in the European Union", (1994) vol. 32:2 *Journal of Common Market Studies* 215-236.

de Varennes, F., *Language, Minorities and Human Rights*, (The Hague: Martinus Nijhoff, 1996).

___, *To Speak or Not to Speak: The Rights of Persons belonging to Linguistic Minorities*, (working paper prepared for the UN Sub-Committee on the rights of minorities, 21 March 1997, published at http://www.unesco.org/most/ln2pol3.htm.

Walker, Neil, "European constitutionalism and European integration", (1996) *Public Law* 266-290.

Wallace, William (ed.), *The Dynamics of European Integration*, (London; New York: Pinter (for the Royal Institute of International Affairs, London), 1990).

___, "Introduction: The dynamics of European Integration" in Wallace (ed.), *The Dynamics of European Integration*, (London; New York: Pinter, 1990), 1-24.

Walters, David B., "The legal recognition and protection of language pluralism: A comparative study with special reference to Belgium, Quebec and Wales", (1978) *Acta Juridica* 305-326.

Ward, Angela, "Effective sanctions in European Community law: A moving boundary in the division of competence", (1995) vol. 1:2 *European Law Journal* 205-217.

Watts, Richard J., "Linguistic minorities and language conflict in Europe: Learning from the Swiss experience", in Coulmas (ed.), *A Language Policy for the European Community*, (Berlin; New York: Mouton de Gruyter, 1991), 75-102.

Weatherill, Stephen, *Subsidiarity and Responsibility*, (Nottingham: University of Nottingham (Research Paper), 1992).

___, "Beyond preemption? Shared competence and constitutional change in the European Community", in O'Keeffe and Twomey (eds.), *Legal Issues of the Maastricht Treaty*, (London: Chancery, 1995), 13-33.

Weiler, J.H.H., "Prologue: Amsterdam and the quest for constitutional democracy", in O'Keeffe, D. and Twomey, P. (eds.), *Legal Issues of the Amsterdam Treaty*, (Oxford: Hart Publishing, 1999), 1-19.

___, and Lockhart, Nicholas J.S., "'Taking Rights Seriously' seriously: The European Court of Justice and its fundamental rights jurisprudence", (1995), vol. 32:1; vol. 32:2, *Common Market Law Review* 51-94; 579-627.

Weinstein, Brian, (ed.), *Language Policy and Political Development*, (Norwood, New Jersey: Ablex, 1990).

___, "Language policy and political development: An overview", in Weinstein (ed.), *Language Policy and Political Development*, (Norwood, New Jersey: Ablex, 1990), 1-21.

Whelan, Anthony, "Fundamental rights", in Tonra (ed.), *Amsterdam: What the Treaty Means*, (Dublin: Institute of European Affairs, 1997), 147-158.

de Witte, Bruno, "The scope of Community powers in education and culture in the light of subsequent practice", in Bieber and Ress (eds.), *Die Dynamik des Europäischen Gemeinschaftsrechts*, (Baden-Baden: Nomos, 1987), 261-278.

___, "Building Europe's image and identity", in Rijksbaron, Roobol and Weisglas (eds.), *Europe from a Cultural Perspective*, (The Hague: Nijgh en Van Ditmar Universitair, 1987), 132-139.

___, "Cultural policy: The complementarity of negative and positive integration", in Schwarze and Schermers (eds.), *Structure and Dimensions of European Community Policy*, (Baden-Baden: Nomos, 1988), 195-204.

___, Cultural linkages", in Wallace (ed.), *The Dynamics of European Integration*, (London; New York: Pinter, 1990), 192-210.

___, "The impact of European Community rules on linguistic policies of the Member States", in Coulmas (ed.), *A Language Policy for the European Community*, (Berlin; New York: Mouton de Gruyter, 1991), 163-178.

___, "Surviving in Babel? Language rights and European integration", in Dinstein and Tabory (eds.), *The Protection of Minorities and Human Rights*, (Dordrecht: Martinus Nijhoff, 1992), 277-300.

___, "Le principe d'égalité et la pluralité linguistique", in Giordan (ed.), *Les Minorités en Europe: Droits Linguistiques et Droits de l'Homme*, (Paris: Éditions Kimé, 1992), 52-64.

Wouters, Jan, "European citizenship and the case-law of the Court of Justice of the European Communities on the free movement of persons", in Marias (ed.), *European Citizenship*, (Maastricht: European Institute of Public Administration, 1994), 25-62.

Wright, Jane, "The OSCE and the protection of minority rights", (1996) vol. 18:1 *Human Rights Quarterly* 190-205.

Wynne Jones, Alan, "New Welsh Language Bill in 1993?", (1993) vol. 10:2 *Contact Bulletin* 1-3.

Zuanelli, Elisabetta, "Italian in the European Community: An educational perspective on the national language and new language minorities", in Coulmas (ed.), *A Language Policy for the European Community*, (Berlin; New York: Mouton de Gruyter, 1991), pp. 291-300.

Index